Praise for *Our Worst Strength*

"Moving, thoughtful and mind-expanding."

> — JOHANN HARI, NEW YORK TIMES BEST-SELLING AUTHOR OF *LOST CONNECTIONS* AND *CHASING THE SCREAM*

"An astute examination of loneliness and isolation that sheds light, finds humor, and provides hope."

> — KIRKUS REVIEWS RECOMMENDED BOOK

". . . an invaluable book for understanding the hidden costs of American individualism."

> — ROB HENDERSON, USA TODAY BEST-SELLING AUTHOR OF *TROUBLED: A MEMOIR OF FOSTER CARE, FAMILY AND SOCIAL CLASS*

"A moving portrait of the loneliness embedded in everyday American life and a powerful warning to younger generations to course correct."

> — JENNIFER BREHENY WALLACE, NEW YORK TIMES BESTSELLING AUTHOR OF *NEVER ENOUGH: WHEN ACHIEVEMENT CULTURE BECOMES TOXIC—AND WHAT WE CAN DO ABOUT IT*

"James F. Richardson's *Our Worst Strength* is a comprehensive and highly entertaining examination of the impact of our unprecedented explosion of lifestyle choices. With humor and care, Dr. Richardson thoughtfully charts the rapid change in social circumstances and attitudes that are contributing to our widespread sense of disconnection. This book is essential reading for anyone looking to better understand the pervasive influence of individualism in modern culture."

> — ANNA GOLDFARB, CALLED THE "NEW YORK TIMES' FRIENDSHIP CORRESPONDENT" AND AUTHOR OF *MODERN FRIENDSHIP: HOW TO NURTURE OUR MOST VALUED CONNECTIONS*

"Richardson's a shrewd, witty, sometimes outraged observer who urges readers to approach individualistic impulses more critically."

– BOOKLIFE REVIEWS (BY PUBLISHER'S WEEKLY)

"Dr Richardson takes us through an amazing and alarming look in the mirror as a society. As a keen observer of human behavior, James is able to find context and simplify the complexity of answering the question—'how did we get here?' in an engaging, provocative, and well thought out prose."

– APU MODY–CPG ANGEL INVESTOR/ADVISOR AND FORMER PRESIDENT MARS FOOD AMERICAS

"*Our Worst Strength* is an exemplary work that makes the familiar strange, enabling us to see one of our most cherished American traditions—individualism—with new eyes. Dr. James Richardson not only reveals the historical specificity and psycho-cultural impacts of individualistic norms but also serves the public interest by illuminating how they shape some of our greatest societal challenges, enabling us to critically evaluate and ultimately transform the values that govern our lives."

– DR. VICTOR BRAITBERG, ASSOCIATE PROFESSOR OF PRACTICE AND ANTHROPOLOGY, W.A. FRANKE HONORS COLLEGE, UNIVERSITY OF ARIZONA

Our Worst Strength

Our Worst Strength

American Individualism and Its Hidden Discontents

James F. Richardson

Social Awareness Institute
Tucson

Our Worst Strength © copyright 2024 The Social Awareness Institute, an Arizona nonprofit corporation. All rights reserved. No part of this book may be reproduced in any form whatsoever, by photography or xerography or by any other means, by broadcast or transmission, by translation into any kind of language, nor by recording electronically or otherwise, without permission in writing from the author, except by a reviewer, who may quote brief passages in critical articles or reviews.

To protect the privacy of those depicted in these pages, the names of the characters, businesses, and places discussed in this book have been changed by the author. Any resemblance to actual persons, living or dead, or actual events is purely coincidental.

Hardback: 979-8-9887680-0-5
Paperback: 979-8-9887680-1-2
eBook: 979-8-9887680-2-9
Audiobook: 979-8-9887680-3-6

Front cover art/photo courtesy of Jasmine Hromjak
Book design by Mayfly Design

LCCN: 2023915829
First Printing: 2024
Printed in the United States of America

To my wife and kids for enduring the author-at-home

CONTENTS

Preface xiii
Introduction xvii

PART ONE—How to Make a Hyper-Individualistic Society in Seven Easy Steps

    1. Unlock the Variables of Lifestyle Choice 3
    2. Silencing the Elders 15
    3. Make Privacy Sacred 23
    4. Make the Individual Responsible for Their Problems ... 34
    5. Reward Productive Antisocial Behavior 43
    6. Distract Ourselves with Personalized Entertainment ... 52
    7. Anchor Our Minds to the Next New Thing 57

PART TWO—How It Became Awkward at Work

    8. Recovering from My Career Fantasy 69
    9. Work-Life Dustups 75
   10. The Great College Divide 89
   11. Career Zigzag 103

PART THREE—How We Got Lost in the American Funhouse

   12. Why I Suck at Parties 121
   13. American Rumspringa and the Risk of Self-Implosion .. 125
   14. How Youth Culture Fractured Fun in Two 136

- 15. Modern Recreational Worlds 144
- 16. Consuming Media Trumps Group Fun 154

PART FOUR—How We Came to Eat Whatever, Whenever

- 17. My February 8, 2000, Panic Attack at Cub Foods 163
- 18. The Erosion of Meal Ritual and the Rise of Obesity . . . 170
- 19. The Oddly Social Origins of Food Sensitivities 185
- 20. Aspirational Diets 194
- 21. Potluck America 204

PART FIVE—How Friends Became Entertainment Devices

- 22. My Biggest Failure in India 213
- 23. Friends as Entertainment 221
- 24. The Fake Business Friend 233
- 25. Sexual Partners as Best Friends 241
- 26. How Pets Edged Out Our Friends 252

PART SIX—How We Shriveled the American Family

- 27. I'm Named After a Very Disappointing Man 261
- 28. The Cultural Triumph of the Romantic Couple 267
- 29. The Shriveled Family Tree in America 281
- 30. From Parents to Life Coaches 290
- 31. Declining Gender Diversity at Home 297

PART SEVEN—The Future of Individualism in America

- 32. American Individualism: A Diagnosis 307
- 33. Growth and the Undoing of Community 319
- 34. The Rights-Enabled Consumer in Social Retreat 330
- 35. Emerging Countertrends 336

Epilogue 344

Book Club Questions and More 349

Acknowledgments 351
Appendix A. 353
Appendix B. 355
Notes. 361
Index 399
About the Author 415

PREFACE

"Do you know that you're a terrible communicator?" our CEO asked me as if my fly was down and I was the last one to know.

I began to tremble in my conference room chair.

Wait! Am I being fired here?

It was 2007, and I was thirty-five years old. My wife of only one year was seven months pregnant with our first child. She earned half of what I did then, so this was *not* the time to lose my job and more than half our income. Not with a mortgage of $2,588 a month ($3,800 today).

*Sh*t! Now, am I completely f**ked? What else will I do with this PhD here in Seattle, the Amazon-badge-flapping tech-tropolis, where humanities majors go to starve?*

And so, my mind continued to catastrophize as I tried to keep my focus during this tense conversation.

Reply! Say something! They're staring at you.

"Um, yes, I guess so . . . uh . . . I don't . . . don't know what to do about it," I stammered out before pausing again. Once more, I had agreed without understanding *or insisting on* clarification. I hate open discussions. All the verbal murk. No structure. Argh!

My head spun, and my ears shut down as my nervous amygdala went into flight mode.

Our CEO waited for me to form my next words because my quivering face signaled that I was trying to speak. But, instead, I began to weep. The mask shattered. The owner held back for a while as I composed myself, but then he got tired of waiting and continued, "We can't figure you out, James. Sometimes you're very effective and persuasive, but there's no consistency. And you piss off a lot of people. Your peers. Clients. We want to see you succeed here, but things *have* to change."

But I don't know what to do!

I was thirty-five years old, and I *often* did not know what to do beyond my laptop's confines. In real human interactions.

My interactional challenges were not new, yet hardly anyone confronted me about them as I was growing up. Not in high school. Not in college. Most everyone tolerated my many quirks. James was just a bit weird. As I would learn soon after the horrendous meeting above, social interactional challenges and hatred of social ambiguity are hallmarks of Asperger's syndrome.

Asperger's is one of the least adaptive neurological traits you could have as an otherwise functioning adult *in one of the most individualistic, rapidly changing societies on Earth.* Modern America requires *enhanced* social skills to navigate. After all, you have tons of choices, and your life journey is basically yours to craft. *On your own.*

Looking back, my interest in cultural anthropology and studying foreign cultures probably stemmed from being a misfit in my own northern New England cultural home. I was loud. I was weird. I talked too much for too long. I made inappropriate jokes and swore a lot randomly. I stimmed—that is, I randomly made repetitive sounds or blurted out of context words (I still say my dog's name when randomly walking around the house). None of these Aspie behaviors fit well into WASP theories of polite decorum or the quiet calm of northern New England culture.[1] When I was a kid, my parents spent so much time telling me to be quiet, I'm surprised they didn't just wear a lanyard sign around their necks so they could flash "Silence, please!" at me on demand while they kept reading. Putting the TV in the basement was perhaps the easier solution.

The most comfortable I ever felt in my twenties was doing my dissertation fieldwork in South India, not because I fit in there so well, but because Indians I met seemed to know how to deal with socially awkward people much better than Americans. The solution is not at all complex. You just "manage" weird people more intently. You keep an eye out for them. You correct them actively on the spot. You tolerate weird responses whose harm doesn't matter much. You don't overreact, alienate, or avoid people because they annoy you. "I like how *you* speak Tamil, James," one friend said . . . and he wasn't being sarcastic. I think?

I would find out way too late in my adult life that Asperger's was a big liability in a society that had only recently expanded lifestyle choice to a degree the Founding Fathers could not have foreseen. Ben Franklin's notion of individualism was not nearly as radical as what exists today in America. Even he might be a bit lost.

But I also had no idea in my twenties that I was part of a rolling, unplanned social experiment—in overturning a hundred different traditions at once, an experiment loosely begun in the 1960s.

I responded to my own overwhelm by shutting the real world out. I obsessed over a doctoral degree curriculum where I could honestly "punt" most of the big life decisions well into the future. I ended up receiving a PhD in anthropology, which plays a large part in why I'm qualified to write this book.

The overwhelm I felt as I wrestled with the myriad lifestyle options available in America was just an Aspie amplification of what many people now experience. This realization became a key impetus for a narrative about individualism in America, and our struggles with the extremely abundant choices facing all of us. I hope it helps you reflect on your own life journey in a new way and have more empathy for your own stumbles and those of others in your life.

Individualism is a very weird value system in the history of human societies, and I hope you'll see it that way by the time you're done reading this book.

Enjoy!

INTRODUCTION

When I was coming of age in the early 1990s, everything in the adult life of most young Americans was *their individual choice* to make. For these substantial life decisions—a sexual partner, career, recreational activities, etc.—there were no *traditional or rigidly enforced rules* to follow. You avoided the patterns of your elders and primarily looked to your peers (and to the media) for clues as to what to do. Moreover, for most Americans in this era, family stayed out of the way until things went south or you invited them in to help. Parents tended to hang back and give their kids loads of privacy. Not providing this privacy was one primary source of parental estrangement. And finally, the scope of permissible lifestyle choices was unprecedented for an urban American. While many coasted forward under traditional rules for some aspects of life, many did not.

As a single young adult American, even today, the number of lifestyle options you are faced with is the most intense of your entire lifetime. Much of your life is on manual and little on autopilot—except grooming, sleeping, and chores. Your daily habits are not nearly as fixed as they may become when you're older. You're open and discovery-oriented. This openness is most true if you've left your hometown for education or work. New social networks. New beginnings. Opportunity, we passively learn, is exciting and enthralling. Yet, it's also nerve-racking for many of us, not just those with Asperger's or other interactional challenges.

The early twenties in America are like a national version of Amish Rumspringa, without the puritanical objective of adult baptism. In the language of cultural anthropology, it is all liminality, all "betwixt and between."[1] In the language of American business, your twenties are all "upside."

America's historically unprecedented gift to its citizens—social freedom from tradition, from the constraints of monarchs, dictators, and elders—is not limited to young adults. It's why we attract immigrants constantly. It's also why middle-aged people suddenly reinvent themselves and shock their friends and family. *You're going to sail to Polynesia with your dog? What??*

There is so little traditional constraint on American lifestyle choices that most adults can determine all of the following and usually do it without the *socially mandatory* consent of anyone:

- Sexual partner(s)
- Spouses
- Career (how many, how many at one time)
- Friends (how many and how shallow)
- Food and drink
- How to be religious (or not to be)
- What volunteering to do
- What to do for fun (media, socializing, relaxation, doomscrolling)
- Family communication patterns
  - Who in the family to ignore
  - Frequency of speaking with family
  - Frequency of visiting family
- Where we shop
- Where we live and for how long we do
- Personal hobbies

Just for some concrete perspective, if you exclude the average time Americans spend in direct human care activities (1 hour) and household chores (1.95 hours), the list above basically covers 80 percent of the average American's waking hours.[2]

This list *is* daily life in modern America. And most of it is subject to our individual choices with minimal pushback from society. Yes, there is still a massive amount of the social influence, signaling, and coordination common to human societies, but without the social enforcers (strict elders, matriarchs, and village-like supervision) common to conservative societies across time. Noticeably absent are the received mandates and the choice constraints of "tradition." Instead, culture influences us primarily through media, peer networks, and consumption, locking us into the next new trend. There's a conscious sense that we're always in flux and that the rates of social and technological change are accelerating.[3]

The enormous *scope* of lifestyle choice is at the root of much of the overwhelm and anxiety young people today face. I call it "imaginative overwhelm." This choice might not matter if we couldn't so easily perceive the options or stumble on new ones randomly all the time; if college campuses, the media, and our social networks didn't constantly present us with other options. It might not matter either if we encountered all these choices suddenly later in life. It would become academic or curious.

It's the anxiety of super-abundant lifestyle choices without many of the hierarchical ordering principles common to premodern societies. Choice without much structure. We are let loose with no clear ritual process to get us to some clear end state. Some of us crash and burn. Badly.

It signals a national Rumspringa with no real end. Certainly not in baptism.

When I first heard about Amish Rumspringa in graduate school, I was having dinner with an Amish refugee graduate student in the International House at the University of Chicago. He had no intention of returning to Ohio. He had failed the test of faith. In Rumspringa, Amish youth are permitted to "go crazy" and take autonomy to its extreme. This period takes place during the late teens, immediately prior to adult baptism, which, in the Anabaptist faith, is a deliberate, adult choice. Some kids never return from Rumspringa.

In that University of Chicago dining hall, I discovered an Amish life stage that drowns young people in the ocean of free will and lifestyle choice without any scope or rules in order to test their commitment to the Amish Order. Most Amish kids quickly realize the value of all that structure and return to take their baptism.[4]

For most Americans, though, there is no mandated path like this. There may be echoes of what your parents did or glimpses of what your peers are doing. But the life paths are now many, and no one's permission is needed to take any of them. Yes, there may be backlash, but *not from people who can stop you.*

As I got older, I increasingly found the society around me to be mostly a disabling force. When I discovered my neurological challenge in my midthirties, I tried hard to knowingly adapt better. Slowly, I realized that my emotional volatility and poor stress management found daily triggers in modern social life, especially its emphasis on self-control and self-reliance. I also noticed that the external forces creating anxiety for me deeply affected others with neurotypical brains as well.

This book is my personal and professional attempt to understand the experience of individualism in a society that has taken lifestyle choice to its logical extreme at the same time that social change has accelerated faster than any time before in recorded human history.

The questions driving this book are:

- What is it like to live like an individualist in America?
- How does it work?
- What long-term consequences does it create for American society?
- Where in our everyday lives has individualism been a boon? Or a setup for trauma?
- How does rapid social change make individualism adaptive or maladaptive?
- And, finally, what really are the hidden discontents of America's national ideology?

To make this productive, I conducted extensive national research among older Americans (now aged forty-seven to seventy-six) in 2022 and 2023.[5]

Why not research everyone? Because older Americans have had enough life experience to say something meaningful about their life choices and the consequences of those choices in a rapidly changing world.

Specifically, I focused on older Americans' experiences of major life decisions (e.g., career changes, marital issues, family cohesion, dietary changes, recovery from trauma, etc.). How individualistic were these decisions? What were the consequences of making nontraditional lifestyle choices? And how have older Americans adapted to social changes impacting them during their lifetimes (such as the rapid rise in female employment and increasing job insecurity)?

This book is not a comprehensive summary of research findings. It is not a scholarly monograph. Playing by those rules would severely limit the audience and the impact of my work. Instead, I want to take the reader on a journey that (a) first makes individualism weird; (b) then explores how individualistic behavior panned out for real folks, including me, and finally; (c) urges us to take a more critical approach to heeding the call of individualistic impulses.

My goal is not to call for a return to some imagined past utopia that never existed. And I won't be outlining some perfect society we should quickly build. My purpose is to get us to question how we live and the broader social forces that individualism feeds on and supports. I want to help curious readers detach from a common belief in the *inevitability, and the inevitable preferability, of a highly individualistic society*. Things didn't have to turn out this way. Something *was* lost. Some things were gained.

This book is unique because no one to my knowledge has taken the individual's perspective and listened to how she navigated a distinctive culture of extreme lifestyle choice that spread quickly in the 1960s and 1970s.

Only once we recognize how adaptive or maladaptive individualism has been in everyday life do we have the power of real social awareness that affords us the wisdom to make collective change.

Now, let's see what happened . . . !

Part One

HOW TO MAKE A HYPER-INDIVIDUALISTIC SOCIETY IN SEVEN EASY STEPS

> The primary function of the term "individual" is to express the idea that every human being in the world is, or should be, an autonomous entity.
> —*Norbert Elias, Society of Individuals*

Chapter One

UNLOCK THE VARIABLES OF LIFESTYLE CHOICE

The best way I can think of to make individualism seem weird or at least seem like an arbitrary way of living, is to pretend you and I are cooking up a brand-new society from scratch. What basic elements do we need to produce a society of individuals extremely oriented to their own autonomy?

In part one, I'm going to share what I think are the seven basic ingredients you would need. But I'll be honest, I don't know the entire recipe.

When I'm done, you'll be ready to explore how individualism and social change have combined to alter American life in dramatic ways that rarely get discussed in one place.

Our Greatest American Freedom

"Don't your children want to come back and visit the home they grew up in?" my eighty-six-year-old maternal grandmother asked my mom in 1991 when she told her they would sell my childhood home in Bedford, NH. She couldn't believe my parents would just sell it as a *lifestyle choice*. She didn't understand the "time to move on" sentiment in modern America, especially among the affluent. She also didn't understand the idea of parents making all their decisions *as a couple* once the kids were gone, i.e., reverting to a romantic couple. Home was a family asset to her, and there was a female obligation to maintain it forever. To my parents, it was just a house, an easily disposed of investment. Home is where the heart is, right?

At the time, my brother and I were in our twenties, adrift in America's open-ended Rumspringa, exploring opportunities physical, intellectual, and income related. We were following no clear life-stage timeline whatsoever. If we fixated on anything back then, it was the possibility-rich future ahead of us as well-educated young people.

I remember the nineties as nothing but a wide-open field of opportunities. So many life choices not yet made. So many choices I got to determine for myself. So many choices whose timeline itself I could set without supervision.

In the nineties, we twentysomething grandkids didn't look backward to:

- A homestead
- A family farm
- A family business
- Family traditions
- Inherited religious practices
- Ethnic customs
- The way it's always been

Any lifestyle choice that tied us to the past looked antiquated, sad, unambitious, and lacking in creativity. *You want to go to law school? How lame.*

As my mom understood well in 1991 when she sold my childhood home, the single most important social freedom in the modern world is the *freedom to ignore the past*. It's less about deleting the past and more about the freedom to pick what little we want to carry into our respective, personally curated futures.[1]

I'm betting my maternal grandmother couldn't grasp the meaning of such lifestyle freedom. Intellectually, I'm sure she could understand it, but I doubt it appealed to her. Certain early feminist freedoms appealed to her: the right to vote, the right to work after pregnancy (which she was denied), or the right to delay marriage (which she did). But the freedom to hook up with random people before marriage, the right to single motherhood, or the right to divorce? I doubt it. For her, the scope of individual freedom stood anchored to the dominant, largely unchallenged moral constraints of the early twentieth century. The scope of *desired* freedom was much narrower than it is today.

In mid-twentieth century America, our nation underwent a rapid restructuring of its social landscape in response to historically unprecedented macroeconomic growth:[2]

- Cities grew and overflowed into government-subsidized suburbs.
- The college degree took off as a social mobility tool.
- National and multinational companies grew fast and moved employees around a shrinking national geography.
- Life expectancy grew, allowing the old to plan long retirements in warm zip codes far from family.
- Young people looked for more comfortable, hedonic lifestyles than their Depression-era parents.
- Everyone needed more and more cash in a fully realized cash economy whose growth was ever more driven by premium upgrades in housing, transportation, and home necessities.
- Friends became more critical than ever in our social lives as sources of economic and sexual opportunity.
- Social networks became more and more curated by individuals, not assigned to individuals by birth or geography.[3]

When entire generations seek out better jobs, better incomes, and a better life, and the economy rewards geographic and social dislocation to pursue them all, the pilot light of a hyper-individualistic society gets lit. Whether any of this is *better* doesn't matter for this discussion. This seeking behavior is about shedding the past for perceived modernity. It's easy to get lost in a reckoning of who got more access to the benefits of modernity than others (mostly whites and Asians). But the larger story has been the unprecedented degree to which any lone individual can now tread life paths dislocated from multiple forms of the past— their geographic past, family past, and ethnoreligious past. And even some of those born into poverty pull it off as well.

In 1968, an aging Frank Sinatra crooned his new hit song, "My Way," to thousands of enthralled Radio City Music Hall listeners. It was the height of America's most significant cultural torment since Reconstruction after the Civil War. The English lyrics of "My Way" are unconsciously sexist, expressing a hypermasculine, borderline antisocial ideology of individualism. Sinatra crooned a mass-market way of interpreting and making life choices, at least for America's middle and affluent classes.

In 1968, unlocking the scope and timing of significant lifestyle choices (marriage, becoming sexually active, first full-time job, retirement, divorce, etc.) was still largely a *male* prerogative in American society. Men could break with many social norms, but not women.[4] Men had been doing this in America since they abandoned the family farm in the nineteenth century to work in urban factories. In some cases, they even left their families to do so. But middle-class women would soon have their moment of lifestyle liberation, one an aging Sinatra could not foresee.

The enormous social forces that permitted men to act like mini Sinatras in the 1950s and 1960s soon became available to tens of millions of young Baby Boomer women.

The *Real* Invisible Hand(s)

In modern American history, there are three social forces we tend to deny the existence of, even though they operate like the Jedi force all around us, all the time.

1. A **cultural orientation to an unknown future** full of emerging opportunities and consumer experiences
2. A steady **temptation to unlock lifestyle choice variables to maximize our adaptation** to a rapidly evolving social milieu for which our childhood didn't prepare us
3. A constant **pressure to self-regulate our behavior** in ever more complex ways as society diversifies and

integrates and as achievement standards grow more nuanced[5]

I want to focus readers on how 1) orienting to an unknown future *distracts* us from the past, making it much easier to 2) unlock lifestyle variables that permit 3) our continual adaptation to accelerating social changes.

This working model of modern American social life makes lone individuals primarily responsible for adapting to change through ever more intense self-regulation and self-awareness. We have repeatedly raised the ante on the individual to be more flexible, adaptable, and accommodating. Yet, we present this reality as an ultramodern superpower—*autonomy*.

The debate over microaggressions is a perfect ongoing example of how standards of self-regulation ratchet ever upward, especially as the modern workplace diversifies.

"I've learned to make no assumptions," a Baby Boomer peer once told me on a business trip years ago. She grew up in a conservative, working-class home. Still, she was thrust into a multiracial, modern multinational apparel company early in her career. She met all sorts of folks from all kinds of backgrounds. The company intended them to melt together as a team nevertheless. This required a lot of self-control. Women no doubt still have an advantage over men in this quiet, relentless social adaptation process. Adaptation, after all, is very close to accommodation and its ally—*pleasing authority figures* (if we can imagine society itself as an authority).

But what if you are an individual whose neurology doesn't suit you to such a world, to such interrelated forces of change and the confusion and ambiguity that result?

What if you have chronic anxiety, autism, or clinical depression?

What if you have past sexual assault trauma, yet find yourself working around poorly behaved men for a living?

What if you have undiagnosed ADHD and can't do deskwork for eight hours a day inside a cube farm?

What if you are a man who doesn't trust your *female* peers because your mother was a clinical narcissist and emotionally abusive?

What if you are being asked to make behavioral changes you can't stand to make for the sake of adapting to new norms?

What if you cling more to past social norms than others and are offended by modernity?

It doesn't take a survey to realize that many people who grew up in the 1950s through the 1980s could answer yes to at least one of the above questions.

To make my point more concrete, let's dive into the great American Rumspringa, the extended premarital life stage that so many young Americans enjoy and get lost in.

The American Rumspringa

"Hey, I heard from Bethany. Remember her?" my boss asked me once in her office out of the blue.

"Oh, yeah. She was really smart. Too bad she left," I replied.

"Well, she just asked for a reference because she got laid off, and her boyfriend dumped her. Everything's in flux! Remember your twenties?" she asked rhetorically while chuckling.

I call this weird life stage the American Rumspringa because it resembles an open-ended version of the let loose phase that Amish teenagers engage in before their adult baptism and acceptance of the Amish Order.[6]

The Amish view Rumspringa as a one-to-two-year spiritual test of loyalty to family and the Amish way of life. They don't want posers to stay. It's a brilliant way of purging bad influences in a conservative, highly conformist subculture. It also allows immature people to see how much trouble you can get into beyond the protection of the order and how unpleasant that trouble *feels*. It lets you experience the *loneliness* of self-destruction and self-absorption.

As a young American adult, however, there is no ceremonial beginning to our Rumspringa, except perhaps one: attending college. College is where many Americans now learn to break with prior traditions, play with their lifestyle, and let loose.[7]

The American Rumspringa is a time in our lives made possible by the permission to delay marriage (or ignore it entirely). It is when Americans focus their energies on a volatile mix of friends and quasi-friends, dates and semi-dates, and the occasional love triangle. The young American's social life outside work revolves almost entirely around their curated friends and sexual partners (inside or outside of marriage). There's a famous sitcom on this topic called—brace yourself—*Friends*. Super creative writers.

Making friends with strangers is a critical young adult skill if you decide to leave your home turf for any reason. And the more educated you are, the more likely you will relocate during your early twenties.

I sure did.

Post–World War II America unleashed an acceleration in the scope of lifestyle choices available to the average middle-class and affluent adult. This did not, however, evaporate conservative notions of family, gender roles, household composition, who should work outside the home, or sexual behavior. It just enabled the erosion of the dominant constraining forces governing lifestyle choice. Someone came around and loosened all the screws or unlocked the breakers.

By the 1970s, most American men and women now had unprecedented lifestyle control over the key domains that govern daily life.

Choice is a tricky concept, though, and I want to define some terms for the rest of this book because I hope they will help you see individualism from a new perspective. This is the bottoms-up perspective of everyday life, the stuff of cultural anthropologists and urban sociologists.[8]

We do not make all our life choices consciously. If we did, we would go insane by late morning each day. And just because we perceive that a choice is possible does *not* mean we feel we have the power to exercise it. Historically in America, this state of adverse constraint has held for the poor, the Black, the Indigenous, the homeless, and women. The white male has *always* had more choices available to him in every given era.

Here are the stages of *choosing* stuff as an adult human (in any society):

Stage 1—Perceiving a choice exists at all. Before the 1970s, choosing not to marry was rarely perceived as a valid lifestyle choice;

it was the reserve of priests, gays, madmen, and wealthy eccentrics (who literally could buy sex).

Stage 2—Perceiving the full scope of possibilities. A conservative evangelical may understand that society will let them delay marriage. Still, they don't see this as an option.

Stage 3—Being open to part or all of the permissible scope. Just because I know I can have an open marriage since adultery is no longer a crime does not mean I believe I am comfortable with this option or would ever bring it up with my wife even if I was. Which I'm not.

Stage 4—Making a choice (at various levels of conscious awareness). Marriage is a conscious and deliberate choice in all societies. What minimum level of food quality you adhere to at the supermarket is much less so.

Stage 5—Accepting your choice. The therapists come in here! Don't laugh. A lifestyle choice in America is not always one permanently made. The perception that even a marital choice is reversible (i.e., divorce) adds a modern level of anxiety to our lives. This is the stage in the choosing process that your parents or grandparents may still not understand (and many never will).

If I can force a review: Stages 1 and 2 are where cultural and familial influences linger from the past to varying degrees. Stages 3 and 4 reveal how much agency a person feels when making this or that perceived choice. Stage 5 is increasingly where we confront past choices we made years ago that are now maladaptive to a new present no one we knew could anticipate.

As you'll see in this book, it is *not* just Asperger's sufferers who walk around scratching their heads these days, totally confused. It is many of us.

Now, I'm ready to share a fun little thought experiment that will make much more historical sense out of choice theory and America's modern Rumspringa (I hope).

How to read this table:
Choice domain =
    a *category* of choice most Americans perceive as available
Scope of choice =
    a set of choices widely known and perceived as available

Table 1. Modern Lifestyle Choices c. 1970

CHOICE DOMAIN	SCOPE OF CHOICE		
	Choice #1	Choice #2	Choice #3
Household composition	single	couple	family
Women's career/work outside the home	full-time	part-time	none
Marriage	yes	no	
Marriage timing	early	average	late
Divorce as option	yes	no	
Loyalty to patriarchal gender roles	yes	no	
Having kids	yes	no	
Caring for elders	yes	no	
Relationships with extended family	none	weak	strong
What to eat/drink	basic quality	basic and premium quality	premium only
Transportation expenses	low	medium	high
Daily hours spent in leisure activities	normal	above normal	

Unlock the Variables of Lifestyle Choice

This table is insufficient for a sociology dissertation. It is a *Reader's Digest*–friendly thought experiment that offers a fundamental contrast between the world I was born into in the early 1970s versus the world of my grandparents (born between 1902 and 1919).

Let's look at the options in table 1 and calculate the number of unique *lifestyle choice combinations you get*. There are 30 options across 12 mandatory choice domains, yielding *46,656 possible lifestyle combinations*. Math is fun stuff. I'm sure there is a nerdy board game concept in here somewhere.

But, if we eliminate choices and options that *the majority didn't perceive before 1970*, here's what we get. Are you ready?

Table 2. Lifestyle Choices c. 1920[9]

CHOICE DOMAIN	SCOPE OF CHOICE		
	Choice #1	Choice #2	Choice #3
Household composition	single (men only)	couple	family
Women's career/work outside home	part-time	none	
Marriage	yes		
Marriage timing	early		
Divorce	no		
Loyalty to patriarchal gender roles	yes		
Having kids	yes		
Caring for elders	yes		

Relationships with extended family	weak	strong	
What to eat/drink	basic quality	basic and premium quality	
Transportation expenditures	low to none	medium	
Daily hours spent in leisure activities	normal		

In this premodern world before World War II, *we only have six of the original twelve choice domains available to most adults.* There are fewer perceivable lifestyle choices and fewer feasible choices in this era (permissible without major social ostracization in a highly networked, more conservative society).

The choices available to most of America in the early twentieth century yielded only *144 combinations or individual lifestyles.*

Americans witnessed an exponential increase in lifestyle choices in only about 50 years (from approximately 144 different lifestyles to more than 44,000). That's a 324 times increase in lifestyle options in three generations.

Wow. I mean, just wow.

Humans are incredibly adaptive animals, probably the most skilled *conscious* adaptors in the animal world. That's because we can adapt within complex social networks, not just in crude, alpha-driven packs. And we can adjust fast, if necessary. But, still, what I just outlined is an incredible explosion of lifestyle choices in a short period.

For much of human history, many adult choices we take for granted were not choices, especially the most critical choice: who you will marry and when you will do this. Most American college students gasp when they first encounter East African ethnographies describing the practice of bride price among premodern groups like the Nuer or the Masai. In these communities, the groom's parents negotiate a price for a young woman (in cattle and other goods) and offer this amount to the bride's parents. Marriage in these tribes is an explicit economic transaction, not a romantic one.

In contrast, the twentieth-century American social experiment has been a massive experiment in *multiplying* choice, proliferating it, and socially deregulating it for a broadly defined middle and upper-middle class.[10]

In this historical context, neurodivergence like mine becomes a social liability it would not have otherwise been. The sheer complexity of life escalates when choices increase. This creates cognitive overwhelm, ambiguity, and confusion that did not exist at a similar scale before the 1960s.

Parents raised in the pre-World War II era could not foresee what their young adult children would have in front of them as they entered adulthood. No one can blame their parenting from this perspective.

My ordinarily mild-mannered grandfather was livid, maybe even apoplectic, when my oldest aunt divorced her abusive, alcoholic husband. Livid. She didn't take it personally and ignored him. But I'm sure it hurt to get that stern, patriarchal letter.

The multiplication of lifestyles in America has not been a monolithic, simplistic transition from a conservative society to a liberal one. Hardly. It's about the proliferation of lifestyles across this entire continuum. If you want to cling to a 1920s lifestyle, go for it. If you wish to pursue a niche lifestyle combination no one can fathom, go for it. If you want to be a polygamous Mormon, fine. If you want to be a BDSM "slave" on the weekends, whatever. In both extreme cases, you'll lose some friends, but you'll have the perfect cultural air cover: it was *my* choice and it's none of your damn business.

Chapter Two

SILENCING THE ELDERS

I remember big bear hugs from my maternal grandmother every time we visited her musty, hillside 1930s Dutch colonial in frostbitten northern New Hampshire. She looked delighted when we showed up every Thanksgiving Eve. Kids can tell. When we were young, she always pointed us quickly to the candy bowl full of Werther's Originals, recently bought for our visit and lying on a fresh doily (!). If you just googled "doily," you are young.

While we were grabbing the candy (hey, never refuse a gift), my mom always looked anxious. Kids can tell.

We had two annual visits with her each year while Grandpa was alive and well. Then it was just one at Thanksgiving. Then, once we kids were in high school, it became none. My mom would continue to visit independently, but only once a year. Their relationship had plenty of scars; again, none of *my* business. Kids learn not to reopen old wounds out of curiosity and allegiance to the cultural code of silence known as privacy. Don't get nosy with her unless you want her to butt into all of your life—mutually assured privacy.

I can confidently say that, in my parents' worldview, fostering deep relationships between grandkids and grandparents was *not* a priority. It was a very low priority, given that the individuals only lived two hours away from us. I mean, gasoline and time were cheap.

So, like so many Caucasian Americans in my generation, I grew up to understand that my grandparents were friendly folks who were irrelevant to our daily existence. And so, we ignored them.

When elders only have sporadic holiday contact with their living descendants, the focus of any rare interactions becomes hedonic: fun and enjoyment. Latent concerns about their kids' parenting skills or their grandkids' swearing tend to fade to the background in favor of listening to the verbal equivalent of boastful holiday family update letters. It's all performance on both sides. And the performance is easy to sustain for one to two days. OK, maybe just one day.

We forget that this detached relationship between elders and the youngest generation is very modern. In traditional societies, the patriarchs and matriarchs controlled most of your life until they expired. If you work in your family's multigenerational business, you are part of a small minority of Americans who may still experience the power of the aging elder at work. But there aren't many of you (mostly on family farms, ranches, in the local trades, or the food industry ecosystem).[1]

Silencing the elders is critical to delinking oneself from an inherited past of prior choice patterns. It involves the following components (at least):

- Obtaining financial independence from them
- Geographically abandoning them
- Implicitly threatening to cut them off
- Limiting lifestyle interventions to low-stakes areas

Obtaining Financial Independence from Them

Leaving the family farm was a half-century process for most Americans from 1860 to 1920. This gargantuan mass migration set up the fundamental microeconomic requirement for silencing and neutering the social power of elders later.[2] It ended the default practice of working for the family.

Most Americans today work for *nonrelatives* in professional settings (white collar and blue collar), even if the company they work for tends to be a family business.[3]

Working for your family's business is one of the more awkward things an educated adult could ever confess to anyone beyond the family. Nepotism is a gross sin in a modern, hyper-individualistic society. It is the butt of endless jokes like the lines from a recent Upwork commercial, "I could be hiring talented people from all over the world. Instead, I'm sourcing talentless people from inside my house."

Ouch. Tasteless, maybe?

As working for the family declined after World War II, becoming financially independent from one's parents became a broad middle-class mandate. Once Mom or Dad can't "cut you off," they can only *comment* on your lifestyle choices.[4] They can scream and yell or refuse to see you. That's about it. And this behavior doesn't tend to yield visits or returned phone calls. The power of estrangement is not the same as the power to decimate your cash flow. It is a nuclear option with blowback mostly for the elders.

Geographically Abandoning Them

Abandoning one's hometown for a preferred lifestyle is not a twentieth-century idea. It began right after the Civil War as America industrialized. Urban factories offered time-bounded shift jobs that a) paid more than the farm did, b) offered liberation from broken family dynamics, and c) often boosted daily leisure time (if the one factory wage was a living one).[5]

Putting geographic distance between you and your natal kin has usually been essential to achieving lifestyle freedom across the modern globe. And that is why many Baby Boomers and Gen Xers in America grew up wanting to "get out of Dodge!" Not all did this, for sure, but certainly the most ambitious or alienated from their parents.

Before the internet and cheap, unlimited long-distance phone calls in the 1990s, there was always the "expensive call" excuse to reduce telephonic contact with annoying relatives, including your parents.[6] And letters, though cheaper, were super easy to ignore (a pile of ignored letters is a staple movie trope). This relative communicative isolation before high-speed internet added to the phenomenon of geographic abandonment—a double buffer of silence kept any unwanted elders at bay.

Increased connectivity to family today may be changing some of these dynamics. But let's be honest. You aren't going to avail yourself of FaceTime with jerk parents just because it's cheap and the audio is good. The power of the relationship trumps the cost and ease of communicating with anyone.

Implicitly Threatening to Cut Them Off

Some children end up "disappointing" their parents. Some disappoint massively and are a constant source of problems and stress. I know a retired couple across the street raising their grandson because their son (and his wife) are drug addicts. Raising a grandkid was *not* how they planned their golden years, trust me. Their massive RV bus collects dust when it should be barreling down Route 66.

A lot of parent-child estrangement is due to intergenerational shifts in values related directly to the c. 1970 lifestyle choice table I showed you in chapter one. And it appears from my recent research among older Americans that, during the rapid individualization of lifestyles starting in the late 1960s, some parents miscalculated severely and lost contact with their grandkids. This, in a way, became their version of individual choice: the *choice* to disown the forsaken child.

During a typical rambling phone call with my parents years ago, my mom brought up, yet again, the heinous behavior of a friend's daughter-in-law. The rude comments. The selfishness. The sheer obnoxious disrespect every time they brought the grandkids to visit.

"She always hated her, even before she married David," my mom said.

"Why didn't she intervene to block the marriage, then?" I asked naively.

"Because he might not speak to them again, and then they might never see their grandkids," my dad responded as if this was a logical and sane response.

This is the *implied* estrangement threat we hold against our elders. You can comment but be careful what you say because we don't *need* you in our lives.

Although I suspect many grandparents exaggerate the likelihood of their own behavior triggering estrangement, the fact that so many feel this way poignantly reveals their disempowered structural position as elders.

Years later, in another epic telephone banter session with my parents, the same dark, twisted soul emerged in the conversation.

"Why don't they just cut this woman off? Tell her she can't visit anymore unless she behaves differently," I asked with similar premarital naivete.

"What if she cuts them off in response? How would they see their grandkids?" my dad responded almost identically.

The power of the implied estrangement threat works pretty well if we invert a simple statistic. Ten percent of American adults with living parents are wholly estranged from one of them.[7] But that means that 90 percent are *not* estranged from either of them! As lifestyle choice constraints unlocked in the late 1960s, parents witnessed shocking behavior they did not know how to tolerate, let alone accept as usual. The elder learning has been *extreme* tolerance, primarily to maintain sporadic access to the grandchildren and their biological contact with the future.

Grandparents will do a lot, it appears, to keep access to their grandkids (even before they arrive). Why so much effort to bite one's tongue? Well, because a) they see them in person so rarely, and b) biology is how humans have traditionally perceived the future when we didn't do it by tracking technological change and modeling retirement nest eggs. Staring into the young eyes of your living descendants is the original time machine (even a niece or nephew counts). Your pet can't ever offer you this feeling.

It's intoxicating.

In a society drowning in media and consumer temptations, connecting to the future has shifted culturally from connecting with our kids and grandkids to connecting with the next new thing to *consume*.

In the Academy Award–winning movie *On Golden Pond*, Henry Fonda plays a grumpy older man named Norman living with his wife in New Hampshire. Norman is desperate for a grandchild his only daughter has not yet delivered due to her career priorities and late marriage. He only heals when he finally meets his daughter's stepson. Finally, Norman has a connection to the future beyond his imminent death. Someone to whom he can teach fishing. And when he does this simple thing, he realizes he can now die with an imagined bridge to the future.

Limit Any Lifestyle Critique to Lower Stakes Issues

While Baby Boomers bolted from the cul-de-sac to pursue opportunities and new lifestyles, they did not abandon their elders entirely as they aged. Grandma moving in with the family continued to happen after the cultural revolution. However, it hasn't been the choice of most adults.

If a parent does move in with you, though, there is a dramatic cultural test that unfolds pretty quickly. It tests a parent's willingness to let you set different parenting rules with the grandkids (i.e., these are not your kids, Mom and Dad). Believe it or not, the number of homes running this multigenerational cultural test has been growing steadily since the 1970s. As I write this, around 18 percent of households are multigenerational in America (three or more generations under one roof).[8]

What grandparents have learned living with their grandkids is that they need to confine their behavioral critiques a) to the ears of their kids and b) to low-stakes issues. Things like *Your kids watch too much TV*, or *Your kid eats too much ice cream*. And *not* stuff like *Your daughter dresses like a flirt*, or *YouTube is a covert agent of the great Satan* (which it is, but that's not the point).

Here's a telling anecdote from my recent research I suspect has repeated itself in many multigenerational homes after Grandma moved in.

> *There was something with Sarah [our daughter] about two to three weeks after my mom moved into the addition we built for her. My wife and Sarah were having an argument, and my mom tried to get in the middle of it. I took her into her bedroom, sat her down, and explained that Sarah is our daughter and that she couldn't get involved in parenting her. She was pissed off and didn't talk to us for a few days. But it never happened again.*[9]

Grandma is no longer a matriarch. She is a source of bear hugs and candy. And encouragement. That's it. Honestly, is it so bad being Mrs. Positive all the time?

It's fun for both sides if Grandma can tolerate biting her tongue until it bleeds.

Capitalism *Wants* the Elders to Back Off

Ironically, the growth of the middle class in America almost predestined the silencing of our elders. Pursuing career opportunities exposed tens of millions of working- and middle-class Baby Boomers and Gen X adults to new lifestyle options beyond the sheltered suburbs of their youth from the 1950s to the 1980s. Unless you were going to choose not to perceive these opportunities, your chances of leaving Dodge were high during this period.

Growing economies from 1950 to 2000 required citizens to disconnect from rigid value systems and extended family bonds that would otherwise have kept them locked in geographically confined, ascribed social networks. Fast-growing economies need most adults to disconnect from the past, from the conservatism of elders that would encourage them to ignore anything new.

Growing consumption-led economies like ours continually feed the desire to consume more by increasing the desire to earn more so one can recycle last decade's everything for this decade's more expensive everything. In some categories, like home decor and automobiles, this cycle is turning over every five years, and even faster for clothing and media.

Some of America's largest industries relate entirely to exploring our curiosity (travel, media) and loosening our inhibitions (alcohol, porn, nightclubs, music venues). The leisure industrial complex we have developed has little use for uptight grandmothers.

Commitment to *consumption* competes unfairly with commitment to the family for most of us (beyond the trust fund elite). This is why most Americans detest inherited wealth but have no problem with the nouveau riche, with wealth generated in one action-packed generation (cue my father's biography).

It's not that we have silenced our elders *literally*. You can take candy from them on Thanksgiving in Miami. You can hug them on Christmas morning in Milwaukee. You can light the menorah with them in LA. You can light oil lamps with them on Diwali in New Jersey.

America's elders often object to what their grandkids do, but immensely less than an Amish parent would in a similar situation. Rumspringa is Rumspringa. Then it stops. Or we will shun you. Then we will banish you. Amish kids have one chance to cut off their parents; parents do the estranging. This is the way of most conservative, premodern societies where elders rule until death. These are not societies engineered for rapid change. One could argue they are engineered to slow down all attempts at change until the elders reflect further (much like church ordination timelines).

Most American elders pick their battles with their kids (and grandkids). And what else can they do? There is no real social force that they have left to compel you to follow their rules. Accepting this fundamental impotence of modern elders forces us to realize, by the logic of inversion, that the single most efficient, compulsive, and powerful way to inhibit individual freedom of behavior is by *ensuring that a choice is not ever perceived*.[10] Once we perceive a new choice and believe it is feasible (e.g., divorce in the 1960s), then social change can be so rapid that society is not at all ready for the individualistic consequences.

Chapter Three

MAKE PRIVACY SACRED

On my second day in Tamil-speaking South India in 1995, I ventured into the old city of Madurai. I wanted to visit the massive Saivite temple in the center with its stunning two-hundred-foot towers covered in painted statuary. After I got my sandals off and stored them, I went through the south gate and hired a temple guide to take me around and explain things in English.

After the "tour," my guide, who spoke in broken English, asked if I was hungry. I nodded, and he offered to take me to a nearby restaurant just around the corner. I didn't know where the hell I was, so why not? Now playing cultural guide at the restaurant, the man noted that there was always a traditional fixed lunch in Tamil Nadu (i.e., you don't order off a lunch menu). In seconds, I had a fresh banana leaf rolled out before me, sprinkled with water by a different person and topped with a pile of steaming rice from a bucket from another. Seconds later, another kid plopped three side dishes on the far side of the rice pile. Finally, another kid ladled thick yellow dal stew and poured it on my rice. It took five people to get me served!

I was so busy trying to figure out how to eat the food with my right hand, I didn't notice that my companion hadn't ordered his own lunch. About ten minutes in, I began to fall asleep from some medication. It was a sudden, unnatural sleepiness. I had been drugged with something akin to quaaludes. I assume it was via the water they gave me. As I turned into a pliant zombie, my "friend" escorted me outside to an autorickshaw. I still have no recollection of who paid for lunch, if anyone.

My captor asked me to tell him where my apartment was, info

which I have no recollection of giving to him or the driver. I do remember trying to push him out of the rickshaw and get home on my own, but my muscles wouldn't comply. The scene had turned into "get the sick white man home." The temple guide was now playing the part of my "rescuer" to everyone we encountered. No one else around seemed to suspect anything.

I remember unlocking my apartment gate and being "helped" up the stairs behind it. When we both entered my apartment, I passed out on my mattress, with him sitting behind me in my living room.

When I woke up hours later, he was long gone. It was now early evening, and the gate to my apartment was swinging open at the bottom of the stairs. I first checked that I hadn't been attacked, sexually or otherwise, then searched the apartment for missing items. My traveler's checks, all $2,000 worth, were gone. But I still had my passport in my neck pouch. The checks were worthless in the legal banking market without that ID. A silver lining?

I was sitting there in my apartment with about 500 rupees in cash. I had to solve my money problem because I had two more months in India. I desperately wanted to call my parents due to the shock of everything. But I couldn't bear the humiliation. Plus, there wasn't anything they knew that I didn't know about how to solve this problem. I just had to get to the nearest Amex office, which could reissue the checks, which, when I called around that night, was a five-hour bus ride away. And they wanted a copy of a local police report to prove I'd made some feeble attempt to recover the money.

When I recounted this tale years later to my Tamil friends where I was doing fieldwork, one of the otherwise mild-mannered guys blurted out, "Where is this idiot? We'll go beat him up!" These were church choir boys, just to be clear, so I was shocked to hear their suggestion of violent retribution. And they weren't exaggerating for effect. Trust me.

The Tamil response to my drugging, abduction, and robbery highlights, by magical inversion, the power of American middle-class culture to make everyone feel solely responsible for their own problems. Instead of pointing out what I did wrong to get myself in trouble (the American response), they just wanted to defend their friend and protect the *group* against a threat. Clearly, to my friends, I was taken advantage of and bore no responsibility for simple naivete. Not once did any of them suggest I was an idiot for letting it happen. And Tamil culture is not shy about interpersonal confrontation about anything.

I didn't call my parents that day because I didn't want to hear them lecture me about being more careful. They may not have done this, but I was culturally primed to think they would. Like most survivors of trauma, the last thing you need to hear is, "You got yourself into this mess." Yet that is precisely how we are all taught to think when this kind of thing happens. A proud, urban culture of self-help (and self-help books) almost requires that we solve our problems alone. Eventually, you come to believe that you caused most of the problems in your life, which, as with your successes in life, is an absurd illusion I hope to burst open in this book.

Learn to Conceal Your Interpersonal Trauma

By defining interpersonal failures, traumas, and tragedy (whether failed relationships, getting conned abroad, or old-fashioned physical abuse) as *personal* outcomes, American cultural ideology convinces us that we are individually responsible for what happened. The social context that created the perfect conditions of possibility for a bad social outcome, fades into the margins of our moral memory. *We didn't speak up early enough. We didn't prepare. We asked for it.*

In the 1990s, the modern rape survivor expression, "You did nothing wrong," did not exist. I would wager most older Americans still believe that the individual is primarily responsible for entering a dangerous social context and then suffering trauma there. "You had to *know* it was dangerous. You didn't do your homework." This thinking is still everywhere, even as younger folks challenge it.

The key word here is "know." Is it reasonable to expect that everyone understands what could go wrong in any given social context they are freely allowed to enter with zero preparation? Freedom of mobility would then imply a hell of a lot of foreknowledge (via Neuralink?). Yet, who holds that knowledge before entering new relationships or social spaces? And how would this critical knowledge get to the naïve effectively anyway? And why, oh why, do we always rely on *prophylactic* education to prevent *individual* missteps?

"You should have done your homework" strikes me as an impossible standard in more than a few situations encountered in modern urban life. This is especially true in a rapidly changing society when individuals are straying far beyond their family's knowledge base. "Do your homework" is an introverted librarian's approach to social policy and the social protection of individuals.

Only in the extremes of natural disasters and mass shootings do we seem to look first to context and *not* blame the victims.

The result of America's culture of hyper-individualistic moral reasoning is that trauma survivors learn to hide behind a self-imposed veil of privacy. Too many bury the trauma for years or even forever. And the more privileged the individual, the more that shame hardens that veil of privacy and the threat of embarrassment.

One question still haunts me about that blistering hot day in June 1995: Why was I, a naïve graduate student from abroad, *allowed* to wander into central Madurai alone? After all, the local college year-abroad program run by the university I was affiliated with gave their students thorough introductions to local risks. The university knew I was going there. But their obligation ended with getting their local contact to set up an apartment for me and send me an address. That was it. I was otherwise on *my own. Why?* I still have no good answer decades later.

Being *alone* with the temple guide opened up the opportunity for a con game. Nothing would have happened had just one additional person been with me. This is why Tamils always go to new places with companions, preferably a posse. It's tough to con an entire group unless you are the CEO.

I later learned that the Meenakshi temple was known for doing nothing to prevent unauthorized guides from operating on the premises. *Would have been nice to know.*

Making Privacy Sacred Leaves Us Very Alone

We are encouraged to say, *Leave me alone* in defiance to anyone who objects to our individual quests in work, romance, or leisure. In return, we do not ask society to accept responsibility for bad interpersonal outcomes. We asked for freedom, so society essentially checks out and hopes for the best (or remains indifferent). We only invite society back in to help us pick up the pieces. Perhaps. And this is more likely if we are female or grew up with strong family values.

The sacredness of privacy in American culture requires us to bury our personal traumas and failures, to confess them to no one (or much later when something in our lives blows up). *Suck it up, kid, and move on.* If we don't want people all up in our personal business all the time, we kind of have to keep our problems to ourselves. We must keep everyone out, letting them receive only a filtered version of our life. This is what I might call the *LinkedIn performance of recent professional achievement*. If you choose to reveal your trauma, it's your choice. But society has no *right* to access this personal knowledge, despite how useful it would be for your boss, spouse, parents, etc., to know it.

The sacredness of privacy makes it impossible for society to *prevent* needless trauma at the individual level. Most of us don't grant society the authority to edit our personal wanderings *in advance*, which is when guidance is most beneficial. Society intervenes mainly in *reaction* to individual moves.

In modern America, we have all manner of privacy protection tools to protect a thin layer of foundational ID data about ourselves, data that can be used to "steal our identity" in legal and financial terms: data-wiping software, search history deletions, credit freezes, personal data deletion on Google, cache wiping, and incognito browser tabs. We live in a world where we interact ever more with impersonal systems and bureaucracies run by people we will never know. And as a result, our foundational ID paranoia has never been higher as a society. And honestly, the financial risks of identity theft are measurable and growing.[1]

Yet, media coverage of database breaches has only ratcheted up the privacy mania in our country, making it harder for any of us to question the deal we have made with the devil of alienation.

What am I talking about?

By making privacy sacred, we hide our biggest problems from all but one or two people (or everyone if it is very humiliating). The result is that fewer people than ever actually know us deeply. How can we claim to know someone well without knowing their failures, most profound flaws, and deepest low points? Premodern village communities, where everyone is all up in every family member's business, share this interpersonal knowledge. We seem to have conveniently forgotten that this means that these quaint villagers are fully known by a lot more people than we ever will be.

Most Americans have decided it's better for our boss, colleagues, industry peers, and weak ties to know just a thin layer about us, the "happy face." Given how often you work with your core colleagues, this seems very odd. On the nineteenth-century family farm, the family knew everyone's sh*t and worked together all day. When the eldest son had a tantrum on the tractor, everyone knew it was just a bad temper (or something else). Family members did not freak out and see the signs of a man about to grab a gun and shoot people. They understood the individual family member's behavior patterns well. They had loads of context. There is no substitute for knowing people well.

Changes in social structure and local residency tenure in modern America mean we have a smaller circle of close people who have deep knowledge of us than ever before. The related epidemic of self-reported loneliness many feel in modern America results from curating a problem-free self to 99 percent of our social network, including those we spend hours with daily. At the same time, only a tiny few get to know what is really going on.

The disconnect between these two selves is the tragic source of our loneliness. And if we lie to our spouse or partner, the loneliness could be maddening.

Here's the apparent truth many modern Americans have forgotten. Humans don't trust those who we don't fully understand as individuals. That's what Edward Snowden reacted to in his whistleblower rage back in 2013. What if an NSA analyst drank too much cold brew and misinterpreted what someone said about Iran on the phone last Sunday, and that someone's name is *Muhammed*?

Our fear of privacy invasion rests on the fear of someone passing judgment on a scrap of our behavior with no real context. And because we insist culturally on keeping people out, we actively willed the possibility of this fear into being. We authored it. We invited it into our lives. We love it. Most of us do, at least.

We would have to become massively confessional to a much larger audience to pull the privacy curtain aside and not be afraid. Then, we would have to hope this broader audience would not use that information against us (which some obviously would).

In a weak tie, consumer society like ours, the last hope is a pipe dream.

Stigmatize the Busybodies

At the neighborhood level, we can see how extreme privacy beliefs cripple our communities and, in turn, individuals in trouble. Sometimes, it takes an extreme example to make out the dynamics. I want to share a story of how racism and privacy beliefs combined to hide a monster living nearby.

It was the early 1990s in a predominantly black neighborhood in West Milwaukee. A thirty-six-year-old black mother named Glenda Cleveland saw suspicious behavior multiple times across the street at the Oxford Apartments. She called the police to intervene directly when the weird white guy seemed to be dragging a very young, visibly uncooperative, and drunk Asian boy toward the entrance of the building. The police proceeded to believe a young white man over a middle-aged, middle-class black woman and let the man, serial killer Jeffrey Dahmer, take his drunk victim home. Dahmer knew what to do. He wore the mask of the kindhearted friend caring for a drunk buddy. Why question this performance in a free society, where getting drunk isn't suspicious? In which we protect the *white* stranger's privacy above all others?

Glenda was a concerned neighbor who wanted her street to be safe. She was engaged in organic surveillance of her surroundings, common in neighborhoods where objective crime rates are high enough to warrant more heightened vigilance. She was aggressive and angry because you would be too if you wanted a neighborhood like this not to decay further.

In her astute mind, white men don't tend to bring Asian *boys* home in her neighborhood. It was understandably odd. And Dahmer's child victim didn't look able to consent to anything.

The Milwaukee police had ignored Glenda repeatedly in the past. She was branded a busybody who often called them with "overblown" concerns. She was also an "angry black woman," one of the most marginalized identity positions you can have in urban America.

Had Glenda been an angry white woman, I think the police would have responded differently, but only to a point. There is no precedent for police to "investigate" anyone's residence without probable cause or a warrant . . . or . . . with resident permission. That's convenient for violent sociopaths or even generic abusers. Just talk your way out of it and close the door on the police. Tell a story to maintain your privacy. Ask for a warrant.

There is no database of "nosy neighbor incidents," let alone one broken down by type (e.g., nighttime noise, excessive barking, human screams, gunshots, etc.). We don't know how many false alarms get generated in America by the well-intentioned Glenda Clevelands of this world. We don't know how common "busybody behavior" is or how often it gets ignored by authorities.

A few years back, though, I researched an analogous behavior which explains in part why so many of us distrust the Glenda Clevelands of the world—reporting child abuse. My trigger was learning that a neighbor had their kids taken away for a mandatory forty-eight-hour investigation period based on an ER nurse's "concern." When I dug into the Washington State data, I found that, in 2022, roughly 82 percent of child abuse complaints didn't pan out as valid (i.e., it didn't lead to validation of the initial claim and intervention).[2] Most of these abuse referrals came from third-party professionals without real context on the parents involved. That's a frightening degree of inaccuracy, almost as bad as the record of indicting witches in seventeenth-century Salem, MA.[3]

Yet, as a society that believes in the sacredness of privacy, we continue to favor and believe in the judgment of state-appointed surveillance agents to solve hidden, domestic problems.[4] Glenda Cleveland called these agents of the state because she couldn't rally a Hatfield versus McCoy posse to confront Dahmer. And then the state authorities ignore the Glenda Clevelands of the world, the neighbor, but *not* the ER nurse? We must really want *our neighbors* to stay out of our lives if this is the bargain we've struck.

Perhaps we want the neighbors out of these interventions because they have the most opportunities to misinterpret a random comment (i.e., from across the fence line). They are closest to the source data for a complaint and yet don't know us any better than our boss, actually probably much less.

Americans hate neighborly busybodies because they avoid direct confrontation by *tattling* on us. Yet our radical approach to privacy and declining community ethos in local neighborhoods only encourages us all to tattle *to the police* as we are not really comfortable confronting people we barely know. So, *we tattle on the people with absolutely zero context*. It doesn't take long to imagine why black folks are the least likely to file a noise complaint and why so many black people have been killed or jailed due to irrational complaints given to police with no real context.[5]

What does all this privacy yield? A lot less interpersonal verbal confrontation in our everyday lives. Instead, we outsource this confrontation to the bureaucratic state.

What else do we get? A lot of hidden domestic violence. Around 4 percent of the US adult population experiences violent domestic assault yearly.[6] This highly conservative estimate is *twelve times higher* than the rate of identity theft we worry so much about. Yet, we barely talk about domestic assault. It's carefully hidden from standoffish neighbors. And the more income and wealth, the more separated you are from your neighbors physically, making the concealment of abuse even easier.

Our Grand Bargain with Law Enforcement

We live in a society that has made a grand bargain with most of its citizenry to maintain their domestic privacy, especially, and most ironically, privacy from our neighbors.[7]

We let law enforcement handle antisocial behavior and don't deal with it ourselves. This is even more true across lines of class and race. This outsourcing of local dispute management includes domestic abuse right next door to us, which needs detection and intervention in minutes to prevent injury or death. The latter would truly be a head-scratcher for the Yanomami of Venezuela and most tribal communities I have researched in my career.

The Yanomami, for example, still live in circular ring shelters with their extended family (dozens and dozens of people), all present and visible to each other more or less. Privacy occurs in the jungle, if anywhere. Since the jungle is not a safe place for a lone person, privacy is not a priority.

This grand bargain absolves us, as modern individuals, of the responsibility to intervene with our family members in return for gaining privacy from these very friends and family.

We "don't butt in" on family members' problems.

We "let them solve their own problems" and "stay out of it."

We "mind our business" even with the folks closest to us.

And, let's face it, we relish this fundamental *irresponsibility* to them. It not only saves us lots of time intervening in high-conflict situations. It saves our emotional energy for other leisure pursuits. In the history of humanity, deliberate social irresponsibility *in the service of individual privacy* is bizarre at best and pathologically self-absorbed at worst.

If the bad actor doesn't live with *us*, we presume not to know what is happening nearby. We don't *want* to know in many cases.

Sadly, in the case of domestic abuse, our grand bargain places an enormous burden on a victim's nonresident family and friends. The victim often lives in fear of reporting their partner. So, the family/friends of the victim have to pierce the sacred veil of privacy and report abusive individuals to the police. Reporting is not likely to happen if the victim actively hides the abuse (sadly common). You can now see the Achilles' heel of our privacy beliefs. It makes no sense. And, when an individual has threatened to harm a victim if they break the grand bargain, these situations can fester for years and years. And they do.

Social science has an old concept called "the conditions of possibility." The conditions of possibility for a behavior or an event are the social variables that permit it to be more likely than not.

The conditions of possibility for *rampant domestic abuse* include our small household structure, soundproofed dwellings, and, most critically, our belief in the sacredness of individual privacy.

Due to highly private residential settlement patterns, older Americans have gained a fair amount of wisdom about the ripple effects of abuse in families and communities. They understand that individuals who are abusers rarely get caught, reported, or dealt with swiftly by the local law enforcement we claim to trust so much. Even prosecuting these cases is notoriously tricky, given the lack of witnesses in our privacy-obsessed society.

I understand why many older Americans I surveyed recently are tired and fed up with violent men and domestic abusers getting away with their behavior despite multiple calls to the police (who rarely do much initially).[8]

Here's what I found in my recent survey:

- Sixty-one percent of older Americans (those most likely to have already experienced abuse in their lives) believe that convicted domestic abusers should be monitored by local law enforcement.
- Fifty-one percent of the same folks want local law enforcement to monitor those who merely *threaten* others with violence.[9]

These older Americans think *local law enforcement* should be the primary monitoring force even though neighbors live nearby. Do you agree?

If you do, note that this is not what our legal system is set up to handle. And the second item above would violate our constitutional enshrinement of domestic privacy. It wouldn't even be legal.

Chapter Four

MAKE THE INDIVIDUAL RESPONSIBLE FOR THEIR PROBLEMS

In 2001 I presented my first paper at an anthropology conference. I slept for about an hour the night before my presentation, tossing and turning, unsatisfied with the paper I would have to soon read in front of my peers.

I was having a panic attack. I didn't understand this at the time.

I managed to get through it without being mocked, and we all retreated to the tame, nerd-heavy after-party in a nearby room. I met a fellow graduate student from the University of Wisconsin–Madison there, and we sat down to catch up.

At some point, the commiseration of the weak turned very dark as Paul revealed he had just broken up with his latest girlfriend because he was moving on to a new visiting position, the fourth in five years. Just to survive. He was an "academic hobo," as one of my relatives called it back then. He *should* have lived in a railcar to eliminate the annual moving expenses.

Listening to Paul's lament, I thought I heard a foretelling of my own dark future. Soon, I would be pursuing the lone radiologist in some rural Iowa college town, wrecking her family to obtain a stable relationship, and convincing her to follow me from job to job.

Chasing tenure will kill me slowly, like it's killing this guy. How the hell did I get into this position? I'm smarter than this. I went to Harvard, for hell's sake!

That night, my birthday, I realized I had aspired myself into a psychosocial spiderweb. The academic spider was sitting patiently at its center, waiting to crack open my skull and eat me as fuel for its tuition industrial complex.

Just jump and figure it out. You went to India and figured it out. You were almost killed three times. Ending this dream can't be more challenging than that.

This was the time in my life when I finally learned that a typical Western male's expression of grief is barely controllable rage. So, that night, I thrashed myself to sleep alone in a rage. And I began the process of divorcing my academic career. It went on for six months before I made the final decision. I quietly continued to finish my dissertation, so I would at least get the credential. I defended my research to an unsuspecting faculty committee used to depressed-looking grad students.

When I chose to leave academia in 2022, while living alone in Chicago, my mental health was sliding fast. I'd already been to the ER once for a massive panic attack. Aspie brains quickly lose it without structure and predictability.

I had run out of time to get a life, so I jumped off the train. This was my choice, but it was also my problem alone to solve. This was my first taste of the incredible loneliness of modern work, the thing we spend most of our time doing.

In fully realized consumer capitalist societies like America, the tacit distribution of responsibility for addressing individual-level problems (job loss, work-related issues, mental illness, addiction, loss of friends, divorce, estrangement) rests heavily on the individual. This is most acutely true, I believe, for men, because society has trained us to treat life as a lonely survival game in which you never admit defeat or weakness.

In America, our weak ties generally hang back as we "figure it out."

"We're here if you need us. Anytime."

"Call me whenever."

"I'm here for you, man."

"Dude, I know you'll totally figure it out."

Many of us have trained ourselves *not* to butt in or offer unsolicited advice when we catch wind of someone's big problem (except with our spouses/partners). Our spouse's life problems affect us too much to hang back. Yet some parents and close friends continue to fire off unsolicited advice in their social networks. I suspect they represent ghosts of the American past. Unsolicited advice annoys most of us, not just your resident teenager.

The cultural rebellion against this proactive invasion of our privacy is ongoing, decades in the making. Type "unsolicited advice" into Lord Google's search bar. You'll get page after page from modern psychologists and psychotherapists about how to shut down unsolicited advice, how negative and hurtful it tends to be, nasty grandmothers, evil stepmothers, clueless uncles, etc.

Rejecting unsolicited advice by cultural default preserves an extreme level of privacy by shutting down any proactive social intervention. It also relegates the intervention of society to *reactive* handouts—to welfare for the poor and information pamphlets/book suggestions for everyone else. Then, when we throw up our hands as lone architects of private solutions to our problems, we reach out for help to clean up the consequences. Although some of us, mostly white men, do not even do that.

This oddly monkish orientation has deep roots in the history of monotheism, especially Western Christianity and its ironic promotion of charity/philanthropy as the way to handle the flaws of society. The cruelty of charity is that it's reactive rather than preventative.

I loved this reactive, leave-me-alone cultural setup as an Aspie adult for a long time. I react the *worst* of anyone if you try to intervene proactively to head off a personal fumble of mine. I have often exploded at well-intentioned people.

"Leave me alone!" is inscribed on my forehead and tongue.

It wasn't until I was about thirty-five that I discovered how dysfunctional this is for people like me. The Aspie brain needs *more* proactive social intervention, not less, to head off much more frequent social goofs, conflict triggering, and interpersonal trauma. Oops.

I don't want to claim that the desire to head off someone else's train wreck in a superhero act has disappeared. It hasn't. Many of us have intervened, or tried to, before. It's just that we know up front that doing this is very risky for any relationship. You have to intervene gently, in a certain way. Or not at all. We're not flippant about it, except with our spouses.

"That's a stupid-ass idea" is not on the list of helpful intervention phrases.

As individuals in America, though, we tend not to seek comprehensive, detailed *foreknowledge*. We love to wing it in this country. The more privileged we are in terms of wealth, the more we take this kind of risk, like my PhD education, pointing to no real job opportunities (or ones a sane human would want).

Instead, our broad, middle-class ethos in America honors the individual's right to make a substantial personal mistake privately. Others in our lives stand prepared to offer gentle help, only if asked later.

When someone shares a life decision they are about to make, we:

- Offer emotional validation (however disingenuous)
- Help out with the mess later if asked
- Point quickly to the professionals

Offer Emotional Validation

It's common to use friends or family as an initial sounding board when faced with significant life problems (often due to decisions we made in relative cognitive isolation). And there appears to be a common middle-class ethos when someone discloses a big problem they're facing: a) you should listen first, b) suspend judgment, and c) avoid weighing in unless asked.

If any group in America is prone to violating the American hangback ethos, it would be our parents (while mindful of the implicit estrangement threat if they go too far!). This ethos may erode as permissive, highly involved parenting spreads into the middle classes. But it certainly was in force when I was growing up in the 1980s.

Suppose you're not going to jump right in and help solve someone's problems, though. In that case, you have one thing left to offer: emotional support and validation of the *individual's* ability to pull it off. You could even provide some super trite, canned validation phrases.

We are primed in America to boost individuals' belief in themselves as autonomous problem solvers. We actively reinforce the idea that they "can do this" or "you got this" rather than try to open up a joint problem-solving approach (unless specifically invited).

Phew. We're all off the hook.

And let's remember, if you live in a society where *you* are the go-to solution architect to your own biggest problems, then you don't have time for anyone else's problems, right?

Gulp.

Help Out with the Mess if Called On

I do not have data on how often Americans ask other people to help them initially *decide* how to make big life decisions. I imagine it would be hard to collect since we have a cultural bias to take the first stab at any adult decision autonomously. But I recently collected data from older Americans about how they have approached thinking through major life *problems* and finding the best solution.

Roughly 40 percent of my national sample of Gen Xers and Baby Boomers prefer to think through *and* solve their life problems mostly or entirely *alone*.[1] How *American*. Sure, a bunch of these folks live alone, but this shouldn't affect major life problem-solving, since most people are not hermits.

Remember, the topic here is life *problems*, not the initial decisions that may or may not have led to the problems in question (!). So, among older Americans with the most life experience, we have a crazy hardcore group of hyper-individualists who will decide and suffer the consequences alone. I'll call them the Super Stoics. Let's send each of them a copy of Thornton Wilder's *Our Town*. These are the folks who rarely ask for any social assistance at all with significant problems.

The rest of us happily "drag" society in to deal with the "mess" of our initial decisions *later on*. The jerk boyfriend. The sh*t job we had so much hope for. The dud of a first husband. The bipolar, philandering wife. The PhD degree pointing to virtually no academic jobs available that require it. Argh! A rapidly changing society offers no shortage of new problems to solve.

And let it be known that only 12 percent of our wiser elders *prefer* just to canvas the opinion of *relatives*.[2] We'll call them *codependent*, using the modern pejorative term that most of us have tossed out before to judge someone. Don't deny you've flippantly tagged someone as codependent. I have.

If you're one of the Super Stoics, don't get comfortable. You're weird in the context of human societies. Dragging in the family would be the default human way of solving individual problems. I saw this happen all the time when I lived in India. I was shocked at how urban people dragged their friends into dealing with all sorts of messy, ugly, embarrassing stuff that I, the ultra-private American Stoic, thought should be contained deep in the emotionally repressed heart of the nuclear family fold.

Here's an example from my fieldwork years. In 1999, to be precise. It involved a close friend of mine in Tamil Nadu, Selvam, who was a business owner. A few years earlier, he had divorced his wife, with whom he shared a young daughter. Until then, Selvam lived a wobbly life as a bachelor, hanging out with foreigners and artists. One afternoon, after drinking, he fell off his motorcycle at an average (i.e., slow) urban speed. He wound up in the hospital for several days. His relatives stepped in to run the retail store. Friends, including me, spent time with him in the hospital, keeping him company. Per local norms, we all wasted no time slapping his wrist for the boozing and told him it was out of control. His community offered comfort and censure in equal measure. As far as I know, it never happened again. The community reacted swiftly, a community of people who knew him well and had been seeing this problem building.

Professionalize the Solutions to One's Problems

What is one positive outcome of the otherwise nightmarish, dysfunctional, enraging annual performance review in American workplaces? Virtually no one who has received one can claim *not* to have heard some community-based critique of their behavior patterns.[3]

This means there is an elevated level of self-awareness among American workers compared to past generations. The level of self-awareness may still be very low and highly selective for some folks. Still, the baseline has moved up by light exposure to ritualized behavioral critique.

The problem with life problems in American society is that our dominant culture pushes us to find our solutions mainly by ourselves, or at least assumes we will. Society waits for people to "figure it out." We plant seeds of behavioral change gently and hang back.

The more traditional approach of family proactively getting "all up in our business" is the target of decades of sustained media and professional vilification. Americans extol the virtue of making big decisions free from meddling family members. Nothing better exemplifies this virtue than the intense stigmatization of the *codependent* female in America. This dark archetype demonstrates the extremes we are willing to go to as a society to let people figure out their own decisions and solutions to life problems without regard to their relative ability to play the individualist game.

Here is the US Army's definition of codependent behavior—one I find honestly bewildering as a lifelong student of human societies. It represents a perfectly mass-market definition of the term, one full of received assumptions.

A codependent person will:

- *Feel anxiety*, pity, and guilt *when other people have a problem*
- *Feel compelled—almost forced—to help that person solve problems*
- Feel angry when their help isn't effective
- *Anticipate other people's needs*
- Do things other people are capable of doing for themselves

- Feel bored, empty, and worthless if they don't have a crisis in their lives, a problem to solve, or a person to help
- *Believe deep inside that other people are responsible for them*
- *Get superficial feelings of self-worth from helping others*
- *Try to catch people in acts of misbehavior*
- *Become afraid to let other people be who they are and allow events to happen naturally*
- *Think they know best how things should turn out and how people should behave*[4]

I've italicized all the behavioral signs of codependency that, in reality, are signs of healthy communities in the premodern world. By premodern, I mean a world where individual privacy and agency are *not* the top cultural priority and where the elders are the keepers of the moral order.

To keep "codependent" meddling family members out of our problems, starting in the 1970s, increasing numbers of Americans have sought out *professional* solution providers. This new breed of shaman offers solutions such as cognitive behavioral therapy (CBT) and addiction rehab.

It should not surprise readers that self-improvement has become a professional enterprise. The civilizational process in America has slowly professionalized almost everything from birth to burial, so why not our emotional breakdowns too?

Active therapy recipients skew toward the eighteen to forty-four set today, which includes many white and black females, since women tend to go for mental health treatment more than men by a substantial margin.[5]

But did you know that around 40 percent of Gen X and Baby Boomer adults have been to therapy? One savvy Boomer in my recent research noted a faddish uptick in therapy experimentation in the 1980s in NYC, such that "everyone was doing it."[6]

It took me a year in therapy to come to my breakthrough insight. It was painful and jarring to have a professional stranger eventually cut right through your bullsh*t more effectively than any friend, parent, boss, or wife could do.

"James, I've heard you repeatedly talk for months as if high intelligence and social skills were mutually exclusive. But I know several people just in my own network who exhibit both. Do you want to be one of them or not?" Ouch.

Therapy blew up my plate armor of excuses. In American culture, though, therapy has a singular bias: you have control over how you react to the world. If you *like* playing the sad victim, therapy will be very unpleasant for you.

Therapy teaches you how to gain psychological control even when you feel reduced autonomy. This is why it may be one of the more adaptive innovations to the underlying problem of individualism as the basis for making big life choices more autonomously than many human societies would allow. Americans who experience dustups with bureaucratic constraints on autonomy or the sudden collapse of a relationship don't always handle this attack on autonomy very well. Our belief in our own super-agency is constantly confronted with counterfactual experiences that require us to adapt and pivot.

Chapter Five

REWARD PRODUCTIVE ANTISOCIAL BEHAVIOR

It's lunchtime on the set of *Fitzcarraldo*, Werner Herzog's award-winning biopic featuring Klaus Kinski, his go-to lead actor. Klaus is super pissed. He's irate about the "inedible" lunch on set in the middle of the Peruvian lowland jungle.

"Worse than prison! Pig sh*t!!," Kinski blurts out in German in the middle of a long, semi-coherent tantrum that lasts for fifteen to twenty minutes.

Here's Werner's recollection, years later, in a documentary about his most loved employee:

> *The cause was trivial, and I didn't bother to interfere . . . These ravings were frightening and a real problem for the Indians, who solve their conflicts in a totally different manner . . . Normally, they speak softly, and physical contacts are gentle. They were afraid. Towards the end of the shooting, one of the chiefs came to me and said, "You probably realized that we were afraid, but we are not afraid of him [Kinski]." They were actually afraid of* me *because I was so quiet . . . the Indians offered to kill Kinski for me. And I said, "No, for God's sake! I still need him for shooting. Leave him to me."*[1]

I'm not an expert on these tribal communities in lowland Peru. My inference from Herzog's ex post facto narration is that the native Peruvian extras were primarily terrified of Herzog. To the Indians, Herzog had abdicated his *responsibility* to contain a low-level threat from within *his group*. He was a lousy leader.

Tolerating Kinski's behavior (or letting it fade out each time) to the Peruvian natives seemed insane behavior for a "chief." The implication is very old in human societies—you do *not* tolerate this behavior, since it harms the group. Emotionally first, but if the person gets violent, physically. Due to frequent interclan violence, the communal ship must be tightly managed in societies requiring semi-militarized readiness. Defusing unnecessary internal conflict becomes a fine art.

Traditional human cultures promote strict group harmony that seems almost militaristic or cultish to modern Americans. Leaders of these societies will eject the unmanageable, antisocial person. In rare cases, some societies killed them quickly. Disposing of the sociopath makes sense when your society, a hunter-gatherer tribe, has no feasible way to deal with someone with severe mental illness. Tribal people do not medicalize antisocial behavior as we do; they tend to spiritualize it. It simplifies the process in moderately violent societies with a narrow margin for *individual* error.

Many in Germany believed Kinski had an unmanaged mental illness for most of his life. Kinski was also a man who allegedly raped his daughter and never showed any public or private remorse for this crime.[2]

We might call Kinski a sociopath because his behavior displays extreme non-empathy for others across his lifetime. Americans, like most humans, still tend to spiritualize the problem of an extreme lack of empathy. We point to it as the problem of "evil" and handle it through religious rituals. This is true even though mainstream psychology now suspects that sociopathy, like autism, is heavily neurological.

Whereas the lowland Peruvian Indians wanted Kinski *dead* as a broken human in a society where modern scientific mental health treatments had not penetrated, Herzog, the artist, was willing to tolerate extreme antisocial behavior because, frankly, Kinski had to act less. He could just release his inner torment through the script. Most of Kinski's roles in Herzog's oeuvre seemed oddly tailored to his extreme, misanthropic tendencies. Kinski was what we might call a highly functional deviant and was rewarded with a salary and a great deal of fame (in Europe, at least).

I also get no sense that Herzog feels the slightest responsibility for routinely employing a man who should have gone to prison for the crime against his daughter, *if he was indeed guilty*.[3] The typical Western rationalization for such enabling behavior is that a productive worker's *personal* problems are his own and none of the employer's concern. *Hey, as long as he's still productive for me.*

Antisocial behavior for the sake of *art* is oddly easy for many Americans to justify, whether Kinski's rages or Hunter S. Thompson's drunken pranksterism and self-aggrandizing orneriness.[4] For many reasons, we have come to believe great artists feed off madness though no scientific evidence supports this.

But what about antisocial behavior in the modern office? What is the value of this kind of individualism and eccentricity at work? At best, I think we are very conflicted as Americans. The phenomenal success of the TV series *Mad Men* originates partly from our growing distaste for uber-narcissistic white-collar workers willing to lie, abuse others, and steal ideas to get to the top or stay there. And yet, many viewers deeply sympathize with Dick Whitman, the abused boy who grew up in a brothel and managed to lie his way straight into the 1 percent of urban America. We sympathize with a con artist *trying to better his condition*.

On the proverbial pre–World War II family farm, I'm confident that there was one behavior you wouldn't find: *maneuvering for a promotion*. Although, upon second thought, without a system of primogeniture, the favored son spot is indeed negotiable from the start. There's an exploitative reality show premise in here somewhere. *Farm Wars? Inheriting the Farm? Agrarian Backstabbers?*

Jokes aside, today's office workers looking to grow their salary above cost-based inflation adjustments must maneuver for promotions, i.e., for limited spots up the organizational hierarchy.

This gives an advantage to those who arrived first in a growing organization. The need to calculate, plot, and charm your way upward only grows the later you onboard, the more peers you have, or when the company's growth stops.

The literature on how to get promoted is growing daily. There are now even consultants who specialize entirely in training you to be *more promotable* (huh?). Use of the phrase "getting promoted" has grown exponentially in the printed English language since the end of World War II.[5] Not surprising.

Promotions are something I've been fortunate to experience on a number of occasions. I was promoted five times at the only firm I've ever worked for. I was also employee number 14, who came on board before a rapid growth spurt in company revenue. And those promotions came despite a colossal meeting gaffe in a company-wide meeting in my first month on the job! White male privilege? *Probably more than a bit.*

Promotions are the most favored way to achieve significant salary increases (i.e., 20 percent or more) that either maintain your lifestyle or make substantial lifestyle investments possible (a new home, vacations, private school tuition). Promotions have become an odd necessity in modern America.[6] Suppose promotions at your current employer are scarce by definition, the labor market, in that case, nudges you to seek a salary promotion with a new employer or a new career. And either of these options represents a jarring, anxiety-filled process of leaving a work community you may like for something unknown, maybe even in a different city.

Chasing salary increases is one example of the Darwinian aspect of current urban life that pits individuals against each other in a competition that subordinates communal obligation. There are at least two other, very common forms of productive antisocial behavior in modern office life. These are behaviors that employers directly reward, again and again:

- sociopathic manipulation
- jerk jiujitsu

Sociopathic Manipulation

The debate on whether or not there is such a thing as a broken brain, one that cannot feel empathy (or thereby commit to any moral order), continues unabated. In the 1960s, the FBI unveiled a class of people known as serial killers. The serial killer profile helped medicalize our understanding of antisocial behavior that human societies traditionally called "evil" or "demonic."

Most Americans still use the word "evil" to describe what mainstream psychologists now refer to as antisocial personality disorder or sociopathy. My vernacular take on sociopathy is this: interpersonal conniving using commonly available social skills and devoid of any perceivable empathy.

As I write this, the debate still goes on as to whether a sociopathic profile stems from genetic traits.[7] But, as far as society goes, why does it matter if we resolve the question of nature/nurture for sociopathy? Would we somehow cut sociopaths more slack if we could prove it was mainly neurological? I don't get more slack as a neurodiverse adult. I can tell you that.

Part of the challenge with psychopathologizing anyone is that it relies on a questionnaire or interview *alone* as the source of evidence. Yet this was *not* what the FBI did when they created their *behavioral* profile of serial killers, the original dataset for the sociopath label. Instead, they first looked for behavioral patterns linked to individual homicides. Then, they eliminated the possibility of the typical motives for homicide—jealousy, greed, or vengeance. They were left with the inexplicable as the motive: *boredom*. Sociopaths are engaged in aggressive play without conscience.

The premeditated misleading of other people to obtain some transactional advantage is standard human behavior. We're not such a nice bunch of primates. To connive in this way without remorse for the interpersonal consequences of one's actions or even to delight in the misery created is very rare. To be unable to stop doing the above even when others complain is perhaps the classic sign of someone with a disordered behavior pattern.

When we meet this kind of person, we often describe them as "sick" or "evil."

The interesting thing about America is that, whether violent or not, adults can display vaguely analogous conniving behavior and achieve what we might otherwise describe as "success."

Don't believe me?

Studies have shown that CEOs and executives over-index for sociopathic behavioral traits.[8] A book called the *Wisdom of Psychopaths* has sold pretty well, spinning some of these traits as "functional" in highly competitive organizations. A successful corporate attorney even wrote a memoir loosely normalizing her diagnosed sociopathy as functional.[9]

So, why would a sociopath excel in the modern office?

Simple. The abundance of chaos and insecurity. Most of this chaos is caused by the high level of mergers and acquisitions (M&A) activity in corporate America, where deal flow grew exponentially in the 1990s. M&A activity has sustained geometric growth since the end of the dot-com bust and remains at a very high baseline compared with twentieth-century norms.[10] Corporate M&A activity eliminates the absolute number of upper-level positions in the private sector, including many of the middle ones. As industries mature and consolidate, promotions become less likely, not more likely. And any acquisition itself leads to internal corporate panic and anxiety, as do the constant "reorgs" inside larger companies. How regular are corporate reorgs? One recent survey-based estimate found that 50 percent of 10,000 surveyed corporate executives were in the middle of a reorg and that 70 percent of reorgs failed to meet their intended business objectives—all that stress and anxiety for naught.[11]

Sociopaths thrive in the organizational chaos and anxiety caused by events like corporate acquisitions and reorgs because most of today's employees are quietly panicking about them. In smaller private companies, the panic stems more from the wild swings in monthly revenue that keep putting salary raises out of reach.

Chaotic organizations don't have the stability to enforce ethics either. Only healthy, stable corporate cultures do this well.

Increasingly, the manic emotional rhythms of Wall Street bankers create insecurity in the American corporate employee. There is also no job security at any level of the organization, least at the top.

But in the words of Dr. Robert Hare, "The psychopath has no difficulty dealing with the consequences of rapid change. In fact, he or she thrives on it," he explains. "Organizational chaos provides both the necessary stimulation for psychopathic thrill-seeking and sufficient cover for psychopathic manipulation and abusive behavior."[12]

I suspect that one reason sociopaths do well in chaotic times and organizations is that they don't look to a functional community or leadership to help solve their anxiety. This is not a need they have. As others reel from the chaos, the functional office psycho remains unaffected and more focused on work than everyone else. Their emotional imperviousness to chaos would make them more productive in a corporate sh*tstorm. Ah, there's that word—productive. It seems a powerful absolution for deception, better than the forgiveness found in your local confessional booth.

Sociopaths hate it when others term their behavior "manipulative" because they don't see anything problematic with conniving, transactional behavior, including lying, to get what they want.[13] And, in our current capitalist moment, it's hard to see a clear line between functional self-promotion and sociopathic manipulation. I have worked in and for corporate America for twenty years and still can't see a clear differentiation.

If actual upper-level positions are declining due to M&A, large pay raises become more rare or undersupplied. The office ecosystem then encourages most of us to act like sociopaths in pursuit of an undersupplied resource, even when, deep down, we might regret what we said or did in the office to get that promotion.

Here are some examples of common sociopathic behavior in the office:

- Lying about a job offer to extract a raise when you know you are temporarily irreplaceable (high risk!)
- Concealing opportunities from peers so you can get first dibs
- Spreading gossip about a competing peer to damage their reputation and promotability
- Taking credit for another's idea to advance one's image (when the other person is not present)
- Backstabbing a former ally to curry favor with more important executives

Jerk Jiujitsu

The sheer volume of essays and articles on "jerks" in the modern office and how to handle them reflects the broad prevalence of the problem (which is admittedly very hard to measure).

The common status of jerkism also reveals itself in the ubiquitous portrayal of this antisocial behavior in media. The Wolf of Wall Street was a classic, modern jerk. Bankers, doctors, and lawyers are entire occupational classes routinely portrayed as replete with jerks. We even have a mobile video game, "Office Jerk," that allows us to sublimate our hatred of our jerk of choice. You can't insert a picture of their face yet, though.

The volume of clickbait articles railing against negative office behavior does not indicate that change is underway. It simply means a *rebellion* is underway. In the absence of other data, that's all you should conclude from the mountain of counterfactual advice pieces on any one negative office behavior. There would be no audience if the behavior were rare, right? We click on these articles because the sh*t behavior just happened ten minutes ago on a Zoom call!

Here's a story that didn't make the news, though, because it almost sounds made-up. It's that jerkish. And it came from a Gen X woman I interviewed who lives in Arkansas. We'll call her Emma. Roughly fifteen years ago, when she was working in a secretarial pool for a nondescript corporate headquarters, she had a female boss who had her marked as the naïve one.[14]

One day, Emma was at her secretarial desk and her boss, the head of the secretarial pool, wanted to see her lover and asked that Emma call him and invite him over specifically for a sexual encounter. You read that right. Emma balked initially and told her boss to call the guy herself. Her boss pressured her to call her boyfriend anyway, so Emma called the number of this married man and told him her boss wanted him to visit her office right away. She didn't say why. Emma was raised in a strict Baptist home and was offended that the behavior was happening at all, let alone that her boss thought it was funny to get her involved in the invitation (perhaps a way to implicate her witness?).

When the "lover" arrived, he exposed himself to Emma at her desk before heading to her boss's office. Emma signaled to the cleaning lady to come over and listen at her boss's door as they proceeded to have sex. The cleaning lady was Emma's witness.

Later that week, Emma reported her boss to HR, whose representative said they would look into it. Of course, nothing was done. Instead, about a year later, Emma was abruptly fired with no cause.

The literature on jerks at work is getting academically deep, with one scholar identifying *seven* types of office jerks (kiss-up/kick-downer, credit-stealer, gaslighter, bulldozer, micromanager, the neglectful boss, and the free rider).[15]

Although often stereotyped as a *male* behavior problem, the latest research reveals that jerkism at work is unisex. Jerkism has expanded well beyond older men having angry mantrums and geeks being arrogantly dismissive know-it-alls.

The office jerk is often *productively* jerkish and not systematically punished or penalized by the systems that promote or protect individuals. I suspect this is why so much of the literature focuses on "how to handle jerks" instead of calling for collective action to get them fired. They rarely present any employer with legal cause for termination. The voluminous self-help literature on engaging in jerk jiujitsu implies that you are stuck with them.

Modern societies use legal systems as the means of legitimate interpersonal violence, so we do not have to engage directly in violence ourselves to resolve civil conflict. Is not office jerkism a similar, "civilized" sublimation of a desire for physical violence in a highly individualistic society where your work peer competes with you for undersupplied promotions and salary increases? Isn't being a jerk adaptive to a labor ecosystem in which no one has your back at work, and loyalty does not exist?

Chapter Six

DISTRACT OURSELVES WITH PERSONALIZED ENTERTAINMENT

If you could use a time machine to return to the basement of my childhood home on a random Saturday afternoon in 1982, you'd find my brother and me slumped horizontally on Pier 1 furniture and binging a cultlike serial TV show about time travelers—*Dr. Who*. My brother has a plate of Oscar Mayer hot dogs (cold) and a mound of Skippy peanut butter he is dipping them into. I have at least two stacks of Premium saltines in my lap. And we are sharing a two-liter bottle of ginger ale or Coca-Cola.

This was the TV cave. It was also the VHS movie theater. To Mom and Dad, it was the kids' room. Parents had minimal authority in this space. They determined only the biggest picture details of that room (the furniture and finishings). Otherwise, they stayed away. *Far* away.

We had no cable (i.e., no Cinemax, Playboy, or HBO), so my parents never felt the need to censor the TV content much. They also didn't seem to screen the VHS movie rentals that came in the home much, either. *Scarface*? Rented by a fifteen-year-old and watched by a twelve-year-old? Hmm . . .

VHS tapes were the wink-wink back door to R- and X-rated content for America's teens. *The Cook, The Thief, His Wife, and Her Lover* came out when I was seventeen and introduced me to the concept of scatological torture, which I honestly didn't need to learn. Seriously, good grief.

VHS tapes expanded the video content universe into all sorts of imaginary spaces *The Lawrence Welk Show* did not offer. I had many VHS-fueled coming-of-age realizations in that TV room.

I remember being plopped in front of *Sesame Street* at four as Mom cooked dinner (or had some alone time). This was when I met one of my early "adult" role models—Oscar the Grouch. Oscar was real. He didn't care what anyone else thought. He spoke his mind. He was "legit." And mistakes of the mouth were made.

It was, dear readers, the early beginnings of *permissive* parenting among highly educated (primarily white) families.

America's Video Entertainment Revolution in Brief

Generation X learned to surf television channels from an early age because we were the first to have access to a meaningful array of eighteen-hour-a-day operating channels on VHF and UHF. This modern scope of viewing choices made choosing what to watch a potentially drawn-out process. It was especially true if you were *alone*, operating under zero social constraints like a latchkey kid.

My darling Gen Z kids may not realize that that old, ugly, low-resolution CRT machine from the late twentieth century was the first device to push video content into American homes all day. It was the original video streaming device. It just wasn't portable (at first). And you could only *choose* content by rotating a cheap plastic handle.

When TV began the *video* revolution in the modern world in the 1950s, it was a revolution in socially coordinated, ad-sponsored, *multisensory* distraction. Unlike broadcast radio, which only had *one* sensory pathway to tease, television brought the abundant sensory magic of the minstrel show or theater production into our living rooms, basements, and bedrooms.

Until television, we all had to go outside the home and engage in a social ritual to witness audiovisual storytelling or entertainment. I suspect nostalgia for the campfire story accelerated during the 1980s for this reason.

The primary reason it took so long for TV to overtake Americans' daily leisure time was the minimal scope of content until the 1990s and the low quality of the broadcasts until the 2000s.

In the 1950s, only four television channels in the United States had broadcast content: NBC, CBS, ABC, and DuMont. In 1969, PBS started broadcasting in Boston and select markets. Cable television also began to roll out in the late 1960s. By 1980, cable offered another 35 channels, but only to 23 percent of households. By 1990, cable provided upwards of 80 channels to 60 percent of US households.[1] By 2000, cable and satellite TV content funneled video content into 84.4 percent of US households, much like today (after consolidation). Today, the average cable/satellite plan offers almost 200 channels. And the eight major on-demand streaming channels offer seemingly unlimited storytelling content (hundreds of thousands of content items) to entertain and distract us all.[2]

The ability for any one of us to curate a never-ending stream of personalized video content all day long *is very recent*.

As of 2021, the average American spends 2.86 hours a day watching video content (any screen), more than half of their daily leisure time.[3] When unemployed, this surges to four hours!

In 1965, the average daily hours of TV viewing was only 1.48, almost one-half of the daily viewing time today.[4] It took about a half century for daily TV viewing to double, *a rate of change that we cannot perceive as human beings*.

It was a slow creep.

Radio is to TV as Presence is to Absence?

Why do we care about the slow creep of daily video content consumption in American life? It has to do with the potential for any media that immerses and seduces us, encouraging withdrawal from social interaction.

Before the spread of mass-market radio broadcasting in the 1930s, the primary at-home media that allowed adults to escape reality from the comfort of their living rooms was—printed stories.

Reading was the original activity that gave you permission to become socially absent (even while in the presence of others). *I'm sorry, hon, what were you saying?* is a phrase as old as reading at home.

Radio was the first mass-distributed escapist medium to distract us from leisure reading. And it introduced two major experiential innovations to domestic life in the 1930s:

- A live stream of music into your home
- Escapist audio entertainment (including new, engrossing forms like quiz shows and comedy shows)[5]

In the 1930s, when the radio went mass-market, Americans listened for an average of three hours a day, not too far off the common TV watching average today.[6] When TV went mainstream, however, radio as a channel became a music jukebox for Americans.

But listening to music is not nearly as immersive as either reading or video. If this is true, then reading and TV compete for similar cognitive immersion in everyday life. They are equally good at drawing us out of reality and making us socially *absent*. But they compete unfairly with each other. Reading is an active process of imagining based on symbolic input and processing for which the human brain did *not* historically evolve. Video watching, on the other hand, is much more passive; it is something our brains handle easily and is potentially much more engrossing to virtually anyone.

If you talk to folks in their eighties and nineties, they may or may not be avid readers, but, on average, they read three times as much each day as the rest of us, even with all that TV watching they do.[7] My experience studying age cohort differences for consumer marketers would suggest that this age difference is mostly about never having been *habituated* to TV consumption as a child. TV, like soda pop, was originally a treat. So, their reading habit was dominant for longer during their early lives and survived more intact upon retiring.

In the last twenty years, the slow creep of immersive video has affected something else that should give us pause. The average hours per day Americans spend socializing have declined in *inverse correlation* to the increase in television viewing, no matter how you measure it.[8]

Americans spend about thirty-five minutes daily, on average, socializing and communicating (i.e., face-to-face with those beyond their home). Yet, we spend roughly five times more minutes each day watching that irresistible, near-infinite video content.[9]

The slow, steady decline in socialization is hard to fake in datasets like the American Time Use Survey. Other everyday behaviors have been moving up and down in frequency during the last twenty years, so this highly linear time usage trend stands out. Of course, correlation does not mean causation.

That's why I prefer the word "distraction." TV (and any video) is so easy, engrossing, and so effortlessly escapist that we get distracted from more energy-intensive activities like casual social life.

There's another way to think about the daily influence of television. Activities requiring deep immersion (social interaction, reading, and video viewing) tend to compete for our time.

But when one of these immersive activities is passive, i.e., participation is low complexity, it will subtly win out, or at least dominate, in the name of sheer behavioral ease.

America is awash in video content, coming at us conveniently on multiple screens all day. It. Is. Just. So. Easy. To. Watch. Getting your friend or relative to come over on any given day is much harder.

The unfair behavioral advantage of video is enormously important to remember as we explore together the experience of individualism in a landscape of unparalleled lifestyle choice.

In our growing videographic passivity, we project, sublimate, fantasize, and emote more of the day *privately*, absent from direct social engagement. And this growing chunk of our day does nothing to reinforce social bonds, even if it doesn't actively undermine relationships.

Infinite video tempts us with escapist absence as an alternative to emotionally more taxing social presence. If modern media is having an effect on our society that warrants investigation, it is not the quality of the news. It is the sheer fire hose of escapist content we continue to gravitate toward instead of calling friends or hanging out with them. Yes, I mean on a random Tuesday night. Your Netflix binge is *not* that important, seriously.

Chapter Seven

ANCHOR OUR MINDS TO THE NEXT NEW THING

My maternal grandmother lived in the same house for fifty-five years until her death from a burst aneurysm while she was writing in her journal in the sunroom. The year was 1995. Her home decor had not changed since the 1960s. Even her dinnerware was essentially vintage upon her passing.

That charming four-bedroom house on Hillside Avenue was a time capsule. And she liked it that way. She also had limited monthly income from social security (surviving spousal benefits) and minimal savings.

My parents, on the other hand, have lived in three different houses since I left for college: about one new home every ten to twelve years. Each has had a new, renovated aesthetic with new appliances, kitchen setup, paint colors, and celebratory dinnerware. Yes, they are more affluent than my late grandmother. A pile of money doesn't force you to modernize your aesthetic. However, internalized social values and interactions with those who share those values will make what outsiders see as arbitrary seem necessary. It's possible to move between houses and keep using the same dinnerware. It really is, folks.

Behind my parents' behavior is a grander impulse that America's peculiar version of unbridled capitalism gifted unto the modern world: the *consumer trend*. I now have about eight pages to prove to you, dear reader, that chasing consumer trends is a critical behavior we all use to maintain our escape velocity from the past. It is a collective religion, crudely put, whose primary tenet is that the next new thing should be ritually honored and contemplated, not ignored. In this religion of rapid turnover consumption, we anchor ourselves perpetually in a near-term future of unending possibility and becoming. We disrupt our preferences in lifelong consumer categories with relative ease and enormous social encouragement.

Though trends are clearly social productions spread by media and our social networks, they lead to a continual questioning of our individual habits and preferences. They ironically keep us focused on ourselves as individual consumers—on how we are changing and *should* change. We have become not unlike mobile phones requiring ever more frequent software updates.

Need a concrete example?

I learned about Corian countertops when my parents built their first spec home in the early 1990s. Then, in 1999, they built another house. I learned about Miele and Thermador appliances and handmade Italian dinnerware (i.e., brought back from Italy). Then, in 2012, they downsized, and I watched them join the kitchen cabinet refurbishment trend and learned about quartz countertops. In an oddly ironic way, my parents have always been two steps ahead of my wife and me in the domain of "kitchen reno." We learned the latest kitchen trends and possibilities, in part, from *them* because they had the desire and money to absorb the next new thing *early*.

Capitalism doesn't silence the elders if they can be used to disseminate the next new thing.

The Birth of a Mass Orientation to Consuming the Next New Thing

Modern consumption patterns in the West began in late eighteenth-century Britain with home goods like soap, tobacco, candles, pottery, printed fabrics, utensils, furniture, and limited beverages like spirits, ale, and tea (over which some people initiated a revolution).[1] These were the first categories to be purchased by ordinary folk as branded items in return for cash. The number of categories you sourced for cash was much smaller than today, but steadily it would grow. And grow. And grow.

Before the 1920s economic boom, most adults used to buy things largely according to static social class positioning and regional buying patterns linked to locally made items. There was usually both a local and a fancy/imported version of most household items (think Shaker furniture vs. Chippendale). You bought furniture from a local furniture maker, produce from a local produce supplier, and pottery from a local store. Local retail *was* retail. And during this time, only the rich routinely went for truly fancy versions of essential household items. We might read about this behavior and trade up very little ourselves. The original magic of modern consumption was the idea that you and your wife did not have to make all these home goods anymore (i.e., the candles, the soap, the linens), cash permitting.

After the Civil War, new consumer brands appeared routinely (e.g., Coca-Cola, Pepsi, Campbell's tomato soup, Nestlé baby formula, Hormel tinned meat, Jell-O, Kellogg's cereal, and on and on). Their adoption was slower than most realize (mainly because the unit prices initially operated at the level of gifts or luxuries). And the pace at which new consumer items appeared was not as fast as industrial innovation.

My maternal grandfather was a boy when horses and trains were still the primary modes of land transportation. By the time he was out of college (1925) and working, Model T cars were selling as fast as Ford could make them. In fact, from 1909 to 1924, the price of the Model T collapsed from the $850 original list price to only $260 or only $4,500 in 2023 dollars. In 15 years, the original factory vehicle had become as cheap as a motorcycle today.

Automobiles were one of the earliest case studies of *ultrarapid* mass adoption beyond the 1 percent. A pace of 15 years surely beats the 150 years (and slave labor ecosystem) it took for sugar to become a staple household commodity in American homes.[2] Categories explode today by using rapid supply chains, production technology, and global economies of scale to reduce prices relatively quickly as volume grows.

At least two things were different back then, in the early phases of mass consumer innovation:

1. The perceived "need" for the new thing did not spread as fast as the price lowered. For example, despite the excitement about cars in the 1910s and 1920s, by 1930, only about 20 percent of Americans owned one.³ I could make a similar argument for soda pop, which did not become an everyday consumer item until the 1970s, long after the price had declined from luxury levels.
2. In the early twentieth century, new categories of goods appeared regularly but *did not go out of existence during our lifetimes*. The pace of category creation was accelerating in the late nineteenth century, but the rate of category death was not yet measurable (transport horses came first).

That is not true anymore. Don't believe me?

Do you know where your CD and DVD collection is? How about that tiny digital camera (with the teeny APS-C sensor)? Or your touchtone phone? And how about malted milk? Worcestershire sauce? Wine coolers? Woodstove home heating? Vinyl wall paneling? Hand-crank car engine ignition? Kerosene lamps? Incandescent bulb lamps? CRT televisions? Home radios? LP players? Draperies? And on and on the creative destruction goes. In the new consumer era, we are not impressed that we don't have to sew our own table linens; we are impressed when we can buy new seasonal table runners every couple of years as we get bored of the old ones. All this for a dining table we use once or twice a year.

The faster we chase it, the faster modernity just recedes into the distance in this new consumer world. It's exhausting enough to make you want to type, "How do I join the Amish?" in the Google search bar. Hint: they don't want you.

What began in the 1980s and has accelerated since is a new level of innovation that has embedded chasing the next new thing into virtually every consumer category in our homes. This new level of innovation, of trend formation, occurs *inside* each socially entrenched category of consumption. It began in vast sectors of consumables that we constantly display to a social audience—automotive, home decorating, and fashion.

The potential for hairsplitting seems nearly infinite when you stare at the nutrition bar shelf set at Whole Foods or even your local Kroger store. David Brooks thought the bourgeois bohemians were a niche tribe of elites who by 1999 saw the need for a course correction on unbridled individualism (social and economic).[4] This course correction has still not come. What they unleashed is now a way of consuming and living for the country's majority.

The key to selling us on the next new thing is to a) make it initially exclusive based on price and distribution, b) convince us that its modern design attributes are the better way to achieve this or that outcome, and c) make us afraid of being out of date. Yes, the fear of modernity receding over the distant horizon and abandoning us is deeply unconscious for millions of us (if not all).

But there was another component to developing the creative destruction of modern consumer societies—*we needed a lot more cash to spend.*

A Super Brief History of Modern Consumer Spending

To understand how we got here, we must understand our economic orientation to frugality at the beginning of our modern consumer culture—the sheer lack of fun money we once had to spend. So, let's look briefly at early twentieth-century consumer spending anchored to today's dollar and made equivalent to a standard, per capita spending basis (see appendix A). *Phew, what?*

I promise that this geeky metric allows us to understand how little cash wiggle room your average early twentieth-century household had in a world without payday advance companies, pawnshops, check cashing stores, or portable bank credit cards.

In 1901, the average per capita consumer spending *was $388 per month* in 2023 dollars.[5] *And only 20 percent of this sum was for items beyond housing, clothing, and food.* Food alone was 43 percent of consumer spending in an era before highly processed and government-subsidized food production. My grandfather's parents thought about the price of food with the same stress you feel about your rent or mortgage. This cash situation doesn't motivate anyone to binge-buy from the Sears and Roebuck catalog. That catalog was mostly for drooling.

Even during this age of tycoons and mass industrialization, the average American household could only afford about $77 of nonessential leisure spending per month in today's dollars. Gulp. No Starbucks for these folks. They could have benefited from a Netflix subscription. I think they read books instead. Or (gasp!) they talked to each other? *Do you think they actually did?*

Jokes aside, in the early twentieth century, America was not the society you might imagine. It was not a similarly structured, but a less spendy America. The country's social structure was steeply stratified, composed of a small class of wealthy owners and an enormous mass of low-income laborers and small-scale farmers (with a large, black underclass living at the margins). The heavy-spending middle class we see all around us today was only 5 to 6 percent of the US population. Yes, you read that correctly. What we see around us as half the country today regarding income generation capability ($63–$155K) amounted to only one-twentieth of America when my grandfather was a boy. These cash-rich folks worked primarily as small business owners, private sector administrators or executives, or licensed professionals. America was still mostly a working-class, blue-collar economy with a wealthy and tiny educated elite in critical industrial cities.[6] And your forefathers probably weren't part of it.

Today, though, we see a very different consumer spending story, one in which Americans spend a lot in categories my grandfather would not have understood growing up in the 1900s. The list of "necessities" has expanded, partly due to technological advances in transportation and healthcare and the location of work relative to our homes. Healthcare (and improved labor conditions) has extended our life expectancy to the point where the importance of retirement savings and life insurance has broad middle-class relevance.

Modern life *is* more expensive per capita because we insist on a more complex, convenient, and leisure-oriented lifestyle infrastructure than our forefathers did.

Housing is now 30 percent *more* expensive per capita than in 1901. In part, increased home costs are because builders, developers, and banks keep pushing larger and larger homes to juice their profits. And because rental properties are undersupplied.⁷ But supply and demand alone can't explain the quarter-trillion-dollar home renovation space. Only media-infused desire and the constant presentation of modern alternatives can explain our current renovation nation. Seeking alternatives is also a key sign of an impending divorce (!).

Media and marketing are vital reasons why we spend more than our forefathers on all sorts of "necessities," not just because we have more cash to burn. We want to do what innovative companies and brands tell us to do. We desire the premium version. Our social networks constantly validate this desire to trade up. We take out debt to obtain premium whatever. Spending fast is the collective experience of being modern. If we started to live like my grandmother ended her life in her time capsule, the specter of social death (real or not) is what we would fear.

Our greater disposable income allows us to make more consumer transactions per year, and make them individualistically, further constraining our perspective on life to chasing our "personal" choices and desires.

Shopping is socially influenced but executed largely as a playground of individual choice.

The Foot Soldiers of Creative Destruction

I worked closely with several modern foodies when I lived in Seattle years ago. One was even a trained chef. One had written one of those ingredient-based culinary history books like *Salt or Spice*. One was simply a knowledgeable wannabe desperate for the approval of the others. The four of these folks chased the latest new thing in the Seattle restaurant scene on their own time, attended oil tastings in people's homes, and ate in underground, unlisted "restaurants" with fixed, whimsical menus made up earlier that morning. They didn't always agree with each other, but they rigorously defended their right to wear the foodie hat.

One of the critical boundary-defending questions foodies use is a mirroring retort. The foodie will take some food culture terms you used and hand them back to you as a skeptical question designed to make you doubt your own knowledge.

"What do you mean by *concept* restaurant?"

"What do you mean by *chef*?"

"You found the recipe on *AllRecipes.com*?"

I could go on and on with a description of this insecure, faux snobbery. But I won't. What's important here is that my foodie colleagues in Seattle weren't very active *creators* themselves. They weren't the chefs confabulating the next new thing on Seattle menus. They weren't opening concept restaurants or writing cookbooks. Foodies are the next rung out from the wizard creators—the initial fan base who get the word out about the latest restaurants and amuse-bouche. These folks actively create the next trend through word of mouth and raising a new restaurant's profile. Foodies are expert restaurant-goers.

If you dare try to "impress" one of these foodie darlings, one of two things will still happen. Invariably, you will learn that you are a good five to ten years out-of-date with your "new" discovery, or they will stand there silently unimpressed. In the latter case, you have one-upped them. Still, they refuse to acknowledge it as necessary or legitimate simply because you are not a member of the tribe. Good grief.

This is the behavior David Brooks describes in all its pseudo-intellectual, adolescent insecurity in his famous book *Bobos in Paradise*. A form of primal insecurity is displayed when grown adults try to defend these arbitrary tribal boundaries of elite, ever-changing consumer knowledge. David Brooks introduced us to bourgeois bohemians in 1999, at the front end of a growth curve in upper-middle-class consumption that has still not stopped. But what Brooks didn't focus on was the mechanics of *spreading* desire for $400 kitchen mixers you never use and $25 artisan dinner plates (that don't chip).

Clever, nuanced language wielding is definitely vital to being included as legitimate in lifestyle tribes like foodie-dom. But the open secret to birthing these upper-middle-class bohemian trends are tiny social networks of category geeks who incubate and sign off on the new symbols that may or may not eventually flow outward into the mass market. These are highly democratic, yet viciously exclusive, social worlds based on denying others the ability to participate in trend-identification so that their selected "trends" become rare by default. This leads to lots of unstable cliques chasing this or that hot symbol.

It's not that every new food trend a foodie points to spreads. It's often a matter of sheer volumetric trendhunting. And, as soon as something catches on, it must be replaced with something else in the foodie hopper. The geeks always need something new to discuss to maintain their standing in these tiny social networks, but also because they have a primal terror of being dated. This fear causes them to chase the next new thing. They take pride in their role in the social order: selecting the next new thing from available restaurant menus, often operating at the edge of obscurity.

Destroying yesterday's trend or drowning it out with talk of the next new thing becomes a deliberate social act of status reproduction and a way to calm the ever present anxiety that they may soon be out of touch.[8] If you destroy the old and replace it, you control the trend. You have avoided social death in your tiny little urban lifestyle tribe.

Perversely, foodies are simply the foot soldiers of consumer capitalism itself. Their creative destruction keeps consumers constantly on the lookout for the next new thing and fuels demand for arbitrary consumer innovations. It also keeps consumers ready to pay a premium to access trends early (in the context of their social network).

In modern America, individual consumers remain in a permanent state of destabilization when it comes to their own individual consumer habits. External forces are constantly pressuring for change in those habits. And as a result of all this rethinking and trading up and trading across, we develop a high opinion of ourselves. As shopping gods.

Part Two

HOW IT BECAME AWKWARD AT WORK

"Your sister died, and you're not acting appropriately. You need to cry," she said and then shoved two boxes of tissues at me.
—*someone's nursing colleague, greater Denver metropolitan area*

Chapter Eight

RECOVERING FROM MY CAREER FANTASY

It was March or April of 1987 in Concord, New Hampshire, and I'm positive classical music blared in the car as my dad drove me home from the PSAT test site. "What do you want to do for a living, kiddo?" My dad blurted out randomly with no lead-in. This is a habit we share. Radical non sequiturs. Hey, we started the conversation in our head minutes ago; you just didn't see fit to join in.

Most fifteen-year-olds tend *not* to have crystal clear career plans. I have since realized they were probably the smart ones. But not me. Nope. Mr. Straight A Nerd had it all planned out. I wanted to study religion and become a professor somewhere.

Yes, yours truly aimed for the ivy-draped halls of the academy at a young age. As anyone alive who knew me back then understood too well, my then-idol, Professor Joseph Campbell, inspired me way too much. Campbell was one of the twentieth century's most prolific synthesizers of humanity's mythic corpus and author of the classic mid-century literary theory text, *The Hero with a Thousand Faces*. Campbell authored the classic "hero cycle" in modern literary theory: *separation, initiation, and return*. Campbell's hero cycle is embedded in the mythic narratives of preliterate and classical civilizations. And in Hollywood films like *Star Wars* "Episode IV."

Notice that Campbell's theory of the hero is cyclical, not linear. This befuddles the Western, post-enlightenment mind. We prefer lines to circles. Progress to eternal reversion. Nevertheless, the early career arc of most professional cultural anthropologists like me features the entire arc of the hero cycle.

1. We *separate* from home in graduate school.
2. We *initiate* ourselves in a far-off country "in the field."
3. We manage to *return* in a transformed state, knowledge in hand.

The problem with returning, as Odysseus found, is that you may not recognize your native culture anymore. You may not like it. You may not trust it. It may *disgust* you.

And this is certainly how I felt about my field when I returned to the American Anthropological Association conference in the fall of 2000. I wandered from panel to panel and felt less at home than in India. That's a form of cross-cultural irony I cannot describe unless you have experienced it yourself. The papers were boring, self-involved, and disconnected from fundamental human concerns. No one was talking about real people. They were philosophizing on top of scattered field notes loosely related to human existence.

The politics of how to discuss human societies mattered more to most conference attendees than the courageous act of making assertions of empirical fact.

But I wanted to spend my life making smart social generalizations, not demonizing anyone and everyone who dared to assert any.

Something was deeply wrong. As an American, my top priority social identity, work, began to flicker like a UHF channel I wasn't meant to receive in my zip code. The white noise of identity confusion was intruding.

Since the advent of Generation X (1965), getting a PhD in fields tied mostly to academic employment has continuously revealed the limits of letting individuals do their own thing as a choice ideology. Trying to become a professor is no different than setting out to become the next Jimmy Kimmel.

Not that telling me any of this when I was fifteen would have dissuaded me.

Killing a Career for My Mental Health

As of 2000, I still hadn't thrown in the towel on my professorial goal, not after six and a half years straight of intense studies (think two thousand–plus pages of dense reading a week for the first three years), including two and a half years of language training and fieldwork in which I nearly got myself killed three times by in-person attackers.

Not to mention the thousands of hours of reading, paper writing, and hoop jumping that all dissertation candidates go through. When I started the program, I had the naïve assumption that the faculty were engaged in a brutal winnowing process, and that those of us who made it to the end would be supported in our job hunt and early career. I had a romantic master-and-apprentice view of the process.

The opposite turned out to be true. At no point in my doctoral program did I ever feel that the faculty or university felt any obligation to me other than setting up hoops to jump through *in return for tuition*. Highly sporadic, take-it-or-leave-it advice was thrown at you. But there was no mandatory ritual process to initiate students into a career, even once we had returned from fieldwork. There was certainly *no* presumed faculty obligation to get PhD holders a job as in the old days of American academia. I had a professor who had his advisor literally secure a tenure-track job by phone before his dissertation was even completed. This was in the late 1950s. In the early 2000s, on the other hand, we were all alone in our battle for tenure security. It was entirely our responsibility. When I later saw how MBA programs fight hard for even the most mediocre graduate to get some kind of full-time position, I knew anthropology was anchoring the zero-obligation end of the professional education continuum.

The PhD had quietly become an elite consumer product, not a ritual initiation into a career, as I had expected. Almost on cue, around the same time I came to this disillusioned realization in 2000, a faculty member candidly described a PhD to me as a "meal ticket." Nothing more. That was a nicely chosen consumer metaphor from a comfortably tenured academic who could be brutally honest.

For the prior nine years, I had been essentially an apprentice with no master. The Karate Kid received more meaningful guidance (and structured coaching) than I ever did in graduate school.

In late 2001, when I decided to bail on my academic career, less than ten tenure-track jobs were open nationwide in cultural anthropology, and only three were ones where my specializations fit. At the same time, well over ten years of PhD holders had backed up trying to find these jobs. My intel told me that each tenure-track position was getting six hundred to eight hundred applications! That's far less than a 1 percent chance.

My advisor had urged me at least three times from 2000 to 2002 to start publishing. Since I did not even submit anything, I'm sure she lost interest in my career, thinking I had rejected her advice. The reality was that I needed to finish the dissertation *analysis* to have the material thought through well enough to cherry-pick something for an article. Or so I misunderstood. She never once set up a meeting to get me unstuck. The latter is what masters do with apprentices. They structure an intervention. They insist. They don't treat the student's behavior as *their personal choice*. They don't just shrug their shoulders and walk away from the young grasshopper.

But this is how leaders in a hyper-individualistic culture behave. Advice is cheap, even when correct, but sitting down to guide the newbie through the process is a ritual investment of time and energy. You must care. A lot. About. Community. And its members. You have to feel obligated to someone to spend this kind of time with them. And there needs to be some kind of chemistry in the advisor-advisee relationship. We were like oil and water, doomed from the start.

Here's why none of the above matters in the end. The issue with my fading academic career was structural. And my advisor was not in a position by herself to change the macro-forces involved.

Anthropology was one of the first fields to purposely diversify its tenure ranks by limiting the number of slots filled by white males. I supported this in principle at the time. Our field is *the* field focused on honoring cultural diversity, after all. So, I competed for jobs with an ocean of white male PhDs, including folks ten years out with a long CV, even for basic positions. This is because white men were still far more likely to enter these doctoral programs, finish them, and have the financial safety net to take this career risk.

Throughout the 1980s and 1990s, anthropology departments had been overproducing PhDs for minimal tenure-track slots even though it was already clear to faculty that there were *no academic jobs* for most doctoral students. If that doesn't strike you as ethically dishonest, I don't know what would. It is sickening that some of these misled students took out student loans for their graduate studies. The older tenured faculty lived and worked longer in tenured positions than ever as they refused (as a field) to set demographic quotas *on admission* to align with each department's informal diversity goals and undersupply of open positions. America's anthropologists certainly felt no obligation to retire early. As a field, tenured faculty took *no* responsibility for the problem they were enabling.

But wait. If a degree is a capitalist *product*, you would never set a cap on admissions. Capitalism seeks never-ending growth. Capitalism hates caps. Capitalism is also the muriatic acid of community-centered ethical obligation anywhere it goes. Capitalism encourages you to think about your family and yourself, mostly yourself. And so, America's social science deans allowed some anthropology faculties to bloat as long as there were enough graduate students willing to pay tuition to cover their salaries. Fascinating.

Luckily, the ridiculous oversupply of PhDs in anthropology was a tangential variable in my decision-making process. But it was the final straw. It made moving forward nearly suicidal for someone still trying to find employment and a life partner and settle down his autistic brain. And, contrary to my advisor's urging, publishing one or two articles wouldn't change anything. How did I know this? Remember my buddy, Paul (from chapter four), who had just broken up with his girlfriend? He had published *four* articles and still couldn't get an associate professorship.

And then, amid this theater of the career absurd, I watched a white male friend with *no published articles* get a tenure-track anthropology position at Yale. Why? He was a master networker at major conferences. Everyone knew him. He was an extrovert in the field par excellence of pathological introverts. In an ocean of white males, he had the critical edge I would never have. Not someone with my poor social skills.

And that was my fundamental "mistake." I needed to have spent more time networking with tenured faculty who make hiring decisions *and* building a super-strong relationship with my advisor. I did not have a rising star *brand*. No one was advocating for me, and somehow it was my job to motivate them to do so. I was invisible in a vast ocean of white male applicants. An excellent dissertation had long ceased to be enough to get you even an initial shot. There was no "meal ticket" anymore. *Finding a dining hall was now the challenge.*

Yet not a single faculty member I asked would admit this.

And not one tenured faculty member had ever mentioned the critical role of networking or the fact that the priority candidates in a white, male-dominated field were now women and minorities (my advisor incidentally ticked both boxes).

When I chose to leave academia, I was living alone in Chicago. I'd been to the ER for a massive panic attack. Aspie brains quickly lose it without structure and predictability. Without any semblance of control. Even prior to receiving therapy, I could intuit with my gut that chasing tenure in anthropology through a series of noncommittal teaching jobs all over the country would have destroyed me.

Let me summarize. At no point in my doctoral journey did anyone in authority offer *formal* assistance in finding academic or nonacademic jobs. There was no felt responsibility to help PhD holders obtain *any* job. Only to write a recommendation.

You were on your own. And you always had been. Those in authority bear no responsibility for your future—tough sh*t. Solve your own problems. Deal with it.

Hey, your tuition is due.

Sounds like a great, loving community.

Chapter Nine

WORK-LIFE DUSTUPS

One of the first things Germans note when arriving in the United States is how much time we spend working each week *compared to them*. American workers work 30 percent more hours annually than Germans. And we have far less paid time off than the Germans too. However, overall, our average annual workload places America in the *middle* of the global pack of nations. On the other end of the continuum are Indians, who work 21 percent more hours than we do![1] Farmers work hard.

We're not workaholics in historical terms, either. Our American ancestors worked far more hours per week. Let's follow the experts and accept that nineteenth-century American farmers worked, on average, 10 hours a day, 6 days a week.[2] That's a 60-hour work week, roughly. Or roughly 3,120 annual hours . . . versus the 1,794 hours that the average American works each year today.[3]

America has *reduced* its average annual work hours by 42 percent in 140 years. And most of this reduction occurred in about 50–60 years surrounding 1900, due to federal and state regulations (and the transition of millions into factory shift work). Every generation alive *today* has worked under this leisure-forward standard of work.

Most Americans are *not* overworked. And yet this does not mean we are happy at work. Or that work doesn't interfere with the rest of our lives.

What's fascinating is that American workers today who put in the longest work weeks work in *elite* occupational roles or desperately entrepreneurial ones.[4] For example, today's management consultant or investment banker trying to make partner works significantly more

75

hours than ye olde farmer types. I know some of these folks. Burnout is high. Eighty-hour work weeks are completely normal. A question often arises: *Why am I working so hard to make old rich guys even richer?* It's a legitimate question for one's therapist.

Table 3. American Work Hours Across Time[5]

Nineteenth-century farmer: 60 hours/week
Factory shift worker pre-World War I: 60 hours prior to labor laws
Factory shift worker, 1920s: 50 hours/week (with overtime)
Modern worker: 40 hours/week (5 days)
Professionals: 45-60 hours/week (5-7 days)
Management consultants: 70-80 hours/week (6-7 days)
Entrepreneurs (mostly self-employed, small teams): 80+ hours/week (7 days)

Source: Robert Whaples, "Hours of Work in US History" and my estimates.

As a card-carrying member of the neurotic upper-middle-class tribe, I have worked roughly 50–70 hours a week for my entire career since it started in 2003. Sadly, the higher end of this range has been recently as a solopreneur. *What am I doing to myself?*

Upper-middle-class professionals work more than their nonprofessional peers and, on occasion, more than the nineteenth-century family farmer. We sad folks are the only ones who can claim that work hours conflict with other aspects of our lives. This is not a call for sympathy but to understand the prevalence of overwork. It's actually not prevalent. At all. Mostly, it is the affluent who voluntarily choose their overwork or wake up with golden handcuffs tying them to jobs that fund equally optional, overwrought lifestyles (and mortgages).

The problem with work-life conflict in America is *not* our long work hours, despite elite media outlets writing increasingly about (their own) workism.[6] Only a tiny percent of adults—*professionals and entrepreneurs*—work crazy hours. In my study of older Americans, they represent perhaps 3–4 percent of everyone I researched, probably less. And, no, "authors" don't influence these numbers much (even if they work like hell).

Work-Life Separation Is an Absurd Cultural Expectation

The problem with work-life interaction in American culture is about something else that reveals the limits of individualism as a sensible way to frame our lives. The conflict between work and life is mostly about the rest of our lives requiring more flexibility, sensitivity, and understanding than your average employer has typically offered anyone, except their top (white, male) executives—that is, until the COVID-19 pandemic.

For example, it doesn't take a long workweek to generate:

- Partner conflict over who has the most post-work energy to cook dinner
- A painkiller addiction that affects work performance
- Abusive or mismanaged work environments that generate Sunday scaries
- Insensitivity to off-hours work availability
- Insensitivity to working parents' longer commute times (due to childcare drop-offs)
- Daytime availability expectations conflict for remote workers due to a plethora of residential situations
- Limited sick leave, despite a wide range in variation of immune system strength—hurting employees who empirically get sick a lot (cold/flu/COVID)
- Bereavement and grief overwhelm
- Conflict over how to accommodate workers taking care of the disabled, children, or the chronically ill
- Finding time for doctors' appointments
- And on and on . . .

I'm just old enough to remember when precisely no one openly complained about these sources of work-life conflict with their work peers, let alone their managers. When the former CEO of a company I worked at asked me to take two days out of my fourteen-day *unpaid* paternity leave to help with a client presentation, I said yes, thinking this "was what you do for the guy at the top." I was offered extra paid time off in return. Yippeee! I should have renegotiated my salary on the phone when he called because, apparently, *I was pretty valuable.* We older folks were trained to look at the latter as employee *extortion* that could easily backfire (i.e., leaving a sour taste in the CEO's mouth).

Until recently, and throughout the careers of older Americans, employers have tended to behave not unlike high-functioning autistics: they've been incredibly *insensitive* to the diversity of the personal worlds of their employees. Without careful leadership, bureaucracy has a fantastic ability to undermine the basic rules of human community bonding. Honestly, most leaders have little real idea of what individual employees are going through at home. Nor do they ask. Remember the sacredness of privacy from part one? Workers have also trained employers *not* to ask about their personal lives.

Increased lifestyle diversity among employees increases the likelihood of employee A being offended by the atypical lifestyle behavior of employee B in ways that my grandparents' generation could not have possibly foreseen.

And our corporate answer to this has been: "Don't ask. Don't tell."

This adorable phrase signals an old behavior that did *not* begin with managing homosexuality in the military. "Don't ask. Don't tell" started as soon we left the confines of family businesses in the nineteenth century and began trading our labor full-time with total strangers. I once had a boss who repeatedly told me, "I don't want to know about anyone's personal life. Work is for work." I bet you know someone who *still* thinks like this at work. It might even be *you*. Gulp.

I now want to use an anthropologist's perspective to illustrate how this rigid belief is weird and show you what it enables.

For the rest of this chapter, consider the possibility that a rigid separation of work from life is simply impossible for the human mind, let alone the American mind. Human beings don't have a magic wand to keep emotional problems from intruding onto their work existence. For most of human history, humans didn't even have a concept of "work" as a distinct domain of activity. You lived and existed all day with your clan. Work was *family* labor. You knew exactly where you fit in. All day long. You had no reason to hide your personal life from your family who knew everything anyway.

Ever since factories drew us away from lives working for family farms, stores, or trades, Americans have had to decide what to share, or not share, with their colleagues at work. Coed offices only complicated any desire to share personal beliefs or activities. Better to keep things at a minimum. Especially, if you couldn't stand your work peers. Don't give the office gossips any more ammunition.

We are good at keeping our personal lives behind a veil of privacy; we have become skilled in pretending while at work that everything at home is OK (even if it is a nightmare). We can fake contentment when colleagues ask us rhetorically, "How are you?" We can repress negative emotional impulses using that enormous neocortex designed for precisely this thing, up until a limit. Ironically, when we do break down at work, we become undeniably human to our colleagues. And we find out blindingly quickly if we work in an inhuman, toxic *Reichsministerium*.

The best way to prove that no one is pulling off anything like pure work-life *separation* inside their heads is to share a few common scenarios:

- The mysteriously exhausted peer who shows up for work, but, from your chair, looks like someone who should take two days off, minimum
- A sleep-deprived new mom not able to pay attention well in meetings and who needs more support at home (and a sick day)
- Someone who partied too hard on Thursday night and can't contain their hangover the next day
- The ridiculously sick worker who, absent sufficient sick leave, shows up anyway and coughs his way through the day, turning his sleeve into a wet mess and otherwise being

supremely slow and unproductive as well as making at least two other people ill

With the spread of hybrid work, white-collar workers now have the luxury of concealing some low-productivity days. Yet, I suspect that for hybrid workers, these hidden, unbalanced days squander valuable opportunities to become human to your colleagues in return for reducing embarrassment and maintaining the sacredness of our privacy. We like the concealment power of remote workdays and forget the bonding power of being human in front of others.

We Are Fractional Humans at Work

My business clients know I'm a vocal opponent of fractional executives in fast-growing companies. Aside from accounting, there is too much to oversee in any major business function (sales, marketing, operations) to believe that ten to twenty hours a week will get it done. It's naïve to think an impressive résumé applied part-time solves the problem.

I've often meditated about why insensitivity to workers' personal lives is so unbelievably rampant in American offices and other places of employment. And part of the complex answer is that we are never fully realized people in an office.

We are fractional humans at work. We are slivers of ourselves walking around, wondering why our colleagues don't "get us." We only know scraps about a few of our peers' lives. And only if we listen or ask. We primarily work with strangers we know only in so far as we observe their *workplace* behavior patterns.

We then "upsample" this tiny stream of data to create a misleading picture of who an individual peer is.

We casually say things like "Jack is really tense," but all we know is that Jack is tense *at work*. We don't see him at home to understand how he behaves there. Or with his friends. Or with his parents. Or with his labradoodle puppy. Or with the kids he coaches on his youth soccer team.

Whenever I read the phrase "bring your full self to work" in some idealistic career advice piece, I laugh. Not only is this *not* possible even with your "work spouse," there is also absolutely no structural incentive to do this in a modern American work environment unless you are on the leadership team. It is tough to do it and not eventually get punished by your frenemies or the office sociopath. Although most Americans do not work in larger government or private sector organizations (five hundred or more employees), it only takes a company with more than three to four employees for a conversational veil of privacy to appear between one's personal and work lives.

Let's retake a look at some of the common personal intrusions into work time mentioned above and examine how common cultural attitudes preclude us from acknowledging or discussing them at work:

- In a society where meaningful pay raises involve competing with your colleagues to be more productive (even overproductive), *there is little incentive to share the extent of your many personal distractions (i.e., sources of low productivity)*.
- In a society that stigmatizes mental illness, *why would we discuss our mental health challenges with anyone at work*, especially someone who could start looking for our replacement in an at-will nation?
- In a society that psychopathologizes individual complaints as individual in origin, why would you ever point to context-specific problems at work like a) lack of training/coaching for new employees and new managers, b) gender imbalance in staffing, c) class imbalances, or d) similar sociological "facts" in the workplace. *You don't need coaching, Sally. You just need to get your sh*t together. You can do it!*

Verbal Work-Life Separation Is a Factory of Loneliness

I have a friend who teaches at the University of Arizona, where, in 2022, a hydrology professor, Thomas Meixner, was assassinated while walking back to his office from class. The assailant was a disgruntled graduate student *who had been expelled for sending violent messages to faculty members.*[7]

When my friend expressed his trouble sleeping, his anxiety, and his dread of returning to campus in a faculty meeting, multiple colleagues, including his boss, later came to his office, one at a time, to *make sure he, as an individual, was OK.*

His colleagues didn't acknowledge the events or grieve the trauma publicly. They did not discuss it or confess their concerns in the meeting (they only discussed helping the students cope as individuals). There was no shared grieving ritual, no group processing of the heinous act of terror that never should have happened on a modern campus.

My friend wanted a ritualized acknowledgment that something heinous and evil had transpired, that they *all* had the right to be very upset and afraid, and that they would get through this together and fight for change to ensure it never happened again.

Not only did *his faculty* not do that, but the university also did not do it. Instead, the university issued customary condolences to the family of the slain professor. And, days later, there was a *voluntary* candlelight vigil held. Ah, yes, the voluntary vigil for the concerned minority, the highly distressed. The rest of us stoics have moved on because we're tougher than you. *Good grief, what an obnoxious delusion.*

What better way to dismiss a tragedy in one's community than stage a *voluntary* memorial?

- Hey, if you want to play pool, come to my place at 7:00 p.m.
- Hey, if you want to light a candle in support of a professor *who was f**king shot in the hallway yesterday*, come to the plaza at 5:00 p.m.
- Or go watch Netflix, it's all cool.

Is it all cool, though? Really?

Our Dysfunctional Reactions to Hurting Individuals at Work

Later in the year, local Tucson journalists discovered that not even the U of A hydrology department members, where Meixner taught, were immediately informed of the shooting. It took hours for some of his colleagues on the campus to find out. They just kept working in ignorance while medics removed the body. The university just went on . . . like the restaurant bombing scene in the movie *Brazil*. It was a communication fail when it counted the most.

Bureaucracies hate anomalies. And this is why a healthy bureaucracy needs built-in community-preservation rules and policies. Or it will act against the public health interests of *everyone—every* time. It's what they do. The larger the employer, the more this is the case.

If you're having a bad day at work in America, we presume it is your problem . . . we psychologize you. And we isolate you in the process of doing so. Sally is depressed. Let Sally have some alone time. She'll feel better. Don't bother Sally. There is no science behind advising a grieving, let alone a clinically depressed, person to go into social isolation. This is a *culturally* arbitrary, socially transmitted reaction based on how the sacredness of privacy makes us afraid to know our colleagues intimately. It is also a legacy of the Super Stoic subcultures that have dominated the country's institutions and public life for four hundred years. This widely distributed attitude is also *inhuman* in the context of the history of most world cultures.

What your average American does not do is embrace any traumatized person asking for help, acknowledge that a *community* is being affected, and then bring that person into a mandatory *group healing process*. We partly avoid this because we are incredibly incompetent at these emotionally vulnerable healing rituals. Ancient group healing rituals feature raw, intense emotions that violate the public performance of a Super Stoic self that so many older Americans, especially, grew up thinking was normal.

Why do we avoid *group* healing?

Well, for one thing, we are mostly irreligious and terrified of publicly admitting our dark emotions related to tragic events. The more educated and whiter we are, the more I fear this is true. Older Americans, especially, descend directly from or grew up in a public culture overly influenced by the Super Stoic cultures (Nordics, English, Slavs, Russians, and Germans) who immigrated here and created most of our current leading institutions. They did this in a resource-rich agricultural country that tempted many to see community as less necessary. When land in the West went for pennies per acre, individual men could realize grandiose ambitions by paying for stray labor.

The devaluing of community is very old in America. Our individualistic, work-first, W-2 ethos teaches us daily to see the individual as the site of their own healing because the individual is the source of its own sustenance.

Instead of group healing, we heal like individuals. Older Americans lived under this harsh shadow as if it were entirely normal.

If you've ever been to a charismatic Christian church (think rock-n-roll worship services), you will never see people isolate another hurting person. When someone confesses their pain or trauma, multiple people will stand up, go over, and lay hands on that wounded person. Intercessory group prayer may freak you out if you're an atheist, but it's just one version of thousands of rituals of healing well-known to anthropologists.

Instead of labeling the individual as depressed, anxious, or having a bad day and then "giving them space," traditional human cultures quickly form a circle, embrace the individual, and go through a ritual that processes and expunges the harm. In our society, ironically, this ancient behavior is best represented by evangelical prayer groups.

Instead, most American workers in distress experience a potpourri of well-intentioned, obtuse comments, offers, and minimal empathy. This is true even in workplaces filled with women, the gender we associate with greater compassion.

Read Sally's story of receiving the worst possible phone call at work anyone could get and how her Denver hospital's nursing department reacted:

> *One day in 2014, I was at work and got a phone call from the coroner's office. My sister had been missing. I'd filed a missing person's*

report on her, actually. I remember the cops at the time saying to me, "Why do you care? She's just a drug addict and an alcoholic. . . . She'll show up eventually." Well, she did show up eventually. She was a Jane Doe they found dead in a park.

The coroner said, "We found that Jane Doe and identified it as your sister."

I was at work when I got that phone call. I remember dropping the phone and screaming and collapsing on the floor.

I remember somebody else saying, "What's going on?"

I said, "My sister's dead."

I remember sitting on the floor and three other nurses huddled around me.

But I work in a very toxic work environment.

Because she was a coroner's case, we couldn't have the funeral right away, so I took a few days off, and then I had to wait for her to be released. . . . We're Catholic, so you have to have the body present for the funeral.

[Meanwhile] I went back to work. And I remember somebody coming up to me and saying, "Is something wrong, Sally? You're acting differently."

I said, "Are you joking? My sister just died." And they're like, "Well, you're just acting kind of strange."

What amazes me is that nobody ever came to me and asked me, "Would you like to go to employee assistance?"

And then, another person comes up to me and says, "You're acting kind of weird."

I will tell you I was angry. I had this angry reaction to my sister dying.

I remember this one person coming up to me. I'm not making this up. She came to me, handed me two boxes of tissues, and said, "You need to cry."

"What?" I replied.

"Your sister has died, and you're not acting appropriately. You need to cry," and she shoves two boxes of tissues at me.

And I said, "Get the f**k away from me."

Then I got pulled into the boss's office and lectured about how I *shouldn't have said that to her. Nobody addressed the shoving of the tissues at me or anything, right?*

So, my sister died in October. We had her funeral at the beginning of December.

[During this time] I get pulled over by the boss after Christmas, and she goes, "Well, we're getting some complaints"—she pulls me into a closet, a broom closet—and she says, "You are like having anger outbursts, and you're behaving inappropriately at work."

And I said, "Oh, my God, my sister just died, and they buried her about two weeks ago. I was like, and I remember I just started bawling. That's when I start bawling, and then that's finally when somebody says, "Have you gone to employee assistance?"

And I said, "No, I didn't even know this was an option for me."

So, they wait all this time to send me to employee assistance, so I show up at employee assistance. And the first thing they tell me is:

"It's important to understand that individuals vary in how they respond to traumatic occurrences. This is normal, not a sign of psychopathology by itself."

The problem with your coworkers' lack of empathy is not their gender, race, or class background.

It's that they know next to nothing about you. You're just a walking sliver of a human, playing a role, wearing a narrowly imagined mask. Your colleagues don't see you as an individual. They see you as a role player in an office game. The game might be fun, terrifying, or a mix of both. It's certainly fun until you have to share your cancer diagnosis, your brother's seventy-two-hour psychiatric hold, your parents' bankruptcy, or your child's arrest.

What's so tragic about Sally's story is that at no time was the entire nursing ward informed adequately of her personal tragedy so that people had the chance to react differently. At no point did all her peers grieve with her ritualistically. And finally, she was not granted paid bereavement leave proportionate to the situation.

No one even knew what the situation was. See how the next paragraphs of context change or don't change your mind about Sally's grief-stricken rage at work.

Sally idolized her older sister growing up. They were best friends at home and even during college. They played, watched TV, and went to the movies together. Sally's sister initiated her into adulthood. She taught Sally how to navigate a party safely as a young woman. They loved each other in a way that not all sisters experience.

In 2012, Sally dropped her young daughter off with her sister, who routinely babysat for her. When she did, she saw that her home was oddly unkempt. The kitchen wasn't as clean as it usually was. And, whoa, there were broken beer bottles on the floor. The scene was very off.

Over the next eighteen months, her sister revealed herself to be an alcoholic, lost her job as an elementary school principal for being drunk at work, began experimenting with OxyContin and heroin, manipulated money out of their parents multiple times, began turning tricks for drug money, and finally was found dead of a drug overdose in a nearby park not far from Sally's home.

For eighteen months, Sally watched her older sister, her best friend, transform into a raging monster, an alien, and finally slip away in the dead of night, all alone.

Would that make *you* angry?

Or could you sit at your desk and work calmly and speak *appropriately*?

Would you want someone to shove a box of tissues in your face and walk away?

A perfectly functional middle-class citizen vanished from society, but at her work, this person's death was Sally's personal problem. Sally, the walking sliver of a human, had a problem *at home*. No community took immediate responsibility for helping her. The "community" showed more proactive responsibility for her sister's corpse than it did for her. Not until she broke down. At work. Months later. Where it was oh-so-embarrassing for everyone else to witness.

In female-dominated work environments, there is often tighter regulation over how you communicate than on a male-dominated stock trading floor. But tight regulation of etiquette, tone of voice, emotion, etc., is a regular feature of modern, bureaucratized offices and organizations (private and public). It's a performance of civility with a well-intended function *when employees aren't hurting*. It works well for modern coed offices too, since women often don't enjoy listening to locker-room banter from men.

But human life is full of hurt and tragedy. No amount of modernization will eradicate suffering from human lives. If the COVID-19 pandemic didn't remind you of that, I don't how to make it any clearer.

Americans do not know how to deal with personal tragedy at work because we are so intent on the HR performance of civility, communicability, niceness, appropriateness, etc. Our fanatical belief in privacy means that Sally and her colleagues have perverse incentives to never learn about the eighteen-month implosion of her sister's life or the decades of friendship that preceded it.

What's impressive is that Sally made it through that fall herself. After her behavior irritated her colleagues, you'll notice, only then was she asked if she had gone to "employee assistance" for therapy. Interesting that no one suggested this proactively or formally upon learning of her loss months earlier. With the help of her workplace's professional psychologists, she recovered. This is a privilege most American workers do *not* have in place at all. Nor do they have access to free, premodern group rituals of grief (i.e., prayer circles or intercessory prayer) like many evangelical Christians can more easily find in their social networks.

Instead, American workers in mental distress get interpreted at work as any combination of the following: annoying, irritating, disruptive, or unproductive. Unless the worker produces a formal diagnosis of mental disability, there is no legal obligation for employers to accommodate the kind of temporary situation Sally found herself in. And the relevant federal law protecting those with a mental health/neurological disability only passed in 2009. I doubt most employers out there have any clue as to their real obligations here.

But how many even care?

Chapter Ten

THE GREAT COLLEGE DIVIDE

When my grandfather went to college in 1920, he might as well have been seeking a PhD as far as the ordinary American was concerned. Less than 1 percent of adults obtained a four-year degree in any subject in that era, even the practical ones like chemical engineering. Only about 17–20 percent of Americans even graduated from high school that year.[1]

Tocqueville's description of American higher education in 1831 was still accurate in 1920: "Primary instruction is within reach of each; higher instruction is within reach of almost no one."[2]

The much-revered four-year liberal arts college degree took off in America after World War II because the GI Bill paid tuition for millions of first-generation college males. Private companies also needed workers with more advanced knowledge, skills, and the ability to sit for hours and hours *at desks*.

Before World War II, most Americans joined the family business, performed factory labor, or learned a trade they could sell in their local communities. Little of this work relied on more than a fourth- or fifth-grade formal education. This is why high school completion was rare before the Depression. It was the Depression surge in high school graduation rates (from 29 to 51 percent in ten years) that provided a national foundation for a whole new educational attainment competition that we take for granted today.[3]

So, how did this college thing pan out for older Americans born after World War II, when some form of postsecondary education was a mainstream career-enabling goal that over half of the population attempted to obtain?[4] How did work pan out for those who *didn't* get such a degree? And how did our belief in individualism hurt some but not others in the process?

In my 2022 national survey of older Americans (aged forty-five to seventy-four at the time), I asked a simple question up front:

How much do you agree/disagree with the following statement: My formal education is directly relevant to my most recent employment position.

Only 31 percent of my sample of older Americans agreed or strongly agreed with this statement. This implies a reasonably *nonutilitarian* relationship between curricular content and specific classes of adult employment after twelve to twenty years of schooling. Perhaps this is why so many middle-class parents today find the increasing college prep orientation of your average public high school to be tone-deaf at best and a blatant disservice at worse.[5] Even today's less skilled technical careers require both a high school degree *and* a two-year vocational/technical degree (an investment of nonworking time and money). A blue-collar existence requires more investment of time and money than ever. Only the truly unskilled sector (e.g., farm laborers, housecleaning, fast food, etc.) is available to the terminal high school degree holder.

But wait. This crude nonalignment of curriculum to final employment does not isolate how a college degree fits. So, let's dig deeper.

Roughly 73 percent of older Americans graduated from high school (as of 1997), but only 36 percent graduated college from a four-year degree-granting institution. Twenty-five percent of older Americans tried college and *dropped out*, receiving no added social proof to future employers.[6]

Whoa. Wait, what? You read that right. Twenty-five percent of older Americans are college dropouts! This astonishing number shows, in part, how powerful the college degree aspiration was for these generations. It drew in millions of students who were not prepared to reach graduation in such a self-directed curriculum and for whom unexpected childbirth also got in the way.

Among the four-year college graduates in my sample, however, 81 percent believe their formal education links well to their current/last job. Among terminal high school degree holders, unsurprisingly, only 22 percent said the same thing. So, the four-year degree's value finally becomes clearer.

If a college degree links so well to one's job, is it because of a tight connection between curricular content and the daily responsibilities of this or that career, or is the linkage about something else? My survey lacked space to dive deeper into why, but my life history explorations confirm that a four-year degree primarily *qualifies* you for modern, white-collar jobs paying middle and, to a lesser extent, upper-middle-class wages. A narrow "content" connection is a tempting conclusion. But it only holds for the minority who majored in finance and entered banking, majored in hard sciences and entered research and development labs, majored in physics and joined NASA, majored in accounting and joined a local CPA firm, or majored in engineering and joined a local civil engineering firm, etc.

A four-year degree has another filtering function when it comes to employment. It filters crudely for folks who can read and write at above-average levels of competency and sit at desks for hours and hours (without losing their minds).

For Baby Boomers and Gen X, a college degree was a *modern* marker of middle-class status. But you didn't need one to get a middle-class wage at a union factory, become a postal carrier, or even a corporate salesperson. And it was not evident in the 1960s, for example, what the downsides of *not* having a college degree would eventually be. Let alone the downside of not having a *postgraduate* degree.

College degree attainment divided post–World War II America into those with access to more stable middle-class incomes versus those without this stability. But it was hardly a magical affluence-producing certificate. Around two-thirds of four-year degree holders in my survey, like my father-in-law, never earned elite incomes ($100K or more in 2023 dollars) during their lifetimes.

The college degree assisted more in directing older Americans to modern forms of office employment (eventually) and offering them social mobility into the middle classes. The degree has had an adaptive function primarily.

What gets lost in our cultural worship of the college degree is that *most older Americans never obtained one*. And some who got one failed to build on their parents' wealth with it in hand, while others experienced extreme career instability despite hanging a diploma on the wall.

To understand the complicated impact of the college divide on older Americans in a culture of almost self-righteous individualism, I want to explore the work histories of two individuals I met in 2023.

Contrasting the experiences of these two people, *both of whom never got a four-year degree*, exposes the sadly unequal outcomes generated by letting individuals figure out their careers autonomously without significant structural guidance, coaching, (and even therapy) from the broader communities in which we live and work.

Women Without a College Degree Floundered

In the 1960s–1980s, older men without a college degree could always deploy their basic social skills and tap into various old boys' networks mainly based on interpersonal, referred trust in their natal towns. These men just needed to figure out how to do this beyond networks of blood kin that used to give men their initial entry points into the workforce in prior generations.

After World War II, "Bob's uncle helped him get a job at the factory" transformed into "Bob got that factory job after a buddy at the Elks club put in a *good word* for him." This was a gradual transition for men as family networks became less and less valuable in sourcing any employment. For *modern* forms of employment, which require a college degree, even your friends might initially have little to offer.

Women entering the workforce in the 1960s, 1970s, and 1980s, however, entered more or less *alone*, on their own. They had a résumé, initiative, and a presumed gender orientation (or societal expectation) toward pleasing authority, empathy, and agreeableness.

What's critical to acknowledge is that these women had no sizable generation of female mentors preceding them regarding modern employment. And they certainly had no old girls' network to access optimal white-collar positions. Some perhaps had a one-off sister ahead of them. That's about it.

Moreover, older women today had no allies at work either, for the most part. Instead, they had *competition*.[7] In some cases, the toxic female-to-female bullying behavior reached levels made famous in movies like *Working Girl* (1988) or my personal favorite, *The Business of Strangers* (2001).

I believe the following tale happened to millions of Gen X and Boomer women who failed to get a liberal arts college degree. They did not get a degree that would have catapulted them well above the mass of women working in low-status, female-dominated functions/roles *inside male-dominated organizations*.

With limited chances for promotion in a secretarial pool, for example, and no intrinsic career support from male leaders, the potential for women to eat their own was not only high but also fits into a known pattern of stigmatized groups attacking each other at work to angle for limited upward opportunities.[8]

Nancy is the forty-seven-year-old only child of now-deceased parents who were dependent on Section 8 housing in Alabama all their adult lives. Her father only had a sixth-grade education and delivered newspapers reliably for decades on behalf of local news outlets. Her mother stayed at home due to undiagnosed and unmanaged mental health problems. Nancy's mother most likely had severe anxiety in an era when little help was offered to poor women suffering from it.

Her parents didn't drink or get into trouble. They kept to themselves. Nancy had a sheltered childhood in the 1980s, but not due to wealth and snobbery. It was a Southern Baptist kind of moral sheltering. Her parents did not let her wander around alone, anywhere, even as a teen. And she couldn't afford a car. In her childhood, she described an atmosphere of order and calm so palpable that you would swear she was comfortably middle class. There was no hint of the corrosive stereotype we tend to have of the working poor on public assistance. Her family was the audience we created Section 8 funding to benefit—working families *with no means to escape* minimum wage employment. At some point in American history, we accepted that social mobility was not a mass phenomenon. That millions of people need housing or income support. Our modern media seems to have forgotten this.

Nancy thought a terminal high school degree with a vocational office admin certificate would give her middle-class security. Here was her impressive plan in high school.

> *Well, I didn't wanna work in a factory. I knew that. I thought: I got to figure something out. I won't be stuck at a restaurant somewhere serving hamburgers to people. I knew I didn't wanna do that.*
>
> *And so, I thought, Office work! . . . I was kind of apprehensive about the typing class. But I aced it. I did great and everything, which got me interested in office work. And so, I applied for the vocational school secretarial program, which I got into pretty quickly and got my secretarial diploma. It's a certificate, not a degree.*[9]

The fact that there even *was* a plan is a testament to extraordinary individual initiative given her circumstances. Her parents certainly didn't have much advice about surviving in the modern working world. And Nancy worked hard to make this career path work. She was poor by contemporary standards but not malnourished or poorly clothed. Her parents were levelheaded, decent people who kept to themselves and appeared to focus intently on protecting their daughter from bad influences. As a teenager, she was not even allowed to walk to the nearby convenience store without a companion. They didn't let her do typical summer teen jobs either since this exposes you to even more potential distractions (i.e., pregnancies you don't need).

But the "protection" her parents defended also came with a cost. It meant that she didn't socialize much with middle-class kids. So, she never lost her deep working-class drawl. She would be forever marked by the way she talked and interacted.

> *I remember I would argue with my dad and tell him, "You know that I don't have a whole lot of friends" . . . that I felt I was being treated differently for living in government housing. And he would say, "I buy you nice clothes and dresses just as good as they have. Well,*

maybe if anybody doesn't like you for where you live, the hell with them!"

I didn't accept him saying that because I thought, "Well, he can afford better." . . . As I grew older, I realized he's exactly right.[10]

The linguistic and interactional code of middle-class conformity was not something Nancy's family could teach her. It was accessible primarily from her teachers at school. I believe this lack of social skills *upgrading* initially marked Nancy in middle-class circles, despite her work output or work ethic. It would take her time to acquire those social skills *at work*. If she could.

Let's think about her state of alienation as she entered the modern workforce. Nancy's parents couldn't give her any cash safety net between adult jobs OR any meaningful advice/encouragement based on white-collar experience. Nancy would have to figure *all of it* out on her own.

Attempting to shift social classes like this was and is one of the loneliest journeys in American society, and we do little to recognize the difficulty. We do not ritualize it or manage it as a society. And it is vastly easier for men, especially men like my dad, son of a semi-employed carpenter, who then married an *upper-middle-class woman*.

Take a look at Nancy's exhausting work history in an individualistic society in which women are entirely on their own to find portals into the middle class without much, if any, family support at all:

1. Miscellaneous low-end admin jobs (18–20)
2. Daycare worker (20–23)—searching for higher pay
3. Community college (24–26) with part-time admin job and public assistance (and a young child)—searching for higher pay
4. Construction office admin (28–30)—searching for some kind of decent pay
5. Administrator at a grocery chain HQ (30–42)
    - Got that higher wage!
    - Laid off without cause or explanation after being internally transferred due to run-ins with several female bosses, one who was simply abusive

6. Apartment complex property manager (42–43)
    - Fired with three days eviction notice for refusing advances of male resident (boss believed rent-paying resident's false narrative, not hers)
7. Remote customer service during COVID (appliance company) (43–45)
    - Fired for not escalating angry customer call properly
8. At-home customer service (briefly) and laid off for structural reasons
9. Unemployed currently

The critical office role for female secretaries—executive secretary—required a four-year degree. These elite white-collar women attached themselves to specific high-status executive men. They could even follow them around from company to company, avoiding any real competition with other women in a traditional secretarial labor pool or within any pool of female-dominated roles in an organization. I had an aunt who did this masterfully. Her social skills were also masterful. She did *not* grow up in Section 8 housing.

But you had to have near *upper-middle-class social skills* to get these executive-admin positions, social skills you could possibly acquire in *college if you came from a middle-class family background* but ones not likely to be obtained by someone emerging from a sheltered, working-class home (lacking a middle-class mentor).

Nancy was set up to fail in her attempt at class mobility, despite her mature plan at age eighteen.

When communities cannot reliably reward the earnest, organized, and willing, we have to step back and ask where we went wrong.

Upper-Middle-Class Men Could Ignore the College Degree and Do Just Fine

Todd is a sixty-nine-year-old retiree, a classic Baby Boomer in that Beaver and Cleaver sense of the phrase. His dad was a salesman and then a small copywriting agency owner. Mom stayed at home. They lived in a superficially idyllic southern California suburb with a backyard pool. The only wrinkle with the perfect veneer was that Todd was adopted, and his siblings weren't. And, oh yeah, his dad ignored him, while his mother openly resented her decline in lifestyle with an "under-earning" husband (i.e., she was born into the Midwestern 1 percent).

Reading between the lines of our interview, I believe that Todd took his dad's aloofness as a personal rebuff of *him* as an adopted child. He became an angry teen who thought his dad avoided him as *nonkin*, a very natural fear for adopted children around the world and across cultures:

> *I had an attitude and an arrogance that it was like, "You know what, [Dad]? Whatever you say, I'll take it into consideration, but it has the same weight as Sam's parents or Alan's parents because I'm as much related to them as you."*
>
> *The other kids' fathers would talk to them for the most part, and I had a couple of kids' fathers that would really sit down and talk to me where my own dad wouldn't.*
>
> *He was raised as a German, and they just keep their mouth shut and glare at you.*[11]

Todd's allusion to his dad's ethnic background is not trivial here. Anglo-Saxon and German American men from the Silent Generation and earlier were notoriously noncommunicative people, especially with social subordinates (that includes kids!). These are very hierarchical ethnic groups whose approach to the patriarchal family structure was aloof and laconic, not cuddly, backslapping, or boisterous. Obviously, fathers in these families varied in their behavior patterns, but the general image holds for these historically high-status ethnic groups in American society.[12] Watch Tennessee Williams' *Cat on a Hot Tin Roof*, starring Paul Newman, for an entertaining fictional portrait of this ethnic archetype.

Todd's anger at his father's aloofness is understandable whether he was adopted or not. The anger reached such a point in his early teens that a Presbyterian minister at their church realized it was heading to a bad place (apparently before Todd's parents did). The minister recommended an eccentric chain-smoking therapist when Todd was just fourteen. *Reader, do you see how functional social surveillance led to a successful, organic intervention beyond the confines of the nuclear family?*

Here's what the therapist said to him in 1966:

> "Why don't you go to Peru? You strike me as the kind of person that would really do good there, and they need earthquake help."
>
> The Sendero Luminoso people in the more rural areas. You could trust them. So, I spent time learning about their traditional ways of medicine. I spent most of my time with a retired headhunting tribe that had switched to tourism. My maternal grandfather collected shrunken heads, so this was all in the family!
>
> I fell in love with Peru. I fell in love with the people. And sometimes I regret not having stayed.
>
> I stayed for five months that summer and even missed the first two months of high school.
>
> I learned a lot about how other people lived and died.
>
> We were there with the YMCA to help with earthquake relief. When I came back, I didn't need any more counseling.
>
> As far as that goes, it's like, okay, now I know how the world works. And there wasn't an arrogance anymore. I knew how the world works. That it was about being human, you know. I have so much more sh*t than everybody else in this part of the world has. I was living a luxurious life, and I didn't even realize it. And you people don't have things, and yet you're loving and accepting of me, regardless of what I have. And so that changed my whole outlook on life, and really got me to the point where the most important thing is to find loving people rather than money people.[13]

Todd became a proto-anthropologist without knowing it at the time. He disconnected from his family's upper-middle-class materialism as well. Todd certainly had the requisite qualification for anthropology: supreme alienation from his natal culture—in his case, from the most primal of human identities—*family*.

As a form of healing, Todd spent the next few high school summers abroad in Peru, working among poor, indigenous peoples who had "real" problems, like recovering from the massive 1969 Junin province earthquake in the central highlands. He was trapped in a cold, well-educated family where a wife verbally resented her husband's inability to earn as much as she grew up used to spending. The Peruvian Indians, on the other hand, offered a window onto nonmaterialistic, premodern family relations, relations *focused on intimacy, communal sharing, and emotional availability*. Not the accumulation of things by individuals.

Todd's dual-layer alienation from his family is no doubt why he broke his life into stages related to *family*, not career, as the majority of my other interviewees did.

Todd's Self-Described Life Stages

1. Exploring
2. Married
3. Family
4. Search for Birth Family
5. Grandpa!
6. Exploration Again!

One thing Todd did not do early in his life was to graduate from college. His parents certainly thought he would. As upper-middle-class Americans, they raised him and his siblings to pursue college degrees. But Todd struggled to focus in traditional liberal arts college settings that American society put on a pedestal of modernity back in the 1960s. After two years floundering in a University of California chemistry program, he transferred to the University of Montana in Bozeman and met his wife in an anthropology class.

This is how he narrates his admittedly entitled approach to college,

> *I attended college. I didn't go to classes.*
> *. . . If I wasn't getting anything out of a class, I just didn't go. I'd write the paper, take the test, and go. The only downfall to that is I failed chemistry twice. You had to go to class, right? I mean . . . you had to be there, and you had to be in the labs. . . . But you know, it's like I'm never going to pass chemistry, and to get a degree . . . I had to have the science course.*

> So, I eventually said, "Screw it! I don't really need a degree to do what I want to do, anyway," which, looking back on it, was . . . a classic mistake.
>
> . . . I kind of developed an arrogant attitude that did me no good service.
>
> My wife and I met in an anthropology class on primitive American religions, and I think I went to class three times and got an A. I even wrote her paper.
>
> I always thought I'd be a great anthropologist, but having kids kind of took that dream and put it off to the side.[14]

Todd recounts a classic behavior common to many upper-middle-class adults—a built-in class confidence in his future that allowed him to treat what most Americans considered a rare opportunity (college) as a toy, a mere option. This is no different from his contemporary, Bill Gates, son of a corporate attorney, throwing away a Harvard diploma to found Microsoft.

This is rich kid stuff. And Todd is very aware of this now.

In context, though, Todd also had deeper unconscious priorities, like building a family—a very different family from the one he grew up in. Marrying at twenty-three and having a kid right away not only shifted his priorities, but I also suspect this was the plan of his unconscious mind all along, the next stage in his healing process as a confused, adopted child.

As I listened to his retelling, it was clear that creating a nonmaterialistic, loving family became far more important to him than the content of his career, which ended up being relatively mundane (manager/director in a logistics firm and then operations director for a retail store) until his kids left the nest and he joined a Native American tribal public health agency.

Todd sacrificed his upper-middle-class birth status for a comfortable *middle-class* existence with different priorities. And he does not see it as a failure at all. He used his class privilege to dodge the upper-middle-class rat race that others blindly joined autonomously. And he found a life partner who was OK with the income trade-offs her husband made.

When we dive into the lived experiences of older Americans, we find that the real college dream in the 1960s–1990s was less about becoming rich than it was about a) escaping working-class misery where you trade limited skills for cash as a non-owning, easily discarded employee *or* b) reproducing the middle-class comfort your parents had managed to achieve and raise you within.

In my national research, I learned that your average older American was vastly less pretentious and upwardly obsessed than some of us might assume. If they did become wealthier, it was more a consequence of various decisions they made than a conscious (or ruthless) plan. Despite his working-class origins, even my wildly successful father claims he did not set out to become wealthy (just comfortable). The folks who actively *chased* wealth in this older age cohort were mostly born into the 11 percent upper-middle-class slice of it (like many of my Harvard undergraduate peers in the early 1990s). Honestly, this elite group is where access to the social capital required to become a successful entrepreneur is found. Todd chose to exit this tribe and seems incredibly happy with this decision. As an ambivalent member of the upper-middle class, I'm not surprised by his happiness.

Comparing Todd and Nancy's career journeys reveals how both gender and class origin profoundly affect the emotional and economic reality of having loads of autonomy in one's approach to career and education.

Nancy was set up to fail as an upwardly mobile autonomous actor.

Todd was set up to thrive as he made autonomous decisions. He didn't need a college degree because he was smart *and* had upper-middle-class social skills. He is socially *hyper-skilled*, in my view. He should be a TV anchor.

Individualism as a choice ideology favoring autonomy in major life decisions sounds intrinsically unassailable to most Americans. For a long time, I agreed. But the reality is that it favors neurotypical, white men from upper-middle-class backgrounds the most. The ability to thrive while throwing away a college degree opportunity is a powerful sign of:

- How a moral compulsion to be an autonomous individual does *not* yield the same outcomes for everyone in an individualistic society
- How powerfully this ethos lets down otherwise well-intentioned adults by encouraging a false belief that you are the origin of all your problems and certainly the solution to them
- How this ethos of naked individualism encourages a communal disinterest in those who are essentially set up to fail. Nancy is an "embarrassment" to our collective imagination of self-reliant social mobility.

Instead, outsiders see your "failure" and just point a judgmental finger, looking everywhere they can for how you screwed this up. Judgment instead of stepping in to mentor and help where natal families simply cannot. This is where our communities and state governments let down the millions hovering just above the poverty line.

Chapter Eleven

CAREER ZIGZAG

My dad spent his entire thirty-year career as a corporate attorney. He had three positions and applied only twice for jobs. Who sprinkled pixie dust on *his* crib? My dad's idea of career insurance was to accumulate three high-value specialties (Securities and Exchange Commission law, mergers and acquisitions, and healthcare/HMO law). But he never once had to think about leaving the law *profession*. He would always be in demand.

Let's unpack the unconscious logic of his work life: my dad picked a highly regulated *profession* (law) and pursued a corporate legal *career* within that profession involving only three *"jobs"* in thirty years.

A profession. A career. A job. The difference between these three terms is how you approach acquiring your income. Professions modify careers. Careers modify a string of jobs. You can easily string together jobs without having a career or a profession. Language is fun, isn't it? Yet, we don't view someone who has worked on and off as a waitress as someone with a "career." People doing minimum wage jobs don't consider their work a *career* either. They are trying to survive.

A career is a term we reserve for jobs that are a) modern and b) pay more than minimum wage plus tips, even though plenty of minimum wage jobs have a wide bandwidth of skill competence (ever had a lousy waitperson at a restaurant?). "Careers" differ in the a) experiential knowledge sets accumulated, b) formal knowledge/jargon required to fit in, and c) categories of "job" that fit within them. Jockeying for this or that career sucks you into a modern status game from which it is difficult to extricate yourself. A career also implies you believe you have *options for upward mobility*, which many, but not all, Americans have had since World War II.

The professional route to employment remains the most secure (and expensive) way to do this income-generation thing. It's like taking a rocket to orbit. My dad rode the equivalent of a Saturn V (in the 1960s too!). The problem for America is that very few of us will ever be *professionals* in anything. It's a tiny tribe. Among older Americans in my research, only 6 percent have an elite professional degree (MD, JD, MBA, or PhD).[1] The architects don't add up to many folks, so I left them out. That's less than one out of ten folks with the career security of a professional degree. If *all* your friends have one, you now realize what a ridiculous social bubble you live in and why you may think this book is about another country.

With or without a professional degree, many of us will try to find a "career" because building on a consistent, compounding skill set (with or without certifications) makes us more employable and promotable over time. It gives our adult existence greater meaning and symbolic power in conversation too. A punchy career tag has more impact on our social lives: "Oh, you're an anthropologist? Wow. How *interesting*."

Whether your work is interesting (anthropology) or dull (corporate law), the benefit of planning one's career too far in advance eroded by the turn of the twenty-first century. Career instability has overtaken most of America and remains an under-discussed source of individual mental health challenges.

Why?

American Individualism Pivots Around the Concept of the Career

One of the modern behaviors signaling an upwardly mobile American has been pursuing a *career* instead of a) defaulting to the family business or b) stringing together unskilled or semiskilled jobs. Tens of millions of Americans still do the latter and often suffer inflation-adjusted wage decline as a result. "Careers" are for individuals who don't feel they have to view their lives as survival. I assure you that the old-time family farmer saw his life as *survival*. He didn't "retire" to compose his memoir—*Fieldwork: How Farming Taught Me the Value of Resilience and Grit*. The latter requires a frighteningly self-absorbed careerist person as its author. Know any?

But let's get real: the entire notion of pursuing a career is a profoundly *male-biased* concept, as Micki McGee aptly puts it:

> *This model of human action, which emphasizes the individual's independence or "agency" over the impact of the social milieu, was a profoundly masculine model . . . it was rooted in the values of a commercial sphere that had heretofore been dominated by men.*[2]

I would go further than McGee and say that women have only recently had the luxury of planning a life *entirely* focused on their careers. Men have had that luxury ever since they abandoned the family farm (or trade) in the great nineteenth-century kickoff to industrialization. They just dragged their families with them to factory housing or urban tenements. In patriarchal societies, therefore, individualism took off among urban *men* first. They got to "have it all" from the start. But, for older women, *not* having children was *the* critical lifestyle choice that made a *pure* career focus possible in the late twentieth century. They could not rely on men their age to stay home or do significant chores. Not having children still makes a strong career focus far easier for younger women. All working moms alive today have been tugged this way and that, battling guilt and resentment (and exhaustion) for eighteen to twenty-five years until the children leave home (if they do!). They still do not have as much career autonomy as individuals.

Another critical facet of modern career seeking is that, as McGee notes, we divorce our careers from community commitments or obligations (unless the "job" is tied to local government institutions). Careers bear no inherent social responsibility other than to contribute to the house "kitty." Even doctors have no broad community obligation in our society, simply a Hippocratic oath to their patients. There is a frighteningly archaic clannishness to how we pursue, manage, and reinvent our careers. We are like hunter-gatherers in an urban savanna chasing wild paychecks (not gazelle). It's worth considering if the growing desire among Millennial and Gen Z workers for social impact careers has to do with filling the massive emotional void our dislocated, trans-local jobs create for us as humans. The work of our careers has no direct impact on our social lives outside of work.

Americans most easily believe that we are lone actors in our careers, battling for our sole survival first, secondarily for a family standing behind us with open palms. The community value of what we do doesn't enter our field of view. Work is the one everyday cultural activity in which we positively *worship* our individuality as cultural beings. The W-9 form legally enshrines this. This is true even when class privilege, gender privilege, and racial privilege (or the stigmatic inverse of each) are clearly *at work behind the scenes* of our journey.

The Problem with Career *Planning*

Back to Dad. Dad is eighty years old. He's sick of being mentioned in this book too. Nevertheless, I'm sure he would tell you not to expect the charmed, simplistic career path he had to fall in *your* lap, even if you can afford Harvard Law. My dad was a professional outlier in terms of career security.

The real shocker that fell into the lap of older Americans was the end of the *single-career*, middle-class existence during their lifetimes. Nineteenth-century family farmers and cobblers had more "career" consistency than we do. This is one of many historical ironies that make our modern, individualistic society far from a simple endpoint on a glorious, happy journey of constant improvement ending in a righteous angelic chorus of joy and happiness for all.

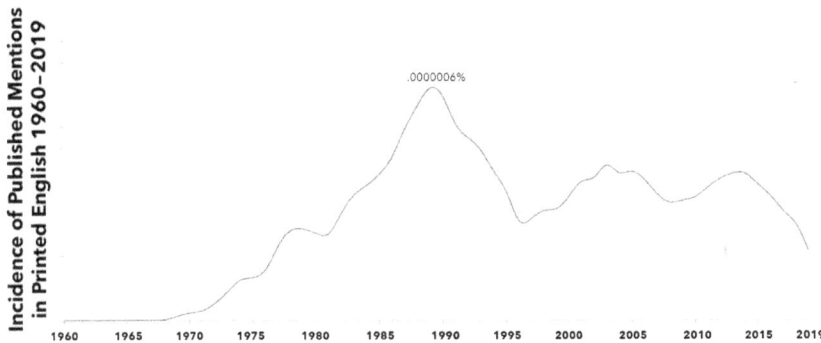

Figure 1. Printed Mentions of "Career Change" in the English Language. Table data sourced from Google's Ngram service.[3]

The phrase "career change" exploded in printed English in the 1970s and has been consistently in use ever since. Millennial and Gen Z children have now grown up watching at least one parent switch careers. I do not believe any prior American generation can say this other than the ones that watched their parents leave the family farms for factories from 1880 to 1920.

A massive increase in life expectancy due to modern medical care is also a supporting factor in the likelihood of a career change. We have more decades to either get fired/laid off or to decide to make a bold change. It's amazing that we don't talk about career change more. A lot more. After all, work is our number one priority social identity in America. If you believe Tocqueville's 1831 "research," the primacy of active labor in our cultural self-concept has existed since the initial immigrant surges of the early nineteenth century. *This* is our single greatest national tradition—our work ethic. We love work. *The best proof of this is the fact that the highest-income Americans work the most hours!* They don't surf dinner parties like the Gatsbyesque rich of the 1920s.

Were older Americans ready for this massive shift in the reliability of our primary social identity? Within their own lifetimes? Did they see the tsunami of career changes headed their way?

Fifty-four percent of Americans aged forty-seven to seventy-six, like me, believed they would have just *one* career. Remember the professor of something I intended to be at the age of fifteen? My wife, though, was in the "change-is-a-coming" camp, thanks to an up-to-date

California high school guidance counselor in the mid-1980s. As you may have quietly suspected all your life, *everything* is indeed better in California.

So which faction turned out to be right about the likelihood of career change? Well, ahem, it wasn't me. I had a bad role model (see Dad story above) and an irrational belief in my own upper-middle-class control over the universe. We're seriously confused about causality and risk. We also took our entitled social position for granted in a broader society with plenty of reasons to root for our downfall.

And so, I now feel compelled to release one nasty histogram to make my point. I beg your liberal arts pardon if you were bad in math.

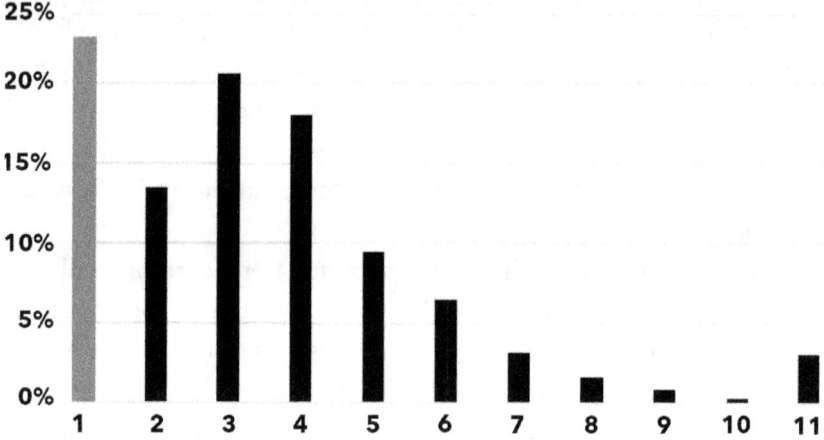

Figure 2. *The Number of Times Older Americans Changed Their Careers. Table data sourced from SAI Older Americans National Study, 2022.*[4]

Almost 80 percent of older Americans changed their career at least once *but only 46 percent of them thought they would be doing this*. That's one out of two folks, mostly middle-class people, who found themselves making big, unforeseen changes to their number one priority social identity. Among this 80 percent majority, the median number of career changes (to date) is 2.5.

The growing prevalence of career change as a mass social reality in a matter of a few generations is one of the least properly analyzed topics in modern social history and yet one of the most aggressively marketed via a wide-open fire hose of self-help literature predicated on the concept of "reinvention."[5]

As I mentioned earlier, there is a strong, upper-middle-class bias toward any concept of an autonomous career *journey*. This "journey" contains a vision of a lone individual wielding a polished résumé. She boldly drives her sensible yet stylish sedan to an office park to engage in a conversational battle for positions in an idealized, zigzag career path.

The reality for older Americans is that a great deal of career change was *not* voluntary but performed in emotionally volatile, financially distressed circumstances. Almost 80 percent of older Americans who have changed careers have experienced a firing or layoff before one of their career changes. That's 60 percent of those aged forty-seven to seventy-six today. Wow.

Getting fired or laid off doesn't force you to do anything as grandiose as changing a career. It's not like rain triggering you to put on a coat. You may find another position elsewhere in the same career box. But, wow, getting fired/laid off sure makes you think about every variable related to what you're doing with so much of your daytime hours, doesn't it? Indeed. Indeed, it does. It's brutally painful in a society that teaches you to be the self-sufficient source of your own sustenance.

When Americans get laid off or fired today, there may be a ton of paperwork and a clinical, inhuman mass Zoom meeting. But there is no ritual group process leading you to your next job.

Instead, employers hand out papers, point to resources (a small severance check which is your parachute), and run the other way, primarily back to their workflows. They couldn't care any less about your fate, to be honest, beyond a token letter of recommendation. Today, lawyers often keep managers from contacting you, lest they disclose something that could be used against the company in a wrongful termination suit.

Employers certainly feel no obligation to reseat you in another job. Hardly. If they had such an obligation, they would think much harder about how they hire and fire, wouldn't they? Callous firing and sloppy/near-sighted hiring go together like alcohol and date rape. *The victim is always fully responsible.*

When I was a teenager, I listened at dinner one evening as my dad described how he and his partners went to lengths to secure a new nonprofit position for one of their more incompetent legal colleagues so that his family would have a decent income when they fired him. Wow. If you can find me even one anecdote in the past twenty years of any professional services firm doing such a compassionate, kindhearted thing for an employee they need to fire, please e-mail me (address in the appendix), and I'll send you $500.[6]

While employers have come to think of workers as entirely disposable, including white-collar workers, the concept of employer responsibility has shrunk to meeting payroll (and benefits). The employee's *career* is of no consequence to them. The tech world has witnessed some of the most egregious inhalations and exhalations of human capital in human history. Mature companies hire tens of thousands of new employees annually and periodically spit off ten to twenty thousand to meet Wall Street quarterly earnings expectations.

The callous approach of modern employers doesn't surprise you, but have you ever dwelled on the lack of *moral* obligation implicit in all this firing and impulsive laying off?

Such moral chaos might make a small, privately owned family business seem like a safer place for your career. Except, as I've discussed in part one, this is precisely where you will almost surely never get a lifestyle, inflation-conquering promotion. Ever.

Stagnant or slow-growing organizations will fight against any employee's attempt at careerism to keep your productive self right in its place . . . *forever*. About 90 percent of all small, privately owned family businesses function this way; they are career dead-ends for anyone. And they also become economic dead-ends in a constant inflationary erosion of your lifestyle.

The Lonely Reality of Solving Career Problems

A career change is a cognitive choice with social stakes too high to be unconscious. We make career changes very intentionally. Deliberately. Of course, this doesn't mean we do it competently. And it doesn't mean we change careers without being influenced by the broader culture and social networks we live within.

In many cases, adults are making a very *intentional* escape from a toxic, wage-stagnant, or simply defeating situation at work. As older women became more confident and experienced, they increasingly gave the symbolic middle finger to "the man" and moved on to something completely different. But changing a career based on one hellish job/organization does not come quickly. It takes a lot of deliberation and soul-searching. And support. And guts.

For older Americans, though, many career changes followed firings and layoffs. The intentional career change occurred in a volatile emotional context where money is now more scarce. The first thing fired/laid-off folks do as they move through Elizabeth Kubler Ross's stages of grief is to decide whether they should remain in their specific *industry. Do I stay in Software-as-a-Service (SaaS), or should I be a marketer of RVs?* Only when that fails, do they think bigger—about leaving their career in (insert current industry) behind. Those who choose to leave a career behind do it because of the "transferable skill set" concept popularized by the godfather of career change—the late Richard Nelson Bolles, founder of the publishing enterprise *What Color Is Your Parachute?*

We are so used to this chaotic, stressful process today that we forget that career change was uncommon in the mid-century period. And it was more likely to be entirely voluntary in all social classes before the 1990s acceleration of the involuntary drivers (M&A, cost-cutting mania, reorgs, etc.). The 1944 GI Bill also helped smooth over some of this change for fifteen million GIs who didn't want to or couldn't bear to return to their Depression-era employment.

If we follow the logic that career change was far less prevalent in the 1960s and that it has always been less common for the upper-middle-class professionals that Harvard produces with factorylike precision, then, in 1968, Richard Bolles himself was most likely without a dense group of friends "who had done this before." He was born into the last generation (the Greatest Generation) that believed in and experienced lifelong, single-career lives.

In addition, until very recently, career changes out of duress were not something you confessed to many people. Getting fired and making these kinds of pressured changes was embarrassing. The stigma of being fired (*Oh, he's incompetent*) or being laid off (*Oh, only the jerks get let go*), or working remotely for yourself (*Totally unemployable idiot, most likely*) is still with us, but it's weakening. In part, LinkedIn and business media outlets like Forbes have allowed professionals to zag and reframe their work identity with tons of content that distracts readers from even caring about their résumé, let alone looking at it on LinkedIn.

I can prove the persistence of career change stigma/suspicion to you indirectly by asking you to recall someone you know who recently told you they resigned from a job to pursue something else. Freeze that person's image in your mind.

When they told you about their "resignation," did you, even for a second or two, suspect they may be covering up the fact *that they were fired*?

I remember meeting with an entrepreneur in Seattle the year I resigned from my last W-2 job (2017). As I narrated how I voluntarily left my old company to start my consultancy, he interrupted me and said with surprise, "Oh, you *resigned*."

For context, if you look at LinkedIn profiles, one of the more common cover narratives for "Sh*t. I was fired and have no idea what I'm going to do and am quietly looking for the next position," is to label yourself as an *independent consultant*. "Richardson LLC" or "JFR Consulting LLC" or something similar with no corporate website link.

And this is the state of play in 2024.

I can't imagine the stigma in 1967 when Bolles told his friends he got fired. A man, the sole earner, who gets fired was a double failure. He failed as an individual and as a provider. I imagine you never, ever told anyone but your close family. You buried the story, including the firing, until the new job was lined up. You got good at bullsh*t nonanswers to "How's work?" cocktail questions about the job you hadn't been to in seven months.

Career-changing adults in Bolles's generation were not only lost at the margins of social change, but they also faced enormous stigma when applying for that new job in the new career:

Those resumes which have the greatest difficulty in getting through this Screening Process are those belonging to Zig-Zag people, Second Careerists who've accumulated much experience in their old Zig profession, and now are trying to Zag.[7]

The deeply painful heart of career zigzag is probably why 60 percent of older Americans describe it as something they figured out exclusively or primarily *on their own* (without much input from those close to them).

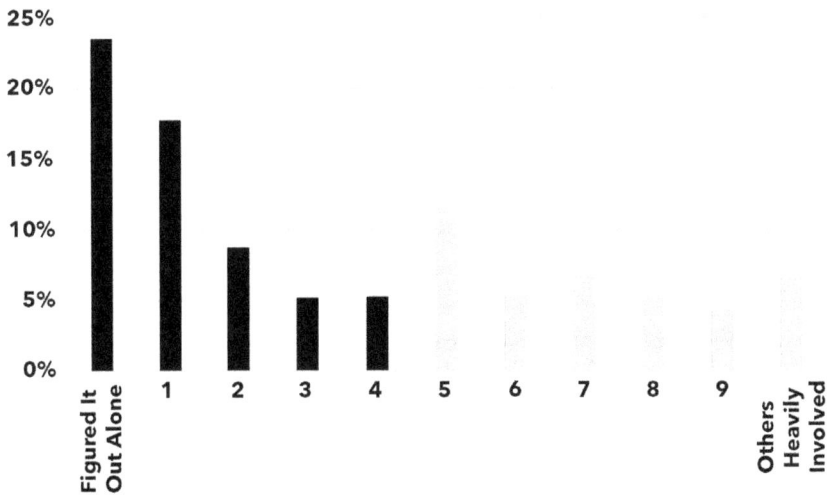

Figure 3. How Older Americans Figured Out Their Most Recent Career Change. Table data sourced from SAI Older Americans National Study, 2022.[8]

Remember that this age cohort (forty-seven to seventy-six) is overwhelmingly white (82 percent) and heavily populated by people from Super Stoic European ethnic groups averse to interpersonal drama and socially distributed emotional burden sharing.[9] These particular older Americans have real problems "dragging" other loved ones into their big, problematic decisions. Maybe their spouse. Maybe.

Self-knowledge and self-awareness are the secret sauce of Bolles's parachute method, not family therapy. This is a lot of work, folks. And dragging your spouse into a job or career hunt is only sometimes helpful since they have a significant conflict of interest. They need your money. *Get the money!* They are not necessarily on your side.

The tragedy of this lonely thing called a career is that, when we get laid off or fired or must jump off a moving train that is slowly killing us, there is no ritualized process to help us through the limbo, the betwixt and between, the shadowy tunnel leading to our next position. We have no ritual process for a career change, like an Amish barn raising or a church confirmation. Bolles cleverly reveals that third-party agencies repeatedly fail (from the 1960s until today) because a) they either work for the employers or, more importantly, b) they do not know *you*. At all. A résumé is not a document that produces self-awareness. It's a calculated performance.

There are tons of websites, blogs, coaches, and books. Oodles of resources for the individual . . . *to figure it out herself*. . . . It is a Stoic, librarian's approach to the problem of life itself. But there's a reason we don't ask librarians to devise social policy or healing rituals.

There are at least four cultural reasons why career problems become so alienating for Americans:

1. We don't tend to marry or partner with people in the same career or industry,[10] so *there is no domestic source of consolation and implicit understanding.* You may not be in a relationship if you have never listened awkwardly to your partner vent about career problems you don't understand. Check with your therapist. This wasn't true for the nineteenth-century family farmer. Everyone in the family was a farmer. They all lived on the farm.
2. *Throwing away the sunk cost of time/money invested in existing skills is emotionally tragic* and devastating to the individual who acquired them. You have no idea how many professors out there wanted to quit but couldn't get past the sunk-cost barrier. So. Many.
3. Therefore, *only the individual can fully understand* the emotional hell of remaining in their mainly messed up career situation.
4. *Career satisfaction is the perfect storm of social science complexity.* It exists at the emotionally charged intersection of career, burst personal fantasies and

dreams, desired economic reward, and whatever drives your fulfillment in a work-first culture like ours.

It is more than possible that we invest too much of our identity in work when deciding to pursue a *career*. I've had this conversation with colleagues before—the conversation about the possibility that we're wildly overcommitting too much of ourselves to "our work sliver."

From Reactive to Intentional Zigzag

If you want a vivid example of what it feels like to find yourself in the wrong career due to your own choices, read Anna's story about working for three years in a suburban Kansas City police department run by what seemed like a sociopath:

> *The people that I worked with were crazy. They were all crazy, I mean, I could write a book, and I have often thought about it. But I don't want to relive it at all because it was just a horrible time. They were horrible people. . . . I mean I worked with people that hated each other. And they were always trying to undermine one another. . . .*
>
> *There was this Hatfield and McCoy feud being played out in this little, tiny eighteen-person department. So, you had to be very careful who you were with because you would get put into groups that were on the chief's side or not. He [the chief] had two people he [really] didn't like, and they were older policemen. . . . They didn't ever go to a full police academy training. And so, he researched and found out that he could make these men go to the police academy. So, he sent them. Both of them were in their late fifties. And because it was such a low-paying job, they really needed it, and so they went [to the academy]. It was embarrassing for everybody. I mean, it was just horrible cruelty to do that. He's trying to humiliate them, and they're going to the academy with all these [young] recruits. They've been police officers for thirty years.*
>
> *[The people of the town] wanted someone that would do anything to protect them. There were certainly lots of legal lines that he*

> would cross to do whatever it took to make his citizens happy, and they liked that about him. Other people came to the department, and maybe they had no other job prospects. So, he either drove them crazy, and a) they stayed, and now they were crazy like him or b) some people left, like me. Yeah, there was a lot of turnover.
>
> I had left my teaching job to go into [the police force], not expecting it to be like this, and very quickly, in the first couple of years, I realized I did not want to stay in law enforcement. I had made a huge mistake, and I blame that mistake on television as well. I think I got into it because I thought being a cop was like on TV. . . .
>
> You know my parents were not in favor of [my being a police officer]. Of course, they didn't want it, and they were very happy that I [left].[11]

Anna ended up recovering and stabilizing with a new career in IT, a track I sensed was more suited to her introverted, quiet disposition.

In an individualistic society, though, Anna's stumble is unsurprising. We encourage career choice that is disassociated from our parents' careers, our family's experience, and the lived experience of even our close friends. We put ourselves in the position of chasing something without any easy ability to preview what could very well be an alien, moving target. Or even a complete disaster.

What happens to many like Anna and me is that we confuse career *fantasy* with career dreams, merging with some idealized person in the career as presented by media, merging mindlessly with a fixed object versus identifying intimately with the journey to becoming proficient in X or Y.

My teenage fixation on becoming a professor was more about wanting an intellectual career focused on deep thought and writing. I tried to merge with a fantastical image of the professor. I had no clue what professors spent their time doing every day. It never occurred to me that I should even find this out.

It's not shocking to learn that the "career planning" industry is now an $18-billion industry in the United States, growing annually.[12] It should probably be a $200-billion industry if our society cared about planning the way it should. There are specialists for every industry and for every stage of career planning. Amid all the modern infrastructure to advise us on our careers, I'm still haunted by a passage Richard Bolles wrote in the 1972 first edition of his famous book:

> *Our society has taken pity on the job-hunter and career-changer and invented all kinds of help for him or her: federal-site employment agencies, private employment agencies, classified ads, job counselors, computerized job banks, and so forth. None of these works very well. In fact, the number of people who turn to any one of them without getting a job, as a result, is simply mind-blowing... Stop giving the job-hunter a fish, half a fish, or no fish; and instead, teach him how to fish.*[13]

I suspect Bolles was reacting to the last gasps of an old tendency in America: looking for a networked social authority to land you a job. This used to happen all the time in America *inside large family networks*. During my research, I collected several anecdotes of Baby Boomers' parents receiving this kind of help from older relatives. This worked very well for blue-collar jobs (at your uncle's auto-body shop) but not for the "college jobs" that careerist Americans tend to seek. And not for *new* jobs or careers of any kind. Market research survey analyst? Daycare administrator? At best, your friends might *help* you get the job.

Maybe. But probably not.

It's a human tendency to seek networked-based help for any survival need. And W-2 income is no different. But Bolles is telling young Baby Boomers in the 1970s that those days are over. No one is going to get you the job. There is no Uncle Bob who can help you in most careers. We have scattered to the winds of hyper-specialized jobs.

In our cash-based society, your income begins and ends with W-2 employment as a solitary activity. You must figure this out yourself. You must acquire job-hunting *skills*. Individualism. Pure and simple. Deal.

To me, though, the real lesson of older Americans' experiences is that a "career" is a fantasy-laden trap at worst and a weak form of personal branding at best.

The infuriating and beautiful simplicity of living without any career ideal is that you can never be let down or disappointed by a long-term dream that blows up in your face. Your toil, your labor, is always and only a means to an income or survival.

The long-term clairvoyance of Richard Bolles's book is that it teaches you how to *know yourself well enough* to monetize what makes you happy and content, without regard to concepts like "job descriptions" and without making yourself subservient and psychologically dependent on employers' mercy, on the mercy of strangers who just do not give a damn. They don't care, because society does not obligate them to think deeply about your situation. Employers don't think like communities or families.

It has taken way too long for Americans to realize that working in an environment of rapid social change requires more self-awareness than ever before, or external forces you barely understand will knock you around repeatedly.

I get now why my dad retired as soon as he could.

Part Three

HOW WE GOT LOST IN THE AMERICAN FUNHOUSE

"A guy I knew wrapped his car around a pole south of town and was dead. I think that was kind of a jolt to me."
—*Kevin, age fifty-six, Pennsylvania*

Chapter Twelve

WHY I SUCK AT PARTIES

I may be an unreliable narrator regarding the American concept of "fun." I suck at parties and was not often invited to them. I went to about four in high school. One was the senior graduation sleepover (the invitation was public, the parents were home and took our car keys). I didn't attend many more parties in college either because I didn't drink until junior year.

In high school, multiple teachers routinely told me to "smile more" as I walked around campus with my Aspie blank face. And this was at a school in relatively un-smiley New England. My behavior would have probably triggered a child welfare visit in the South. I'm Mr. Serious most of the time.

I don't know of anyone who thinks of me and "fun" in the same sentence. I honestly didn't care then and don't care now. But, under the theory that marginal status (vis-à-vis the domain under discussion) gives you an enhanced perspective on norms, this is probably an asset in my discussion of this jazzy little English word.

How I Discovered America's Master Symbol—Fun

Having lived abroad in Asia for several years, I will go out on a limb and say that America's most influential export is *entertainment* (mainly music and film). Hollywood films consistently earn two to three times their domestic sales in international markets.[1] I can prove it without numbers too by describing the maniacal enthusiasm for Hollywood films in India. India is a very proud, relatively chauvinistic, classical civilization. This is, in part, why British colonization was more *economically* successful than culturally so. When I lived in Tamil Nadu (southern tip) in the late 1990s, I quickly lost track of the random strangers I met who tried to bond with me immediately over this or that foreign "film" they had just seen.

- "You are liking Bruce Villis, no?" *Absolutely!*
- "How many times have you seen *Titanic*?" *This movie played for over a year at one local theater.*
- "Mr. James! You look exactly like blond hero in blue film I saw yesterday!" *"Blue film" means pornography. He meant well.*

And so on. All these exchanges were a shameful mirror to my doctoral candidate elitism, as I recoiled artistically at basically every film title they mentioned.

I also dreaded standing in the thronging press of non-deodorized male bodies that filled the metal-caged ticket lines in my chosen Tamil city. These caged lines even had metal bars *on top* to deter people from running across everyone's shoulders to cut the line (you laugh, but I went through this once). I swore I would be crushed to death in one of those lines and become an international spectacle of flattened, sweaty jingoism.

My Tamil friends thought it was "fun." I felt like a ninety-year-old white man.

The earliest English language usage of the word "fun" dates to 1699, when it was a Scottish reference to "a cheat or slippery trick."[2] Fun entered English-speaking culture as a marker of a practical joke or prank.

By 1726, though, the bawdy eighteenth century in England allowed the definition to broaden, becoming closer to what we mean today by the noun "fun":

- Lighthearted pleasure, enjoyment, or amusement; boisterous joviality or merrymaking; entertainment.
- Noteworthy or exciting activity, esp. when providing entertainment for onlookers; action. Sometimes used with ironic force.[3]

Henry Fielding's footloose, sexually promiscuous main character, Tom Jones, epitomizes the modern meaning of "fun" in the first, rambling English language novel, published in 1749.

The early eighteenth century usages of "fun" focused on *group* merrymaking, live in person. "Fun" was never solo in common usage.

Then, the Victorian era hit, as well as the evangelical revival movements of nineteenth-century America. "Fun" took a big hit in culture (and in English printing) only to rebound from the 1980s to the present.[4] I believe the revival of "fun talk" coincided with the 1978 release of the movie *Animal House*, a high-brow favorite of literary types everywhere. Pluto for president.

Now, in 2024, *everything* is supposed to be "fun," including work. Work happy hours. Work parties. Office birthday parties. Emojis in e-mails. GIFs and memes in Slack. And on and on. If you're struggling with the standard, you can even take a course on *happiness* at business school.

Yours truly, Mr. Serious, was *not* prepared for the acceleration of fun in American life during his own lifetime. It has taken a long time to adapt. Living on the West Coast was invaluable.

Why I Suck at Parties—It's Not What You Think

I don't like parties that much unless they're less than ten people and hosted at someone's home. Aspie brains get overwhelmed not only by the noise of your average party but also by the sheer ambiguousness of rapid-fire, dyadic (i.e. one-to-one) chitchat with no purpose other than bonding.

It got no easier in adulthood. In fact, I wager it got harder for me because teenagers are amazingly tolerant of inappropriate language, tone, bad form, lousy etiquette, and all manner of things with which we Aspies get charged. By "tolerant," I mean they won't stop talking to you. They may declare you sexually unattractive, that's about it.

At least 50 percent of my reputation as "funny" is due to my consistent, unfiltered, inappropriate social commentary. Insightful, yet inappropriately timed (and aimed).

Most parties in America involve a chaotic ping-pong of dyadic or triadic interactions that keep switching up every few minutes. These conversations accomplish very little other than generalized impression-making. Just when I want to go deeper, my interlocutor is ready to move on.

This. Is. Not. Fun! It wasn't that fun in high school. It's not fun for me as an adult.

At least in college, I was socially permitted to drink so much that I could just sit by myself on a couch, in silence, with a propped-up Woody Allen grin on my face. I was recuperating.

Chapter Thirteen

AMERICAN RUMSPRINGA AND THE RISK OF SELF-IMPLOSION

American youth have so many different words for "party," it boggles the mind. New ones appear in every generation. While researching this chapter, I collected over one hundred different synonyms and slang references to this common English word. Why is "party" such an elaborated linguistic world? Why all this endless party talk?

One reason is that "parties" are *the* major social activity young Americans associate with "fun." And this association starts in early childhood with the preadolescent birthday party. The connection is innocent, but it sets a foundation of expectation that only intensifies during adolescence and college: parties are informal rituals to drink, eat, and *goof off*. Even the most uptight WASP mother in the 1970s allowed her kids to bend the rules of decorum at their birthday a bit. Kids could be loud. Messes could be made without rebuke. Self-expression was honored. The birthday celebrant could choose the cake, the activities, and the friends to invite (per Mom's strictly enforced audience cap). Generation X was the first to have *retail* birthday parties at Burger King (me) or the trendy Chuck E. Cheese arcade (my friend).

A lot of the behavioral elements of the American birthday party reappear later at the high school party: the ability to be loud, violate normative standards of decorum for one's age, goof off, play games, eat abundant snack food, have the freedom to declare one's eccentric preferences for whatever. The added elements in high school and college are really tools to get you in the flow: alcohol, cigarettes, and sometimes drugs.

If eight-year-olds require no alcohol to lose their inhibitions, it is because they have very few onboard inhibitions to begin with. Adolescents and college students, however, use alcohol and drugs to reenter a childlike state of unencumbered autonomy for which they have conscious memories. In more formal eras, I suspect that children did not grow up with these experiences. They worked on the farm from very young ages. They had group fun *without age-segregated parties*.

Modern adolescent and college parties have also been a playground for sexual experimentation and sexual *predation*—whether the charming Casanova or the malevolent Ted Bundy. Learning how to navigate a coed alcohol-infused party *safely* is a major rite of passage for American girls. Hint: you do it as a *group* . . . not as individuals. Among older Americans I interviewed, this learning appeared to happen mostly in college unless an older sister inducted them earlier.

Finally, youth parties have a major performance aspect as well in the modern world. Showing off, doing something impressive, or even just acting weird becomes part of loosely ritualized "fun" as an *attention-capturing game*. Taking behavioral risks to show off one's individuality is part of the "fun."

To summarize, American youth party culture is about:

1. Returning to a childlike sense of autonomy *temporarily*
2. Garnering social attention through performance (verbally or John Bellucci style)
3. Sexual adventure, flirtation, and experimentation

College, Not High School, Is When Most People Start Partying

Partying is as old as the inception of humans allowing men to go off and drink together. What is most modern is the *coed, youth-only party (with music and alcohol/drugs)*. Putting sexually mature boys and girls together without adults present and then adding mind-altering substances is *not* as old as humankind.

In my in-depth interviews with older Americans, I had a good mix of Boomers and Gen Xers from whom to learn about when all this partying tends to start. I noticed that anecdotes of "partying" became common for everyone when they got to college (or otherwise left home), but most were not doing much if any partying in high school.

High school partying is about more than escaping parental supervision. Nonpartying kids already had lots of ways to avoid adults: the mall, the movies, the 7-Eleven, or a public park. Avoiding parents didn't require coed fooling around or alcohol. High school partying in the 1960s to 1990s mostly involved a small clique of the "usual folks" at every school (as I too remember it in my own school) who usually wanted to drink and/or smoke pot.

I always observed that it was my peers who struggled in school (at least one D or multiple Ds all the time) who seemed to value partying the most. For them, school was a constant, daily reminder of not living up to parental and class standards. School was humiliating for them, really. Parties became a periodic "middle finger" to an educational system that was driving them nuts. Looking back, it must have been really f**king annoying to bump into straight-A punk nerds like me, for whom school was enjoyable and *even attractive*. Remember, a lot of kids before 2000 went all the way through college with undiagnosed and unaddressed learning disabilities but were otherwise smart. Millions of kids suffered like this. Partying had a desperate attraction for these kids.

And these academic misfits preferred to party with equally alienated peers. In fact, when one kid in my high school with a B to B+ average tried to host a keg party, *no one showed*. He wasn't a nerd either. Unlike movie representations of the small party that the entire school shows up to, parties were not contagious phenomena in high school, like a bag of Cheetos or two-liter bottles of soda. You almost had to disqualify academically to host a high school party. And doing well in school more or less disqualified you from attendance in most cases (or at least made it harder to discover where the hell the party was). I usually got the invite last, whenever I did.

The primary reason that partying (i.e., letting go with alcohol and drugs) was not more widespread in high school was pretty simple—a parent was generally at home all the time. Only the most educated professional elite would leave town as a couple, creating an open "party zone," featured in interviews for this book, but more broadly seen in films like *Risky Business*, *Heathers*, and *Fast Times at Ridgemont High*, and even at the house of "that rich kid" from your local school.

In college, things change, a lot. The lack of structure, high degree of student autonomy, and higher expectations than in high school combine to stress most students out. And now there are no parents to be seen. So, it's not surprising that a lot more of us start partying at this point.

It took me a while in college to realize that the attraction of a raging party is exactly that: *losing control*. College parties are far less about overt rebellion (a cranky adult's interpretation) and more about a desperate need to vent frustration during the very long, drawn-out process of becoming a highly autonomous adult *under very high social expectations*. More specifically, the cultural objective of a college party is to dispense negative thoughts, energy, and frustration from the prior week so one can return to work or school "fresh," "in control," and "productive." With the right limits and peer supervision, parties can be a very functional weekly ritual. Too often, though, it winds up like the nutzo Holiday Party my roommates and I hosted in 1992. This raucous event featured some secret punch recipe (rum, juice, sugar, vodka) borrowed from a residential dean and which sent all of us running to the nearest trash bucket or toilet bowl between midnight and 1:00 a.m. At least the next day was Sunday.

The alcohol-fueled, drug-assisted party is a well-honed human ritual of liminality designed to restore psychic balance. Shamans know it well. Rituals of liminality are about dissolving the existing social norms *temporarily* to come out transformed and ready again for those same annoying social norms:

- College kids drinking too much from red Solo cups at an off-campus frat party
- Sleep-deprived moms going on a wine-infused, out of town girls' weekend

Basically, the same structure for both events. We call the former a "party" and the latter a "getaway." Whatever, Moms. A *reset* is the point, not open insurrection (even with the moms). This is why raucous parties happen far from authority figures or places of authority.

America's Rumspringa Can and Does Go Very Wrong

As I discussed in chapter one, America's national Rumspringa is an open-ended period of life that no one forces you to end. You are drowned in all manner of lifestyle choices and allowed to come to your own senses at your own pace. This includes when to rein in the partying. As friends settle down, Americans say, *They got their sh*t together*. In your early thirties, the peer pressure is subtle and pervasive to end your partying years. Showing up hungover at work when you're thirty-three has a different look than when you're twenty-two. In traditional Amish settlements, Rumspringa lasts one to two years at most. You either flee or seek baptism. Some of us never leave our version of Rumspringa. We just tone down the partying. Others become suspended in it. We call it "arrested development." And some lose all control early on.

Partying is a mode of "fun" that can easily become a lifestyle. And this lifestyle of Thursday to Sunday imbibing with friends can devolve without too much effort. Fun can morph into something sinister, something that destroys careers, lives, and poisons social networks.

Americans expect each individual to "know their limits" and stay on the right side of the line. This assumes a very high degree of self-control, of impulse control in the face of peer-induced invitations to have yet another round. The problem is that the ritual of American partying encourages eccentric, wild behavior, so there really isn't a clear line at all when it comes to demarcating "out of control." When does behaving drunkenly morph from funny to tragic? At any one party, there is no universal way to tell. Onlookers may also have little context, when individuals who cannot control their drinking go unnoticed by slipping between nonoverlapping social networks. Was Alex just letting loose or does she have a problem? If she self-identifies as an alcoholic later, we still blame her though. We, the onlookers, the "responsible drinkers" at all those parties, are never responsible. If we do feel responsible and intervene, we are noticeably the "good friend . . . such a good friend." We frame intervention more as heroic than obligatory.

College party culture is mostly innocent, but it is also now a known factory of adult alcoholism. The three primary behaviors correlated with onset of adult alcoholism are a) drinking before the age of fourteen, b) binge drinking between the ages of eighteen to twenty-five, and c) a mental health collapse.[1] We don't admit the rather obvious role of binge drinking, because we desperately want to believe that binge-drinking individuals are just going through a phase. So, we ignore the minority whose lives are destroyed later by permitting a lifestyle of binge drinking to emerge, flourish, and keep going without much social intervention.

Anyone who binge drank in their twenties and later suffers a severe depressive episode is at very high risk of alcohol use disorder (AUD). But do their friends really pay this kind of attention to them? Enough attention to surveil their mental state and keep them away from drugs and alcohol? It means punching right through the sacred veil of privacy we are so proud of as Americans.

In 1985, near the peak of US alcohol consumption (see figure 4) the CDC estimated the population of alcoholics at 10.6 million adults or 6 percent of the US adult population at the time.[2] Today, even though alcohol consumption is down overall, it is getting more extreme. The current incidence of adult alcoholism is 11.3 percent, almost twice as much as in 1985, and is harming the lives of 29 million adults.[3]

We have reduced alcohol intake but watched alcoholism take off.

If an electronics or parts factory had a 10-15 percent defect rate, it would lose most of its customers and quickly go bankrupt. If a food factory had a 10–15 percent incidence of bacteriological contamination, it would probably destroy most of the brand's value through mass recalls and consumer rejection. There would also be enough hospitalizations to lead to bankruptcy through class actions. Yet, alcoholism is one of these dark secrets about American life that we accept with a shrug and then blame the individual for messing up their life. *Where did he go wrong? So sad. . . .*

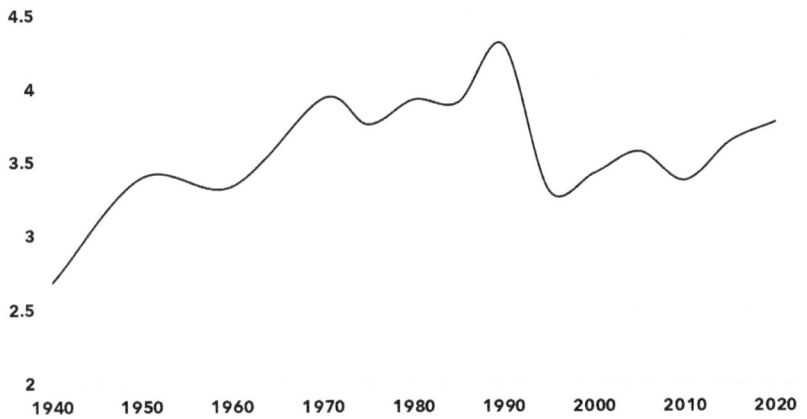

Figure 4. Alcohol Consumption per Capita Among US Drinkers. My analysis of data sourced from Gallup and the National Institutes of Health.[4]

We don't take an ISO 9000 approach to alcohol parties for youth (of all social classes), even though there is nothing stopping us from doing this. College kids could still have their buzz, still goof off and have fun without enabling binge drinking and the incidental, quiet nurturing of future alcoholics.

College partying is a great example of how American culture teaches us to ignore a harmed minority whose later behavior ripples out to affect many others in their lives. Hey, if 90 percent aren't harmed right now, it's fine. The 10 percent who are harmed later by X, Y, or Z, just need to figure their own sh*t out. They had plenty of time. They're outliers we can ignore.

We measure social harms like we measure day trades. Instantly. *This is a failure of social imagination.* Some behaviors do lead to a high likelihood of future problems. We have the data to prove this with regards to alcoholism but refuse to act socially in the present to safeguard the hidden minority.

In my life history interviews with older Americans, most folks reported to me that they put an end to the low self-control, college-style partying in their twenties, sometimes early (if kids came early).

But not all of them. In fact, I interviewed two recovered alcoholics out of twenty interviewees. I had no screener for substance abuse either. Both of these men were lost in their early twenties. Very lost.

Kevin's story below illustrates the risk of letting everyone do the American Rumspringa their own way. In 1985, Kevin was an eighteen-year-old single male who had just inherited his trust fund. It was his first year at Michigan State. His paternal grandfather was a businessman and bootlegger during Prohibition, when a few families made fortunes in untraceable cash. Kevin grew up in an eight-bedroom house complete with a quarantine room and enjoyed a well-heeled upper-middle-class upbringing with seven other equally privileged siblings. He had the epitome of a perfect head start in life.

When he entered college he began partying immediately. Able to fund his own excessive drinking, he also could buy rounds of drinks for others. Throwing this kind of largesse around as a young person is a social intoxicant for the giver and for young women who don't meet many young guys this wealthy. Buying rounds at the bar or tavern has long been an expensive way to make many weak-tie friends in America. And Kevin was happy at the time to spend his trust fund money doing this.

Reflecting on these years with me, here's what he said:

Kevin: Am I ashamed of my life? What I did then? Yes, absolutely. I hurt a lot of people. . . .

JR: How long did it take you to come to that realization?

Kevin: Around 1993, when I finally entered rehab and got my act together, got cleaned up and realized that. Hey, I gotta be a father, and then, I'm going to be a husband. I also knew someone, a guy I knew, one of my running buddies in college. We had all gotten loaded one night, and he got in his car and shouldn't have, and I later found out—I think it was a couple of days later—that he had wrapped his car around a pole south of town and was dead. I think that was kind of a jolt to me. I think that kind of helped me wake up [to the fact] that that [same thing] could happen to me. I had a daughter who, at that time, was about seven years old. And I wasn't being a good dad to her at all. But if I want to be [a good dad], I gotta be alive to do it.[5]

Not long after his friend's death, Kevin got into a bar fight and was arrested. He had no family to call because they had disowned him. They had stopped communicating years earlier. So, he called an old friend, Allan, who had earlier stopped associating with him due to his drinking. He didn't know who else to call. In America, this is our version of Amish banishment. We pull away and stop communicating. We abandon the wounded individual. We give up on people.

Here's how Kevin got rescued, not by himself, but by a fateful phone call to a friend who had not given up on him completely.

> *Allan's dad owned some retail or apartment rental properties, and he had come down to Michigan State too. He bailed me out of jail.*
>
> *He was a big physical guy. He was strong. And he grabbed me. He had been lecturing me about my behavior. And finally, he grabbed me out of the chair and pulled me up, took me over to the mirror, and he kind of slammed me up against it and said, "Look what you've become! If you continue down this road, you're not going to live very long. If you let me help you and you take it seriously, I'm going to take you over to Cloverside Rehab."*
>
> *[The facility] was connected with a hospital. It was a twenty-eight-day program, an inpatient program. So, I was there for twenty-eight days with follow-up care after that, and then twelve-step Alcoholics Anonymous.*
>
> *"I'll take you there, but if you continue like this, I just simply won't talk to you anymore."*
>
> *So, I agreed to go, and I took it seriously, and I got my sh*t together [starts crying as he remembers it].*[6]

Kevin is an alcoholic. One out of ten Americans are with him.[7] He will die an alcoholic because we now know what his parents did not know when he was born in 1966. Alcoholism is a lifelong disease (declared so in 1956) whose only cure is *total sobriety*. We now know what alcoholism does to families, to spouses, to children, and to innocent bystanders on our roads. We also know how it fuels domestic violence. Alcoholism can turn a relatively functional person into an alien monster. The emotional damage ripples outward in ways we continue to discount as a country.

And we also know that alcoholics must reconfigure their social networks to survive. They have to banish their drinking buddies for one thing. If you're single, cutting out your drinking buddies forms real conflict with the Rumspringa stage of life in which friends are *the* focus of your nonwork time. This is not easy for most adults to do. It was near impossible for Kevin, since he was surrounded by enablers all the time. The lure of a friend calling you out for a round of brewskis is like the lure of an ear-piercing ceremony in a tight-knit Tamil village family. Saying no is almost impossible when your core social network is calling. It takes an unnatural degree of self-control and emotional independence without the help of a spouse, an AA sponsor, or the pull of a family.

Alcoholism is also not super attractive. Attracting a partner who will help cut you off from your friends is not a realistic plan, let alone a fair social policy. It easily traumatizes another person and solves nothing.

This is why Kevin could have easily died in his twenties. Very easily.

Unbeknownst to any of us, Kevin was part of a rapid national acceleration in heavy alcohol consumption in the 1980s due in part to a rise in binge drinking among young college students. Ever since the 1960s, more adults, especially women, were drinking than ever before. Alcohol prices were dropping even when adjusted for inflation.[8] Until the 1991 recession. That was when a perfect storm of inflation, unemployment, and a sharp rise in liquor prices (9 percent) reduced a lot of heavy drinking to moderate drinking. Permanently.[9] Kevin entered rehab in 1993 as America collectively recovered from its 1980s hangover.

Kevin was set up by circumstance to implode. He was predisposed to alcohol abuse, something that was known in high school (but not addressed). He had access to virtually unlimited trust funds in a town far from home. And he lived in a binge-drinking, campus town environment. The 1980s made dozens of campuses infamous "party school" destinations—Ohio State, Michigan State, UW—Madison, Arizona State, and on and on. All became quiet factories of adult alcoholism in a privacy-obsessed, hang-back, hyper-individualistic society like ours. You won't find this addressed in their alumni magazines.

In a sense, Kevin is only really an extreme example of what happens to predisposed binge drinkers when you take the price of liquor out of the behavioral equation. In an individualistic society, you architect your own social world largely under the influence of the media and your peers. College partying may seem like groups of sheep running around in herds. In reality, it takes place in a social context where the adult is, for the first time in their life, truly managing a network where they are at the center of things. This very precocious, modern approach to networked individualism allows anyone to stumble into danger zones they might not stumble into otherwise. If you're the CEO of your social world, who will challenge you effectively? Any ideas?

When no social limits are put on Rumspringa, you get millions of Kevins. Guaranteed. And by making Kevin responsible for controlling himself, it may never end. Kevin gets the blame. Kevin takes the fall for society's lack of obligation to protect him. From himself.

And who is as wise and long-term in their thinking as Kevin's friend Allan? Is such a person in every alcoholic's life after they've alienated so many who once loved them? Someone who can remind them of what they are throwing away?

Kevin was very lucky. He could unravel for eight years straight, but the memory of his high-self-control, affluent upbringing was always there, waiting for a social intervention to force its urgent recall.

Chapter Fourteen

HOW YOUTH CULTURE FRACTURED FUN IN TWO

The silent diktat of the American Rumspringa life stage is that fun is for your age peers. It's possible this could include college students mixing with high schoolers and vice versa. It could even include college kids mixing with young graduate students in their twenties (considered bad form when I was in graduate school).

"Fun" *can't* include college kids with *retirees*. Or grandparents. Or parents. Or even aunts/uncles. That's a boring family occasion. Snore. The reason the movie *Dirty Grandpa* is so hilarious is that it is wildly unlikely to occur in real life. The humor lies in the ineligible social actor—Grandpa—trying to crash spring break parties in Daytona Beach with his grandson. I won't say this has *never* happened, but you understand my point.

"Fun" *can't* include your boss or superiors either. That's an office party. There's too strong a hint of obligation to show up and too many limitations on goofing off. However, "fun" at an office party, if it happens, is most likely going to happen among colleagues of similar age to you (filtered for title and rank of course).

Ever since the 1960s, youth fun has been about tight age ranges of peers avoiding society for a few hours. Stepping outside of society's rules and norms is critical, especially stepping away from any kind of mature supervision. One reason sexual assault is so common at youth parties is not just alcohol. It's that there is no vastly more mature adult there to step in. For youth, fun must be *un-surveilled* liminality, i.e., not ritualized with elders present.

Beginning with the spread of high school, America began a social experiment that immerses every cohort of young adults in a "society of peers" for years.[1] *Years of* deep immersion with each other and with the mostly sympathetic teacher or coach as the primary adult role model.

Prior to the mass adoption of high school during the Depression, American youth *worked* as soon as they hit adolescence. I know this is hard for many of us to accept. Teens apprenticed in the trades. Teens worked on the family farms. Teens went off to the factories. At no point in the nineteenth century did most teenage adults spend all day with their age peers outside of work (i.e., in a school). For most of human history prior to industrialization, adulthood began more or less at puberty.

As the scholar Paul Howe correctly identified, the high school *created* "adolescence" and enabled the youth culture that flowed from it all the way into college and beyond.[2] High school age segregation and the delay of adulthood's onset created a unique laboratory for rejecting or rethinking elders' wisdom. In the film *Dead Poets' Society*, we see how boarding schools (and private day schools like mine) took this even further by creating *teacher heroes* who espoused values diametrically *opposed* to those of your parents. *What am I paying this tuition for?*

The idolized high school teacher is the first one who encourages teenagers' separation from the values of a prior era of classism, racism, conservative values, and low relative lifestyle autonomy. My teacher idol was a Baby Boomer English teacher who taught electives on philosophy, Zen Buddhism, and Native American mysticism (e.g., the works of Carlos Castaneda). I took them all. I drank it all up to argue more effectively with my Reaganite, corporate attorney father at dinnertime. He was in good spirits about it, luckily. Nothing an extra glass of whiskey couldn't solve. *Again, what am I paying this tuition for?*

The *vilified* high school teacher, on the other hand, is the one most like your father or mother. *Horrendous. Scandalous. That a parent could possibly know something of value to you, a living emblem of a brave new future? Perish the thought.*

High school is like organized *cultural resistance to the past* (i.e., whatever your parents do or think). A lot of it is just venting, but not all of it. This separation process requires cocooning yourself along with your age peers against the outside world.

For the students, high school is a relatively large chunk of their lives, almost a quarter of it by age eighteen. For the parents, high school is over in a blip. *What the hell happened to my kid?* is a common parental remark ever since World War II ended. This proportionality makes high school social life incredibly influential on one's twenties, on how adults approach the American Rumspringa.

Most of us pick and choose from our parental value set as we grow up. And we do it in ways parents may not be ready to accept or even be aware of until years later. This was the case in the 1960s–1990s across the United States as music-fueled youth culture took over the teenage years and became a multibillion industry vested permanently in reproducing a dissenting adolescent peerage. Intergenerational cultural warfare is very profitable in multiple industries that sell things. Otherwise, we could share more. *God forbid.*

How Fun Got Cracked into Two Age Groups

In my 2022 survey of older Americans (now aged forty-seven to seventy-six), the very generations who made high school an iconic cultural life stage had, by middle age, drifted far away from the idea of "fun" as a party or any kind of group activity at all (see figure 5).

How can this be? How can the people who pioneered modern partying for four to eight years have turned into a bunch of relative social isolates?

Too *much* partying? Are they just *tired*? Too *broke* to party? Or are they in a life stage when the gregariousness of youth culture becomes irrelevant?

Well, the answer is *not* that older people have become antisocial recluses. They prefer to socialize differently and without a maniacal focus on age-peer parties. Family fun, specifically, looms large in their older worldview, much larger than among youth in my survey data (see figure 6). Older Americans do *want* to socialize even if their time diaries don't reflect it.

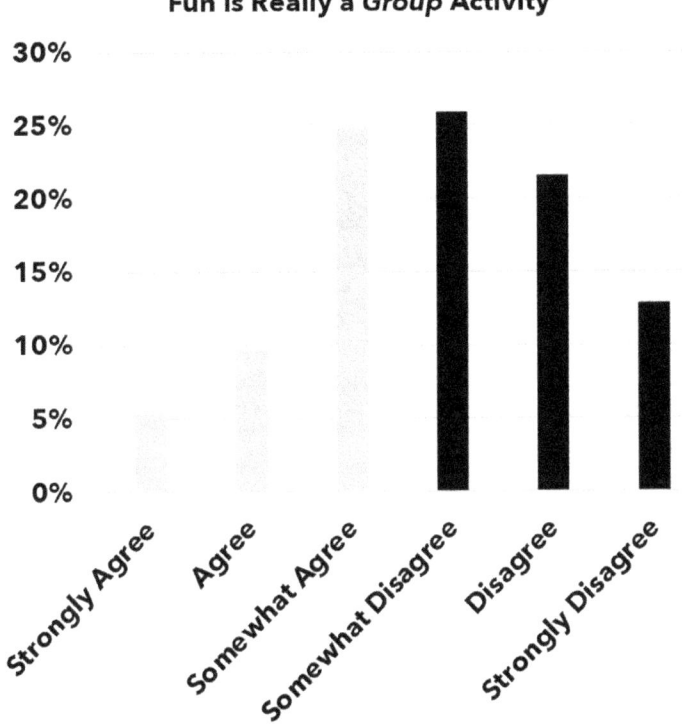

Figure 5. Older Americans Are Happy to Party Alone. Table data sourced from SAI Older Americans National Study, 2022.[3]

The reason older Americans disagree with the statement, "Fun is really a *group* activity" is twofold:

a. *They live alone or only with a partner in very high percents—* so their ideal notions of fun have altered to accommodate life with far less overall social interaction and more focus on the individual preferences small households permit. Solitary fun is much easier, not necessarily the most preferred.[4]

b. *Americans of all ages tend to define "fun" most often as some kind of emotional outcome.* In other words, how we get to the happy/joyful outcome is secondary in American culture (see figure 6).

Americans define fun firstly as 1) an *emotional outcome*, then as 2) *doing a specific thing*, and finally as 3) *just being with human beings they love* regardless of the activity.

Americans' Definition of "Fun"	Old (45+)	Young (<45)
Emotional Outcome (e.g. happiness)	44%	51%
Being with People	27%	15%
Specific Activities (alone or with others)	25%	26%

Figure 6. *How Americans Define "Fun." Table data sourced from SAI National Poll on Americans' definition of "fun," 2022.*[5]

Americans of all ages seek fun because *we want an emotional transformation* of some kind. Only a minority of us primarily see fun as being with other people. So, we can easily have fun *alone*. And we do. Look at that big screen in your living room. It's probably on right now.

This data suggests that it is not inevitable that old and young remain largely separate in their fun seeking. Yet, age-based segregation is how American social structure functions. Real estate trends since the 1990s confirm a strong, conscious allegiance to age-based residential segregation. America has 27,000 fifty-five-plus retirement communities (from independent/active to highly medicalized/nursing) generating $100 billion in annual revenue.[6] Many of these HOAs have tight restrictions on how long children and grandchildren can even visit. They actively *prevent* multigenerational homes. Whoa.

From what do all these old folks have to hide, I wonder?

Music Keeps Youth Culture Alive and Separate in the Public Sphere

Music may actually be the cultural fuel par excellence that sustains *age-based* fun in American life. In doing so, it fractures a key axis of community in human societies, making individuals far more able to exercise individual autonomy.

Unsurprisingly, there is passive resistance among older generations to new youth music content from the youngest generations. And conversely, it is only the cool youth music du jour (mostly hip-hop and rap) playing at all the venues where youth party, congregate, or even just hang out. I see youth music (new artists in the youth-oriented genres just mentioned) as a perfect social shield to get rid of stray older folks.

And this strict age segregation is exactly what the entertainment industry wants. A constant refresh in what is cool youth culture means they can keep their media brands from becoming the *Lawrence Welk Show*. And ultimately sell more.

We have to accept that "cool" equals youth culture in America, even though, technically, the backers of all this "cool" are middle-aged white and black men (the ones with money in the music industry). For every Olivia Rodrigo (age twenty), there is a John Janick (CEO of Geffen Records, age forty-eight).

If we look deeper at music, we can see that older Americans prefer to listen to what they've always listened to *since they were young* (classic rock, rock, and country/western), despite easier-than-ever streaming access to any genre you could possibly imagine. There is less friction than ever for older folks to shake things up and listen to Taylor Swift, Lizzo, Bruno and Olivia if they want to. It's a few clicks away.

Yet, the only musical genres today where young and old meet are R & B, classical, show music (e.g., *Hamilton*), and folk music. I guess you should play these genres at the Fourth of July town parade and your family reunion.

If you play the Rolling Stones, the Gen Zers at the family reunion will start screaming "Boomer," and the party will soon end. If you put on Lizzo at the same reunion, the Boomers will run for the cocktail bar and complain.[7]

Either way, the "fun" will end, and only awkwardness will ensue.

Ironically, Baby Boomers are the most active concert attendees today because they can afford to go! It's just that they go to different musical events than their kids do—ones with really old people onstage.[8]

Older Americans' Approach to Fun

What's interesting is that, when we look at the data, older Americans' idealized definition of "fun" does *not* match up well with their fun *behavior*.

Percentage of adults aged 45–74	Fun Activity Performed in the Last Twenty-Four Hours
71%	Watching movies/TV
48%	Thinking/relaxing
38%	Reading
36%	Texting/calling/video calling with a friend
28%	Playing video games/computer games
25%	Exercise (running, biking, walking, etc.)
21%	A personal hobby (photography, metalworking, art, writing)
17%	Going out with family (those living with you)
14%	Going out with friends
13%	Having family members over to hang out
13%	Sex
9%	Having friends over to hang out
7%	Listening to podcasts
4%	Volunteering in my community

Figure 7. What Older Americans Do for Fun Every Day. Table data sourced from SAI Older Americans National Study, 2022.[9]

If "fun" equals leisure time, then we know from the American Time Use Survey that most leisure time is spent *consuming media*, mostly video content. And this is also what my older survey respondents most commonly did in the last twenty-four hours (71 percent of them!).

Yet, in my open-ended definition challenge (i.e., define what "fun" means to you"), only about 1 percent of older Americans define "fun" as consuming media![10]

What?

Even though 27 percent of older Americans define "fun" in terms of human interaction primarily, socializing is much less common in their past-twenty-four-hour behavior.

What is going on?

When behaviors (e.g., watching TV) inside a cultural domain (e.g., fun) happen more often than they get pointed to as ideals, it's because it's a low-ranking, overly common behavior. TV watching is fun, but not that fun because it's too ordinary and commonplace. When a behavior (e.g., hanging with friends or grandkids) happens *less often* than we point to it as an ideal, it's because it's high-ranking behavior we want more of than we get.

It's entirely possible that Americans define "fun" unconsciously in terms of the peak emotions they experience *during rare activities and events*. This aligns with a nation of partyers who grew up partying as a peer-based emotional transformation. It's also in line with a nation that depicts (and talks about) sex much more than we have sex. On any given day, around 13 percent of older Americans are having sex (I rounded up, sadly). Sorry. It's the TV again. Sex only takes three to five minutes, but the emotional ramp-up takes *days* sometimes. Hard to pull off, honestly, when you're forty-five or older. And then there's the sciatica.

I strongly suspect that most older Americans would prefer more fun via social interaction than they have, though perhaps not vastly more. They appear to have become so accustomed to defaulting to media instead of "getting out there" because the extended family just isn't as available as in pre-World War II generations now lost to history and because friendships have become harder to maintain as so many forces pull them away (more in part five).

When an entire society defines "fun" most often as a context-independent emotional outcome, an individual-centered view of social existence means the individual is free and subtly encouraged to engage in solo fun (including *that* kind as well).

By allowing ourselves to leisure with or without social interaction, we also set up group leisure for a major historical transition. It becomes less about affectionate bonding and quiet presence amid deeply loved people who know each other well and more a form of competitive theater for individual outcomes and "look-what-I-did" storytelling. I realize this is merely a difference with no moral outcome. But it has consequences nonetheless. It makes socializing itself as optional as this or that TV show.

Chapter Fifteen

MODERN RECREATIONAL WORLDS

Civic engagement and volunteering have declined a lot since the 1960s, whether you look at voter participation, membership in formal associations, or any other metric.[1] What few seem willing to examine is how our approach to fun may have a lot to do with this. Our leisure time and "fun" approach have become incredibly individualistic and self-absorbed. And let's face it: I've never heard anyone say "volunteering" or voting is *fun*. Although, I used to do the former to meet women (face-palm). This is ironic since there is much research to suggest that freely choosing to help others does make people *happier*.[2] And "happiness" is the number one way Americans of all ages define the desired emotional outcome of having *fun*.[3]

Part of the reason we have a blind spot that keeps "fun" dissociated from civic engagement is that music-filled partying dominates our definition of "fun" from a very early age. Our definition of "fun" comes pre-loaded with a focus on mania, especially the mania of eccentric goofball behavior in social settings.[4] And some older Americans never outgrew this definition.

Don't believe me? Then explain why I got a text one day years ago from a fifty-something-year-old entrepreneur who bemoaned, "All my friends want to do is come over and get hammered and microdose." This is what happens to your adult socializing if you allow the college definition of manic partying to continue through your parenting years (with a probable assist from your own alcoholism). High school has never ended.

By contrast, the Amish have learned to embed fun into civic obligation. Heard of an Amish barn raising? Not *fun*, you say? That's because it lacks the manic, boisterous semi-structured ethos of an American "party." And it is neither alcohol-fueled nor age-segregated. And the Amish don't want eccentric goofballs at the barn raising. Not helpful.

From Formal Social Clubs to Informal Recreational Worlds

Robert Putnam has chronicled the decline of formal membership in local clubs and associations as a social change and *as a likely contributor to declining social trust in America*.[5] Bowling league membership declined, even though bowling was more popular than ever. This is, in part, because the informal "party" culture of Boomers and younger cohorts had taken over more formal recreational organizations. The modern definition of high-school-like fun means you can't have all those damn rules and formality.

The concept of a voluntary, local social association has yet to die in America. Its focus and structure have simply shifted to adjust to a more noncommittal, individualistic, urban, twenty-first-century culture.[6] Voluntary associations in America have shifted from business associations, veterans' groups, and men's clubs (celebrations of fixed/former social identities) to achievement-oriented recreational groups, some of which involve spending a fair amount of money on branded equipment and very little (to nothing) on membership fees. Examples of these modern recreational groups range from a self-mocking Meetup.com "Hot Dads" running squad to a local road cycling club with a real organization (and 501(c)(3) status). Most major metropolitan areas have thousands of local recreational clubs, including more activity types than my grandparents could have conceived.[7] As far as I've determined, no one has ever tried to count them comprehensively.

Recreational worlds in modern America have developed informal boundaries with professionalized or pseudo-professionalized centers.

You may be a runner with your runner group composed of supposed "hot dads." But recreational running connects those groaning, "hot dad" runners with Masters-competitive runners in the same age group who attend USA Track and Field public events. Some Masters athletes compete in national and global events with impressive personal record times. They are serious amateurs, folks. Not the "hot dads."

Recreational worlds remind me of Jupiter, a massive gas planet with a tiny rocky core. The certified, professionalized core is the critical difference between your local track and field club event referees and administrators and the "hot dads" who have never been to the registration website for anything more intense than a 5K beer run.

None of this modern recreation resembles the Elks social club your grandfather attended for decades. Serving in the Elks club was not connected to some profession; it was not achievement-based. The Elks was an ecumenical Christian service organization for local communities. It was wholly volunteer staffed. Being an Elk did not progressively cost you more time, energy, and money based on your individual ambition inside the community. There was a hierarchy, yes, as with my grandfather's Masonic lodge. You gained status through service activities. And, sure, there was an administrative elite. But these older social clubs never presumed most members were in some individualistic competition for *self-improvement*. That wasn't the point of the Elks. The point was to serve locally and to do it with people you knew outside the Elks. It was about maintaining your good Christian social status locally, not becoming a badass mountain biker to differentiate yourself from the chubby slobs at your office.

Overall, I see essential differences between the contemporary recreational *world* and the old-style social *clubs*.

Here are the essential contrasts I observe:

Table 4. Twentieth Century Social Clubs vs. Recreational Worlds

Twentieth-Century Social Club (e.g., Rotary Club, American Legion, Elks)	Twenty-First Century Recreation Group (Meetup.com, running group, USA Track and Field)
Membership screened heavily for *character*	Just show up! Little to no screening for newbs
Focused on celebrating a fixed social identity as pretext for organized public service	Focused on a core activity, around doing it to varying degrees of excellence
Membership is *required* to participate	Membership generally *optional*, but grants you "perks" like event participation, swag, hosting events, and networking status
Activities highly *formalized* (e.g., catered dinners and fundraisers), centrally planned and authorized	Activities more informal, even ad hoc, *not all centrally approved*, except for annual events; frequency varies
Local members know each other personally quite well	Only the administrative elite know each other really well; participants may or may not know many others
Most participants are *heavy-to-moderate users* of the community	*Most participants are light users* of the community (dipping in and out when they have time)
Friendships deep and long-lasting	Friendships fewer, often shallower and fleeting
Dues cover more of operational budget (like a private school)	*Corporate sponsorship common* because dues are low to boost list sizes
Financially successful rise to the top	*Advocacy/competence/excellence* a key reason to be voted into power
Club networks often overlap with local business and social worlds	Connects people who would otherwise *never meet*
Freely share personal lives and issues with member friends	Shoptalk only (with limited exceptions)

The Author's Experience with Mountain Biking

Modern recreational clubs and associations started in the late 1980s and the 1990s as sports and fitness culture took off. The West Coast was the pioneering region here (as early as the 1970s Venice Beach bodybuilding scene). And credit goes to Baby Boomers who introduced entirely new fitness activities like aerobics and competitive running. We can even pinpoint the geographic origin of some of these worlds: mountain biking literally began with a clique of Boomer "dudes" riding up/down Mt. Tamalpais in Marin County, CA, in the late 1980s.

And this is where I fit in. For the Seattle mountain biking club that I participated in from 2003 to 2006, "joining" consisted of creating an online profile with a picture, *not paying a fee*. You had to pay to host rides but not to attend rides. Early on, public rides were even publicly displayed (but not *who* was attending). Ride hosts never screened for membership status at the ride sites either, so unaffiliated folks routinely showed up via cell phone or e-mail chains. It was all public land that we rode on, unlike the Rotary Club building or Elks lodge.

The leadership of the mountain bike club I joined in Seattle in 2003 was super intense, intense at advocating for mountain bike trail access in Washington State. They were *not* at all intense about meeting club members. In fact, they were downright passive-aggressively elitist for the most part, even at major events like annual meetings. Most of us were there functioning as names on a list to assist with legislative and other governmental advocacy. This kind of attitude is common in Seattle recreational worlds: a desire to appear casual and informal while strictly enforcing a social hierarchy based mostly on *tenure*. I call it hypocritical friendliness (more on this in part five).

But for American adults today, modern recreational communities skew toward the informal with internal gradations of status and commitment. My personal, nonscientific experience is that they tend to be filled with single, college-educated people who are a) new to town, b) romantically unattached, c) involved with a sexual partner who is into the activity too, or d) permanently single blokes for unknown reasons unrelated to their sexual orientation. What you often do not find are married/partnered adults with kids at home, especially in anything that requires hours and hours of weekly training or hours to engage in a single activity (e.g., cycling). You may see recreational subgroups of older folks, as is common in the running and cycling worlds (who wants to try to keep up with a twenty-four-year-old cyclist punk?). Fitness communities neatly reproduce the age-based segregation of America's broader leisure society. We *work* with all ages, but we do *not* want to *recreate* with all these folks. Generally, no.

Recreational Worlds Are About Achievement, Posturing, and Performance

Modern recreational groups also have a *competitive* approach to "fun." The degree of competitiveness varies greatly from minimal (pottery studios) to gonzo, elitist jackass (downhill mountain biking). The groups for older folks tend to be minimally competitive. But, on the Rumspringa end of the age spectrum, it gets cuckoo crazy. I remember skiing once with a female friend near Seattle in 2003. She was a ski instructor and pointed to a group of male colleagues carving parallel slalom arcs on the ungroomed part of the slope in front of us. "Those guys are snobs. They're just comparing the shape of their slalom arcs with each other," she said with a wink.

Add too many men into any recreational world today, and it will inevitably get competitive. Not necessarily our stereotype of male boasting but more like a lot of competitive *storytelling*. And teasing.

- "Dude, you can downhill five thousand vertical feet without stopping but still can't nail a bunny hop? WTF?"
- "Man. I nailed that berm. Smooth as silk. Not like during the mud fest we had here last month."
- "Mike, I saw you bail, as soon as you saw it was a gap, not a drop. Trail newb!"

If you're confused, that's because you don't know the mountain biking rider's technical dialect.[8] To be seen as committed in any recreational world, you must accurately deploy technical jargon in your stories. You must know the gear and the brands and the terms. The more dangerous and technically complicated the activity, the more dialect strengthens and separates the newbs from the hard-core. Rock climbing and mountaineering are similar here.

The inclusive power of deploying recreational lingo is so seductive that I met more than one individual who was not very athletic or "good" at single-track riding but knew precocious amounts of technical jargon. That's called posturing, folks. Talking beyond your "game." Sad.

Using the jargon as a committed participant is a natural part of joining any recreational world. It's essential to bonding with your buddies during the activity and the craft beer refreshment afterward. A lot of recreational worlds feature post-activity celebrations. After a long, single-track ride in the Cascade mountains off Highway 410 in Washington, almost every backcountry ride group stops in nearby Enumclaw for some beer and food. In these post-ride socials, the point is to remain silent until you have a story to share or a technical comment about the ride or your equipment's performance. The event is a stage for the narrative performance of your experience level and commitment to the activity. This defines authentic post-activity socializing. It's a performance of communal bonding but is slightly off and inauthentic because of the posturing element. Buddies who recreate together frequently will get past this posturing eventually and function more like a bunch of close friends who happen to do X activity (more in part five on how to tell the difference).

No matter how well you get to know your ride mates, your commitment to the sacredness of American privacy means that, just like at work, they know very little about you. At these post-rides, you are primarily a smelly, sweaty, dirty recreational sliver of a person . . . having a beer. Every Thursday evening for two years, like some mad superhero, I transitioned from a work sliver into a single-track sliver in the bathroom of my company's office. Then, I drove to a weekly post-work ride leaving the old Redhook Brewery at 6:15 p.m. (It's light until 8:30 p.m. four months a year up there.)

"And you have *fun* doing this?" one of my completely nonathletic, foodie colleagues replied when I described an eight-hour ride from the prior weekend with four thousand vertical feet of gain and shoulder shredding descents. I never brought up mountain biking with him again.

Recreational Worlds Offer Respite from Rumspringa Loneliness . . .

Recreational worlds play a major role in replacing the time young people would otherwise have spent with family generations ago. With so much of the educated person's life span spent outside of child-rearing and with Rumspringa's alienation of you from your extended family, *most of your life* is now open to this kind of recreational community.

For those who delay marriage well beyond college graduation, recreational worlds offer one way to find some sense of social security in the otherwise chaotic, frequently disappointing worlds of work and dating. If you lose your job and dump your boyfriend close together, nothing could be more important to your psychological health than having some kind of routine community to immerse into as you recover. Recreational worlds are a modern solution to episodic loneliness for anyone but especially the lonely Rumspringa wanderers. I used to hear people at the trailhead spontaneously say things like "Needed to get out of the house" or "Was *sooo* bored," both common urban euphemisms for loneliness.

What starts as a desire for human connection may then progress organically into moderate-to-heavy participation like it did for me in the Seattle mountain biking scene from 2003 to 2005. Then the activity embeds itself in your weekly social routine. You bond with the activity first, then the people doing it. But, often, folks dabble and fade away quickly. This is mostly true in recreational worlds with low costs of entry (e.g., running, track, ultimate frisbee) versus those with high entry costs (e.g., cycling, kayaking, and mountain biking).

Indirect proof that loneliness was the primary driver of joining these worlds of group fun is that many fade away as they get romantically involved with someone outside the "community." The individual who "flakes out" may or may not return with their new partner (a new convert!). But since modern coupling in America makes the romantic leisure couple the dominant entity in most adults' social lives, they probably won't return. Kids also become a final cutoff choke point for many formerly intense recreationalists. I explained this to one of my mountain biking friends like this: "If I spend ten hours out of the house every weekend riding my bike, she'll divorce me, man. I might as well marry you."

. . . But Also Train Us to Be Noncommittal

Modern individuals dip in and out of recreational communities based on their schedules and, importantly, their moods. When so many recreational participants are childless singles, empty nesters, or childless couples, you must wonder what causes their busyness and "crippling" lack of consistent availability. House chores? Hardly. Work? They are not all entrepreneurs or CEOs. Trust me. Working eighty hours a week is *not* the reason for their flakiness.

I've never in my life witnessed so many men behave as if they are having a migraine or their period and cancel on people at the last second as I did in the Seattle mountain biking scene: "Hey, man, I know it's last minute, but I'm just not feeling up to riding today. My bad, [insert name]. I'll get the beers next time." The fact that his "friend"—you—had scheduled his whole day around a three-hour ride doesn't compare with their pseudo-depressive world-weary "mood" that suddenly erupted that afternoon. Half the time, I could smell the weed across the digital airwaves connecting our mobile phones.

This last-minute bailing behavior is a perfect sign of what we can see all over America regarding weakened community building—a lack of deep obligation to others at the most basic level, including to spots on their schedule *that you put there*.

The sacredness of privacy enables the rise of Mr. and Ms. Noncommittal Recreationalist. Not everyone. Not even most. But, the noncommittal adult is *not* banished or even admonished. I wonder if the Elks would kick out members for bailing, flaking, or ghosting. They might have, given that a character reference was required to join.

If adults approach recreation this casually, some will also approach dating the same way. Dating, after all, is just a sexually charged form of serial *recreation*.

Noncommittal dating behavior is the number one sin of young adult males, as any straight female knows. I swear modern recreational behavior reinforces noncommittal male dating behavior.

Recreational worlds generally do not create the strong obligation to *serve* that you'll see in the Rotary, Elks, or American Legion organizations of the twentieth century. The Seattle Mountaineers is one of these service-oriented recreational clubs but is routinely mocked by many for this very ethos (as too rigid). Americans today treat recreational communities like dating. You can be as noncommittal as you desire; no one *can or will* stop you. They can judge you and gossip. The hard-core folks will shun you, but it doesn't change your life much. You can ditch those people and find another recreational world to emerge in, if needed.

This bizarre, noncommittal vibe is reinforced by a very simple code of silence, especially among men. Don't get too personal in the post-activity chatter. It is "uncool" to talk about your job, family, or other things that might take the focus off the "shoptalk" and storytelling. Maybe a little, but not much. This keeps things "light" and "fun" and "not heavy."

The most awkward experience I had as a mountain biker was spending a three-day weekend in a rental home with a bunch of biker friends because, as recreational slivers of people, we ran out of sh*t to say to each other, *and* we *weren't* close friends at all. So, when people tried to get personal, it got awkward, even nasty, a few times. As mere cycling buddies, we had not bargained for such exposure to each others' actual lives. It was a bad idea.

The riding that weekend was great, though! Super *fun* . . . the people, not so much.

Chapter Sixteen

CONSUMING MEDIA TRUMPS GROUP FUN

Americans have more leisure time than ever before in our history. Five hours per day on average.[1] This leisure time dips as adults enter the workforce and grows as we age into retirement.[2]

We certainly have more leisure time than the nineteenth-century farmer who worked 50 percent more hours than we do and whose proverbial wife spent more time on basic chores in her appliance-lean farmhouse (think churning butter, sifting flour, and using a washboard).

Despite all this leisure and relaxation time, American adults do not spend much of it in face-to-face interaction. Half an hour or so *on average* per day.

Wait, what?

Our real-world leisure face time was already low in 2003, the year the American Time Use Survey launched, long before we accessed FaceTime, Facebook, YouTube, Instagram, TikTok, and Snapchat on our smartphones. And real, human *face time* has decreased from 5.39 *hours per week in 2003 to 3.99 hours per week* as of 2021.[3]

That is a 26 percent decline, slowly and steadily, in the early twenty-first century. A big social change, indeed, one that is surprising we do not ponder more deeply.

But, wait. Perhaps we see this change recently because younger generations who adopted internet-enabled mobile apps most heavily became very antisocial or simply *digitally* social? Maybe there's a bunch of hyper-social old folks buried in signal noise.

Nope.

Following our cohort of older Americans, I found that when we compare this age cohort in 2003 (when they were age twenty-seven to fifty-five) versus 2021 (when they were age forty-four to seventy-three), the same story holds. In fact, it's even *stronger*.

Older Americans have seen their total leisure time *grow* as they have aged in the twenty-first century—from 4.05 hours per day to 5.39 hours per day. The influence of retirement and nest emptying is huge here, of course. *Overall, this is a 33 percent increase in daily leisure time for the same age cohort. However, older Americans have seen their real-world face-to-face social time decline by 43 percent during the same period!* From 18 percent of their daily leisure time to 10 percent of it.[4]

This "face time" decline is not because we're retiring earlier. We're retiring later than ever (unless you are rich). This decline in face time is largely because most of our free time is about consuming media, and older Americans are more happy than ever to do this *alone*. Solitary TV watching competes very effectively with the energy level required to organize, recruit, and attend any social event. This is an embarrassing truth we can poke fun at and make jokes about, but the laughter stops quickly.

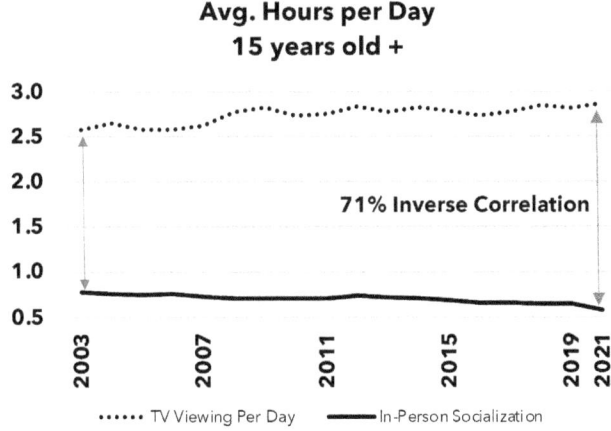

Figure 8. As We View TV More, We Meet Less. My analysis of data sourced from the American Time Use Survey.[5]

The overwhelming ease and immediacy of home video stimulation encourages older Americans to just do fun alone in front of the TV (or iPad or mobile phone) instead of making an effort to get together with friends, neighbors, or family. And if others are feeling the same unconscious prioritization, it's not surprising that so many folks can't seem to "find the time" to get together. There is oodles of time, folks. Sorry. Older Americans, especially, cannot "blame" younger family members alone for less family time. This lack of effort is socially well distributed with causes on all sides, most of them cultural in nature (more than logistical).

America's consumption-first leisure society enables ever-expanding solitary media consumption by:

- Making large screen TV consumption *the cheapest consumption experience* we can engage in (*only 75 cents per hour of viewing*)[6]
- Fracturing and *dispersing the extended family*
- *Dispersing "friends"* across a *digital* network rather than concentrating them in one's neighborhood (making it more time intensive to meet them)
- *Separating the young and old* (thereby reducing the sheer number of people who will likely gather)

In fact, American adults watch social groups assemble and interact in scripted television and movies more than in real life. We spend 2.90 hours per day watching TV/movies versus only 1.8 hours per day interacting socially in real life (office meetings plus face-to-face leisure interaction).[7] The difference is even greater for older Americans, who tend to be retired.

The overall rate of decline in our face-to-face socialization is frankly shocking for a social species (he writes as he sits alone in his writer's shed, ignoring his children and friends on a Sunday). Today's sixty-five-plus set in America is *four times less likely to attend social events today (only thirteen minutes per week at events) than they were in 2003.*

If the average social event older people attend lasts, say, two hours, then time use data suggests they attend an event about every five to seven weeks, perhaps seven to eight *a year*. And these folks are *mostly* retired and have the fewest barriers to group socialization of any age group (aside from preschoolers). They should be partying vastly *more* than the rest of us.

If *watching* groups (and group fun) is predominant over being with groups, then we have a media culture in which we quietly supersaturate ourselves in both idealized and dystopic group behavior every day to a degree unprecedented in human history. This no doubt leads to very distorted perceptions about American society and culture based on what you are watching. If humans are essentially mimetic social creatures, then the ratio of *watching* fictional group behavior to participating in it ourselves should concern us.

Do we learn to mistrust and discount the stranger through watching endless hours of cynical, jaded, and just plain violent group interactions on TV? Or is it all innocent escapism? *Why not escape more into group fun like we did as young people? What is stopping us?*

My twenty Gen X and Baby Boomer interview respondents had four hours to confess a burning desire to socialize more in real life than they do. But they didn't complain much about this at all. This intrigues me since, as kids, most of us learned how to have fun in real life by playing with siblings, neighbors' kids, or at preteen birthday parties. The peak of childhood "fun" was not *watching* a party. And, if you've ever been to a modern trampoline park, you'll see that kids have not lost touch with the power of group fun. Not at all.

Older Americans Consume Media Alone and Are Fine with It

In my national survey, 53 percent of older adults claimed to have watched movies/TV *alone* in the last twenty-four hours.[8] Sixty-two percent of these folks do *not* live alone, though. Wow. Watching TV alone is cultural in origin. We permit it socially as Americans. Americans have multiple screens per household to make this easier than ever. Eighty percent of American households have more than one television. The average is 2.3 TVs. The secondary TVs are mostly in bedrooms, which skews strongly for viewing alone.[9]

Eighty-five percent of Americans own a smartphone, further enabling solitary video/media consumption (and it remains annoying to watch content on someone else's tiny phone screen).

The ecosystem of media availability has changed radically since 2007 and the invention of the internet-enabled smartphone. If you have a phone within reach all the time (in addition to your work computer), it is undeniably lower friction to have fun alone by consuming any manner of media on it. And if an emotional outcome is all you define "fun" to be anyway, well, video content on a screen can deliver this anemic "fun" as quickly as scrolling for a meme. My father-in-law once posted ten to fifteen memes a day on Facebook before moving down to Arizona and gaining some friends again. Coincidence? Increasingly, this is what we *all* are doing, having fun mostly alone.

What is sadly ironic is that older Americans are almost twice as likely to explicitly define "fun" as hanging out with friends or family as the younger portion of America.[10] I believe this reflects how they grew up in America: in a far less signal-saturated and media-saturated world, where fun led more to in-person group activities.

Remember that much of my sample are Baby Boomers who did not grow up watching as much television as Generation X. Or consuming nearly as much video as my Gen Z kids (!). And when Boomers did watch TV, my interviews suggest it was generally a group affair. I didn't speak with any Baby Boomers in my one-to-one interviews who mentioned watching TV *by themselves* in a room when they were young. There was at least a sibling present. Only the Gen X respondents mentioned solo TV bingeing in their bedrooms. Or their basement "kid caves."

In the world of media, age has the most pronounced effect on frequency of consuming only one genre of content: *cable news* (Fox, CNN, MSNBC). I'm not sure this is actually "fun" for older Americans, but the fact remains they are the primary viewers of these shows. I can tell you that watching cable news is definitely *entertaining* for them (and blood-boiling?).

Time use data indicates that older Americans spend twice as much time alone per day as teenagers,[11] the *inverse* of their cable news watching. The two age-related trends are correlated well. *Is cable news perhaps a modern portal to some semblance of community, however imperfect and saturated in fearmongering negativity?* I don't know.

But bingeing Netflix and Hulu is clearly *fun* for older Americans. That's hard to doubt. It delivers a happiness outcome, however fleeting. But is it really as potent as group fun?

Coordinating Group Fun Is Harder in a Culture Obsessed with Individual Preferences

It takes time to plan group fun. Maybe not a lot, but far more than deciding by yourself what to watch on TV right now. Or even to read a book. When I polled older Americans about the relative difficulty of coordinating group fun with friends or family, I got a fascinating set of findings. About 30 percent of older Americans skewed to the harder end of the scale. Twenty-three percent were equivocal. And about 47 percent skewed to the easy end of the scale.

My take is that a society oriented strongly to having fun *mostly* in group settings (let's say the Italians or Indians), would not show 30 percent of people in *any* age cohort having problems coordinating group activities. But that's not American culture anymore. Unless we change those priorities deliberately, the socialization data won't change any time soon.

As we do group fun less and less, it worries me that we may be becoming ever more *incompetent* at casual group fun. And that is, sadly, my anecdotal experience of adult behavior at parties I've been to over the last twenty years.

Cognitive psychologists have extensively researched how human social skills *decline* due to age, as early as the thirties and forties. Social skills that rely less on memory and inhibition (i.e., empathy for physical pain) don't decline. But empathy for *social pain* apparently does decline as people age.[12] In an aging society, this might explain the growing lack of empathy for the homeless, the immigrants, and the marginalized in our society. Partly.

Coordinating group fun requires lots of inhibition of our personal preferences (e.g., I hate Thai food! No way!). And, as we age and spend more time alone or with just our partner, this inhibiting effort may slowly become "annoying" to us, when compared to just ordering takeout for two and watching Netflix.

Scholars believe it requires training to overcome these non-empathic tendencies in older people, which is an interesting concept to consider. Could we invent training to counter this? Video games perhaps? *Rescuing earthquake victims? Feeding hurricane survivors?* This training would become more critical if older people are drowning in perceptions of groups and society distorted by media outlets (instead of going down to the public pool and chatting with real people).

Part Four

HOW WE CAME TO EAT WHATEVER, WHENEVER

"Hey, man! I just went off wheat!"
—*former colleague's roommate, a thirtysomething male, Seattle, WA*

Chapter Seventeen

MY FEBRUARY 8, 2000, PANIC ATTACK AT CUB FOODS

Reentering middle-class life in America after a few years of living in a less-developed country is a surreal experience. One anthropology faculty member advised me, "Take it slowly, James."

How slowly did he mean? Think of a NASA astronaut preparing for a space walk. Very. F**king. Slowly.

I landed in Boston on December 9, 1999, after nearly twenty hours of travel from Chennai. Thirty-five hours of travel overall if you count the journey by rail from my field site in Madurai. When you are twenty-seven, this is all exciting, exotic, and thrilling. At fifty-one, my back hurts just editing the words.

It was a long trip by air travel standards but was hypersonic in its cultural shock value.

My relieved parents picked me up at the airport and took me to Bertucci's Pizza for lunch—just me. I was hungry, but I also think they wanted to prove to themselves that I was still alive, and eating is pretty clear evidence of life. Although Bertucci's menu was emblematic of excessive restaurant choices in American food culture, it was also very pizza-heavy. And this made it easy to dig into my unconscious memory, point to a favorite pie, and be done. My body thought it was 6:00 a.m. the next day. I wasn't going to last much longer, and you can't eat pizza when you're asleep (although I'm sure some college male has tried).

For the next two months, I lived at home, preparing to transition back to Madison, WI, for the final phase of my doctoral work—writing the beast. The dissertation. It was an extended layover because I needed several weeks to complete archival research on the community where I did my fieldwork (at Harvard's lesser-known Houghton Library).

The Tamil Origin of My Panic Attack at Cub Foods

What does my transition at home have to do with Cub Foods, a Wisconsin-based supermarket chain, you wonder impatiently?

I had to get groceries on the February day I moved into my new dissertation pad in Madison. It seems like an unremarkable move-in task, right? So, I naively set off in a cab, thinking this would be a pretty straightforward exercise. I didn't intend to buy that much food since I lived alone. I needed breakfast items the most. What could go wrong?

The last time I shopped for groceries was in 1996 (about four years prior). In South India, I ate out in restaurants sometimes, but mostly I ate food prepared from raw ingredients by a hired cook who came to my rental home where I did my fieldwork. For my cook—Aachi—I paid a monthly cash fee that did not include the ingredients she bought. She asked for reimbursement once a week, and I never asked for receipts (because there are none at a public, open-air food market in India). It was so little money to an American that I have no recollection of how much I spent on the food as I write this. No clue.

Every morning at 6:00 a.m., Aachi would arrive at my early twentieth-century one-bedroom home via a local bus. In her right hand was a thickly woven shopping bag with thin plastic bags of ingredients and raw produce protruding out the top. After unpacking the day's ingredients on the small, unpolished granite counter, she would make fresh coffee (with milk from a local cow delivered by bicycle at 5:30 a.m.), cook my breakfast, lunch, *and* dinner, leaving the stews and sauces covered on the kitchen counter. Due to their high acidity and total lack of sugar, South Indian stews don't spoil very fast. It's incredible how irrelevant the refrigerator was back then, culturally.

Aachi made all my condiments and sauces from scratch every day or every other day according to traditional recipes common to the affluent Chettiar community (Tamil Nadu's premier mercantile and banking caste). Everyone I met was jealous of my food for this reason alone. From the market, each day, Aachi would bring ingredients like carrots, tomatoes, potatoes, cumin leaves, curry leaves, mustard seeds, tamarind fruit, lime, red chilies, dal, rice, wheat flour, and so on. People in Manhattan pay $200 per person for meals made this fresh. The only "processed" foods I ever saw Aachi use were: *rasam* powder (for a sauce), butter, milled rice, and unbleached wheat flour. She even bought my eggs every day as needed.

My Indian rental house was about eighty years old, a traditional one-bedroom village dwelling with eighteen-inch-thick plaster and mud walls coated with low-quality pastel paint that rubbed off on your fingers. The home was not sealed to the outside, especially the kitchen, which was sitting on the back patio and had only a metal mesh screen to keep the big mammals out. If you had left a box of crackers in that kitchen area, it would have been an insect and rodent party by midnight. So, there was nothing in my kitchen at any given time. It filled up for two hours of frenetic activity and then emptied. No snack foods lying around. No boxes of stuff. No fruit bowls. No bags of anything. No jars or bottles in the tiny micro-fridge either. No bins full of empty plastic bottles and cans. No Ziploc bags of leftovers.

Whenever these "kids" these days talk romantically about sustainable lifestyles, I laugh and think of that empty kitchen.

After I returned to New Hampshire, my mom became my cook for two months. I was twenty-seven, single, and needed somewhere to transition back into American society.

As in India, I did not do any grocery shopping during my family layover. Food just magically appeared then too. I had no idea what food cost anymore. In a way, my seven weeks at home were like returning to high school. I ate whatever Mom cooked. I chose only my snacks. It's how I grew up. And, since I didn't have a car yet, I didn't drive out to fast food either. Therefore, my reintroduction to American food choice was gated, slow, and 1980s retro.

But even this slow, seven-week home care transition didn't prepare me for what happened on Feb 8, 2000, when I passed through the electronic sliding doors at Cub Foods at 7455 Mineral Point Road (now shuttered).

The first thing that triggered me was all the electronic noise. The endless beep-beep-beep of the barcode scanners, the intercom announcements, the metal rattling of shopping carts moving around, and the chatter of hundreds of shoppers and associates doing the supermarket thing in America.

Beep. Beep. Beep. Rattle. Squeak. Beep. Beep. Beep. Rattle. Rattle.

It only worsened from there as I awkwardly grabbed a shopping cart and tried to orient myself in that vast warehouse. I had not brought a list, so I had no structure for navigating that 60,000-square-foot maze of American groceries. I had no plan of attack. No mission intel.

Beep. Beep. Beep. Beep. Beep. *Turn that sh*t off. Jesus!*

As I set off with my empty cart, I noticed that the store was lit like a surgical OR with excessively intense light. Everywhere. Painfully high kelvin, blue-white light reflected off the white linoleum floors. The store was immaculate, almost too clean after three years in a country where buildings were not adequately sealed by Western standards, and dust lay on everything.

My Tamil-adapted brain sounded another alarm, one you may never have heard: *This is a f**king factory. There's no food here. Where is the f**king food?*

I had entered through the side of the store farthest from produce by accident. Remember, I'd never been there before. So, when I entered, my eyes did not land on any raw food ingredients at all. Nothing was living. Not even a flower.

All I could see was dead sh*t in cardboard boxes and pricing signage. Everywhere. Symbols. Symbols. Everywhere. But. No. Food.

I had come to the store with some eating occasions as my only navigational aid. I just needed breakfast food and dinner food, and some snacks. For one person. As I pushed through the din of supermarket sounds toward the cereal aisle, my brain amplified the alarm. *Seriously, there isn't any f**king food here. So, just leave. Now!*

In Tamil Nadu, in that old village home, food came in only two formats: raw ingredients and cooked food. I never saw anything in between while I was there. Fresh food required material labor and skill every time. At every meal. Every day. There were no shortcuts. No heat-n-eat pseudo-foods.

But more critically, for my ill-conceived trip to Cub Foods on a cold February afternoon, I almost never saw any foods in branded packaging while I lived in India. I occasionally saw Lay's chips and Horlick's cookies hanging from clip strips on narrow storefronts and at bus stalls. But that was it.

I had lived in an unbranded food world for years, as most humans have since our species branched out from their primate ancestors. In India back in the late nineties, branded consumer items were personal care products, toys, electronics, appliances, or vehicles. The abundance of inexpensive female cooking labor in the home delayed the processing, packaging, and branding of India's food supply until the late 2000s.

As my cart entered the Cub Foods cereal aisle, my cognitive alarm system went truly berserk. I was a white man standing at the entrance to a sixty-foot-long aisle of cereal products. But my brain was Tamil, and it saw a blur of heavily-branded boxes, a riot of enormous, shadow-font logotypes, jelly bean bright colors, and front panel claims. Endless claims. Thousands and thousands of words and images and fonts.

But, no f**king food.

*This. Is. Not. Food! It's a f**king museum. Where are the ingredients to make food?* Screamed my Tamil brain. *Just get the hell out of here. Dude, run!! This is so f**ked up. . . .*

The average American US supermarket has 50–60,000 square feet, roughly twenty to twenty-five aisles of six-foot-high gondola shelving, and around 35,000 unique items for sale. Though this is all true, it still doesn't capture the issue in my brain that afternoon at Cub Foods.

The issue was the sheer flood of symbolism attacking me from all angles. Thousands of symbols per aisle. Symbols blowing smoke and mirrors between me and the processed food hidden behind them in cardboard, glass, and metal containers.

Before I could enter the cereal aisle that afternoon at Cub Foods, I started hyperventilating, my heart rate shot up, and my brain became overwhelmed. I froze and could not proceed. I couldn't breathe anymore.

*Get the f**k out of here! NOW!!!!*

I released my hands from the empty shopping cart, left it there, and bolted out of the front of the store, where I stood in the cold at the bus stop for a ride back to my apartment, empty-handed. My breathing quickly normalized once I got out of the building.

How Did Supermarkets Get So Overloaded with Marketing and Pointless Choice?

The average supermarket aisle is a pornographic advertising spectacle America has taken to overwrought extremes. Imagine how overwhelmed your brain would be if every restaurant menu item had its own made-up brand name and claims; multiplied by one hundred menu items. At a restaurant, you want nothing between the menu description and real food. In a grocery store, no such luck, folks. You get brand identity symbolism.

As with most Amazon.com shopping today, the scope of choices in front of you in the majority of supermarket categories is orders of magnitude more than any individual needs to see or wants to wade through. Even when using Amazon's filters it can take a long time to get choices down to something your human brain is comfortable handling.

Two historical forces combined to create the excessive choice frying my brain that afternoon at Cub Foods, a scope of choice that would have shocked the manager of an 1890s A&P:

1. Since the 1980s, due to regional and national market research, American supermarkets have increasingly catered to the diverse needs of tiny subsegments visiting each store location. *Small niches at the store level multiplied by hundreds or thousands of stores can form huge target markets.* An example would be shoppers interested in natural and organic equivalents to essential American foods. Organic food does not yield much money to any supermarket, but it is significant across two thousand stores.
2. *Supermarkets make their net profits off fees charged to suppliers—the more suppliers and* new products every year,

the greater the fee revenue. Supermarkets charge slotting and marketing fees for new products, even to smaller brands (that long tail of choice). Retailers have a financial incentive to watch them fail so that they can charge the same onboarding fees again to the next start-up as soon as possible. They make most of their slotting money by charging the largest public firms to slot in thousands of new products every year, most of which won't last eighteen months, if that. Then, they do it again. Ka-ching.

Excessive choice is more profitable for supermarket retailers, like a rancher subdividing his land and selling chunks to high-density urban developers.

Capitalist profit motives at the retail level, including public companies' desire to "buy" shelf space for major brands as a billboard/attention-grabbing device, have driven the insane scope of choice you see more than actual consumer demand for all this choice.

The amount of inefficient linear feet of shelf space that doesn't make money in these stores is unbelievable and has necessitated the supplier fee profit model. It would horrify that 1890s A&P store manager, who made a lot of money in only 6–8,000 square feet.

The competition for shopper eyeballs is intense in the management meeting rooms of consumer product brands. This is why stores are full of shelf signs, shelf-stalkers, promo deal tags, sale tags, end aisle displays, and freestanding displays.

The morning after my panic attack, I took a different bus in the other direction, across the famous Madison isthmus, past the Wisconsin state capitol building, and onto a tree-lined street that once harbored Madison's most popular health food store—Willy Street Co-op.

As soon as I walked into Willy Street, I saw raw produce.

Instantly, my brain felt relief.

OK. *This is much better.*

Chapter Eighteen

THE EROSION OF MEAL RITUAL AND THE RISE OF OBESITY

If there is one overwhelmingly shared social fact among older Americans I interviewed, it is that, during their childhoods, dinner happened every night at roughly the same time, even if one parent had to miss it regularly due to shift work. This was true *regardless of social class*.

For most of the twentieth century, the biggest meal of the day in America was a hot *evening* meal. Then, in the decades leading up to the year 2000, the family dinner lost its obligatory status. Family dinners at home became a choice based on family members' schedules. Today, the children often nix the family dinner for eating while gaming upstairs. Parents must insist and insist hard. A restaurant meal is often the easiest way for permissively structured families to eat together peaceably.

The last age cohort which could broadly claim a highly ritualized home dinner each evening as children—the Baby Boomers—is the same generation that first let this ritual obligation go in the homes they created, setting it adrift like many other "traditions" anchoring them to their parents' world.

Many social changes attacked the sacredness of the family dinner ritual in the 1980s onward as Baby Boomers began to start families:

- *Rise in childless households*[1]: The effort of cooking seems pointless when the "family" is this small and doesn't feel

like a family. Millions of older Americans have remained childless right into retirement.
- *Rise of dual-income and single-parent families*[2]: lack of energy to think through meals by 5:00 p.m. and lack of cooking help from husbands (or kids)
- *Spread of cheap fast food, fast-casual food to go*: the opportunity cost of canceling home-cooked meals is mild in absolute dollars or time.
- *Rise of extensive after-school activities for preteens*[3]: kills the ritual before it can get established in a home by interrupting multiple afternoons/evenings per week. And few recreational clubs schedule practices around some "dinner hour."
- *Three times longer commutes/daycare pickup*[4]: traffic alone can transform cooking into the last straw on a crazy day.
- *Lack of help for preschoolers at home*: most parents today do not have another experienced adult under fifty living in the home and certainly did not when they had young kids.
- *Longer professional workdays*[5]: odds of "staying late" became higher in a variety of professions (e.g., sales, marketing, accounting, VP-level roles, any deadline-driven job in any sector).
- *The rise of permissive parenting*: kids often want to eat while doing something else like watching media, and parents have lost the authoritarian will to fight this in a more permissive era.

An Ultra-Brief History of the American Dinner

In large nineteenth-century farm families, eating a hot meal together was a function of logistics as much as a ritual obligation. The homes were tiny, so eating alone in separate rooms was impossible. The media-driven cultural impulse to separate inside the house was also absent. More importantly, meal prep for six to twelve people was a significant effort that required centralized disbursement (on or off the table).[6] The disbursal process brought everyone into the same room, allowing parents to mandate the dinner ritual for moral reasons. Patriarchal notions of family order did not go easily challenged. And children had no valid choices regarding when and how to eat dinner. They most likely *perceived* no choice about dinner at all. My research suggests that the acceptance of child input regarding dinner didn't get going until the 1980s. And it was limited even then.

The nineteenth-century family farm dinner was operationally similar to our contemporary Thanksgiving meals (just with much less food). The latter is the only reliable day each year when *most* Americans experience a real dinner ritual on the same day, with its obligation to sit down, receive shared food, talk, and remain at the table through the end (sort of).

Before industrialization, the big meal of the day with the American farm family was actually at *midday*, what would later become an abbreviated, hasty factory worker's *lunch*.[7] Farmers are up very early, working hard, and hungry by noontime. If you've ever done a ton of yard work on a summer morning, you know what this feels like.

If we can safely assume that 90 percent of possible nuclear family dinners occurred at home every night in the 1950s and 1960s, what do you think the proportion is today? It's about *50 percent*.[8] If you're in my home, it's 30–40 percent.

The home-cooked family dinner ritual has not disappeared so much as lost its power of ritual obligation. And 24 percent of Americans skip dinner entirely on any given day. It's that lifestyle choice thing I talked about in part one. It is really about the accommodation of multiple individualisms in the home. We use the phrase "your day," "my day," and "her day" to mark out our private schedules and their snowflake-like nature. The kids' schedules are now as valid as the parents' schedules. Given how much time Americans spend alone daily, it's not surprising that we're updating each other about our separately transpiring days with these kinds of phrases. So, it should not surprise you that researchers have discovered that "differing schedules," by a wide margin, are the number one reason for canceling family home dinners today.[9] *Oops, can't make lasagna for us tonight, hon; I have pickleball with the girlfriends! Make yourself whatever . . . whenever. Love you!*

Calorie intake has not only shifted from midday/lunch to evening/dinner and has largely de-ritualized, but it has also fragmented into new kinds of eating moments entirely. The necessity of the "meal" itself has waned considerably in the last twenty-five years.

One primary reason Americans feel fine skipping meals, including dinner (!), is that we now do something called "snacking." And we do it daily. This is probably not at the top of your list of stunning insights this book has delivered. I get it. But what most of us don't realize is that snacking has no real historical precedent in human history unless you were traveling and couldn't stop to cook, were actively foraging for the kin group, or you were a sad, single male. To eat room temperature food by yourself between cooked meals or instead of meals is extremely recent in the modern world.

We need to understand how this snacking thing spread because it represents one of the most powerful consequences of letting individualism loose on an entire society.

The Grand Incursion of Snacking Behavior

I do not doubt that young kids have been stealing bits of food from foraging vessels, kitchens, and hearths since time immemorial. I just can't prove it. High metabolisms lead to shorter satiety time spans, so their motive is understandable. And lack of adult impulse control has constantly threatened any poorly guarded food's survival in a human dwelling. Impulsive munching on leftovers by itself is not worthy of cultural demarcation in most societies, because it was never a primary calorie source.

However, *everyone* raiding the dwelling's foodstuffs for snacks *whenever* they want is a late twentieth-century social innovation. Before modern processing, packaging, and refrigeration, very little ready-to-eat food existed in homes. There was probably more ready-to-eat "snack food" among hunter-gatherer communities who traditionally collected wild nuts and berries and stored them. It's just unclear from ethnographic accounts (which rarely discuss eating habits in detail) if anything like modern, intentional snacking occurred in preliterate tribes.[10]

The word "snack" is ancient in English, but not in the sense we use it now. The first use of it related to edibles has to do with tasting liquor. It was not until the eighteenth century that the modern meaning appeared, around the same time that our modern definition of "fun" also appeared (!). That can't be a coincidence, can it?

> *Snack: a mere bite or morsel of food, as contrasted with a regular meal; a light or incidental repast.*[11]

When we read the early usages of "snack" in a post-Renaissance literary context, it's clear that the word connotes a sad, small meal substitute eaten out of desperation (i.e., no time or person to cook a meal). It sounds like it was a mostly *male* problem—this eighteenth-century snacking.

The eighteenth-century "snack" certainly does not signal an idealized, fantasized, or happily sought-out behavior. It's far from the turn of the twentieth century, beachside snack bars with popcorn, candy, and peanuts (and, later, ice cream). Also, far from the coffee-focused "snack bars" of the early twentieth-century urban landscape, which offered working men the ultimate early "snack"—the sandwich (which was not a foot long). This early American snacking behavior was very far from the everyday couch-bound experience of consuming Pringles or trailside swallowing of Clif bars in the 2000s.

Frito-Lay's growth as a processed snack food company is a great barometer for the explosion of a new, everyday American behavior that is anything but sad, tiny, or full of desperate longing for a hot meal. That new behavior has a historically new verb we use all the time now—"snacking." In 1961, when Frito-Lay merged, the company sold around $135 million dollars' worth of branded, processed snacks annually.[12] This amounted to about $0.74 per capita.[13] By 1989, Frito-Lay was selling $3.5 billion in salty snacks at a per capita rate of $14.[14] By 2022, Frito-Lay North America was selling $23 billion in revenue at a per capita rate of $69.[15] Whoa.

You can also see Frito-Lay's imperial growth reflected in the dietary lives of the twenty older Americans I spoke in depth with recently. There is a measurable snacking incidence increase during their lifetimes, consistent with the sales trajectory of branded snack foods. If you didn't snack daily between meals as a kid, the odds are that you do now. It's almost assured.

In constant, inflation-adjusted dollars, Frito-Lay has increased per capita consumption of its branded salty snacks *ninefold* since 1961.[16] The 1960s, incidentally, is also when the word "snacking" took off in printed English. Usage of the verb grew exponentially until around 2010.[17] The 1960s were also when Frito-Lay and other iconic snack food brands ratcheted their advertising spending to drive consumption. Lay's potato chips turned on heavy advertising with its now iconic 1965 TV campaign and the slogan "Betcha can't eat just one." That slogan will take on a dark irony by the end of this chapter.

Today, 90 percent of adults report snacking at least once a day. Snacks represent 22 percent of total energy intake and happen 1.2–3 times daily.[18] Americans no longer rely on meals to feed themselves as their agricultural ancestors did. Since 47 percent of snacking occasions are solitary, this new way of eating represents our individualistic culture's inexorable pull of autonomy.[19] Americans of all social classes now have access to very cheap snacks at home, allowing them to evade any domestic calorie gatekeeper or mandatory eating ritual easily. If we don't intervene, our youngest son will happily graze on snacks all day long (luckily, they're mostly nutritious).

Among my interviews, I collected stories of Gen X and Boomer teens eating at their friends' homes, grabbing McDonald's on the way home from school, slipping into convenience stores after practices, etc.

Who are you, elders, to confine my satiation to your stodgy ritual mealtimes?

Snacking to Banish the Hunger Sensation

The eighteenth-century "snacker" clearly just wanted a meal but had nothing but leftover scraps of stale bread or whatever. This was snacking as an *inferior* meal. And yes, hunger was no doubt the only motive. Stale bread? Dried out, cooked meat? Come on. This is not the stuff of intentional desire.

When I first entered the business world in 2003, I did in-home interviews and shop-along tours with Americans for corporate clients. In these two to three hour explorations of American foodways, I quickly noticed something odd that was tangential to the stated corporate research agenda. The most exciting material was always off-topic.

Most adults I interviewed in the early 2000s believed that merely feeling hungry, a sensation we have all experienced, is something we should promptly get rid of by eating a snack. They did not put it this way directly with me because it sounds gluttonous or ridiculous. I inferred this social truth because hundreds kept insisting that they snacked in midafternoon because "I felt hungry" *and* some version of "didn't want to wait until dinner" or "couldn't make it until dinner." The surface explanation was usually about "lasting until dinner" or "performing at one's best" until work ended, etc.

But for millennia, humans have happily deferred eating for various reasons. Agricultural humans did not have time to forage all day, so they waited, hungry, for cooking-centered rituals of commensality and food sharing. And you waited to eat if it was not a locally appropriate mealtime.

Interviewees' use of the auxiliary verb can/could (i.e., "I *couldn't* make it until dinner") baffles anyone who knows human anatomy or any hunger relief worker who has aided truly starving people in refugee camps. Humans can last quite a long time without food—up to two weeks. *There is no biological reason to react to a hunger signal faster than the next culturally appointed mealtime.* Confining food intake to meals in a cooking-centered culture is very realistic. Let's face it, Americans have three mealtimes from which to choose, spaced no farther apart than five-to-six hours (when not skipped). It's not the end of the world to wait five hours for more food. Seriously.

Yet, here I had perfectly mature, college-educated adults sitting in their living rooms and insisting on camera that they "had" to snack in the afternoons (two hours before dinner) or even in the mornings (one hour before lunch!). *Had to do it, James. Had to. Wouldn't make it to lunch. Wouldn't make it to dinner. I'd crap out. I'd fade. Wouldn't make it through the meeting. I'd zone out. Lose it. Couldn't think.*

It's not empirically clear, but I suspect this notional standard—extinguishing hunger signals more or less immediately—spread in

American culture during the 1990s. This cultural belief did *not* exist in the 1980s when I was growing up. Only teenage males were thrown predinner snacks to quell angry bellies. Sometimes. My wife remembers being told angrily to wait for dinner by her father: "You won't die!" Mealtime was sacred. Food was guarded. If this panicked need to extinguish hunger the moment we sense it wasn't widespread in the 1980s, but it was by the 2000s, then something happened in between.

I suspect that the cultural banishment of hunger pangs among adults and children correlated to a general intensification of the definition of middle-class *comfort* in America. It is part of a longer-term trend toward extinguishing all manner of physical pain with OTC painkillers, prescription opioids, and THC. It's not my place here to accuse Americans of becoming "royal wussbags," as we called our cowardly peers in the 1980s. I do not believe that snacking to prevent between-meal hunger is about being too *wimpy* to wait until dinner. It's simply a cheap luxury in the land of processed mass-distributed calories. It costs little to extinguish hunger instantly, so . . . we do it. It's just so easy when no one guards the sacredness of mealtime. It's something the anxious and stressed can *control*.

I'm confident that all those helpless eighteenth-century men who couldn't find a woman to cook them a meal and ate snacks of stale bread and cold meat would pass out from ecstasy at the array of snack foods available to us now.

Snacking Gets Personal and Boundaries Blur

Beyond the highly mainstream theory of the ever-increasing desire for pain relief in modern society, another driver for daily snacking is important to acknowledge: the desire for positive health outcomes (now and in the future).

As snacking became common in the 1990s, it makes sense that our culture unconsciously generated a feeling that some of this "snacking" should get redirected to more virtuous ends—i.e., personal health. Once snacking adopted the motive of immediate hunger extinguishment, regardless of the time of day, it became almost assured that notions of healthy eating would infiltrate. Why? It's about the moral logic of meals entering a new eating domain. And meals are where agricultural humans confine the *morality* of eating.

Healthy snacking has become a moral, even an elite, signal of modern autonomy for upper-middle-class Americans and a broader group of the health-conscious of all social class backgrounds. Behavior databases continue to reveal that Americans snack healthily in the morning and afternoon but rarely at night. At night, we revert to the oldest way of snacking, snacks as a reward or treat. We're at the beachside snack bar with our great-grandparents by 7:00 p.m., at least in our minds.

In the first quarter of the twenty-first century, food entrepreneurs spent years innovating new, profitable ways for health-conscious adults to find something other than candy or chips to munch on between meals. And Big Food has been chasing these healthy innovations with its mimetic versions at even greater profits.

Modern snacking's highly solitary nature in the twenty-first century has turned healthy snacking into a highly personalized effort. Baby Boomer women led the way in trying to rehabilitate "wayward," impulsive snacking behavior, however partially, as a component of many lifetime rounds of dieting.

What am I talking about when I say rehabilitate snacking behavior?

An extreme case of weight management through snacking will illuminate my point.

Years ago, the research company I worked at used to do group interviews in people's homes. The idea was to recruit a circle of female friends to form a more honest, self-correcting group than the traditional focus group. In one project we did on weight management dietary tactics among Baby Boomer women, we asked the women to bring us examples of the foods they prefer to snack on. As we went around the room for this bizarre show-and-tell, everyone we listened to displayed foods like energy bars, bagged snack products, or an apple. Then, we got to a woman who pulled a rolling, insulated cooler forward in front of her and opened it up. *What?*

This mom had a cooler full of:

- Mozzarella sticks
- Fruit in little baggies

- Nuts in little baggies
- Low-calorie soft drinks
- Bottled water
- Ziploc-bagged veggie snacks (baby carrots, broccoli, pea pods)

This deadly serious woman had several pounds worth of food in her snack cooler. She looked like she was headed out camping. Then she shocked the room by confessing the following (I'm paraphrasing from memory):

"So, I don't eat all of this every day. But I bring this cooler with me every time I leave the house. It stays in my car. That way, I know for sure that I have a whole bunch of healthy options to eat—something, anything—other than junk. It's my defense against junk. It will keep me from going out to grab crap."

She said "junk" and "crap" like a Pentecostal minister screams "Satan," with a slightly erotic tone that signals the dark attraction that plagues her. It's commonplace for intellectuals to blame "marketing" and "propaganda" for all this "mindless" junk food snacking in America. I wish it were so simple. If it were so simple, we could regulate the ads easily. Or ban them as we did with cigarette commercials.

The challenge is that Frito-Lay's formulas are simply outstanding from the perspective of hooking people and causing them to empty bags at very fast rates. The sensory power of modern carb-heavy snack food is the real tragedy for millions of Americans (though we are taught from all angles to blame them for their lack of willpower).

That cooler was an almost militaristic cry of defiance against a world of junk food snacks this woman felt were oppressing her for much of her life. Throughout that project, I remember hearing searing tales of emotional eating, binge eating, compulsive eating, and a complete inability to say no to that office cookie tray or candy bowl. And failed dieting efforts. So many worthless diets. Here was a woman bringing defensive artillery into dietary battle every day. A cooler of healthy ammo. Because society was doing nothing at all to protect her. No one felt any obligation to keep the dangerous delights away from her. They were pushing them at her all day long, even at night.

At the time, I had no idea there was so much internal strife in America's offices and homes around being tempted by junk food. Especially angry about this were the women I interviewed. In my recent interviews, I spoke with a few Baby Boomer men the same age as this woman who also labeled their snacking as "junk." Unlike their female peers, they had no intention of changing anything about it.

As I reflected on the fear some of these women genuinely felt, it occurred to me that large snack food companies spend a fortune to distribute their snack foods at a level of breadth (per square mile) most of us don't notice as we run around in our daily lives.

Shelf-stable, highly processed snack foods, most with minimal nutritive value beyond carbohydrates that quickly become blood glucose, can be found at several *million* distribution points in America. Vending takes snacks to 4.6 million machines in the country. Two hundred fifty thousand convenience stores and gas station food stores place these snacks at most major arterial intersections. Forty-five thousand grocery retail outlets help you grab them on your weekly shopping trips.

If, for some crazy reason, you do not have any snack foods at home, you are most likely less than a quarter mile away from a branded, packaged snack food product you can buy on impulse and eat in about thirty seconds to two minutes.

If you have ever had an eating disorder or found yourself stress-eating or cannot control weight gain, the snack food industrial complex in America is terrifying in its power to surround you with cheap, quick-to-eat sensations.[20]

Whether you are the slightest bit hungry or not.

Omnipresent Cheap Snacks + Solitary Snacking = Obesogenic Results

When you ask the typical American: What causes other people to become obese? Most of us will attack the stranger's lack of *dietary* control.[21] When people explain their own weight gain, though, they first point to their lack of exercise.

The fact that so many Americans refuse to look first at their own dietary behavior is worthy of more than one psychology dissertation. I'll save the academics the trouble. We don't stare at our eating behavior because we know damn well how and what we stuff in our mouths every day is *completely embarrassing.*

Public health officials aren't afraid to point the finger at the snack food. Professor Marion Nestle, Michael Pollan, and many others have spent their careers attacking the low nutritive content of our branded snack food. Yet, all media interviews and rants (and related restaurant calorie labeling) pushed by nutritionists and dieticians have had no measurable effect on rates of obesity in the US.[22]

If we look at the official CDC list of reasons for obesity in America, here's what we find:

- Lack of physical activity
- Unhealthy eating behaviors
    - [Eating] more calories than you use
    - Too much saturated fat
    - Too much added sugar
- Not enough quality sleep (affects hormones regulated hunger)
- High stress (hormone dysregulation)
- Chronic conditions
- Genetics
- Medicines (antidepressants, birth control, antipsychotics, beta-blockers, insulin, etc.)[23]

I am not an epidemiologist, but I find one of the above drivers consistently under-discussed by the media and the public, perhaps because it is too obvious to be worth examining.

Eating more calories than you use. Why do people do this?

Why do we consume large amounts of calories our body did not ask for in any biological manner? We know that snack food formulas are designed to accelerate the volume of human eating, to empty the bag rapidly in what the industry calls "hand-to-mouth" snacking. But what social forces systematically enable overeating that we aren't willing to confront as a society? Is "mindless munching" really our problem to solve as individuals?

When we use ethnographic methods of inference, an interesting source of overeating is staring at us. But before I jump to that, let's step back and summarize the behavioral triggers for snacking (biological and social) for some perspective. I'm summarizing here from scholarly research and my observations.

- Inner-Directed Triggers
  - Snacking to mitigate hunger pangs
  - Snacking as a planned personal health directive
  - Snacking as bingeing to smother stress/anxiety
- Outer Directed Triggers
  - Snacking out of exposure—high-craving foods trigger impulsive snacking for some (common in offices)
  - Snacking as reciprocity—you were offered food, and it is polite to take it
  - Snacking due to social activity: gaming, TV watching
  - Snacking as anticipatory eating (cheese right before dinner)
  - Snacking as a celebration (e.g., the Frappuccino after the big sales win)

Almost all of the above snacking is *unsupervised, untracked, and autonomous*. There is a habit, but no *ritual*. This describes most at-home and office-based grazing behavior. We select and consume snacks with minimal social surveillance and no intervention. Even if someone sees what you pick up, we have a code of "no-comment" at work in our society (spouses/lovers excepted). One exception is online gaming and group TV watching. These group recreational rituals often feature commentary around what people are eating. Your family can and usually will tease you about what you're snacking on or how much of it you consume. Streaming gamers have cameras on them and are often seen eating stuff. Comments happen. And live internet game streaming has kicked off more than one snacking trend (e.g., boba tea during the pandemic).

Snacking *alone* or *unsupervised* is a primary cultural setup for excess calorie intake. We have very little awareness of how much food we eat unless we train ourselves monkishly to track this information daily. Few people can sustain such ascetic self-monitoring.[24] By adding the possibility of between-meal eating, we invite more opportunities to overeat beyond our daily needs. Doing it alone without social monitoring gives us the green light to lose track and control. *Sh*t, the bag emptied. Whoops. Oh well. Where's that gym card, hon?*

Let me share a story from my old fieldwork days that will illustrate how unaware of our snacking behavior most of us are. It's the story of a young mom suffering from morbid obesity somewhere in middle America. When I interviewed her over fifteen years ago, she was in the process of qualifying for bariatric surgery after years of uncontrolled weight gain. At one point, she brought out a picture of her high school prom photo to show how skinny she had been as a girl.

"I just don't know how this happened," she sighed with deep sadness and defeat at her current situation.

As she described her many failed attempts at weight loss diets, I scanned the first floor of her home for anything of interest as context. Quickly I noticed bowls of kids' cereal in every lower room of the house. They were placed like candy bowls on counters and side tables. I leaned in to ask, "I notice you have bowls of cereal lying out. What is that for?"

"Oh, we like to snack on Fruity Pebbles," she said in a neutral tone as if this had no relationship to the question she had posed not two minutes earlier: *How did this happen?*

Fruity Pebbles have about 120 calories for every 30 grams. One cup of Fruity Pebbles (a large handful) is about 140 calories. By having calorie-dense food like this out and ready to grab like popcorn, this young mother was nurturing her family into obesity, one handful at a time, without conscious awareness.

A lot of snacking from bags happens without awareness of the amount consumed.

Snacking without awareness. Alone.

Research has recently shown that snacking impulsively without hunger leads to increased energy consumption (i.e., excess calorie intake), partly because most snack foods are very high in carbs and don't contribute meaningfully toward biological satiety (i.e., most of the Frito-Lay portfolio).[25]

In other words, if you reached for cake, cookies, or salty snacks because you were hungry, you would not be solving anything per se. You probably won't silence the hunger signal that triggered you to grab a snack. I think most of us have experienced eating salty snacks and then still feeling just as hungry as when we started. But we never learn. Ever.

Before the advent of purposively healthy snacking, Americans only snacked on treats or indulgences (cake, cookies, mixed nuts, and candy). The earliest packaged, portable snack foods for sale were candy bars, chocolate bars, nuts, and combinations of all three.[26] Then came the easily dissolved, salty snacks of the mid-twentieth century we all know well.

We have decades of historical momentum pushing high carbohydrate snack choices as rewards and treats, even when the trigger for snacking is just plain hunger. We often grab for the wrong solution and just keep stumbling along, not realizing how easy and cheap it is to consume an extra 200–300 calories daily without conscious awareness.

Without effective weight training or other metabolism-elevating regimens, these extra calories will build slowly, inexorably over time into pounds and pounds of excess fat, even for someone who was skinny through young adulthood.

Obesity in modern America has been, in large part, a slow-rolling result of unsupervised, autonomous, impulse-driven snacking for satiety and pleasure. This is the easiest, modern way to overconsume in a leisure society. Ritual meals don't prevent overeating or weight gain (as we all know during the holidays). But to prevent obesity, restricting access to food during the day may be the most obvious yet logistically challenging solution our farming ancestors accidentally had in their favor. It was a form of indirect calorie restriction. So was the much higher cost of food calories in the nineteenth century.

Once we let go of the sacred association between eating and cooking hot meals and permitted unrestricted distribution of alluring, low-nutrition snack foods, we opened a Pandora's box of dietary consumption that transcends the supposed willpower of individual beings.

The average person lacks anything like an ascetic impulse implied by the proponents of the "willpower" theory. It takes an enormous support "team" and a structured environment to not overeat in modern America. It takes constant social intervention in a society built on the sacred veil of privacy. No wonder it doesn't work.

Chapter Nineteen

THE ODDLY SOCIAL ORIGINS OF FOOD SENSITIVITIES

"I'm going off wheat!" a former colleague's roommate yelled as they passed each other in the living room of their rental home in Seattle. Soon, the roomie was out the front door but *not* headed to the bread bakery across the street.

"Did you hear that Susan is vegan now? I think she like lost twenty pounds or something. She's gaunt. I don't even recognize her," I once overheard in an office kitchen.

"Yeah, I can't eat dairy anymore. You don't want to know why," I explained to someone at an office pizza party full of dairy. And, no, I didn't want to explain what irritable bowel syndrome (IBS) is, let alone the methane-rich consequences of triggering it with a warm lactose gut coating. A shuddering, bloated methane tube is not pleasant when it's inside you.

All three of these mini vignettes *seem* to be about individual food choices. Each individual chooses to avoid something (wheat, meat, and dairy). Each of these folks is declaring an ascetic choice in the context of a broader American food culture. These darling people appear isolated when standing inside their immediate social network (leisure, work, home). But the latter perception is an illusion of interpretation—an illusion that Americans are unusually prone to falling for because we prefer to see the world as composed of mostly socially unstructured, autonomous choosing.

Seemingly individual food preferences exist on a continuum of autonomy. The vignettes above exhibit it well if you reread them. You could add a fourth at the bottom to represent a true "forced choice"—avoiding peanuts due to a medically verified severe allergy. Anaphylaxis is hard to fake.

These personalized dietary tweaks involve food symbolism and cultural rules of interpretation, which have shifted under our very feet in the past half century. They have shifted in part because of social forces and in part because of murky epidemiological shifts in the US population.

So, how do we come to make such bizarre choices that are mostly without historical precedent among humankind?[1] How do we come to make choices against the relentless, daily tidal waves of food norms that would have us give up and give in to the American norms of taste and supply? *Try eliminating cheese from your American diet for an entire week, and circle back to let me know how it went.*

Or try spending an entire year not eating pizza *and* having a robust, event-filled social life. It's not easy. At my old office, I gave up and just ate my own lunch (or the lactose-free Caesar salad) at the never-ending pizza parties, at least two per month. I wouldn't call this the crux of our modern loneliness epidemic, but it's not helping either. Not when it gets totally ignored because, well, the office is small, and it's only James who has the dairy problem. *Whatever, James. Bring some Lactaid. Take some responsibility. We can't please everyone. Have some garlic bread.*

The case of food sensitivities helps us understand how broader societal changes and cultural interpretation *structure* choices that seem to be purely individual-level, even innately biological, issues to most of us.

Tens of millions of Americans now claim to have food intolerances and allergies and alter their diets permanently as a result. I am one of these folks. So is my Dad. Most of these dietary alterations are *not* the result of a medical diagnosis or a hospitalization event. Some are. For many, there is only a *perceived* correlation between unpleasant bodily symptoms and recently consumed food or beverage items.[2]

This lay correlation has been the eternal frustration of cranky doctors and allergists for the last several decades, as this 1984 framing of the issue reveals (about alleged cow's milk allergies):

> The majority of these reactions are never proved to have an allergic basis, but they are frequently presumed to have such a basis by both parents and physician simply because:
>
> 1. No other reason was found.
> 2. The symptoms improved when milk was removed from the diet.[3]

Among older Americans I interviewed for this book, 27 percent claim at least one major allergy/intolerance to a standard American food ingredient.[4] That's almost one out of three Gen X and Baby Boomer people. The fact that tens of millions (including me) are avoiding dairy, for example, due to perceived lactose *intolerance* (not an actual medical allergy) represents a massive, culturally generated collision with the processed American diet, a diet lathered and frosted with very cheap, high lactose cheese and dairy.[5] Once you try to avoid an ultra-mainstream ingredient in any given food culture, eating, especially dining out, takes on defensive, storm-prepper overtones.

When we adapt to dietary intolerances, we become "weird" in our immediate family and social networks. These dietary tweaks make us stand out, in part, because we can no longer share commonly offered food at public or private events in our social world. We must ask for accommodation from hosts who may or may not know how to accommodate us. We must locate alternative products at the grocery store and recipes for cooking. Eating becomes a pain in the ass at times.

A Super Brief History of Modern Food Sensitivities

When I was a kid in the 1970s, no one I knew was gluten intolerant. I never met anyone with a dairy issue. Or a peanut allergy. We blissfully went to school with peanuts and peanut butter like this was normal.

Today, an entire billion-dollar-plus category of alternative nut butter (primarily almond and sunflower seed) services daycares, schools, and your home pantry to help keep dangerous allergens away from kids.

How did this happen? How did so many choose to avoid some of the *most commonly used* American food ingredients? What's next? An *apple* allergy?

Scientists have established the rise in children's food allergies as real, but the origins are still unclear. A surge in autoimmune reactions due to excessive hygiene is one leading theory, among others. Lots of intelligent people are trying to understand the hard science.

But the *social* science is more apparent.

When discussing food sensitivities, we use the same kinds of medical language and framing whether we have diagnosed ourselves or had a blood antigen test interpreted by a professional allergist. We narrate the whole continuum similarly.

Why do we do this? Well, because we are just interpreting bodily symptoms in a modern way.

We could also choose to ignore these symptoms and suffer silently. And the Super Stoics in my research cohort still do, just like you can train your brain to ignore chronic pain.

We could also interpret the same bodily symptoms as evidence of a supernatural attack unleashed by a social enemy and unlinked to food. Thomas More narrates a seemingly allergic reaction to strawberries by Richard III, which More (and Richard) interpreted as witchcraft unleashed by his advisor Lord Hastings (the poor guy then lost his head).[6]

When we narrate food sensitivities in the medical language of organ function/dysfunction, both we and others now see it as an individual medical *problem*. This specific creature over here gets stinky diarrhea when it has milk.

The more medically we narrate our food intolerances, the more people around us become *tolerant* of our dietary weirdness. Ironically. Especially when they are hosting us in their homes.

Sorry, I can't have your lasagna because I'm gluten intolerant.

Oh, I'm so sorry; I had no idea. No worries. I get it. Can I make you something else?

I call food sensitivities the unassailable modern food preference—a choice to avoid an ingredient that makes us feel bad and makes others feel bad for accidentally serving it to us. Today, few will attack you openly for refusing food with this rationale; almost no one under eighty.

But we forget that self-declared food sensitivities would *not* have been acceptable at a family meal fifty or a hundred years ago. You would have been teased or ignored by the home cook. If you kept at it, they might think you were crazy. Your diarrhea, gas, GERD, and hives were your problem if they occurred. Linking it to food would not have been common. The culture would not accommodate these "minor" issues even if they accepted the linkage. You could find something else to eat or, more likely, just take TUMS, Pepto, or another OTC digestive aid to quell your symptoms.

You just need a digestive tonic . . . heard of Pepsi-Cola?

This is what must have happened at home in the 1940s when the first major spike in food allergies appeared in English print media.

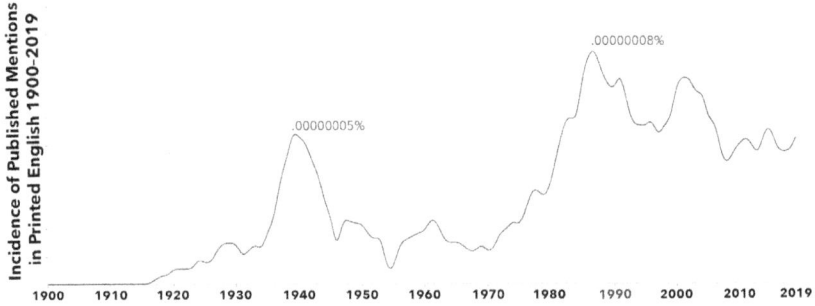

Figure 9. Mentions of "Food Allergy" in Printed English Surge After World War II. Table data sourced from Google's Ngram service.[7]

For the past four decades, at least, the adult *perception* of food allergy/sensitivity has been consistently *more prevalent* than true medical allergies. The difference is that the medical establishment takes food allergies much more seriously than in the early 1980s. Google's Ngram database (see figure 9) reveals that the 1980s and 1990s were crucial for media discussion of food allergies and general awareness building.

> *In the early 1980s, the landscape of food allergy was very different from today: food allergy was less prevalent, there was little public awareness of the problem, most clinicians were highly skeptical of the diagnosis, and there was little active research going on, primarily because many investigators did not consider the field to be "a real science." . . . Thirty-five years ago (1981), the perceived prevalence of food allergy in the United States was similar to what is reported today, i.e. about 20%, but the actual prevalence then was*

thought to be less than 1% compared to more recent estimates today of 3.5%–5% of the general population and 8% of the pediatric population. . . . The reason for this rapid rise in food allergy among industrialized countries around the world remains an open question [my emphasis].[8]

Self-diagnosing adults have become more medically nuanced at interpreting their bodily symptoms. We've progressed from saying things like, "Grandpa has horrible gas after lasagna" to "I need Lactaid if we're going to order pizza tonight." We've changed from reacting-to-your-whatever-problem to let's-prevent-your-valid-condition.

If we look briefly at the top, self-reported food sensitivity in America—lactose intolerance—we can see how real-world changes forced us to adapt our seemingly individual food choices. The rise of lactose intolerance in the US as a perceived issue correlates to at least two major trends: 1) the twentieth-century explosion in dairy in our processed and restaurant food supply leading to more trigger opportunities in our very dairy-heavy popular foods (burgers, sandwiches, pizza, and snack cheese)[9] and 2) a dramatic acceleration of immigration from Lactose Intolerancia (i.e., Middle East, Greece, Italy, West Africa, and most of Asia).[10]

We have learned to mark food sensitivities linguistically, manage symptoms through avoidance, and discuss this openly. This is a profound cultural shift in how we interpret bodily signals, a classic use of language in human societies.

Popping the Illusion of Personal Food Preferences

The average person does *not* have a very large social network in which they know the dietary avoidances of most network members. Try it out. Make a list of friends, family, and colleagues you've conversed with at least once in the last year (digitally or offline). I'd be shocked if the proportion of this broader social network for whom you know their particular dietary preferences is more than 10 percent.

I doubt that most of my colleagues at my old company know that I "became" lactose-intolerant during my tenure there. Honestly, why *would* they remember this? Any more than those who know my favorite PowerPoint template? Or my favorite streaming playlist?

What is my point, you ask?

Anyone who discloses a food sensitivity or allergy to you will appear unique in *your* limited, active social world. For example, you may or may not know more than a few people with the same food sensitivity. Unless they live with you, I doubt you've formed a little club. You're not connected to your fellow lactose-intolerant peers. The broader forces of media and social commentary cause us all to reinterpret bodily signals in the frame of dietary intolerances. The social origins of these interpretations become invisible because these preference tribes don't exist in real life. It's just David's reality. Sally's problem. Alex's choice. It's James's colon woes.

Hotel catering companies are aggressively rude about learning your dietary preferences. They insist on knowing the exact count of every dietary weirdness headed their way. They pursue this private knowledge to minimize food waste and costs and avoid an insane run on the portobello "burgers." What a client disaster that would be. Heads would surely roll. *No one told us that the branding agency was mostly vegan. Sh*t!*

When money is on the line, we suddenly notice how many other people next to us are vegan, lactose-intolerant, etc. The organizers now have something at stake in ritually acknowledging a broader collective issue affecting many individuals dispersed across social networks. We see little catering signs, "dairy-free" or "vegan," next to the food trays. *Oh yeah, I forgot about these folks. I hope it tastes as good as my food.*

Food sensitivities are socially learned interpretations of bodily symptoms. Once honored by society and events, they become ever more legitimate choices. And the latter marks when any of us can transform our food allergy or intolerance into an aspirational dietary hack (e.g., gluten-free for weight loss).

Accommodating Food Sensitivities— Inclusion at Its Best?

Food sensitivities have become a standard theater in which to measure relative social sensitivity/insensitivity to the individual's idiosyncratic needs on teams, companies, and public organizations. Overall, we've become very accommodating to them in the top cities. The hospitality industry led our change of attitude in this area out of a capitalist desire to maximize client satisfaction. It's one of America's better case studies in capitalist-driven inclusion.

These hard-to-challenge food aversion preferences become a grassroots test of tolerating lifestyle fragmentation more generally. Perhaps, food sensitivities are the most basic test there is. If you can't accommodate a dairy-free person in your group event, will you do much better with more charged inclusion efforts?

Food sensitivities and medical food allergies are very different scientifically and usually very different regarding symptomology. But humans interpret bodily signals through cultural filters, whether folk or professional. Cultural rules for interpretation, and the social groups that spread them, teach us how to prioritize the social declaration of our bodily issues. We do *not* discuss every single signal hitting our brains. We prioritize which to conceal completely, which to reveal only to loved ones, and which to reveal to anyone.

America's dietary preferences have fragmented recently, partly because we are empowered more than ever to solve minor bodily inconveniences through dietary avoidance techniques, specialty grocery purchases, and by asking for dietary accommodations from groups.

Instead of resorting to supernatural explanations as Richard III appears to have done centuries ago, we find interfering demons in our food supply. Medical professionals are less prone to corroborate your lactose-intolerance narratives because it's a chemical reaction with your organs, not an immune response (which allergists are trained to diagnose). It's not your average primary care doctor's domain of expertise.

Yet, as a country, we have learned to take these issues seriously in a fairly rapid historical time frame. The fear of legal action in a situation of severe food allergic attack was a major trigger for this tolerance, yes, but it can't explain our tolerance of even the most aspirational, weight-loss focused gluten avoidance from January to March.

Perhaps our experience with food allergies and intolerances is a grassroots learning lab for inclusivity more broadly. Accommodating food sensitivities in a small group takes forethought, knowing people in your social world, planning to include them, and follow-through. It's a lot more work, sure, but in doing it, we honor the diversity in our social worlds. We show we are obligated to care for them. *And* we honor our individualistic impulses as a culture. Interesting that some of us are more willing to include the lactose-intolerant than our black colleagues.

Chapter Twenty

ASPIRATIONAL DIETS

It's not just food sensitivities that divide households and social groups today, requiring them to accommodate individuals or at least listen to their requests. Our interest in aspirational diets and *dieting* also disrupts our collective foodways, at least periodically. And some of these aspirational diets are mimetic reapplications of aversive diets of the food intolerant and medically allergic. Whole30. Keto. Paleo. Low-carb. Veganism. Dairy-free. Low-Fodmap. The list of diets available to pick from has grown over the years. There are dozens of dietary tribes you can join today, most of which my grandmother never encountered.

I call them all aspirational diets. Not because we just talk about them and don't act. Not because only rare individuals can possibly sustain them. These diets are aspirational because we choose them autonomously without social compulsion or insistence by others, and we do it to achieve some *improvement*—personal, social, or environmental.

As a common cultural practice of self-improvement, aspirational diets align with the American economic emphasis on never-ending growth and the fundamental cultural assumption that change is generally wise. We seek the next diet, like we seek the next way to grow our nest egg. Our products and services should become ever more convenient, our bank balances ever larger, and our personal foodways ever more refined. Our alimentary canal has become the site of capitalist energies that focus us ever more on our individual perspective. What better way to do this than get us to obsess over our individual *body*?

This ethos of dietary self-improvement is also an ethos of heightened self-control in a rapidly changing world. In fact, if you don't feel in control of your marriage, family, friends, or career, changing your diet can offer you an intense feeling of control multiple times a day.

Let's see what happens when we let this ethos of self-improvement enter our everyday foodways.

Food Preferences for *Moral* Advantage

The word "vegan" has a known, single point of origin in English. The word "vegan" is a neologism, combining letters from the front and back of the word *vegetarian*. A married California couple, Donald and Dorothy Watson, invented the word in the 1940s as they splintered off from the Vegetarian Society to promote a higher ethical standard of do-no-harm to animals.[1] Veganism in America began as a California thing.[2]

If you intend to eliminate animal cruelty, veganism is the logical endpoint (or Jainism). Protecting animals was also the original motivation for vegetarianism, but I guess "mere" vegetarians can't tolerate giving up milk, cheese, butter, and eggs. Giving up cheese in this country is hard without a solid biological motive (i.e., lactose intolerance and its GI consequences). We spray lactose-infused cheese on everything in this country. I'm surprised we don't have cheese-wrestling contests.

I don't need to convince most of you that, even today, vegan activists tend to be verbally militant. I get why they are. They are frustrated at the slow rate of dietary change in America. Strict veganism is increasing, but not at a rate that reeks of the Bolshevik revolution—ordinary vegan adults, though, range from mellow to militant.

Here's an anecdote of militant veganism in everyday life to ground the discussion. A colleague of mine once went on a corporate research trip to the East Coast in 2004 with a vegan colleague. They arrived late at their hotel, but the second team member was starving. She insisted they go to the restaurant despite it being 10:00 p.m. He accompanied her to be polite and to get a drink.

It was closed. So, she moved them to the bar, which was still serving food. She looked at the bar menu, but it was the usual chain hotel fare at the time (pizza, nuts, chicken tenders)—food for eight-year-olds.

"I need a damn veggie burger!" she yelled at the bartender, who apparently didn't take the hostility well. Nor did I imagine he gave a sh*t about her aspirational diet back in 2003. There was no veggie burger to be had for our hero. And an adult tantrum ensued (allegedly).

When the extreme rarity of your particular lifestyle orientation inspires routine rage at the majority for not accommodating you, you are indeed a *militant*. If you're losing your sh*t in public because your lifestyle *choices* are not being accommodated, you probably need professional help.

Veganism has been around for seventy years as an active lobbying and educational community. Yet, vegan meat alternatives have yet to make a dent in the animal meat marketplace.[3] Americans aren't that into acting on the animal cruelty message and do not respond to it as vegans would hope. I see no way for this to change easily. This is because, in part, we don't care about American livestock like we care about our pets. Pets have created a very high standard that is unrealistic for other animals.

So, personal health improvement remains veganism's dominant motive, driver, and sustainer.[4] We will even consume an alternative food that tastes awful to obtain a healthy outcome. The more personal the outcome, the more personal the sacrifice we will make.

Look no further than the dramatic rise of soy and almond milk, which taste just plain horrendous without flavoring. I doubt your dog would drink either. The driver behind the rise of almond milk was not veganism; it was a) lactose intolerance and b) weight management. Original almond milk has 60 calories versus 100 calories for the dominant milk varietal—low fat. Whole milk has 150 calories.[5] This is a no-brainer for those on a temporary weight loss plan. Milk alternatives are much easier to fit into our diets for health reasons than fake meat (which is very hard to disguise and make palatable).

When cultural rebels, like vegans, persist for decades with an opposing practice or ideology despite having little effect on the majority surrounding them, the primary motive is usually . . . *morality*.

The desire to seek moral advantage through lifestyle choices (i.e., veganism) often originates as an unconscious desire for some elite cultural capital. It is a cry for legitimate social status in a world where social status is often unstable, uncertain, or shifting as frequently as every new job. It can also be simply a dramatic desire for control over something. A performance of moral elitism confers a feeling of control in a world where it is often taken away from you. Social scientists like myself have seen this phenomenon in conversion to morally elitist religious movements across the centuries. There is a powerful emotional comfort and invigoration that accompanies extreme moral beliefs.

When we persist in these extreme, modern dietary alterations, our moral commitment is tested immediately. The strange looks and remarks will start right away. Veganism is a very extreme diet to pick when you live in the United States. Eating meat three times a day is very common. Dairy all day long is even more common. Eggs for breakfast are also common. And we love butter on toast, bagels, and dinner rolls.

So, *who* will likely do something so peculiar as to become vegan? Who has the kind of status ambiguity or lack of perceived control to make any extreme, defiant lifestyle choice attractive?

Well, 55 percent of vegans are under the age of thirty-five! Most are female. And the majority became vegan before the age of twenty-four.[6] These facts align nicely with something called *college*, that time when young adults break from their parents' cooking patterns and many other beliefs and values associated with their parents. When you are single, you live alone, or with just one other roommate, it's hard for anyone to contain or surround your vegan dietary lifestyle with carnivorous excess. There is no bonded group with which you wish to share food, no tradition to offend with your veganism. At the dining hall, your veganism is your private business as you pick and choose autonomously from trays.

The class privilege of obtaining a college education is one condition of possibility for extreme dietary behavior; it permits a total dietary break with little accountability to surrounding norms (even in the college town itself). The American college campus has also become a social laboratory for identity explorations of all kinds. Decades ago, this was when LBGTQ adults could finally explore their sexuality. Today, it's when you can become vegan even though your father is an award-winning North Carolina pitmaster. Your secret is safe with me.

Our broader dieting culture has overtaken and co-opted veganism for its ability to reduce calorie intake dramatically in short-term dieting efforts.

Dieting culture is relentless, backed by billions in annual marketing spending that starts up right after New Year's. Dieting remains the most mainstream cultural theater of self-improvement and self-control. It is cultural theater in which we focus entirely on our body's individual issues. We literally navel gaze. It's important that we understand the power of dieting to focus us repeatedly on our individual food intake *divorced from any consideration of community norms.*

Dieting as Self-Critique

Sixty percent of Americans have dieted at least once in their lifetimes.[7] Fifty-one percent have followed a diet at some point in the past year.[8] The closeness of those two numbers suggests a lot of failures and repeat attempts. And if you interview people about dieting, which I have done hundreds of times, you'll discover women who have made dozens and dozens of attempts to lose weight and keep it off.

The top two reported motivations for dieting in America are: protecting long-term health (35 percent) and losing weight (34 percent). Since weight loss directly influences many Americans' desire for longevity, these two are hard to clearly separate.

If you spend as much time as I once did interviewing adults about their foodways and doing pantry tours of everything in their kitchen, you'll notice that most dietary alterations unrelated to food sensitivities tie back to weight loss—especially in a nation that is very aware it is gaining weight or gaining it back.

Almost all dieting ties back to an American obsession with controlling body composition more than our weight per se. Tracking weight is a mathematically easy proxy for some imagined body image we never had or want to return to. We attempt to eat our way to some aspirational body type. It could be the fit Marvel superhero body. Or the lean runway model body. Or the voluptuous beach body. Or even the Dad bod.

It's not just young people in the long American mating season who aspire to some other body. It could be almost anyone below the age of, say, eighty. And when we aspirationally alter our diet, we drift off easily into fantasy.

Then come the fantasies related to our bodies. The fantasy of not aging. The fantasy of attracting attention in public. The fantasy of re-attracting one's spouse. The fantasy of perceiving yourself as more powerful by physically displaying your elite level of self-control. I don't want to imply that body image fantasy is inherently wrong. Still, it is a dangerous imaginative activity in a leisure society (i.e., with too much time for fantasizing).

The more successful intervention programs for the morbidly obese focus on getting people to *stop* fantasizing. Professionals make these folks set incremental, realistic goals. If you're 350 pounds, lose 25 and keep it off. Then lose another 25. And so on. Medically managed weight loss is not about helping you look like you did on prom night. That's fantasy, not professional advice.

The critical thing to understand with most aspirational diets is that they begin with our dissatisfaction with *ourselves*. Sadly, most adults on a diet do not involve *any* professionals in their attempts, let alone submit themselves to group accountability. Instead, we tend to diet alone in a lonely quest for some other body. Individualism makes our body composition our personal problem just as it makes the solution—dieting—our problem to manage. Americans foster a bizarrely *private* approach to weight loss especially. I say "bizarre" because our food system epitomizes a massive, complex social web of production and influence. Why would we ever think we could battle this *alone*?

We *learn* dissatisfaction with our body composition. It does not arise spontaneously, like an allergic reaction to a food ingredient. The judgmental audience is one we encounter beyond ourselves and our family out in the social world.

This sets up dieting to fail from the start. How? It puts us in an unconscious argument between a defiant, private self that gives the middle finger to conformist social norms such as idealized bodies while goading us constantly with greater attention and social acceptance if we just cave in and conform. I think some of us want the diet to fail as an act of defiance.

A recent analysis of clinical research of over 29,000 adult dieters has shown something truly depressing. It's the most extensive review of dieting efficacy I've ever seen. Most of the top adult diets in the United States don't help you lose weight on your own. And even the two that do (Jenny Craig and Atkins) cannot sustain weight loss for more than twelve months.[9] This is good business for Jenny Craig because all they have to do is recruit you back next January.

My ethnographic research on weight management strategies over the years has revealed that the food ecosystem in the home, especially the habits of other adults not the slightest bit interested in your dieting, easily helps sabotage any long-term macronutrient dietary change effort.

If your husband inhales Lay's chips while you are doing your Jenny Craig meals, it's only a matter of time before your hand slips into the yellow bag again when no one is looking.

"Trying to do this in this house when everyone else is eating all this crap is driving me nuts," one Baby Boomer mom said to me years ago in her home. Not only was the food she was trying to avoid in the home pantry, but she also had to go and shop for it to please her family members.

Asking anyone to sustain highly divergent dietary modifications (e.g., low-carb) in a home overflowing with antithetical foods or beverages is like asking an Oxycodone addict to pursue their recovery quietly inside a drug den. Why would we ever think this could work? Oh, right. Our cultural Hail Mary—willpower.

What the enormous dieting industrial complex has distracted most of us from is the fact that a) how we buy our food, b) what we keep buying, and c) and how we eat *all* need to change in a communal setting if adults want to maintain a healthy weight (below BMI of 30).

What am I talking about? I simply mean that you can't tweak one or two things about your diet in social isolation and expect to sustain weight loss. The science is clear now on what some Baby Boomer women (and men) have already learned from experience.

American women who live in Europe for more than three months often lose weight without trying anything consciously. And then they gain it back (and more) upon return to the United States. The lack of adult snacking behavior is a key component of this, primarily the random leisure snacking and emotional eating that define so much of America's problem with food.[10] Your courteous cross-cultural concierge, the American in Paris Stephen Heiner, lays out the behavioral causes of sudden weight loss in France pretty well:

- No snacking
- Lots of walking every day
- Less processed food
- Small portions of fresh food (higher satiety, less overstuffing)[11]

The challenge for Americans is that fighting our food culture by yourself inside a home with other people who aren't fighting American food culture is simply a naïve gesture.

Even Jenny Craig, which admirably uses calorie restriction instead of culinary punishment, isn't sustainable because you will get bored of the food and drift beyond the box eventually, probably to a restaurant with those Cheesecake Factory portion sizes.

Optimizing the Self Through Elimination

I spend above-average time on LinkedIn every week because it is my consulting business's primary PR/marketing channel. My LinkedIn feed skews heavily toward founders, entrepreneurs, I-bankers, and those who do work insane hours.

Proclaiming one's commitment to sobriety has become a major genre within LinkedIn posts. Yet, almost none of these white-collar professionals mention being alcoholic or suffering from any kind of alcohol dependency.

Here is a nicely written sober boast that just popped up while I'm writing this book:

> As a Software Security Assessor . . . I must be sharp and highly focused. This means being able to read, process, and critically analyze lots of information. I felt that alcohol hindered my performance and slowed me down. Therefore, I prioritized my mental and physical

health by being mindful of the impact of alcohol on my work and overall well-being. Quitting drinking wasn't easy for me; there were many moments of temptation and doubt, especially when surrounded by friends, family, and at events.

But I kept reminding myself of the benefits of sobriety—the newfound clarity, focus, and energy that I experienced. And let's not forget about sleep—I sleep so much better these days. Overall, it made me feel like I was present in the moment and could hear everything.[12]

This is pretty representative of the LinkedIn content I see on elective sobriety. The outcome these ambitious folks seek is not a release from the personal hell of alcoholism. None of the people I see posting about their newly adopted sobriety confess any alcohol use disorder at all, nor could have ever done their jobs easily as an alcoholic either. Very unlikely.

No. These are upper-middle-class professionals and entrepreneurs intent on *higher performance standards* for themselves. It's pretty clear how alcohol might interfere with management-heavy careers that are socially and cognitively taxing. If for no other reason than alcohol will prevent you from doing productive work after 5:00 or 6:00 p.m. (i.e., after the second drink). The evenings are critical catch-up times for all hard-charging elite professionals and entrepreneurs. These folks work right up through 10:00 p.m. or midnight. And they get up early. Being insomniac and completely sober would be a massive competitive advantage for an entrepreneur.

The elite practitioners of what Derek Thompson terms "workism" appear to be the ones most attracted to voluntary, aspirational sobriety.[13] And to any performance-oriented dietary alteration.

Managing one's dietary intake to maximize productivity and energy has mainstream precedents in the lives of tens of millions of knowledge workers. For years, the dutiful, ambitious office worker has been focused on "light lunches" to prevent productivity-sabotaging food comas afterward. The ultimate productivity lunch remains a salad, offering high satiety for a low-calorie count that defends against impulse snacking later.

The privileged sober-curious keep ratcheting up the behavioral standard to remain at the top.

Looking at the ever more fragmenting American diet, it's critical to acknowledge it as a major daily site for enacting personal autonomy or maximum individualism. Is it possible that all this aspirational dieting simply stems from an urge to control our futures in a fast-changing world where so much about the near future, even beyond standard technology, remains uncertain? After all, food intake is one of the most primal aspects of human existence we get to control as individual beings.

Chapter Twenty-One

POTLUCK AMERICA

I've already pointed out that Americans, especially older Americans, do not socialize as much as they used to. Nevertheless, half of all Americans invite guests over at least monthly; a quarter do it weekly or more.[1] I strongly suspect the latter group skews toward households with strong, local family ties. This indeed came up in my life history research. It may even skew toward specific ethnic subcultures where family remains such a vital priority that people are reticent to move away from them during their Rumspringa years (e.g., Mexican Americans, Italian Americans, the Boston Irish, southern black folk).

As food sensitivities have spread into virtually all family social networks, and dozens of aspirational diets have taken off in the past quarter century, the odds are decent that if you invite five to ten guests to your home, you will at least have one to two people who cannot (or refuse to) eat the more commonly served foods and ingredients at American parties (queso dip, guacamole, chips, pretzels, cured meats, cheese, cold cut sandwiches, diet soda, Gatorade, burgers, hot dogs, bagels with cream cheese, muffins/scones, mixed nuts, alcohol, etc.).

How current are you on all your friends' and family members' dietary regimens? Most likely, not really. Adults now go in and out of these alterations in one-to-three-month cycles pretty routinely. The fact that we cannot necessarily assume to know the *current* dietary profile of our closest friends (unless we live with them) is something we should step back and contemplate. Even with these so-called intimate relationships beyond our kitchen, *we must ask before every party where we will offer food.*

Again, this is a reality for virtually any middle-class person, from any ethnic background, who hosts an event with food at their home. Individualized food preferences and our desire to cater to them to make guests comfortable have contributed to a growing shift toward potluck events, even at home.

Hyper-individualization of our food preferences, even temporarily, makes a fixed menu dinner party increasingly burdensome to stage. Even two weirdo guests (e.g., a vegan and a gluten-free) would triple the entrée burden of a dinner party event at your home. Find new friends?

And thus, we have adapted.

A Brief History of the Potluck Meal

The word "potluck" dates back to what seems like a sarcastic sixteenth-century English joke. It originally referred to taking whatever was "in the pot" when you knocked on a home's door for a traveler's meal.[2] The nineteenth- and early twentieth-century American tradition of feeding hobos loosely fits into this old tradition.

The modern "potluck" group meal ritual is much less ad hoc. It began during the Depression to distribute the cost of dinner parties:

> *One thing the depression has taught us, if we have learned nothing else from it is that we don't have to have the "fads and frills" to enjoy life. Back in the heyday, when money came free and easily entertaining was carried on in as elaborate a fashion as possible and simplicity was more or less frowned upon. Now the tables have been turned and hostesses are devising new and novel ideas for parties which can be staged as simply and inexpensively as possible.*
>
> *One of the best suggestions for a "depression" party is a "pot luck" dinner . . . the idea . . . is to have each guest contribute to some part of the meal. For instance, one hostess recently had six couples to such a dinner, the main course of which was beef stew. . . . Several went together in helping to prepare and also to pay for the stew and the rest joined in contributing other parts of the feast.[3]*

I imagine that dishes (or ingredients) brought to these 1930s events were simply oriented to regional and ethnic food traditions and served to narrow, mono-ethnic groups of guests. Americans back then tended to socialize in tight-knit worlds of ethnic affiliation (because that's how neighborhoods formed). Most Depression potlucks, therefore, would not have featured much *diversity of food desire*. The food was an excuse to be together.

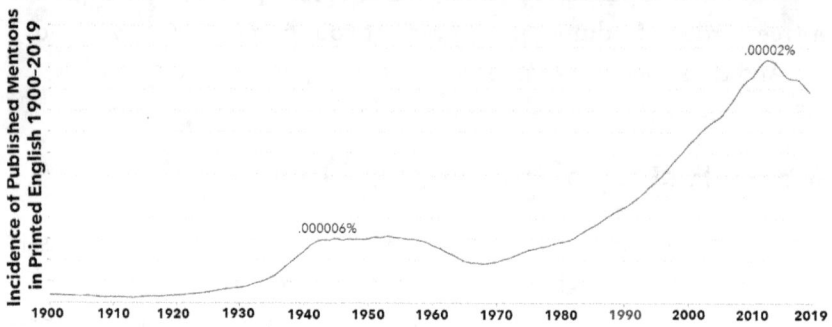

Figure 10. Rise of the Word "Potluck" in Printed English. Table data sourced from Google's Ngram service.[4]

And for many potlucks today, the point is also *not* the food or drink. They often occur at public events run by clubs or associations to reduce catering costs for the host organization. The broader event is the focus, and food functions simply like a gift. Potluck formats avoid the nightmare of trying to accommodate the dietary preferences of eighty-five people.

But potlucks are also more common now at private home parties. Asking guests to bring any more than wine or flowers to a dinner party when I was growing up just did not happen. And a "potluck" at home would have been too informal in New England, at least. You might be asked to bring a side dish to a summer yard party or barbecue. But not that often.

What's fascinating is that most of us do not go to that many potlucks annually—perhaps one to two times a year as a cultural practice. Exceptions include those working in larger bureaucratic workplaces, such as nursing wards, where life events happen regularly (e.g., baby showers, birthdays, holiday parties, etc.). For most of us, potlucks are almost as *infrequent* as the infamous cooking day of the year—Thanksgiving—in which our collective inability to cook for multiple people reveals itself annually. This relative infrequency to potlucking would best explain why there is a continual stream of "how to" potluck pieces in the internet media. In fact, Google trends data on "what to bring to potluck" and "potluck" have steadily increased over the last twenty years as newer potluckers familiarize themselves with a ritual that spikes the most for the December holidays and again around the Fourth of July.[5]

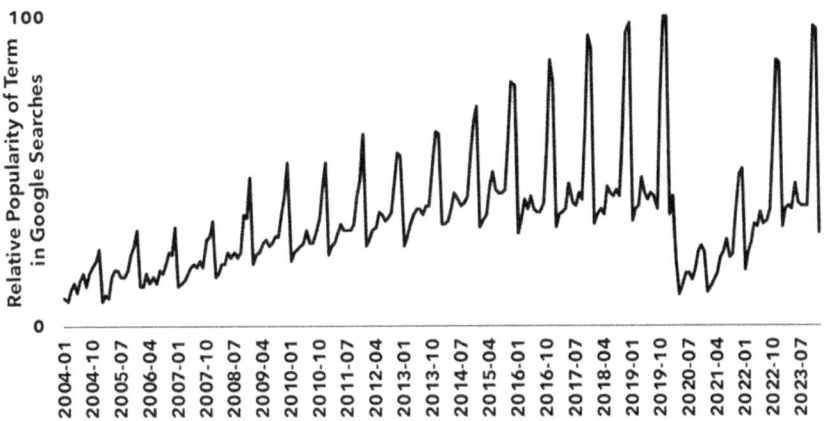

Figure 11. The Persistence of Potluck Etiquette Confusion. Data sourced from Google Trends, an online service.[6]

Potluck Etiquette—Don't Burden the Host

Home parties *and* scratch cooking are rare events (only 6 percent of American meals are for friends).[7] We simply don't do this very much. We are collectively out of practice, especially when we no longer even cook fresh meals every night for dinner. So, distributing the labor of episodic party cooking is a great cultural innovation. Yet, it can easily clash with the rising desire to avoid this or that ingredient in our diet (regardless of our guest status). One best practice is to make the allergic or dietarily weird folks bring their own thing to eat (plus enough for ten). In some cases, it can literally turn into a table full of carried in food.

When I looked at a smattering of early twenty-first-century potluck guidance articles, I came across multiple warnings to the effect of: "Label your dish so people know what it is and what's in it."[8] The host today doesn't even have to have a conversation with you about what is what when you arrive with your side dish. They just function like a catering manager arranging bowls and pans in a logical sequence on counters or tables.

Hosting home parties today, when we increasingly have such fragmented preferences within our social networks is a challenge fit only for catering companies. Potlucks allow us to avoid burdening hosts with the bother of cooking in this context. *The host is no longer obligated to make anything at all.* They too can run out to the Whole Foods and buy five rotisserie chickens if they want. How graciously we accommodate the informal, potluck party format in someone's home reflects how much we recognize the *host's cultural right* not *to cook for us.* I would argue that this empathic winking is strongest among the white, upper middle class, who also form the heaviest shoppers at Whole Foods Market. We seem most likely to not want to cause the host a fuss.

After almost three years in India, I believe this desire to "save the host from kitchen labor" would be anathema there. For one reason, catering is just not that expensive if you're a wealthy person who wants to check out of cooking. But the Indian solution to the tired "housewife" is to assemble *multiple* adult women in the kitchen to distribute the annoying labor of preparing food for twenty-plus people. I saw this for the first time at a local "coming of age" (i.e., first menses) party for a young girl in the local community where I lived. On my way to find the bathroom, I stumbled accidentally into a bustling galley kitchen with at least four women seated and standing in various positions, chopping and prepping ingredients for the common meal to come. They smiled, and the oldest woman continued to peel onions and laughed, "Here to help, Mr. James?" I smiled and made a quick exit!

Cooking everything for close family is one thing. We don't force them to potluck usually. But when a home party starts bringing in random work colleagues, extended family (e.g., in-laws), a smattering of "friends," the charming homeless guy off the street who can cite Robert Frost from memory, or even a "frenemy" from your past, then you are much more likely to invite everyone deliberately to a potluck. You will probably not cook everything for a party for six-plus nonfamily members who come to your home. If you have always cooked regardless of the size of the guest list, you are a saint. The rest of us mortals will distribute the cooking across our guests with, hopefully, an organized division of labor. Hopefully.

Why do we choose *potluck* meals when the guests extend beyond our closest circle of family and friends? Potluck dinners are less about saving the money of people who know each other really well, as it was during the Depression, and more about *saving on the host's labor in front of guests to whom we don't feel that socially obligated to in general*. Frankly, the folks who show up at these larger, "weak-tie" potlucks probably change every five to ten years anyway. Especially at work. Why kill yourself for transients in your social network?

But, there's another social change driving the outsourcing of barbecue and dinner party production to the guests. *Today's party host is* not *interested in missing the party by spending all his/her time in the kitchen cooking and assembling dishes*. If someone does this today, you can be assured they are choosing to do so (i.e., out of some foodie self-identification), not suffering under the constraints of a gendered division of labor. Women, the traditional "hosts," are tired, working, and want to socialize with their guests (whom they do not see that often in most cases). The older tradition of having female guests help you in the kitchen still occurs at some events, but *depending* on this labor is not in vogue. It's not always clear that you even want this help, if your network of friends are not any good in the kitchen. And, increasingly, kitchen incompetency is on the rise (refer these folks in advance to the prepared foods cases at Costco and Whole Foods).[9]

Remember, "fun" is about an emotional outcome, not relationships. This is why the party host insists on doing little work so they can have fun. Cooking for ten-plus people and cleaning up afterward is *not* fun—anywhere.

The host's individual autonomy is now paramount in potluck America.

Part Five

HOW FRIENDS BECAME ENTERTAINMENT DEVICES

"All my friends want to do is come over and get hammered."
—*a rich, Baby Boomer entrepreneur, 2018*

Chapter Twenty-Two

MY BIGGEST FAILURE IN INDIA

In graduate school, I read one of Tamil literature's classic works, *The Kural*, by one of its most revered poets, Tiruvalluvar. The book was a modern English translation of his classical Tamil aphorisms (from the first millennium AD).

I made it glibly and cheerfully to page one hundred, upon which I gulped at the following line:

There is nothing worse than rash friendships. For friends once made can't be abandoned.[1]

Can't be *abandoned*? What?! I've personally abandoned more friends than automobiles and bicycles combined! Americans discard friends like used clothing and furniture. Or worse, we let friendships decay, rot, and blow away in the wind by not trying to remain in touch. We easily *neglect* our friends. And everybody in our outer friendship circle seems to be on the verge of being "toxic" or "too much" or "annoying." Sometimes, we routinely hang out with people we don't even know or like that much as long as we're having *fun*. These are friends-as-props. We feel zero commitment to these people other than to show up routinely as a prop when they ask.

I read the rest of Tiruvalluvar's section on "choosing friends" that day and was stunned at every line. Why did I *want* to agree with him so much, even though his depiction of a culture where friendship "entraps" you with the wrong crowd was the Platonic opposite of what I've experienced living in the United States.

The short answer is that I agreed with Tamil culture's most famous poet because I was adopting a multilayered critique of American society based on my deep immersion and observations during fieldwork. I had started to see my American friendship habits from a *Tamil* perspective. And I wanted access to the kind of friendship I saw there.

In Tamil society, especially in its large towns and cities, friendship can get very intense. Male friendship is incredibly fierce. Adult friendships *often* last a lifetime and are seemingly much more accessible than in America today. For one thing, friendship is highly reciprocal. Friends routinely do inconvenient stuff for each other at the drop of a hat.

Here are some examples of things that friends do for each other in Tamil Nadu:[2]

- Need help finding jewelry? *I'll take you to my friend's shop directly.*
- Need a ride into town? *I'll take you.*
- Injured and in the hospital? *I'll come to hang out with you all day.*
- Need help moving? *I'll help find movers and lend a hand.*
- Need to move furniture around your house? *We'll come over whenever you need us and help.*
- Need to find a moving lorry today? *I know the guy who won't gouge you for being hasty. He's my cousin.*

Tamil men are known to hold hands as a sign of affection, not erotic interest, and lay arms around each other's shoulders as they sit on a wall together. And they respond quickly when a friend needs help. In most of urban India, friends are a crucial networking tool across lines of caste (and class) to obtain access to better healthcare or the best deal on a Samsung washing machine (in a country well known for highly variable, case-by-case customer pricing) or the "inside" price on jewelry for a wedding.

When I lived there, at least, India was still not set up for a genuinely impersonal, zero-contact everyday existence. You couldn't just throw rupees around and obtain everything you needed or wanted; you had to have the right network to get almost anything done properly with your rupees—or you would get taken or screwed. Piles of rupees just make things happen faster, but without a network of friends, you can't navigate a world where prices aren't fixed, and service availability and quality depend primarily on who you are or whom you know—i.e., not licensing and regulatory enforcement. Friends became indispensable in a developing economy full of uncertain, low trust transactions.

Tiruvalluvar's warning points out the inherent *weakness* of Tamil-style friendships (which are not exclusively found in Tamil Nadu, to be precise). Because Tamil friendship is highly transaction-built, it is not hard to force these relationships into existence simply by doing an initial favor for someone you barely know anything about. Oops. This is especially true for VIPs who need to be careful about from whom they *receive* any initial favors. Receiving obligates you to do something for the giver . . . eventually, unless you want to suffer reputational harm. *Tamil friends, once established, don't have the habit of politely refusing offers to reciprocate.* People kill friendships by not reciprocating, but this is dangerous behavior for your public reputation if you do it too often or flippantly. Refusing gifts of time or money from the unknown is a better strategy. The most common way to refuse the relationship is to *immediately* reciprocate and close off what is supposed to be an open-ended cycle.

Let me explain how I repeatedly screwed Tamil friendship up, so you can learn by contrast what we (especially men) no longer have access to in American urban life.

How I Was a Bad Tamil Friend

Indians tend to embed themselves in tight-knit neighborhoods over time, even in major cities. Entire extended families have proliferated residentially to accomplish this. Most Indian families prefer to live near relatives, even in the cities. People generally avoid being residentially isolated on some central identity axis (religion or caste) unless they are super elites living in neo-European apartment buildings in Mumbai (i.e., the Indian 1 percent whom I'm not discussing here). This allows lifelong friendships a much better chance of survival. Most Indians don't desire to move all over India for jobs.

In the Tamil community I lived in, your primary social identity as a male reveals itself in whom you hang out with in public spaces. One of those places is the roadside coffee stall. If you show up and some of your "friends" are sitting there, buying them a round of coffee or offering to do so is polite. They will generally say yes even if they don't want another cup because giving is so honored in Tamil culture that the receiver learns to submit (and the tumblers are only four ounces). Rounds at the coffee stall happen frequently because friendships are vital to thriving as an urban citizen in India. Having dozens and dozens of friends that extend your social influence is critical.

This kind of inexpensive public gift-giving gesture is not only a way to begin friendships but *also a way to sustain them*. Being stingy at the coffee stall is either a sign of poverty *or* aloofness and social nonalignment.

Because my dissertation research at the time involved bridging two communities that were not super aligned (Hindu and Christian, also divided by caste), I felt it was improper to be seen buying drinks for either group routinely. I worried it might generate tension. I voted for aloofness. I was mistaken.

But, let's be honest: I also *forgot* to do this. Bad social skills in America also transferred abroad.

The second way to screw up a Tamil friendship is to receive a *big* favor from someone you know *weakly* (referred to you by a closer friend) and then fail to do what the giver asks in return later. Yes, in Tamil reciprocity, the recipient gets to tell the giver what they want in return, whether a close friend or a mere acquaintance. And when they want it. And this is where Americans, unused to this kind of friendship reciprocity, get confused.

Let me share a story to explain. In 1998, I needed a place to live alone in the community I was researching near Madurai, India. I wanted to live alone because I knew I would be collecting sensitive private information about many residents and could not possibly secure this information in someone else's home. Privacy works differently in a Tamil home than among my WASP peers.

The problem with my "need" was that Tamils (in the 1990s) were suspicious of men who lived alone. One of my bachelor friends described the local stereotype to me like this, "You are either a pimp, a criminal, or both." Every respectable unmarried male remains living at home. Or they might live with respectable bachelors in an urban apartment. But not *alone*. So, no one wanted to rent to me. I asked a local extrovert friend in the community to vouch for me in person with the octogenarian owner of an old village house. It was the house the old man had grown up in during the 1920s. I sat in the "negotiation" with the old man, who openly admitted that his concern with foreigners was someone holding parties and the like. He didn't understand that *James sucks at parties*. After some hemming, hawing, and deferential promises from me, I was allowed to live there based on my Tamil friend's admittedly shallow knowledge of my character.

A year later, when I had to leave India temporarily for my brother's wedding, my friend got word of the trip. In public after church, he asked me if I could get a nice boom box in America for him when I was back there. I was taken aback. He had no intention of paying for this. *This* was his return favor. A gift he had the right to choose.

This seemed egregious to an American mind from New England WASP circles—to demand a *specific* gift. Even if I could fit a boom box in my luggage, it would cost as much as six months' rent or more in local currency. I couldn't understand why he would specify the exact gift he wanted. I awkwardly stood there and said, "OK, I'll try."

When I returned after my trip with a cheap souvenir for him, he got really, really mad and laid out the entire friendship cycle that I had dishonored. He didn't want to hear the excuse of "no room in the luggage" or "my parents wouldn't lend me the money to pay for it" or anything else. It was clear to him that his help finding me an apartment, against the owner's better judgment, wasn't worth much to me. And I see his point. Argh! Mistake number two.

The third way I messed up Tamil friendship was with my closest friend—a local shopkeeper in downtown Madurai. I needed to get my new motor scooter appropriately registered early on. Selvam was willing to be the registered owner (since this wasn't possible then for foreigners on research visas). I would be driving Selvam's scooter, and then, when

I left India, he would have a free vehicle for his daughter! Win. Win. He found someone he trusted to travel to the neighboring city where registrations occurred for my suburban postal code. I supplied the various fees, including payment for the "agent" to travel there, stay overnight and spend hours in an endless line (and offer some bribe money).

Then, I disappeared. I have no memory of why I got so busy. Before this, though, I would meet Selvam in his shop at least two nights a week just to hang out. This bonding time is crucial to Tamil friendships—it's how you earn the right to ask for any favors. But friendship is not a monetary transaction. You don't earn help with prior time spent and then spend it all down like a savings account. You must sustain the hang-out time after any big favor *as if the favor was incidental*. You can't just get busy and disappear and become self-involved. Not when someone goes to this much trouble.

"I feel like I got 100 percent used by you, James," he growled between cigarette puffs when I finally dropped by weeks later. He subjected me to a rant about my selfishness. Ouch. He was right. Tamil friends don't pull this sh*t. But Americans do, all the time.

Why Anglo-Saxons Get Confused by Tamil Friendship

I don't pick up on social cues very quickly. This was especially true when I was in my twenties and unaware of my neurology. But that wasn't my only handicap in being a good Tamil friend.

I also grew up in an upper-middle-class WASP New England subculture that approached friendship differently. *Not* asking for help from friends is a major ethical value. You don't bother people. Ever. Ever. Ever. You solve your own damn problems. And, because virtually any service provider in America obeys largely transparent pricing that doesn't fluctuate based on who you are, you can buy almost anything in America with a big enough pile of dollars *and zero social connection to the service provider*. As in reliable help from total strangers!

I realize that my ethnic handicap is not universally shared among Americans today. Still, it is widely shared by millions of older Americans, who skew white and northern European in their ethnic backgrounds. Many affluent white East Coasters my age and older will still go through a cycle of gently revealing a need for help they have after being probed (Hey, do you need help with the move?), then refuse the offered help so you, the "friend," are not bothered, then listen to the rebuttal and reissue of the offer, then refuse it again disingenuously, and finally relent if the friend tries the third time to offer help. It's as if we want to test how badly our friends are willing to help. I have no idea. But I've seen this behavior in my family and many others in the Boomer/Gen X age cohort. I believe it stems from older Americans' obsession with the sacredness of privacy so essential to our broader society.

Americans believe in some degree of reciprocity within friendship, because all human relationships are built on reciprocal exchange. The issue that confused me in Tamil Nadu is a different set of rules around reciprocity:

- Formal expectations of a return favor (at some point)
- Recipients get to specify the return favor (time and manner)
- Favors can and often will require loads of your time (you can't complain either)
- Recipients can refuse the gift immediately if they don't want to be in a relationship with you (this happened with one person I had previously upset)

Living in Tamil society, I learned that my approach to friendship in America was not really based on a strong obligation to reciprocate time-intensive favors at all, certainly not by letting a prior recipient specify the exact form of the return favor. That's almost a sibling relationship here in the West (or perhaps just the Anglo-Saxon West).

Most people in America's older, super white, generational cohorts don't want their friends to do anything out of *obligation*. We obsess with a Platonic ideal of a purely voluntary, intrinsically motivated friendship, much like we obsess about an intrinsic concept of romantic love driving a happy relationship. We desire a series of one-way gifts. But this is not how reciprocity operates in the majority of human cultures anthropologists have studied. It's an odd, lonely urban ethos we've created to maximize our own flexibility as autonomous actors. Americans favor generalized reciprocity, better known as "paying it forward." This approach cleverly frees us from the *obligation to reciprocate to the initial giver*. Phew! Obligation like that is such a pain.

Social scientists have long known that happiness stems largely from intense social bonds of mutual respect and reciprocal action.[3] Doing things for each other. Intrinsic feelings and personal motivations are irrelevant to these reciprocity cycles. You just do it. The value becomes quickly apparent when you just do things for each other. Doing creates the social bond and the emotional feelings.

Many older Americans I interviewed described their friendship activities as hanging out and having recreational fun. Few described loads of time-sucking favors for friends. Many also shared anecdotes of their parents engaging in more Tamil-style, friendships, of being open to doing things for each other out of respectful obligation. My father-in-law is a master at this. He grew up in rural Ohio in the 1950s. Mayberry. He's also eighty-one.

An approach to friendship as purely voluntary feeds off a desire by many Americans to be unencumbered individuals with maximal flexibility. On the other hand, if you have fifteen friends on call, one of whom might call abruptly and insist you hang out with their lonely kid in the hospital or hang out with them in the autobody shop while they wait, you don't have as much autonomy anymore. There is less time to binge Netflix or write the not-so-great American novel.

In India, you can't overschedule yourself like the 1 percent and just keep saying, "Sorry, not available." If you do this, you'll have very few friends and become completely dependent on rupees galore.

Chapter Twenty-Three

FRIENDS AS ENTERTAINMENT

A lot of what Tamil friends do for each other gets done today with spouses and romantic partners in the United States. All those tedious out-of-home and in-home irregular tasks that go beyond household chores—getting cars fixed, buying vehicles, buying homes, standing in lines at the DMV, navigating government agencies, checking out new apartments and visiting doctors' offices. Hanging out in the hospital with the injured. And, of course, handling emotional and interpersonal problems and life challenges.

We all have problems in life. No "culture" has rendered moot the key Theravada Buddhist talking point—the inevitability of human suffering, disappointment, and grief. But we seek ad hoc solace and companionship less with our friends than in other cultures. Most of us just don't see the fishbowl we are swimming in.

- *Fifty-three percent* of American adults in one recent survey say *they rely first on their spouse/partner when they have personal problems* (the kind you don't readily admit at the office). *Only 16 percent say they go first to any friend.*
- *Thirty-one percent* of American adults say they *do not even have a best friend* (a role idealized in depictions of American childhood and adolescence for decades now).[1]
- *Twelve percent* of American adults today say they have *no friends at all!*

- The weighted, self-reported average number of "close friends" for American adults was much higher in 1990 than today: 6.4 "close friends" in 1990 versus *only 4.3 close friends in 2021*.[2]

That is a dramatic 33 percent reduction in the average number of close friends we claim to have. And during the same thirty-year period, our friendship circles have contracted to fewer close friends. Sixty-three percent have one to five close friends today versus 52 percent in 1990.[3]

When I asked older Americans (now aged forty-seven to seventy-six) in my 2022 national survey if they felt they had fewer friends than their parents did at their ages, 42 percent, almost half of them, said they agreed or strongly agreed.[4] *This is a shocking historical confession.*

During my life history interviews, I heard echoes of a dying mode of friendship from a long-gone world. In this prior era, before the 1960s, we interacted far less with impersonal bureaucracies to get things done, and we didn't outsource virtually everything (cleaning, tax prep, renovation, appliance fixes) to professionals. I'm talking about behaviors most friendship researchers don't even focus on—*instrumental help getting things done in real life.*

Through their children's memories, America's real elders (now eighty-five-plus) relayed all manner of friendship exchanges of time, labor, and love:

- Helping each other out with yard work
- Watching each other's pets or children
- Making meals for friends whose primary cook is sick (not dying, just ill)
- Working on each other's home remodeling and fix-it projects
- Working on each other's cars and motorcycles
- Hanging out for hours at a time, impromptu
- Showing up ad hoc and not being told to return with a scheduled arrival time (yes, this used to happen, folks. Sorry).

If the list above sounds like the *Andy Griffith Show*, that's because the show was based on actual behavior patterns told through fictional incidents. Writers don't make up this stuff in a social vacuum.

Robin Dunbar's work on friendship has indicated that our de facto, active social networks tap out at around one hundred fifty persons (people with whom we communicate voluntarily every year at least). These networks mix family, friends, and acquaintances along a high-to-low continuum of obligation and intimacy. The fewer family ties we have, the more we rely on friendship networks (but always within this upper limit, which he claims is biologically grounded to some degree) to meet our social needs.[5]

There is disturbing evidence that suggests more friends are indeed better than fewer:

- "The more friends we have, the less likely we are to fall prey to diseases, and the longer we will live."[6]
- Adults with ten-plus close friends are 75 percent more likely to be very or completely satisfied with their friendship network. Only 56 percent of adults with an average number of close friends (4.3) can say this.[7]

Were the whispers of intense friendships from the first half of the twentieth century an initial adaptation to an early decline in family ties? What does it mean if we now have fewer friends and even weaker family ties?

And where is this all headed?

Let's define the history of our key term first.

A Brief Social History of the Word "Friend"

The English word "friend" originated to demarcate adult allies beyond your family and household. Here's how the great *Oxford English Dictionary* tackles a definition:

> *A person with whom one has developed a close and informal relationship of mutual trust and intimacy; (more generally) a close*

acquaintance. Often with an adjective indicating the closeness of the relationship, as best, good, close, etc.[8]

In its earliest printed usage, in Beowulf, our Geats tribal hero uses it to refer to:

- Christ—Jesus as the ultimate friend (post-mortem)
- Leaders of an allied political group—a friend to all in the allied group
- The relationship of a tribal leader to his people—"friend of the folk"

In other words, "friend" originally demarcated nonfamily "political allies and leaders" for the most part, primarily relations forged among leading tribal warriors in the late Viking period of northern Europe.

Humans view strangers first as potential threats in nonurbanized, preliterate societies like the Vikings or the Yanomami of early twentieth-century Brazil. They must quickly transform strangers into friends or attack. Keeping people in the "stranger" box indefinitely is something we only do in urban, complex civilizations, but not in close-knit, clan-based societies. It's much more black-and-white. Urban life today is so dependent on getting along with total strangers that our social skills have evolved to the challenge. Our society requires tolerance for many gray areas.

The social context of befriending strangers may differ today from the age of Beowulf. Still, the foundation is the same: strangers become socially intimate with each other due to repeated exposure and exchanges of social time, goods, or labor. There is some kind of sacrifice required to forge the bond. Modern Americans focus on exchanging social time, primarily.

What's fascinating is that we often modify the word "friend" to indicate the strength of the connection. Yet, we don't do this with kinship terms. We talk about our "BFF" but not our "best cousin" or our "best aunt for life." Maybe because many of us can't even remember our aunts' names? With friends, though, our language makes it clear we feel the need to rank them, however crudely, even if we might not admit this to any of our friends directly. *Hi there, weak-tie office acquaintance whose kids' names I still don't know. Wanna get a beer?* We rank friends because they connect us to the broad world of "strangers," a social space full of mistrust, doubt, and fear. All our friends were once strangers at some point. And they can lose that trusted status as well.

Like Beowulf and his warrior peers, Americans work "friendship" into being just as we work hard at dating (some of us) and using many of the same activities. Family, on the other hand, just happens to us. For Beowulf. For you. For us all. Because family relations are passively acquired (note syntax just used), an individualistic culture based on meritocratic achievement just can't stand "family" as a mechanism for resource acquisition, social mobility, etc. Family is anathema to an achievement-obsessed culture like ours. Leveraging family is cheating. *You cheated, you nepo-baby sh*t.*

We are so good at befriending strangers in our modern lives that we have forgotten how little we rely on family or close friends to get anything done. We do almost everything with the outside world by ourselves using impersonal, "professional" service providers, e-commerce sites, government offices, and retail stores. We drive around alone in our cars to get all this done. Every couple of years, we do the tough stuff (buying a car or home) with our spouses, lovers, or partners. But most of us don't feel obligated to, or often interested in, inviting our aunts or uncles to join these decisions. Maybe a best friend. Maybe.

In societies like India, friendship in urban areas skews to reciprocal exchanges of one's time and labor. The work of Indian male friends is not unlike that of Beowulf and his blade-wielding "friends." Friendship emerges in the reciprocal doing of things and forging critical urban alliances that facilitate all manner of social angling. Friends are constantly introducing each other to new friends and networks.

In the case of both 1990s India and eleventh-century northern Europe, though, the work of friendship was deemed necessary and obligatory. The things exchanged by friends are necessities, not luxuries. Not triflings. Not incidental goods or services. Friends help you get important things done (as I briefly explained in chapter twenty-two). Friends in these kinds of societies accompany you to all manner of conversations, negotiations, etc. They are also just more *emotionally* available, especially male friends.

Romance Conquers Friendship

Recent research on Western friendship supports my view that spouses in modern American society have largely overtaken these traditional benefits of close friends (or social allies). And this is especially true regarding intimate disclosure (i.e., private thoughts and struggles, life dilemmas, etc.). The powerful, dramatic stuff that fills screenplays.

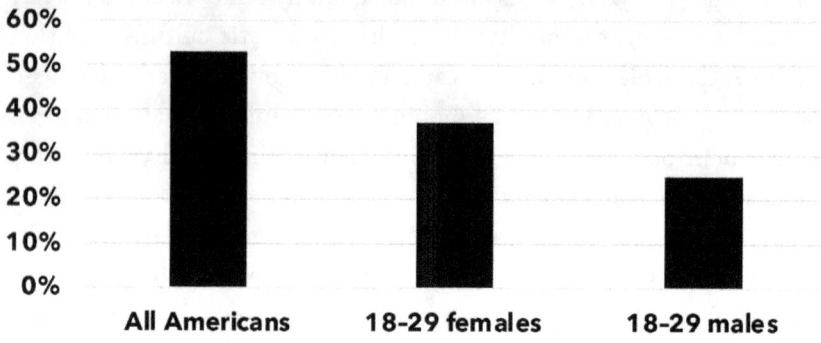

Figure 12. *Percent of Americans Who Go First to a Spouse or Partner with a Personal Problem. Data sourced from Daniel Cox, "The State of American Friendship," 2021, the American Enterprise Institute; chart by the author.*[9]

By inference, we can see from figure 12 that American *men*, especially, start transferring emotional support needs to their spouse or partner as they settle down, removing one of the most potent drivers of friendship in any complex society *not* solely composed of family-based social interactions (i.e., a hunter-gatherer tribe).[10]

The late twentieth-century erosion of family ties among older Americans has created a partial network void that only sexual partners and friends can fill. To the extent that a sexual partner gets viewed as the primary source of intimacy needs, contemporary Americans may tend to view friends more as providers of recreational benefits, *not emotional intimacy*.

As societies modernize and become technologically hypercompetent, it is possible that we strip away the complex needs we once had for intense and large friendship networks (i.e., in the early twentieth century). We remove the need for protection against violence, getting help acquiring and fixing things, and the need for emotional consolation beyond our marriages.

So, then, what are we left with to define modern friendship in America?

I call it friendship for entertainment.

Most of the time we spend face-to-face with friends today focuses on a very narrow range of fun-focused activities—going to shows, events, festivals, a summer barbecue, a holiday potluck, bar gatherings, and restaurant meetups for lively conversation. To have "fun." To laugh. To hear jokes and tell them. To gossip. We're so disconnected from these people that we often use these events "to catch up." If that phrase doesn't now strike you as weird, it should. Are they close friends if you must "catch up" on weeks or months of activities? Probably not. This was very clear in my life history interviews with older Americans. Friends are for fun times, whether the raging college party or the boisterous girlfriend dinner at the Olive Garden.

Indirect evidence for the increasing dominance of friends-as-entertainment is our documented aversion to hanging out with *depressed* friends. And the unconscious gravitation to people in our social network who are doing well and are happy.[11] Americans avoid friends who are depressed because it's contagious. Sad people bring us down. The subconscious attitude, "No one likes a downer," combined with our tendency to pull away from depressed friends is not a human universal in my research and experience. Not at all. It's a *white male, Stoic* reaction to depression. No wonder men like me have fewer friends than ever in recent social history. Women are much better at lending their time to listen and comfort their sad and wounded female friends, *but even they have arbitrarily set cultural limits.*

This strongly suggests that a "close friend" in twenty-first-century America is someone you want to be happy, positive, and cheerful, even when this is entirely unrealistic. And even when we recognize that this is an unfair expectation. We still want a smiley, well-adjusted friend at the Olive Garden. I have experienced this ridiculous problem myself before. Whenever I was most depressed, the more people would steer clear and the *more I felt I should stay alone and spare them (!).*

"I'm not up for going out tonight." The nights on which you say this are the nights your friends should kick down your door and throw you in the car. *Your depression doesn't deserve privacy in a healthy society. And this cajoling is much easier to pull off in a college dorm environment than in a suburb where we live behind soundproofed walls of private homes or apartments.*

By skewing toward entertaining ourselves with happy friends in good mental health, we behave exactly how we do when surfing TV channels. The top-viewed genres of video content are not strange, cynical Werner Herzog rants or soul-crushing tragedies like Cormac McCarthy's *The Road*. The top-viewed video content in America is fun and action-packed! It is *Fast and Furious X*, *Captain America*, *Goodfellas*, or *Dumb and Dumber*. We even mix comedy into a lot of our contemporary drama.

If something is too slow, depressing, or ponderous, we just click to find another show in seconds. We also do this with our friends *when they exist primarily for entertainment.*

If having fun is all you do with your "4.3" close friends, the relationship is also very fragile compared to the one with your spouse or best friend.

While some older Americans I spoke with define "close friends" or "good friends" as someone they have "fun with" *and* with whom they can discuss intimate issues, this really is an idealized definition. We meet them primarily for recreational activities or for entertaining conversations and stimulation.[12] I believe the emotional component of close friendship strengthens as Americans age partly because there is more disappointment and suffering to process. This need for additional solace is more true for older straight women because, frankly, their male partners, as an age cohort, are horrible communicators.

But most of our inner circle of friends (the 4.3) simply activates our recreational social life. This is all fine, but it is a shadowy vestige of a much older, more intense mode of human friendship.

Why Do Americans Have Fewer, More Selective Friends?

As with most social changes, it is not one variable causing shifts in collective behavior. But a contributing factor right in front of our eyes is the person we hold dearest.

The "friends" we feel most obligated to do annoying, time-consuming things for *are our spouses or long-term partners*.

I think the increasingly intense burden heterosexual men place on their female spouses is one reason why Dunbar's work (which skews to research done in the urban West) surfaces a problem in maintaining friendships over time. Many men, especially, have lost a social muscle (confiding in their friends). Many authors have written more eloquently than I about this tragic shift.[13]

The shrinking of friend networks and their desiccation into mostly friendship-as-entertainment goes beyond logistical issues. We have plenty of leisure time to meet our friends. Plenty. Our friends don't all live *that* far away. When seeking solace, they aren't hard to reach with multiple devices instantly.

Yet, Americans don't sacrifice much time for friends, even their close friends, other than an hour or two occasionally.[14] There is no obligation to make significant amounts of time available every week, even to our close friends. Let alone do this spur of the moment, within hours or minutes. Instead, most Americans schedule their friending like concert or theater attendances. Like they schedule any kind of "fun."

Here's a case from my life history interviews that lays bare the severe limits of help Americans can expect from even their closest friends. Tim lives in Connecticut with his ailing wife, who suffers from Alzheimer's. He is her full-time caretaker. His children have their own lives in New York. When his wife was lucid, they both used to hang out and do things with one of his wife's close friends, Sarah.

Once his wife became unaware and required full-time monitoring, the visits from her friend ended:

Our friend Sarah is like, "So, if you need anything, just call. I'll come and help you with it." What am I gonna do, Sarah, have you come here and sit here all day with her?

She's not out of it totally . . . she knows where she is. But if she needs something, she wants something to drink, you have to get it for her. TV turned up or down. They can't do anything for themselves. Now, she's starting to forget where she is in the house.

You need hours and hours and hours of help from people, or it's not f**king help. It's almost like a pain in the ass [to have someone come and visit].[15]

There was an era when the women in the neighborhood would not have let Tim take care of his ailing wife alone. Tim's father was from a generation that would have been discharged of that duty almost entirely by female kin. He would have had hours to himself, unlike Tim, who would spend his retirement as an exhausted caretaker to the shell of his former partner. While family used to intervene in situations like this, *friends do not*.

Taking care of Tim's wife for eight hours is not *fun*. Not the "fun" Sarah associates in her mind with memories of hanging out with her prior to the illness. That is the explanation for Sarah's absence that we all deny, because it's so obvious yet so incredibly shallow.

Dan Cox of the American Enterprise Institute recently shared some insightful drivers of the decline and weakening of American friendship:

- *Later marriages for Americans*—because, in my view, they are trying harder to marry a best friend (and this takes time to find for most of us)
- *More geographically mobile educated adults*—who lose touch with people
- *More time spent and invested into children* (especially among college or post-grad-educated parents)
- *More time spent commuting and traveling for professional jobs*
- *Decline of sources of potential friends after leaving school*—work is the number one source[16]

I would add to this list even more contributing factors:

- *More time every day watching passive video content*—because it's easier than coordinating a meetup.
- *Increasing reliance on our one best friend—our spouse* (even though this exposes us to huge risk if the spouse suddenly dies)
- *Noncommittal recreational worlds creating an unstable, not very efficient way to make friends* (limited hours per week)
- *Decreasing number of friends after childbirth*—Many new moms and dads start to lose friendships as they cocoon with their newborns. It takes a lot of work to fight past this tendency, especially when your "friends" don't have young kids or kids at all. They tend not to offer to help young parents out.
- *Increasingly easy to get "triggered" and dump friends for things like political views*—I see the latter behavior as egregious among my left-wing post-grad educated friends, who seem to curate their close friends like MOMA, unlike an average human with empathy.
- *Increasing fragmentation and political polarization*—incredibly intense among more educated Americans, has created more reasons not to get along with a stranger, a reason to keep them as acquaintances or weak ties
- *Retreating into the uppermost crown of the family tree*—As people age, they want to spend more time with grandkids and their adult children—with family. Sometimes they have no other choice either—such as those who are taking care of alcoholic children, spouses with dementia, or adult children with psychiatric troubles.

American society's support of extreme individual autonomy, its electronic financial systems, transparent pricing, and thoroughly impersonal consumer retail ecosystem mean that most adults can obtain 99 percent of their essential needs without real social networking. Without much human contact at all.

Our lifestyle in America rests mainly on invisible corporate networks based on impersonal trust. Leveraging high-trust friendships to get things done is almost totally unnecessary outside of sophisticated business or investment activities. No everyday socioeconomic transaction requires the help of a friend or even a family member. But more importantly, the more affluent we are, the less we prefer to "impose" on friends for anything (unless we are in college). My WASP peers have an especially bad case of NotImposingitis.

The last time I recall having many friends who did things for each other (reciprocal favors) was in college.

Tiruvalluvar was concerned about Tamil folks naively getting into Tamil friendships, full of reciprocal obligations, inconveniences, and reputational risk.

I'm sorry, but I'd much rather have a culture with that risk than what we have today: friends as entertainment—easily replaced or discarded years before we suddenly realize, *Oh sh*t, if my girlfriend dumps me, I'm alone.*

Chapter Twenty-Four

THE FAKE BUSINESS FRIEND

I've been in the business world for the last twenty years now, and one thing that consistently horrifies me is how one's social network, a thing of beauty that should grow gently and organically, has turned into a transitive verb that has led to horrifyingly inauthentic and just plain crass behavior.

Let's network! So excited to network at this conference! Pumped to make more connections!

The obsession with LinkedIn followers among some white-collar professionals is borderline perverse.

What a disaster this networking thing has become:

- Shoving cards in people's hands
- Unsolicited LinkedIn connection requests
- "Can I scan your badge?" at trade shows (and then spam them with cold sales e-mails)
- Forced conversational move-ins at live conferences
- Aggressively extended hands
- "Bro circles" denying entrance; sis huddles, mocking the bros
- Unsolicited DMs from people wanting to *partner*. I get these almost monthly now. I know people who get them daily. I can't even imagine.

I've been following you and love your posts, man. Do you have time to discuss my latest (purely conceptual) venture (with no funding)? I think you'd be a great partner . . . would love to see if there's a fit . . .

What?

As they say on *Shark Tank*, "I'm out" as soon I get a partner pitch in a message *from someone I know nothing about besides their LinkedIn profile content.*

I'm not here to defame cold-calling or cold-DMing. There's an audience totally prepared to receive these messages in the business world. When I allude to the crass forcing of partnerships or relationships in business, I'm talking about *feigning friendliness to initiate a rapid, transactional business arrangement, almost always weighted in the aggressor's favor.*

How Individualism Promotes Fake Business Friendships

In the parlance of Robin Dunbar, business (or work) contacts generally occupy the outer rung of the one hundred fifty or so folks we interact with each year. They epitomize weak ties, except perhaps for our immediate boss. But they can be instrumental at just the right moment. Research has shown we're more likely to get job offers, introductions, or critical professional information through our weaker social ties (i.e., not our close friends).[1]

There is a growing cultural tendency to inflate one's network of weak ties to gain some notion of commercial or career advantage. This is known as boosting your follower count or connections. LinkedIn even has hundreds of self-appointed "LinkedIn coaches" you can pay to help you grow your "personal brand" and follower count and otherwise be more impressive than the dolt you report to who has worked for thirty years and only has 134 connections. Hah! He doesn't even *have* a profile picture. *Loser.*

Boosting network size is an admittedly shallow form of curating one's social world, highly adapted to a meritocratic mode of individualism that epitomizes white-collar America.

The primary way that I've seen these fake friendships start is by using the language and tone of *old buddies* (i.e., close friends) to shove in a bridge of interpersonal trust where none existed.

- "Hey, man, has it really been a whole year since this conference?"
- "So great to see you. I've been thinking about your LinkedIn posts."
- "How's Tucson? Family doing well? . . ."
- The easy laughter at even the mildest of jokes.
- The moral imperative is to smile, agree, and froth in a standing huddle of amiability.

Getting all intimate and chummy very quickly is a known sales tactic that sales pros use to build an artificial empathy bridge and nudge people over the line of indecision. I have even done this by looking up some personal details I have in common with a client and highlighting those early in our first conversation. We do this because it *works* in a society where we spend most of our days *not* interacting with people face-to-face. We quickly get flattered by personalized face-to-face attention. Very easily.

As actual reciprocal friendships have declined in America, a highly diluted, self-interested favor cycle has reappeared farther out in our social networks in the zone of weak ties (e.g., colleagues, clients, and prospects in the business world).

We do this to "maximize" opportunities. If you do enough light favors at the edge of your social network, you easily replace those who have become unuseful and maximize odds of someone thinking about you for some venture, project, consulting gig, etc.

Performing friendliness becomes a way to boost trust where it normally does not exist. Pretending there is more trust than there is in business has a critical downside: It trivializes the clock time it takes to make a new, close friend truly. It plays right into the hands of the con artist. What has resulted is a desiccated, zombielike form of favor-based pseudo-friendship that sets up partners for conflict and blowups.

This fake business friend performance has become a hidden epidemic in American business. I see start-up founders desperate for cash engage in this performance with investors. And vice versa (which is just plain creepy). Broadband internet (and on-demand, single-serve coffee makers) have empowered us to seek our greatest possible internet opportunity through a much larger set of weak ties than most modern citizens have ever had. And it's vastly easier to pretend to be friendly in a quick LinkedIn direct message.

I have almost twelve thousand followers on LinkedIn right now, which apparently makes me a top 3 percent thought leader on the platform. Whatever. How many of these people have I ever met in real life? Maybe a thousand or so. Maybe. I can't put names on all those faces, however. The rest are simply digital followers. No idea who they are.

LinkedIn has probably accelerated the fake friend thing because it has made it way too easy to approach "skills" or "talent" or "resources" online with minimal actual social context available to either party (beyond that dubious profile). *Résumés were always partial, but LinkedIn résumés are quite comically edited (if you know the person well and see what they've concealed).*

Those who get approached quickly by a fake friend easily get themselves in trouble or waste wads of time talking to people who are often one or two steps from bankruptcy, being fired, losing their mind, etc. If we're honest about our business acquaintances, we have no context about these people. You have nothing but a highly edited CV on a networking site and that dubious "mutual connections" information. Think of how thin your evidence pile is about anyone approaching you on LinkedIn. Why do we even respond? Oh yeah, the upside, the FOMO around business opportunities.

Two Faux Friendship Scenarios and What They Reveal About America

The following are scenarios I know intimately enough to narrate. They occur every single business day in almost every sector of capitalism and predate the internet and LinkedIn. They take faux friendship to stratospheric heights of artistry and complete bullsh*t.

1. **Fake Friend Scenario #1—A service provider wooing a subcontracting partner or freelancer.** In this scenario, there is usually some middling service provider (e.g., a branding agency) that relies on contractors to do sh*t work their clients demand as part of the scope but that they hate doing (because it's labor intensive and profit dilutive) and don't want to staff internally. Their disrespect for this "lower-level" activity their clients routinely ask for is evident in outsourcing it. It would be an internal function if they respected either the work or their client's needs.

    For example, clients often force a branding agency full of creatives and fine arts grads to do customer research to "inform" their creative activities. Branding people hate these clients, but they tend to pay well. So, they find some starving graduate student in social science or an underemployed, weird market research person in the area to do the work for them at meager rates.

    When I left my old executive position at a market research company, I had two meetings with branding agencies that went exactly like this. I was looking for referrals in the wrong place. Oops. Neither of the agencies cared about my business or even asked about it. To them, I was just an unemployed research dipsh*t they were used to contracting. There should be a masterclass called Feigning Friendship to Take Advantage of Freelancers. An agency CEO (any of them will do) should teach it.

    In the first meeting, branding agency guys approached me at a conference with the fake friend shtick, looking for a research chump. But, once I smelled it, I immediately clarified my business services. Then I made some snide remark (deliberately) about the fools who would subcontract themselves to people: "They wonder why they can't pay their rent. LOL." Then I chuckled as *they most definitely did NOT laugh* since they now realized I wasn't going to play ball. And that I was wasting their time. Dominant people hate it when you waste their time. Fake friends get annoyed when they realize you can't be played. I said to another agency owner over the phone, "Oh, I don't subcontract to anyone or anything. Not even to God. I do my own sales, thanks." I never heard from them again. Not a peep. They're out of business now.

2. **Fake Friend Scenario #2—Helping *their* friend out by feigning friendship with *you!*** A business introduction is one of the most common theaters of the fake friend performance in modern business. I don't mean to imply total malevolence or outright fraud behind the millions and millions of "mutual intro" e-mails occurring yearly in American business. The motives are usually sincere enough. It's just that the tone taken by so many has become overtly *friend-ist*.

    Here's an example from my LinkedIn inbox:

yo, James—I just had a conversation last week with a startup that is looking to target the CPG space. I'd love to connect them with you—send me your email address, and I'll introduce you! Thanks—[The Dude]

    You have to admit that the tone there is *friendly*!
    What is absent from this *yo-friendly* outreach is any evidence that this former colleague of mine knows anything about what I'm doing. He hadn't looked at my services page, where I clarified that I don't work with companies under $5 million in sales.
    But, more importantly, I hadn't spoken to [The Dude] in about eight years, to be precise, when I got this e-mail. And I only worked in the same office for about nine months. That's about as weak a tie as you can get.
    But the real problem with these kinds of intros is that the weak-tie "intro" e-mails are amazingly lopsided, loudly

advocating for the needs of a third party with whom the author is friendly but failing to understand, let alone respect, the interests of the person (the fake friend) being pitched.

In both scenarios, there is a hierarchical relationship where one party is de-leveraged, and one party is deliberately in control. The dominant client's leverage is the ability to easily walk away from the service provider (in an ocean of similar companies) and move on to someone else. The more significant the scale gap between provider and client, the more this is the case, and the creepier fake friendship becomes. And the more efficiently the subordinate, financially exposed service provider being "befriended" will likely get into silly business relationships just for quick cash. Oh yes. The old colleague who tries to fake friend you into talking with his much closer business ally is also de-leveraged for the recipient. The fake friend knows both parties, but not you. However, it's easier to reject an "introduction" than a potential contract.

We need to accept that feigning friendship is simply a form of stranger love, of basic human empathy. FBI negotiators have raised this to a fine art form when working on hostage negotiations. Fake friendliness disarms the armed suspect through brute empathy. Feigning friendship in business pushes the listener closer to "yes" before they have time to contemplate what is happening and understand their new "friend's" hidden interests. Fake friending nudges you to commit to a call, read a background PowerPoint, and imagine how you could be helpful to your new Insta-Friend.

Friendship in America presumes that both parties see each other as peers and social equals. This is why friendship is an ideal platform for modern, non-patriarchal romance and, eventually, marriage. But in decidedly unequal, contract-based relationships, which many business relationships are, the idiom of friendship is a mildly sociopathic ruse American business culture has let into the building. Being this informally buddy-buddy while standing on steep inclines of power is completely inappropriate. It's dishonest. It also plays on our individual desire to have more close friends in our lives.

Are we so incredibly overcome by Max Weber's spirit of capitalism that we can no longer see the difference between a friend, a business partner, and a conniving sociopath? I'm not so sure we can anymore. I'm not sure it's all that funny, either.

If you'd like a more famous, inexcusable example of deploying fake friendship to get what you want, look no further than the ghastly individual known as Jeffrey Epstein (who I still insist looked exactly like Thanos).

The fact that Bill Gates met with this convicted sex offender *more than once* to discuss philanthropic donations is the perfect example of how capitalist relationship formation trumps any moral stigma.[2] Would Gates have met Epstein if he had *murdered* someone too? Where do we draw the line in business and in life?

Fake friendships work well for sociopaths because these conscienceless people thrive on dyadic relations with minimal background context. Why? They can fill in all that biographical "white space" about themselves very deftly. They are masterful liars, spin doctors, benders of fact into fiction, disguisers of exploitation as friendship.

Friendship in business should be a nice-to-have outcome of a formal business partnership, allowing trust to form normally over time as it does in a real human friendship between autonomous individuals.

In a work-first, careerist culture like ours, it should not surprise us how quickly we have twisted the idiom of close friendship into a manipulative networking performance.

Individualism's latest creation is the instant, unearned fake friendship designed to benefit the *performing individual*. The fake business friend makes the nineteenth-century etiquette manuals that taught immigrants and quick-to-anger farm boys how to interact with hordes of urban strangers look like simplistic kindergarten watercolor books by comparison.

Furthermore, it makes you doubt the medium of friendship itself, even when friendship is the primary access to community that modern individuals have in urban societies like ours.

Chapter Twenty-Five

SEXUAL PARTNERS AS BEST FRIENDS

AMC's Emmy-winning series, *Mad Men*, profoundly affected millions of educated women in the United States. I'm not just referring to Peggy's feminist career bravado in the face of overwhelmingly sexist dismissal at every turn. I'm also referring to how angry this show made many working women I knew by depicting in excruciating detail the treatment of wives as mere social objects, trophies, decorations, child-bearers, domestic servants, and picnic planners.

The *Mad Men* series begins during the cowboy days of American advertising—the 1950s—an era of strict gender roles, female subordination, and male double standards related to drinking, sexual infidelity, and, most revealingly, work ethic (i.e., men didn't need any).

In mid-century America, romantic marriage was the cultural norm as it still is today. But mid-century romance did not always mean husbands and wives saw themselves as equals. The romance was decidedly patriarchal for most couples. To be sure, some couples that formed in the Silent Generation were like my parents, based heavily on friendship and enjoying each other's company as cross-sex buddies. Other husbands, like Don Draper, came home late, ignored their children, let their wives manage the home as "her domain," and otherwise showed up when they wanted to or when family rituals demanded. Home for the patriarchal husband is simply a stage in which to perform "husband" or "Dad" for a few minutes before having a drink.

The Don Drapers of mid-century America represented the old,

condescending romantic marriage model. Romance was a short, chivalrous game where men socialized with women to pursue them as sexual partners. Once married, this male archetype then pursues other women to have affairs. Otherwise, he ignores women during his largely male-dominated day. The patriarchal husband mainly recreates with other men at male-only events or other social venues where couples might arrive together but mostly self-segregated quickly into gendered conversation bubbles. Wives are trophies and child-bearers, not fit for male conversation and company.

However, at the same time, in the 1950s and '60s, a very different model of marriage was already in motion. In this model, married couples formed more intense bonds of friendship before marriage and in the early years of their marriages. The ability for married couples to control pregnancy through female birth control by the late 1960s facilitated this new way of coupling to a considerable extent. Before widespread access to female birth control in the 1970s, there was minimal ability to prevent childbirth in the first year of any (healthy) marriage (other than men voluntarily wearing condoms properly). By the end of the 1960s, after the *Griswold v. Connecticut Supreme Court* decision permitted use of birth control among married couples, the pill provided a temporal runway for serious, intense, *childless* bonding through shared leisure time in the early years of a marriage. Even couples who married relatively quickly after meeting each other could form a strong couple identity *before having their first child* (unless their religious beliefs proscribed birth control).

Anthony Giddens is a sociologist who was early to point out the emergence of a new kind of marital relationship based on love (i.e., romance) *but without the binding qualities of traditional religious marriages in the West*. He calls it "confluent love" (because academics must invent jargon for individual career advancement).[1] In this modern permutation of romance, the sexual relationship must satisfy *both* individuals, requires much more work to sustain, and more easily dissolves once one partner loses interest (because one partner has no longer signed up implicitly to absorb unlimited disrespect or indifference from the other). The rapid spread of no-fault divorce laws in all fifty states in the 1970s helped "enforce" this new standard of mutual happiness. Your wife could now walk right out of the front door any time she wanted. I had an aunt who did precisely this in the late 1970s.

Without strict gender roles, religious beliefs proscribing divorce, or elite incomes and lifestyles as conserving forces in a marital relationship, Gidden's model explains why family sociologists see a much higher divorce rate among middle- and working-class Americans *than among the upper-middle class*. Women are now free to leave men who are economically incompetent or, more likely, draining limited family cash.[2] And there are many such men in America.

As American marriages have become more equitable and mutually voluntary, they have also become more fragile. Though the divorce rate recently appears stable, it is high if one assumes we have the autonomy to choose, wait, and pick the ideal partner for each of us. *Shouldn't we be able to pick better?* As we now know, multi-decade-long sexual relationships take on an internal life of their own that subjects them to greater fragility when anchored in a concept of mutual satisfaction. . . . And few external factors are *forcing* American couples to stay together. There is certainly no reputational risk to being divorced.

One of the most overlooked reasons for marital instability and marital conflict in America, beyond financial stress, is the excessive emotional reliance married partners have on each other. In the concise words of family sociologist Paul Amato and his colleagues, "Spouses [have become] more reliant on each other for companionship, assistance, and affection."[3]

This is a very high standard that is not easy to sustain. It may be the highest marital standard ever invented in the animal kingdom outside of birds.

Marrying Your Best Friend

When Harry Met Sally came out in theaters in 1989, when I was a junior in high school. This blockbuster movie struck a chord with Baby Boomer women who were growing tired of the cat-and-mouse romantic game in the 1980s, a game involving men *feigning* love to get laid and leaving women as the emotional casualties. Repeatedly. These were also the same male beneficiaries of the sexual revolution who feigned romance to get married and then reverted to the old patriarchal marital model. Dating was now also a societal game that meant nonstop overtures headed toward the most attractive women, *including from married men.*

Dumping your spouse now observes many of the same cultural rules as dumping your "former" best friend.

For those of you who have not seen it, *When Harry Met Sally* depicts two college graduates who argue intensely about the possibility of a platonic friendship between a man and a woman on a long car ride. Billy Crystal's character argues the traditional male viewpoint that this is impossible. Men only want to have sex with women (or eat their food); otherwise, they move on. This Don Draper perspective accurately describes the male-dominated world of Baby Boomers' parents and the mindset of many older Baby Boomer men. Crystal's character argues for what is an ancient male view of coupling (romantically triggered or not). Meg Ryan's character argues that women can form platonic friendships with men (even if this is not reciprocated).

Research in the early 1980s among undergraduates by Suzanna Rose confirmed why these characters couldn't agree:

> *Male participants often stated that their interest in cross-sex friendships was sexually motivated. Women reported their own motives for cross-sex friendships as being platonic but agreed with men that men's motives for establishing opposite-sex friendships were, for the most part, sexual. Women also frequently stated that their belief that men's motives were sexual made them mistrustful of male friendship overtures and unwilling to establish friendships with men.*[4]

However, Rose also discovered that women would seek out platonic friendships with higher-status men who could help them *access resources not readily available to women*. And as women entered the workplace, we would soon see how easily the latter motive could go sideways repeatedly as each gender seeks its conflicting objectives.

One older feminist viewpoint requires that heterosexual relationships start more slowly in the context of healthy mixed-gender activities . . . like the three days of witty car banter in *When Harry Met Sally*. One reason is to manage the threat of young male desire for *immediate* sexual gratification and bend it to the democratic ideals of romance. Meg Ryan's character, a Baby Boomer, also represents working adult women with enough income (and easy access to birth control) to cycle through "jerks" for as long as necessary to find an idealized love anchored in friendship.

Friendship. Romance. If the eighteenth century gave us modern romantic couplings (albeit for an affluent mercantile elite), then the late twentieth century gave us marrying your best friend and confidant.

What's fascinating about *When Harry Met Sally* is that their eventual sexual romance emerges after years of sporadic contact and intense conversation. If we run with the notion that it takes roughly two hundred hours or so to make a best friend,[5] then we can see that the new marital model is suited well to relationships that form when you are in school or otherwise structurally brought together again and again with a potential partner (including work).

Otherwise, it will take a very long time in today's world to accumulate those two hundred hours if you work full-time and don't date someone at work. At a likely rate of only two to four hours per week, that's almost fifty to one hundred weeks to gain a close friend. Sex doesn't add a lot of additional minutes per week, but it does cause people to spend the night. (Do unconscious pillow hours count, Professor Dunbar?) Not forever, but the amount of "hang time" to cement a friendship favors speeding things up with a long vacation together . . . except . . . by then . . . you're probably having sex. And now it's complicated. Really complicated.

Recreational Sex and Sexy Friendship

If sex no longer begins with marriage for most adults, sex will get initiated among couples early during a casual relationship, absent a firm ideological commitment otherwise.

Sex became a bona fide adult recreational activity by the late 1960s *and*, more importantly, sex independent of any *committed* relationship.

Hooking up. What this unleashed was a whole lot of sexual experimentation deep into the middle classes, experimentation that shocked the elders watching television commentary on "today's youth." As with most "revolutions," though, the sexual revolution had a well-promoted, sensationalized extreme phase, which doesn't bear itself out in the statistics or qualitative understanding of the broader population at the time. Woodstock and Playboy mansion orgies happened, but these did *not* represent the mass of American youth by any means.

As college attendance grew, millions of couples formed sexually intimate friendships through young adult activities in college and right afterward. Some had unintended pregnancies that shot them into married life ahead of "plan." I interviewed two of them randomly among twenty life history participants. Birth control was available widely by the early 1970s, but consistent, correct usage is another learning curve for society (!). Immature hookups flourished that led to sudden losses of autonomy (due to childbirth).

One consequence of detaching sex from marriage in this way was that it created the possibility of developing and vetting a healthy relationship, however far apart the individuals' respective definitions of "healthy" might be. Possibility, however, is not an inevitability in human societies.

And so, unleashing lots of sexual intimacy *without commitment* sets up men and women for a lot of heartbreak, unintended pregnancies, and sometimes abuse. Looking back on this era, it's incredible that we downplayed all this the way many of us did.

Introducing *recreational* sex reverted Americans to an ancient primate behavior, ironically: sexual activity (i.e., genital stimulation) as a form of social bonding. It's a known biochemical response. And, if repeated, it works. There is enormous cultural variance in how much sexual activity *should* occur outside marriage as a bonding or social ordering tool. Margaret Mead shocked Depression-era America with (unreliable) reports of sexual promiscuity among Samoan teens and preteens. And Alfred Kinsey's initial surveys in the 1940s suggested that almost 40 percent of American men experienced orgasms with another man during their sexually active years (!). This indicated that bisexual *activity* was common among straight men, even though bisexual *identity* is rare.

Over the ensuing decades, there was a very complex landscape of sexual lifestyle combinations. For the heterosexual majority in America, though, sexual activity led to new sorts of relationship negotiation that affected the lifelong options for men and women.

Yes, many continued down the more church-like path toward marriage in their twenties, where early marriage led quickly to childbirth and aprons, etc. But others took birth control as their green light to delay marriage. A smaller group also took these medicines to prevent any kind of sudden parental obligation *ever*.

One new permutation of sexual relationships initially favored heterosexual men. A lot. By the 1980s, it would get an acronym: FWF or Friends-Who-F**k. Some readers would not call these relationships, but I know plenty who did (and still would today). By the 1980s, FWF was a phenomenon on college campuses as young adults explored noncommittal sexual recreation. This acronym is meant mainly as a female critique of men who are (surprise!) just seeking casual sex without bothering to consult the relationship intent of their sexual partner. FWF is a style of sexual bonding focused on hooking up and having erotic fun in the absence of a serious romantic partner (or despite this). The women take all the risk (pregnancy, abortion), not the man.

The boundary between friend and lover had blurred a lot by the time Generation X got to college. *When Harry Met Sally* was the first motion picture to touch on the intersection between eros and friendship and its relationship to gender equality.

We already know from other research that mere copresence in shared activities can generate close friendship over large amounts of clock time (e.g., one hundred to two hundred hours), not with any two random people, but with *someone* in a decent-size social network (i.e., a college dorm or a workplace, a recreational club). And the same is true for sexual relationships, with sexual activity becoming an ancient form of cementing a primate bond, creating a social bond through maximal physical intimacy.

It's not surprising that, without intending anything, FWF couples would form in a sexually permissive modern world. In modern millennial parlance, FWF is simply two people who lean on each other for hookup sex in the absence of a dominant sexual relationship at the moment. "F**k buddies" is another term for this kind of relationship that your parents and grandparents do not want to learn. Oops. They just did.

FWF relationships also signal *unromantic* sex, something we associate historically with ultra-male sexuality (although this is changing among younger generations). And this is why I believe educated Gen X women deployed the acronym as a critique of male partners, as a challenge—Is this a *real*, romantic relationship headed somewhere or some sexually fun stopover?

In the chaos of American Rumspringa in the 1970s and 1980s, most people were a) not that promiscuous and b) not as cavalier about sex as the media made it seem with alarmist pieces designed to activate their readerships. Moreover, the initial popularity of the birth control pill did not magically lead to even accessibility or usage. Or *correct* usage!

In my research on older Americans, none of the Baby Boomers I interviewed confessed to high school sexual activity. College was when they said this began for them. Some of this was due to their innocence and the total lack of privacy in the much smaller homes of their childhood. Carefully executed cohort analysis by the NIH confirms that the years eighteen to twenty were when premarital sex exploded in the 1960s and 1970s.[6]

College sex sometimes led quickly to pregnancy and marriage for older Americans, even in the new age of birth control. This is partly why the average age of first marriage was only twenty-three to twenty-five for Baby Boomers.[7] I also suspect Boomer women were more pressured into sex than today's younger women, given the broadly sexist culture they were living in *and the absence of a public debate around consent*.

If my interviews were representative of both generations, Generation X was much more proficient at controlling unintended births for years and years, had more sexual partners before marriage, and tended to delay marriage more. This was in part because their mothers (now in their eighties and nineties) were the earliest married (and very excited) users of the pill (which helped delay childbirth after their own marriages).

We associate the pill with empowering women to achieve sexual freedom and erotic independence. Still, it appears that the first thing it enabled for a broad population right away was for married women to delay childbirth and learn, intentionally or not, *if they had indeed married the right person (or if they wanted to have another kid with this "jerk")*.[8] I can't prove this linkage was in any way causal. Still, it is very odd to me that the divorce rate in the United States exploded in the late 1960s and 1970s when older Baby Boomers were in the midst of their initial marriages (1964–1980),[9] some of which were just plain awful relationships.

Delaying childbirth, not sexual activity, would become a real superpower for Generation X women, including my wife, who could escape a toxic first marriage much more cleanly without the complication of child custody that many Silent Generation and Baby Boomer women experienced.

But the length of America's Rumspringa also led to years of distraction and heartache for some. Without universally clear rules around how to begin a sexually active relationship, I sense that men obtained the most significant reward initially from a culture of casual sex. Supporting evidence might be that Generation X men (age fifty-four to fifty-eight today) are twice as likely as Generation X women to have ten-plus lifetime sexual partners.[10] You do the math.[11]

If my math is correct, this is also how some (now) older American women got lost in the Rumspringa years by chasing married men through a very, very old cross-cultural lens of maturity (e.g., a man who has kids and a responsible job seems like a better catch than the dufus heads I meet who are my age).

An extreme case of Baby Boomer sexual liberation points to the potential for confusion and chaos in the Rumspringa years. And it also should remind us that there is nothing at all inevitable when it comes to marrying your best friend. Simply handing young people autonomy does not lead to achieving a cinematic ideal (which romantic marriage has held up for decades).

For some Americans, it took many relationships and decades of wandering and healing before they finally "got their sh*t together." One of the lesser discussed reasons why older Americans sometimes struggled to find their soulmate (the one Hollywood keeps pretending is everywhere and that everyone else has) was that their parents often provided no role model for *marrying your friend*.

This was definitely the case for Alison, a sixty-year-old woman I interviewed for this book:

My father was the life of the party. He was so gregarious. He was the best dancer in high school, and he loved music. And he was a big, big spender, you know. He had a lot of good qualities, but being a father at home was not one of them. Not everybody's made to be a parent.

I got married, you know, relatively later [age thirty-nine]. It was very difficult for me. I was engaged multiple times. It's very difficult for me to go through with getting married. I just have trust issues. . . . My sister was divorced once with a husband that cheated on her. So yeah, I mean, I don't really trust men in a relationship. I trust them as a friend. I trust them at work.

I was an international playgirl, really. I had plenty of flames and plenty of boyfriends in plenty of countries. I was young and thin in those days. I looked good. I lived in LA. I made a big salary. I traveled around. I did it all. So, by the time I got married, it was really kind of out of my system.

I went out with guys that were married because they said they were going to leave their wives. They never did. . . . So that goes directly back to my father. I'm sure. I went out with guys that lived in other countries. I mean, none of these things are going to work. I dated married guys more than once, mostly people I met through work. That's where I met most of the people. I dated some guys who said they were single. Then I found out they were married. That, too . . .

. . . Who wants to be with a guy that's gonna cheat on his wife? I mean right there you got a problem, a huge problem. But you know . . . when you're young you think to yourself: "Well, he's cheating because he's with the wrong woman." No, it's not the wrong woman. He's wrong,

. . . I remember there's one guy I went with. Four years I went out with him. I was madly in love with him. He was married. He was going to leave his wife . . . and I remember an older guy at work said to me . . .

"You ought to get on your hands and knees and thank God that he didn't leave his wife."

And he was right, because I would have been in that same position, and he could see it. If somebody could do it to one [woman], they could do it to the next one.[12]

It's easy to idealize (and romanticize) the sexual and marital revolutions of the late twentieth century. But, when you hand young kids this much autonomy combined with that much *privacy, and* the elders have no real experience handling this degree of sexual autonomy themselves, we should expect a fair amount of emotional trauma, not to mention unintended births and traumatic divorces.

It was a difficult, yet exciting, period in American social history, for sure.

But it turns out that unprecedented sexual *autonomy* requires a high level of interpersonal wisdom many of us just didn't have in the 1960s–1990s.

Chapter Twenty-Six

HOW PETS EDGED OUT OUR FRIENDS

Something else happened during the same historical period that older Americans learned to transform their friends primarily into sources of "catch-up" entertainment more than everyday solace and comfort.

We became *obsessed* with our pets.

We turned them into pseudo-children. Sometimes, our pets *became* the children that nature and circumstance would not let us have.

In 2022, Americans spent $12.6 billion on retail dog food for roughly 65 million dogs.[1] That's a crude average of $193 annually per dog (across all dog sizes). That is maybe six to seven large bags of mainstream branded food per doggie. However, if you're more affluent, you most likely have two or more dogs, *and* you may even buy natural, grain-free dog food for them. If so, you will spend more like $600–700 per year for your dog food. The premiumization of American pet food matches the premiumization of human food closely because we treat them increasingly like family members.

In America, we didn't always fetishize our pets as fictive children. My paternal grandmother (who made excellent fudge) was "attacked" by the family boxer in the 1960s while standing in her front yard. After some lousy surgery, her right knee never bent fully again. Her husband quickly exterminated the family dog with the family gun on the family property. This was rural New Hampshire in another era. You did not necessarily take your problem animal to a vet's office for proper disposal. By the 1970s in America, millions of stray dogs and cats were roaming the streets due to the mash-up of unmitigated animal breeding, a lack of animal control departments, and a lack of regulations around neutering or spaying. People used to open their front doors and let unwanted pets run off (!).

In the 1960s, we did not invest much in our pets other than food and some shots at the vet. Pets did not get health insurance. They did not receive costumes or hiking booties. They did not get dental care or cancer treatment. They did not receive anxiety chews or oral hygiene "bones." They did not go to doggie hotels or spas. And they did not come to our coworking offices.

As pets slowly became more childlike in our eyes, we started to spoil them like little kids, including buying them human-grade food, even if we can barely afford it. But not all Americans.

Pet ownership in America correlates loosely to household income.[2] Poor families generally do not have pets; there is no way to spare the extra cash to support their food intake. Recent research has shown that the population of pets has grown steadily in the United States since the 1980s, but the percent of homes with pets has not really changed much.[3] The pet population has grown twice as fast as the human population despite better animal control and neuter-spay incentives from county governments.

In other words, our love affair with pets has led to a *de facto increase in the mammal population of pet-owning homes*. This, ladies and gentlemen, is what is known as a demand increase. And this happened during the same period as wealth inequality grew a lot and our intimate social networks contracted (at least among older, primarily white Americans).

The decline in family-based socialization, the reduction in time spent socializing in general with anyone, plus the small household size of the average American created an emotional hunger by the turn of the twenty-first century that pets excel at filling.

One group of emotionally needy pet owners, those who tend to live alone as singles, are the ones who truly pamper their pets the most. Their pet becomes a mix of child and partner. They even engage in permissive parenting, which drives all their guests mad. Half of these pet owners will even leave the TV on for their pets when they leave home.[4] Again, if the TV is a companion surrogate for *adults*, then it makes sense for us to project this behavior onto our pets *if we truly see them as household members*.

Pet Affection and Bonding—We Bred This Possibility into Them

The vast majority of American pet breeds in homes today appeared only in the nineteenth century after aggressive, highly intentional breeding efforts aimed only at aesthetic variation.

Due to intense mixing and interbreeding, dog breeds have long since ceased to predict behavior. Even purebred dogs fail to show predictable behavior differences according to the most extensive genetic and behavioral database ever assembled.[5]

As an entire subspecies, human-bred dogs share interactional traits that matter for our understanding of their seduction of American humans. They are almost all *trainable* by humans, and most dogs *want* to interact with humans, not just for food. This prosocial docility appeared centuries ago when aristocrats first bred dogs for estate-level functions (hunting, herding, etc.). We also bred horses similarly so we could control them intensely for our purposes.

But no other livestock species behaves this way. We bred cows, goats, sheep, and pigs to provide us with food and to be minimally containable in herds. Pigs are the most docile of our livestock species, but they lack one trait we consider essential among pets: they can't stand to be picked up and cuddled like a human infant.[6]

And that, I suspect, may be the critical thing dogs and cats have on us: *they will let us treat them like human babies*. And, as such, they become perpetual objects of parent-child soothing, touching, and relaxation. Especially for the childless or lonely empty nester.

And pets don't wake up one morning and ask for a car! Or a down payment!

Pets are a major source of emotional comfort and solace in American middle-class life because, like a baby, they require no complicated filtering of *your* emotions at all. We can be unguarded. They won't talk back. Ever. They don't expect much from us and are super easy to please.

And pets are much more independent than human babies. You can ignore them for hours if you want. Well, until they start chewing all your throw pillows or scratching up your drywall.

Dogs Are Master Relationship Builders

I can't prove this, but it does seem that dogs, especially, are vastly superior at nurturing and working at relationships with humans. Better than a lot of American humans. They simply need our relationship more than we ultimately need them. I'm pretty sure that dogs understand that we can get rid of them at any moment. Deep down.

What else explains this:

> *Dogs provide us with unconditional love and companionship. They're at our sides when we're sick, and they always seem to know when we need a little extra affection. They love us without judgment, even when we are ignoring them or not feeding them a second dinner.*[7]

Dogs are also totally reliable and sensorily fixated on us. Your dog is always there. When it's awake, it's always tracking who is in the room and where people are in the house. Neither your children, spouse, nor friends can claim that kind of availability. They have much greater privacy needs. I don't think your dog or cat needs *any* privacy at all.

Greater physical availability and a lack of need for privacy combine to allow pets to shine in an individualistic society. Our individual schedules and notions of personal space make humans a relatively less reliable source of physical touching and soothing. Your dog will put up with a lot of personal space invasion to meet your daily need for touch.

Here's a description of what happens with my beagle almost every night in my home. This should be very familiar to many of you.

At bedtime, I drag Mickey over to cuddle on my bed. He does not like this. Not when he's curled up elsewhere already and ready to snore. Usually, he reminds me of this by uttering a soft groan (of irritation) as I drag him over. He endures the rough belly rub and ear-tickling that only a human hand can deliver and waits for my hand to go limp, so he can stand up, shake it off, and walk back to his "spot," where he lies down exactly where he had been before being so *rudely* interrupted.

During this "annoying" interruption, he doesn't bark, growl, bite, or try to force himself out of my grip. Why?

Because he tolerates his owner's *need* for cuddle love *and* he also knows I'm dominant in the relationship. And he indeed sees the bigger picture.

The good food. The excellent furniture. The nice people. *And* the "magic fingers."

The what? The magic fingers. Human hands, people. Come on. Very few animals on Earth have ten super flexible fingers on two, count 'em, two huge paws. These magic fingers do things no dog could ever do for another dog. Not even your canine buddy's most fabulous ear lick can compare to the magic fingers.

We bred domestic dog breeds to bond intensely with us. Experts call it docility. The magic fingers were a silent but critical part of the process—docility in exchange for access to those fingers. Anyone who gets massages weekly knows what I'm talking about. It's tough to give up weekly massage. Very.

Yes, theoretically, our spouses signed up to provide physical touch to us, but this is where cultural habits can get in the way. It is no secret that most Caucasian Americans come from ethnic worlds where physical touch is just not super common outside of sexual activity and the baby/toddler years. This is even more true if your partner is on the autism spectrum *or* . . . if both partners are on the spectrum.

Older Americans, especially, come from these low-touch cultural worlds and see it as totally normal. But that is not true for younger Americans, who tend now to come from cultures that celebrate same-sex friendly touch much more (e.g., Puerto Rico, Brazil, Mexico, India, etc.).[8]

By getting our tactile needs satisfied more from our pets rather than from our sexual partners and close friends, we distract ourselves even further from human bonding and community. We become more self-sufficient individualists, pursuing our "personal schedules" independently. Interesting. Getting our touch fix from nonhuman animals who have no privacy guardrails (other than the rear door).

Pets + Video = Who Needs Friends?

Have you ever noticed that your pet seems to enjoy TV time? As in . . . *really seems* to enjoy it? You turn on the TV, sit down or lie down, and within two to three minutes your pet is next to you. Just chillin'. We know pets are *not* watching the video the way we are. Their brains cannot convert 2D imagery into 3D brain images like ours can. They *can* follow the audio well, though. They can hear doorbells or dogs barking in our movies and TV shows. But that's not why they're sitting near us during TV time.

As with on-demand video everywhere all at once, pets allow us to escape daily stress, relax, and remove basic emotional comfort requirements from our human social network. It's hard to believe this doesn't minimize our need for friends to play a similar role. I know it minimizes the daily need for spouses to give us physical comfort. Pets are helping keep the peace, folks. But pets are also enabling our continued physical alienation from each other at the same time.

The tragic COVID-19 pandemic created an eerie laboratory in which to understand how strongly we see pets as sources of emotional solace, tactile comfort, and unconditional love. Lockdowns and pre-vaccine isolation from family created enormous waves of loneliness in America for up to a year or more.

There was also a 2020 run on pets once it became clear that lockdowns would last for *months*. We couldn't see our friends or extended family for up to a year or more in some cases. Physical touch vanished from the lives of people living alone. So, many of us now needed cute, furry mammals to process our roller coaster of daily emotions. Over twenty-three million homes adopted a pet.[9]

Pets fit in perfectly as agents of calm and soothing, weakening our need for face time with friends, spouses, and children. In fact, your pet is far more reliable than the average close friend. The latter has "a life" and "a schedule" and "things to do." So annoying.

Your pet is like a high school boyfriend. It has nothing it needs to be doing other than hanging out with adorable you. Certainly not homework. It is simpleminded. It *is really easy* to hang out with. And it also smells and does gross things.

If there's one thing you're picking up on in this book it's that an individualistic society actually goads us to do whatever is most easy, until we cross a social line. Until society pushes back.

But ours rarely ever does.

Part Six

HOW WE SHRIVELED THE AMERICAN FAMILY

"My parents gave us a lot of autonomy.
They would help us if they could."
—*Sam, seventy-year-old retiree, upstate New York*

Chapter Twenty-Seven

I'M NAMED AFTER A VERY DISAPPOINTING MAN

My name is very common in the United States. There are 5,339 James Richardsons to be precise.[1] My name is so common you cannot even purchase it as an internet domain from an ICANN registrar. A large multinational grain company from Canada grabbed *www.jamesrichardson.com* as soon as it could back in the 1990s.

But the most irritating problem with my name is not its common, dull status. It's after whom I am named.

You see, the late James M. Richardson (1918–1988) was a very disappointing man.

I only met him once when I was an infant. I believe someone took a photo of my grandmother holding me with him standing next to her in our backyard.

I never spoke to my grandfather "Jim," because I never met or saw him again after the day my mom took that photo. And not because he died.

My dad never spoke about his father when I was growing up. It was the oddest void. I learned not to ask, because I never got any answers. On a few occasions, I just got a distant stare. Once I was old enough to be curious about why only Grandma came to spend Christmas with us, I somehow realized he was gone. I wasn't sure for years if he was dead or just gone.

It didn't seem to bother my parents and, so, it didn't bother me. But it was an unaccounted-for absence, a hole in the trunk of our family tree.

Ironically, when the rest of America was accelerating high school completion during the Depression, my grandfather chose *work*. The story is that he dropped out of high school in the eleventh grade abruptly. He came home angry because a teacher was having kids give an oral book report in front of the class, one by one. He refused to do it. He never went back. Odd.

Jim, as he was called, was a tradesman most of his life. A strict union-jobs-only carpenter. The union-only stipulation was good for his self-respect. Bad for the home's cash flow, though, because union jobs were not as common in rural New England, generally linked to government spending.

My grandfather apparently had a roller-coaster work ethic. When he was on, he was a hard worker. Despite his high school dropout status, he was smart enough to read architectural plans for complex commercial jobs. He had leadership skills. My dad even worked with him on jobs as a young man. Union work was often government funded back then but tended to require lots of commuting out of town. As Jim took more and more sophisticated corporate foreman roles in the 1960s, he might be gone for days or weeks at a time.

In 1987, I had the chance to interview my late grandmother about her experience growing up in Lebanon, NH, an old factory town built around its noxious tanneries. I intended to dodge the absent husband topic unless she brought it up herself. For a woman who quietly devoured everything Danielle Steele published, her recounting of why she married my grandfather was heartbreaking.

"I don't really know. It was probably because he had a house and good income," she said after a long pause. There was no bodice-ripping Fabio for my grandmother. Working class New Englanders weren't that impractical.

There was a deep, quiet pain in her recounting that day, not made any better by the fact that my earlier questions about "dating" had forced her to admit she had been unable to marry the boy she was in love with in high school. He was Catholic. And she was a Congregationalist. It didn't matter to *her*, but "it just was not done in the 1930s."

So, in 1938, she married Jim because he had income, and they were able to live in his parents' full-size house. Daughter of a single father, she married *stability*, like many working-class women her age. And he was a good-looking man.

At the time of that interview, I was still unaware of how my grandparents split up. I later learned the story in graduate school from my mother and in it you will see how social forces permitting increased autonomy helped split them up.

Temptation Strikes

One drawback to being a union tradesperson in rural America is that you often need to take work that requires overnight travel or even extended stays out of town. This was very true for residents of northern New Hampshire, which, by the very shape of it, disappears as it stretches toward the Canadian border. Living right near the Vermont border led Jim to one out-of-state job after another.

My grandmother was used to her husband doing out-of-town jobs occasionally. It comes with being married to a tradesperson dependent on infrequent commercial contracts. In the final ten years of their marriage, though, my grandfather took increasingly more lucrative and bigger out-of-town jobs. Their kids were out of the house, which made his absence a lot easier. It's also a lot easier, *if* your wife is *not* your best friend.

And so, on one of his out-of-town trips, in the fall of 1975, when I was still in diapers and pushing mini fire trucks around, Jim simply didn't come home. He called once to say he wouldn't be home for Thanksgiving. Then, silence. My grandmother called my dad out of concern. They both knew the town in Maine where his last job had been located. They had a phone number. My grandmother was upset. He wasn't responding to phone calls.

My dad tried to reach him but also failed, initially. Then, one morning, my grandmother went into town to her bank branch and saw her husband emerging. She watched him get into his car and found out minutes later that her bank account was now empty.

This financial emergency led my dad to drive with his mom to Maine to track his location down, get the money back, and get some kind of definitive answer about Jim's intentions. My dad had become a reluctant social worker.

They found Jim living with a new girlfriend. *Quelle surprise!* It didn't require much imagination to see where this was headed. Jim spoke with my grandmother to clear up his intentions. That didn't take long for a man of few words. And he returned the cash she needed to survive on.

New Hampshire was already a no-fault divorce state by this time, so it was relatively easy to cut ties. But alimony was the primary reason to file for divorce in situations of abandonment like this. Remember, my grandmother had never supported herself for one day financially and was still too young to call on social security for assistance.

She was, technically, a destitute, abandoned wife living in a home in her husband's name. My grandfather could have theoretically taken the house from her had she had no clever legal representation. She needed a divorce for economic reasons and for psychological closure.

But she did not have money for a divorce lawyer. Luckily, she had someone better. My dad. He helped secure three years of alimony and ownership of the very small home for her. The home would be in her name as her primary asset. Initially my grandfather had agreed to these terms. Under the alleged influence of his new girlfriend, however, he changed his mind in court and tried to get the judge to dismiss the proceeding, claiming, incorrectly, that my father was trying illegally to represent both sides of the case (by drafting the divorce papers for him to sign).

The latter move was a final f**k-you to the family he had created, I guess.

My dad never spoke to him again. And he did not attend his funeral in 1988. We certainly didn't. I never learned of his actual death until years later, when I was in graduate school. That's how little it meant to us by then.

In a way, my grandfather's abandonment of his wife fit right into a mid-century trend in social evolution in America. I wouldn't be surprised if my grandfather witnessed all the sexual autonomy his own laborers had in the 1960s and early 1970s and suddenly realized he wanted some of that too. We will never know. He was only fifty-four when he left my grandmother. As an expert commercial carpenter, he also didn't need to maintain a moral reputation among local homeowners in his hometown. He got business from total strangers on a highly rational, contract basis. If his neighbors now abhorred him, it would have no effect on his income. If society would not condemn him anymore and if his "reputation" wouldn't suffer . . . why not find someone you now *prefer* more than your current wife?

The phrasing I just used is intentionally disturbing. Autonomy has a dark side that most Americans are the last to recognize.

There has been a creepy consumerization of romance and coupling since World War II. I'm referring to the infiltration of consumer notions of "trade up" and "preference" into what is supposed to be a very serious genre of lifelong human bonding. Trade-up is a consumer behavior that derives fuel from the constant appearance of more enticing alternatives. Trading up is my core expertise as a business consultant. (I even wrote a best-selling business book about how to design consumer brands that cause consumers to *abandon* their current ones.)[2]

My grandparents' 1975 divorce is an important reminder that the weakening of the American family unit first hit generations *prior* to the Baby Boomers. The first practitioners of optional, no-fault divorce had been raised in a vastly different pre-World War II America. They literally saw the heavy weight of social and community obligation to remain married at all costs evaporate rapidly in the 1960s and 1970s . . . and . . . some joined *in*.

When society removes the constraints that keep unhappy couples together, it's not shocking that couples start breaking up in homes you wouldn't expect and not just in hipster urban neighborhoods full of the perennially "difficult" and self-absorbed.

Divorce hit the oldest, most worn-out marriages first when it took off in the 1960s and 1970s. In one sense, many of these men now had a chance for their first "romantic" coupling, however misguided or ennobling. Or embarrassing.

In the 1970s, we, as a country, were not prepared to have difficult conversations about voluntary, no-fault separation. Men especially were not ready for this kind of conversation. My grandfather was, I gather, especially unskilled and insensitive. Throughout his life, he displayed the symptoms of what we today might label Asperger's (level one, high-functioning autism) in an era long before this behavior was seen as anything more than a "moody personality." His middle name was also "Moody." It's easy to blame him. So easy. We all have, trust me. My poor dad has had to see his dad's name constantly for the rest of his life in the form of his son's document trail and digital authorship. "We would never have named you after him, had we known he was going to do this," my mom once said.

Stepping back, from the perspective of a modern therapist, Jim was a person fundamentally unprepared to navigate his own inner life with the maturity we might *now* expect of a fifty-four-year-old man. Yes, he was an "ass," "insensitive," and "callous." But would most other working-class high school dropouts have acted much differently in 1975 had they fallen in love with a new, somewhat younger woman?

Jim was a white male suddenly permitted a lot of sexual autonomy by the surrounding culture. He made his own choices. But they hurt a lot of people.

Still, to this day, whenever someone new in my life calls me Jim, I cringe, and I correct them immediately.

"I'm James, not *Jim*." I'm not that disappointing guy. Please.

Chapter Twenty-Eight

THE CULTURAL TRIUMPH OF THE ROMANTIC COUPLE

The film *When Harry Met Sally* (1989) ended as 90 percent of its audience wanted it to: the arguing "friends" professed their love for each other (after having sex, *of course*). I think street riots might have broken out had Rob Reiner used the original ending scene *in which they went their separate ways*. This film was a mirror to the collective consciousness of millions of educated Americans at the time—*marry your best friend*. Fall in love with your friend. Do your research. Don't settle.

And don't give up on "true" love. "True" love = friendship with a side of lust.

Marrying your friend. What does this even mean?

In the second half of the twentieth century, "romance" was now no longer just a formal "courtship" *phase* followed by inevitable patriarchal condescension or abuse. The nuance that this movie drilled into the heads of impressionable Gen Xers like me was that you now need to prepare for *a long and wandering search for this ideal partner*. Harry and Sally sure as hell wandered. In this new model, sex becomes more than recreation; it can also honor an intense friendship.

The steady increase in the average age of first marriage during the late twentieth century confirms that many Boomers and Gen Xers wandered. And the more educated you are, the longer you do still.[1]

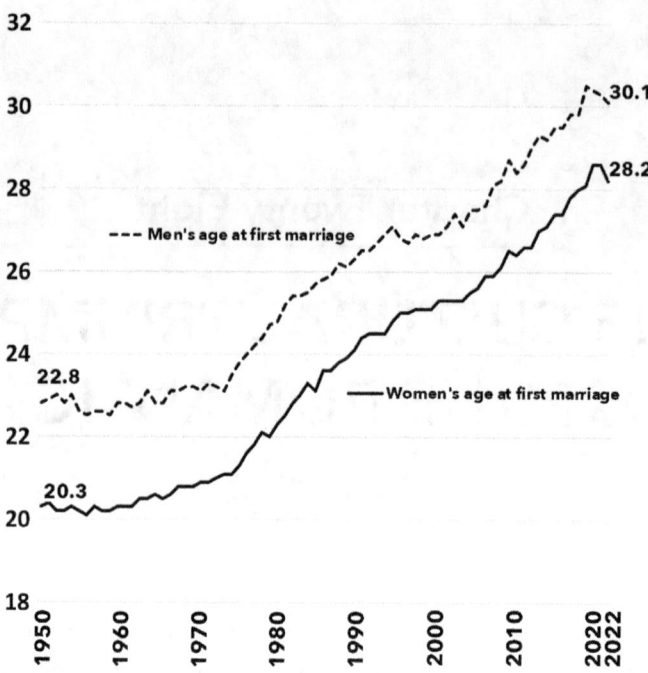

Figure 13. Median Age of First Marriage 1952–2022. Table data sourced from the United States Census.[2]

My Aspie confusion and PhD distraction pushed me *six years* beyond the median marriage age for men in 2006 (the year I got hitched). Not surprising. I'm still amazed I ever got married. Getting into relationships was unbelievably awkward and terrifying for my brain, despite having a solid parental model at home. The motivation was strong. The playbook was, however, missing. I lacked any of the confidence of Mr. Harry Burns. Not until around 2004 . . . I think my platinum status on American Airlines finally gave me some mojo.

Any romantic formula I fumbled with back then assumed that any given woman I met in Seattle even wanted to settle down (!). Bad assumption on the West Coast. The "perpetual bachelorette" was a lifestyle permutation I was not expecting when I came of age in New Hampshire in the 1980s. I had no clue this was a choice. Oh, yes it is.

Despite the best-selling novels of Jane Austen, romantic love has only recently become a mass-market topic and a mass ideal among

American adults. Among *any* adults. Not long ago, "romance" was considered by most to be an indulgence of the rich and dilettantish.

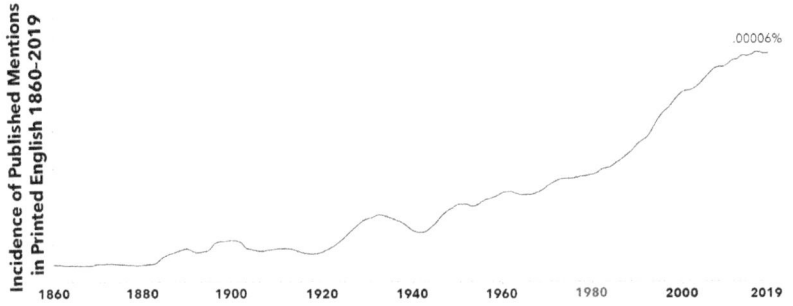

Figure 14. Written English Mentions of "Romantic Love." Table data sourced from Google's Ngram service.[3]

Google Ngram charts continue to floor me in how well they time the appearance of modern cultural trends. What language we *printed* before the internet can reveal the twentieth century mainstreaming of significant cultural values we now take for granted. As women gained control over the timing of marriage and childbirth (and earned a self-sufficient income), wandering for idealized romantic love became more feasible.

The Romance Novel as an Extreme Sign

The real sign of romance's cultural triumph as a mass American orientation to marriage and coupling is something most of us have overlooked—the sales of romance fiction. Romance novels are the number-one-selling fictional book genre in the United States. Over $12 billion in 2022 sales via 19 million units. The number-one-selling romance novel ever is *Fifty Shades of Grey* by E. L. James (approximately 150 million copies sold to date). *Pride and Prejudice* by Jane Austen is number two (at 120 million copies). There is romance fiction for all social classes and dispositions. There is no way a female reader can claim to be overlooked as a reader of romance fiction. Not a chance. If you think so, you just haven't looked hard enough—or at all.

But we need to accept one cultural fact before I proceed. Heterosexual men, at least, do not read or desire anything called romance fiction. This is why you cannot find anything in the genre written for a straight male audience. Only 18 percent of romance novel readers are male.[4] But this fact doesn't stop one genre superfan from making the case:

> *More men should read romance novels because they can serve as instruction manuals for relationships. Romances show how much communication, compromise, and work is necessary for a healthy relationship. Books have the unique ability of letting us live experiences we wouldn't otherwise encounter. And since romance is so woman-centric, it can give male readers a chance to see the world through a female perspective. This builds empathy in readers. It's the closest male readers will come to experiencing prejudices that might not affect them, allowing some men to develop a sensitivity they may not otherwise.[5]*

OK. Noted.

Romance spread among the European elite, in part because the intricacies of flirtation suited aristocrats and others obsessed with nuanced, luxury *consumption* in general. Romance became a form of sophisticated etiquette in which men respected the need for a modicum of respect for the elite women they would marry.

The sales of romance novels signal how important romantic love is today in modern coupling and sexual escapades throughout the broad middle class, not just the 1 percent. The high degree of over-the-top fantasy may mystify most straight men, but ties in to the high interactional standard romantic love sets for courting couples. Romance novels also reveal how difficult this standard for coupling is for most of us and how frequently men, in particular, disappoint. It's easy to point to a Platonic ideal of romance. It's easy to talk about it. Getting any two humans to keep it going is more difficult.

Nothing in evolutionary human biology *necessitates* birdlike bonding in human sexual *pairs*. Rape is just as "effective" as consensual sex in perpetuating the species (and genetic diversity) because survival is a *group* affair for *Homo sapiens* in most cultures. In a tribal setting, you don't rely on your sexual partner as much as we urban types do. Strong, caretaking romantic pair bonds are simply *not* a human universal. In the early twentieth-century Trobriand islands, for example, fathers exchanged yams to initiate and sustain sexual access with a woman, but generally, they focused on supporting and raising *their sisters' children*, not their own. Why? Their sisters' children exist in the same lineage. Their biological children are in another lineage. Strict matrilineality created this structure, a vaccination *against* romance as the sole pair-bonding technique (at least before Christian conversion). Instead, Trobriand women collected yams from their brothers and husbands/lovers and dispersed this wealth as they saw fit. The flow of yams, not flirtatious words, built relations with a sexual partner (often as a gift *after* sex). Interesting how matrilineality empowered women (socially, economically, and sexually) *without* any documented idiom of romance or romantic *friendship*. Ahem. I remain unconvinced that Western romance works to women's advantage the way we all assume. Some men are very gifted at manipulating an idiom of romance to get sexual access, especially married men cheating on their spouses.

The wild success of romance novels signals the failure of our high-minded European romantic ideal as much as its widespread grip on our imaginations. I think the failure is that romantic *courtship* is a poor ritual selection tool to obtain a long-lasting *friendship*. It is certainly not sufficient. Too many abusive men court their "victims" successfully. Year after year. Romantic charm worked as well for Ted Bundy as it does for the average guy.

And, for some women, romance is lifelong tease, a maddening absence or a cruel trick used against their long-term emotional self-interest. The cruelty of the romantic ideal and its tight relationship to conventional notions of beauty lies in making some individuals ineligible to ever experience it. For this minority, often composed of neurodivergent or frankly homely adults, romance is a shameful absence to which everyone else is getting access, but not them.

The Dark Fate of the Unloved

In 1995, I had a graduate seminar on ritual practices, in which I chose to do two months of fieldwork for my final paper. It was a way to challenge myself and warm up my interviewing skills. I chose a charismatic Christian church near Madison, WI. These are the churches where people play rock 'n' roll Christian music, get possessed by the Holy Spirit, conduct live exorcisms, and perform spirit healings.

I knew I would have fun with this evangelical crowd when I showed up for the first service and the pastor handed me a service pamphlet while gulping from a massive twenty-two-ounce C-store coffee. The pamphlet's cover showed a picture of his mug shot from ten years earlier. *Interesting*.

On the second or third Sunday of my ten-week project, I met up with an older woman in the church after the service. Her first sentence?

"James, this is not a church. It's a hospital," she said mysteriously. Word choice does matter in moments like this. She didn't say *"like* a hospital," she said it *is* a hospital. Full of *wounded* souls. Almost all of them were Baby Boomers who had crashed somehow on the rocky shores of the midnineties. Drug addiction. Alcoholism. Traumatic divorce. Domestic abuse.

When recruiting eight to ten participants for in-depth interviews, my healer friend helped me get a good array of "stories." One of the women she sent my way was super quiet. I doubt I would have ever gotten her to agree to an interview without my intermediary's help.

Let's call her Pam.

Most of my interviews featured some kind of born-again conversion narrative, but not a narrative the Amish would approve of. Definitely not.

Pam began hers with a unique opener, "Now, promise me you won't laugh, James," she said.

"Absolutely not," I replied, nervously preparing for a battle with my secular, male diaphragm.

Pam described her abusive marriage and how her former husband eventually abandoned her. Since her divorce, she had lived alone and had not entered any relationships. This was a relationship drought of ten years or more. Pam was obese, in her late forties at the time of the interview, and did not consider herself attractive.

"I'm addicted to romance novels, James," she said matter-of-factly. "I used to go to the bookstore and buy ten to fifteen of them. Then, I'd read them all in one weekend and return to the store for more. I couldn't stop reading them." She began to weep in shame.

When she joined the church, she prayed for assistance. Then, she decided to throw out every romance novel she owned. This involved taking "dozens of trash bags" full of novels to the dump. Whoa. That's a lot of *fictional* love. And, for Christian Pam, it was a lot of *fornication* narratives. At the time, I was oblivious that tens of millions of Americans still frowned on sex outside marriage. Oops.

As Pam told me her extreme story, I thought of my grandmother's unromantic marriage and her constant stream of Danielle Steele novels. *Is this what unloved, lonely women do?* For most women like Pam, romance fiction is a harmless form of entertainment and female-oriented sex fantasy.

Reading romance fiction is polite resistance to the decidedly *unromantic* reality of some women's marriages and lives. It's reaching for something else too—strong human pair bonds in an increasingly alienated society where coupling has become forever voluntary and subject purely to individual whims.

Not all straight men are equipped to fulfill some women's fantasies of romantic love either. That's for sure. Most cannot sustain it deep into a marriage. Yet, they can still be good partners and friends.

I worry that the elevation of romance as the primary way to form a couple has quietly enabled a sort of sociopathic fooling of many women by men who intend to behave like Don Draper once the "honeymoon" is over. This hijacking of romance by bad-faith actors only prolongs the wandering many of us experience in our twenties and thirties.

If the point of modern romance is to marry your best friend, this will happen organically without a game or a sexy performance. Some light social filtering helps a lot. Friendship is not about the dopamine rush of romance (or exercise). It's about oxytocin, the chemical of human bonding. Real friendship takes much longer to form than reading a titillating, dopamine-releasing romance novel.

Which matters more to us? The flirtatious *beginning* of the friendship or the friendship? The ability to "woo," "court," or *talk* a person into a relationship or the quality of the relationship? The *preface*, or the main chapters?

Modern marriage gives us enormous freedom to select and deselect our life partners, but it also allows enormous room for deception and fantasy to distract us from what matters long-term, which is simply consistent loving companionship.

Our culture encourages individuals to overthink coupling like no other I've ever studied. Not unlike we overthink our selection of homes, cars, colleges, etc.

Criss-Cross Class Coupling

By the 1970s, colleges across the United States started to mix "horny" kids from wildly different social classes in a way that had never been seen before in America (outside the military). This was also true at more elite, selective institutions like the one I attended.

In 1970, only 28 percent of incoming first years at America's colleges and universities had a father with a college degree (men generally had the highest educational attainment in families back then).[6] By 2000, as Millennials started pouring onto campus, 50 percent of their fathers had a college degree.[7]

Others have written about the declining class diversity on college campuses compared to the glory decades of social mobility after World War II. It's a real thing and one reason that professors have become increasingly fed up with "entitled" students. These kids are mostly trying to *reproduce* their class privilege (or join the 1 percent), not climb the social ladder.

Yet, America's emphasis on autonomy and silencing the elders still allows individuals from very different backgrounds to meet and form relationships with virtually no interference.

One of the reasons I went into social science was a series of teenage revelations about my parents' own unlikely marriage. This union was so improbable that my own mother has said multiple times, "If I had known then what I know now about your father's family, I'm not sure I would have pursued the relationship back then."

My parents first met in roughly the same way that Harry and Sally did. It's quite eerie now that I think about it. Instead of a three-day car trip to New York, their *histoire d'amour* began with *two weeks* as 4-H camp counselors in New Hampshire in the summer of 1963. My mom was the activities director, and my dad was the archery counselor. (Hey, he never taught *me* archery!)

And *this*, dear reader, is what happened when they bumped into each other at the semi-outdoor laundry lean-to:

[Scene: Laundry shed for 4-H counselors]

[Peggy enters and sees Jon, one of the male counselors, struggling with a hand-operated wringer-style washing machine that has mountains of soap foam overflowing from the bucket onto the slab.]

"What the hell are you doing?" she exclaims at Jon. "Do you not know how to use a washing machine? How much soap did you put in there?"

Some kind of female-dominant conversation ensued in which my mom helped him clean up and restart the load with the proper amount of soap powder (i.e., you don't pour it in like pancake mix).

ARGH! MEN! THEY NEVER ASK FOR HELP!

At some point that first summer at 4-H camp, my mom had learned that laundry-fumbling "Jon" was studying at *Harvard*. Say what?! That's the kind of fact that readily enabled an exchange of phone numbers and addresses back then.

Two years later, they married in northern New Hampshire in May. It was small with mostly family members in attendance. They even ran out of champagne partway through and my mom's father had to run out for more. My parents looked extremely happy in those wedding photos. Extremely.

As the American middle class grew and adults started moving around for college and work, sustaining the entrenched marital bigotries of prior eras within white America became harder. Catholics versus Protestants. Italians versus everyone. WASPS versus everyone. Upper-middle-class adults never marry *down (gasp!)*. America was still utterly racist in its marriage practices, yes, but other boundaries within predominantly white America were breaking down fast.

But how exactly was my mom going to bring home the son of a union carpenter, a high school dropout who was married to a part-time local housekeeper who was living in a six-hundred-square-foot home without either hot water or proper plumbing? Huh? Well, don't invite her to your house!

My mom's father had a bachelor's degree in chemistry, and her mom had a teachers college certificate for secondary schools, both degrees earned in the 1920s! These folks were early educated elites of a sort. Surely, it was unacceptable for my mom to marry this "low" on the social ladder. My maternal grandmother was a very judgmental WASP female from her era. Part of this rough edge stemmed from her own social climbing, having been raised in a working-class home with eight siblings (!). Those who climb in status often do so with an overwrought moral condescension to their immediate family left behind. Not always, but often enough. It's a psychosocial defense mechanism to ensure they do not fall backward.

> *My mother never liked any of our boyfriends. She hated the guy before your dad. When I brought your father home for the first time after our engagement, she asked Jon where he was going to college. I thought she was going to choke when he said, "Harvard." There was nothing Mum could say against that. Nothing at all.*

My father is a man of relatively few words, true to his Northern New England working-class roots. This was his secret weapon when endearing himself to his mother-in-law and father-in-law. When a stranger doesn't say much, the other person projects what they want to see onto them (or they run). I am told this is also an essential technique in spy craft. Sadly, I never learned this skill from my dad.

My parents were insanely well matched for several reasons: they are equally introverted, wanted the same, non-showy upper-middle-class lifestyle, hate partying, and love reading. And they both help soothe each other's pronounced social anxieties. Sharing a key weakness is an underrated bond for marriage. You won't read about that in a bridal magazine.

My parents also brought a very complex form of sociological balance to their unlikely marriage, one that I have increasingly noticed in marriages between individuals from different class origins.

My mom was my dad's tutor in the *ways of the upper-middle class*. Not the only one, but a critical one. Your pillow partner remains the most effective persuasive agent in the modern, couple-focused world we live in.

On the other hand, my dad brought in all the elite income that would allow my mom to live like she had grown up (and better). And this income did not come in an abusive patriarchal package.

As I went out in the world in the 1990s, I continued to meet more and more upper-middle-class individuals who had married upwardly mobile partners from ordinary middle-class or even working-class homes. I have hunted for any kind of sociological survey of cross-class marriages *anchored* in the upper-middle-class elite. Since it's such a small universe I'm discussing, it's expensive to survey such a group in a nationally representative manner. Jane Austen and her elite girlfriends are hard to find. Still. Even after 120 million sales of *Pride and Prejudice*.

Ignoring class origins during courtship is a natural outcome of the marry-your-friend ideal and all of the variables of individualism I discussed in part one. What couples like my parents discovered is that if you marry someone headed for the same lifestyle as you, it doesn't matter where they came from, in the end. In business strategy, this is called a "huge unlock." In sociological terms, it's called autonomy. My parents simply had the autonomy to ignore any family disapproval, had it occurred. They were luckier than many "unusual couples" I met in Tamil Nadu in the 1990s who faced much worse when they broke the marital rules.

In these avant-garde American marital couplings, it takes an intense friendship to pull this off and one that will absolutely dominate the household it forms.

Couples Are More Dominant Than "Traditional Families"

As the authentically romantic couple became the dominant portal to marriage in America, the power of romantic friendship ended up carving out a space to evade marriage entirely. Romance triumphed so much that the couple became the structural anchor of most American homes.

Sometime in the late 2000s, when my former employer peaked in its number of employees, I remember noticing that a measurable number of my Gen X peers (most of the staff) were not married and in their mid-to-late thirties. Some were in long-term relationships too (at least by self-report). More than one unmarried female worker had zero stated intention of ever getting married to their partner. They liked it just how it was.

Coupling and committing take many forms today that my grandmothers would not recognize as legitimate. This is despite the fact that there are substantial financial benefits to getting formally married, especially if you are likely to control a home and other assets. The fact that things like social security spousal benefit transfer does not occur to young unmarried couples is more proof that romantic friendship matters more than economic security in our cultural prioritization.

What's fascinating about marriage among older Americans is something many do not realize—one's generation has had basically no statistically significant effect on the likelihood of your marriage lasting any specific length of time. On the viability of any particular couple. The likelihood of eventual divorce for Americans married between 1970 and 2004 (mostly Boomers and Gen Xers) does not vary by age cohort as one moves through every five-year anniversary.[8] The likelihood peaks early and then hits a ceiling. This implies strongly that it's something else, i.e., the quality of your early relationship itself, that keeps couples going, not the actual act of marrying or romance.

Unconsciously, America's elders understand that a wedding ceremony and a certificate does not keep the romantic friendship alive and well. It is a lot of work. Every day. While most educated couples still tend to get married, we realize that the satisfaction of the individuals inside the couple is paramount, because there is little pressure from society to remain together.

The slow decline in formal marriage, to me, is the final act in the triumph of the romantic couple itself. The romantic couple is now intrinsically motivated or it disappears. Financial stress can easily overcome a weak relationship as trends in single parenthood reveal. Some ask, Why burden the romantic duo with the legal and financial barriers to a quick separation? Why do this *if* the standard is a *healthy friendship*? Marriage is a category of relationship we may idealize but, frankly, many of us now see as optional (especially if we do not intend to have children).

Students of long-term marriages are aware, as are most long-term couples, that the emotional and sexual energy of any relationship's first six to twelve months rarely lasts at that level of intensity. These are the dopamine-heavy months. The latter is why some individuals become obsessed with *starting* relationships, almost like drug-seekers chasing a chemical high. They come in hot and heavy and duck out when the high fades. Romantic love *is* a chemical high of sorts.[9] It's a sexually intense friendship at its most refined level. But not forever. This intensity in early romantic relationships is a chemical combination of sex hormones, pushing physical intimacy, *and* huge releases of dopamine.

What's interesting is that it is another chemical, oxytocin, whose release correlates to *all* intense social bonds, including friendships. It is the chemical of long-term relationships, ascribed and chosen. It is probably the dominant chemical in community formation. We all experience this as humans, whether we are in "dopamine" love. I have often wondered if autistic adults have an oxytocin *problem* underlying their social bonding challenges and their disinterest in human community. The research on this connection is too young and mixed.[10]

The formality of marriage historically had to do with the need to pressure people into responsibility for the babies they made as well as with strict religious beliefs in the West. Socially enforced marriage practices have taken many forms across cultures. Producing children immediately upon puberty was simply assumed in most cultures. But, in a modern, permissive society like America, some couples are still having unintended births while some couples are knowingly avoiding the "children" thing entirely if they would like (99 percent of the time). This is a wide variation both the Yanomami and my grandmother would not understand. While the growing Double-Income-No-Kids (DINK) lifestyle still causes a lot of awkward conversations among Americans, it is the natural outcome of a culture oriented to maximal lifestyle choice and one privileging the romantic *couple* as the dominant axis for initial household formation (*not* marriage or the imminent appearance of *children*).[11]

And the challenger household type in America is the lone adult household (with or without children)—*the anti-couple.*

Couple-centered versus single-adult-centered households. Fifty-five percent of US households (couples with or without kids) versus 37 percent (single parents and singles). It may appear too simple, but this dichotomy accounts now for 92 percent of all US households. The trick to seeing our society this way is to see that a "family" with kids is really anchored in a friendship (strong or weak) plus kids. The kids are no longer heirs to a family legacy but mostly the couple's output, its product, its intensively parented social proof as a good *couple*.

The fact that single parents are 8 percent of households doesn't mean that couple households (with kids) are disappearing long-term (nor does the US Census think so). Yes, there is a lot of diversity within couple households (same-sex, opposite-sex, with kids, no kids, with Grandma, without Grandma, etc.). But the quaint 1950s nuclear "family" with a patriarchal head (not a friendly *couple*) is not the dominant structure sociologically in American homes, even when we poke into couples raising kids (more on this in chapter thirty-two).

I don't even think "family" is the dominant experience of everyday life in adult society any longer, except among religious conservatives. We use the term lazily and without a lot of clarity. If the concept of "family" originally connects to the idea of reproduction, a unit that produces the next generation of kids (even if it takes a village to raise them), then "families" are a minority of American households today. A lobbying group at most.[12]

Regardless of whether you want to use the word "family" or not, the fact that most households have a single adult or a highly individualistic couple as the foundation is an inescapable reality. The presence of kids is culturally secondary and optional. This is our baseline cultural reality, and it partially reflects the primacy of individual autonomy and our assumed right to determine who lives with us at various stages of our lives.

We first live alone or with single friends, then we couple, with kids as optional add-ons who live temporarily with us before we revert to the "romantic" couple again or seek a new partner. We are not, mostly *not*, focused on the family.

Chapter Twenty-Nine

THE SHRIVELED FAMILY TREE IN AMERICA

I took Professor Nur Yalman's famous class on structuralism at Harvard when I was an undergraduate in the early 1990s. If you think that cultural anthropology is a jock major for intellectual lightweights, then you need to account for the mid-century work on tribal kinship. This stuff is like calculus. It's hard to follow and impenetrable until you make a few key insights.

Tamil kinship patterns are famous in cultural anthropology for their bizarre aggregation of global exceptions: a celebration of cousin marriage, status elevation of the mother's brother over the biological father, extremely strong brother-sister bonds, patriarchy without strict patrilineality, etc.

Looking back, though, now I see a complete disregard for the *emotional* layer of kin relationships in this classical oeuvre on kinship. Yalman's mentor, Edmund Leach, was no different. The French structuralist style of kinship analysis took the dry British approach to an even more esoteric extreme thanks to Claude Lévi-Strauss, who created binary labels (+ or –) for various kin relationships and then analyzed the patterns he saw across hundreds of individuals.

However, there is a master finding here. What all these "dull" kinship experts helped us moderns understand was how *reciprocity* functioned in preliterate societies to lubricate specific kin relationships and keep them active. In societies without writing or bureaucratic systems to support the community, the quality and integrity of relationships *gifted* into being is paramount.

What is the big takeaway here for nonspecialists?

Many premodern cultures taught their members to value and *keep track of a bewildering number of structural kin relationships* (by blood and through marriage) and to keep them active through *reciprocal exchanges of time and resources*.

If what I just summarized sounds alien to your family life, you are *not* alone in America.

Kin relations structured almost every aspect of everyday life in premodern tribal societies. Everyone you encountered during daylight hours was a relative of some sort. In societies like this, you do not use personal names. Instead, you address others by their kin relation. This makes sense if society's division of daily labor is also broken out by kinship roles.

The Nêhiyawak people (known by their language Cree) residing in what is now Quebec and Ontario have a classic bilateral kinship system with ultra-specific terms common to many human tribes. Words encode both the direction of the relationship (my/your) and its horizontal placement.

The Cree language they traditionally speak has *seventeen different words for "cousin"* depending on where they sit in the kinship map in relation to you.[1]

- *Nîstâw* or *nîscâs*—my older same-sex cross cousin
- *Kîstâw* or *kîscâs*—your older same-sex cross cousin
- *Nîtim*—my older opposite-sex cross cousin
- *Kîtim*—your older opposite-sex cross cousin
- *Nicâhkos*—my older same-sex cross cousin
- *Kicâhkos*—your older same-sex cross cousin
- *Nîcimos*—my younger cross cousin
- *Nisîmis*—my younger cousin
- *Kisîmis*—your younger cousin
- *Nîtisân*—my cousin
- *Kîtisân*—your cousin
- *Nimis*—my older female cousin

- *Kimis*—your older female cousin
- *Nistês*—my older male cousin
- *Kistês*—your older male cousin

If your eyes just glazed over, you are not alone. Your modern brain was never trained to care about these distinctions. Parsing relationships this carefully may seem academic to you, but it reflects our cultural lack of concern for such relationships. And our large demotion of family relations in everyday life.

Using kinship terms to address people you know well is not limited to tribal communities. I encountered it daily in India. This is how close kin address each other even today in many parts of India.

- "Older brother, come here I want to show you something."
- "Aunt, can you help me with this recipe?"
- "Younger sister, hand me that pot, please."

You can spend much of the day with your family in India and never use anyone's first name. Ever. It used to drive me nuts as a field researcher, because I couldn't just learn names by overhearing. I had to bother everyone, individually. I had to impose my American obsession with individualized identities onto everyone. When I shared this complaint once to a Tamil mother, she laughed at the fact that I thought this was annoying.

It is even common in Tamil culture to address nonkin, i.e., friends, by adding a kinship term as a suffix to their first name. In Tamil culture, you fictively "adopt" your close friends in this way, even strangers you want to nudge into close friendship.

For three years I was called "James-*Annan*" or "James-*Tambi*" by many individuals. *Annan* means "older brother." *Tambi* means "younger brother."

Yet, what I found interviewing older Americans (age forty-seven to seventy-six) for this book was something very different. It's obvious to the reader that English-speaking Americans do not use kinship terms or kinship suffixes at all.

What is *less* obvious to us? The younger the respondent, the less that older Americans seemed to know anyone very far out in the branches of their family tree. Most know the names of their aunts, uncles, and grandparents. Sure. But not their cousins, unless they hung out with them routinely as children (and some did). And certainly not the descendants of their grandparents' siblings. Those branches were a total black spot. A void.

Declining Family Intimacy in America

When I came home from India in 1999, one of the first things I noticed about American life was the deafening silence of extended family, in some cases, the total absence of any blood relatives at all in the daylight hours of American adults.

I'm not including your weekly calls to Mom or Dad or a sibling. That's not particularly impressive intimacy in the history of human family relations. I'm talking about your level of social intimacy with your *extended* blood family (the ones who should pick up the phone when you call). Cousins. Nephews. Nieces. Aunts. Uncles. If you even have their contact info. These relatives share an enormous amount of DNA and family history with you. In most cultures, they remain involved in your life as you and they age. They tend to feel obligated to help in emergencies, even if you do not see each other very much anymore.

Many of us take for granted that hanging with the cousins and aunts and nephews is rare these days. But is it? And, if it is, how rare are we talking? Answering this question became a bit of an obsession while producing this book. First, we need to define relationship intimacy in terms we can quantify to understand what has changed and the burden it places on spouses and our friends.

In my national survey of older Americans, living within a thirty-minute drive of a blood relative at least *doubled* the likelihood of visiting them weekly (or more). The thirty-minute drive barrier surfaced in my histograms as the real barrier to hanging with the fam. If you think about how spread out families are in America, this should make you gulp.

To operationalize my definition of "family intimacy," I actually combine two variables:

- Living within a thirty-minute drive
- Visiting the person *weekly*

The visitation requirement may seem too strict to most of you but wait until I show you what older Americans said about their relatives visiting when they were teenagers. Again, the older generations in America best reveal what has changed.

Extended Family Intimacy Today

What follows is a comparison of intimacy between cousins, aunts and uncles and their nephews and nieces, and grandparents and their grandkids:

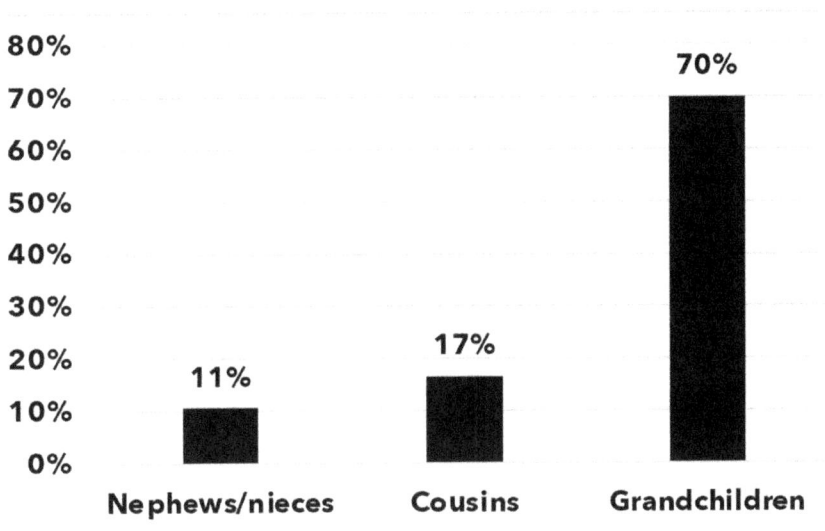

Figure 15. Percent of Older Americans Who Live Within a Thirty-Minute Drive of Specific Relatives and Visit Them Weekly or More. Table data sourced from SAI Older Americans National Study, 2022.[2]

The pull of closely living grandkids is literally *seven times stronger* than the pull of nearby cousins and nephews/nieces/siblings when you factor out geography using a thirty-minute one-way maximum drive. Whoa.

This is our first clue as to what has happened to our extended family "tree" in America. It has contracted *horizontally* back to the trunk.

Extended Family Intimacy in the Past

The second major clue regarding the dramatic changes to American family dynamics in the late twentieth century involves contrasting intimacy *across time for the same individuals.*

Forty-nine percent of older Americans had weekly visits from grandparents when they were teenagers. This is over *three times the prevalence* for today's grandparents and grandkids. This is an incredible statistic to dwell on. That was a lot of grandma time each year back then, probably two to three hundred hours a year at least.

For older Americans who experienced this in their childhoods, how many visit their grandkids weekly *today*? Only 21 percent are continuing this tradition. And even when we roll back in the folks who didn't have grandparent intimacy growing up, only 12 percent of older Americans you bump into today think weekly grandpa/grandkid relations are totally normal family behavior. Not many. It's an anachronism culturally speaking. A vestige. Museum-worthy behavior.

On the other hand, sadly, 74 percent of older Americans have not had this level of intimacy with their own grandchildren, and they are very aware of this. Very.

The primary causal factor here is geographic dispersion of the grandchildren (and children). But culture is also playing a role: the sacredness of privacy. And this is what I heard again and again in my life history interviews—a desire to see their grandkids more while at the same time grandparents appear unwilling to push the issue too far with their "busy" kids. Even the Super Stoics want to see their grandkids more. They just hint at it the least.

Withered Branches Due to Nuclear Family Involution

The intense magnetism of a nearby grandchild indicates how *vertical* the family *imagination* has become in America, vertical and close-in to that all important romantic couple (i.e., the one that is raising the grandkids).

At the same time, a *horizontal* perspective on family, the kind that produces seventeen different words for "cousin," has been lost to the sands of time in America and much of the modern, urban world in general.

The fascination with grandchildren aligns well with our near-future temporal anchoring as a consumer society. It is also an evolutionary impulse to fuss about directly lineal living descendants.

What's also interesting about our vertical, trunk-hugging family imagination is that we only seem to "know" anything beyond our grandparents' generations *if* one of those ancestors had wealth or was a person of prestige in general. Otherwise, the past beyond our grandparents is generally a blank or patchy/cloudy void of oral history for most of us. Even when we sign up for Ancestry to try to fill in this void, we tend to hunt for VIPs, signs of status lost, wealth squandered, curious ethnic origins, or maybe some scandal (her infant girl attended her wedding!). We look for prestige in the shadowy trunk below. What we are not doing is hunting for ordinary social history prior to our grandparents. What is interesting to us in our family past are the same things that interest us about our current family—symbols validating our current lifestyle and social status . . . for something more elite.

Our kinship imagination is not only highly vertical, but it is incredibly myopic in both directions (up and down the trunk). This vertical myopia is the consequence of not needing kinship to function at all in the modern world. It is also a function of how we view time as a society—the deep past is culturally optional and, when gazing forward, we look only at the near future promising the next new thing.

But how did this detachment from the past begin?

One clue emerges from the memories of older Americans regarding how they did or did not interact with their grandparents.

Eight out of twenty life history respondents I interviewed did not have any meaningful relationship with at least one side of their family growing up (due to early deaths or late parental marriages in the mid-century). Yet, all but one had a very close relationship with at least one grandparent, often on the mom's side. When I say close, I mean they saw this person every week or they lived with them during a long chunk of their childhood.

So, even though my survey picked up a lot of weekly grandparent interaction among older Americans, this was largely with just one set or even just one grandparent. In other words, even older Baby Boomers grew up *with parents who had started detaching from their own family past* (in terms of who they spend time with every week), sometimes dramatically. It just took a while for this to become a completely dominant, middle-class reality.

Early detachment from grandparents seems to correlate strongly with a loss in family history and a decline in the value of extended family input into your own life. These are the most closely tied windows we have into the past. Yet, we do not see them very often. And, honestly, I do not meet a lot of grandparents who want to be seen as "windows into the past." Old age = illness and a fixed income in our society. There is little positive we associate with this stage of life, even though it can be very enjoyable if you were able to prepare for it.

For an unknown, measurable proportion of Baby Boomers, though, they grew up with a pre–World War II–style family culture in the 1950s and then watched their parents drift away from extended family for work. Or college and employment separated them forever from their natal worlds.

But not everyone.

Here is what it was like as a teenager in 1970s New York for one Italian American man I interviewed who had weekly Italian dinners with grandparents, cousins, aunts, and uncles. He was the only one of twenty respondents I interviewed who could recount intense, lengthy, and weekly encounters with multiple members of his extended family (vertical and horizontal), *who all lived in the same town he still lives in today.*

> *JR: How much of a priority was it to visit aunts and uncles back then [in his teens]?*
>
> *Anthony: Back in the day it was. It was more of a, I don't know, if you want to call the tradition, but you know, even when you weren't with your parents . . . like. . . . Once I began to drive. . . . Let's say if I was driving by the town, and [my relatives] found out. You know I went somewhere near them, but didn't stop in. You know it was like it's almost disrespectful to do that. So, it was a priority to go visit, you know, brothers and sisters. . . .*
>
> *Back in the seventies, right? Our doorbell would ring. . . . We would go from watching the TV to flying to the foyer and sliding across the tile. . . . Hey somebody's here! Exciting. Blah, blah, blah! My mother would always have cake and stuff on hand. And we would welcome guests. . . .*
>
> *JR: Aside from your parents, did you have an emotionally intense or strong bond with any of your other relatives, adult relatives in your childhood?*
>
> *Anthony: Well, my mother's youngest brother. Vincent. He kind of came out of that hippie era, you know, late sixties, but he was younger than my mom . . . probably around seventy now. He was my biggest influence as far as music and culture. So . . . he was like that jokester guy, he was kind of immature like my brother and I, but he would teach us how to drive his convertible . . . we were like maybe twelve! [Laughs]*

Some of you older readers had horizontal extended family like Uncle Vinnie in your lives. Many of you didn't. If you were born after the baby boom (i.e., after 1965), the odds are higher that you never saw your aunts and uncles on a weekly basis like this. Sorry.

Chapter Thirty

FROM PARENTS TO LIFE COACHES

At the end of college, when it became clear to me and to my parents that I would be applying to doctoral programs in anthropology, I noticed something for the first time.

They changed their tone when talking with me. I can't prove it was the first time they changed their tone, only the first time I noticed it. My parents started talking to me as *coaches*, not as disciplinarians. The tone was supportive as long as it seemed like I had a plan and that I was taking steps. My parents were seeking *my fulfillment as an autonomous individual.* Compared to many of my Korean American Harvard classmates, whose parents badgered them into engineering or medical degrees, I felt emotionally spoiled with autonomy.

"What's the plan?" is the kind of open-ended question a good coach asks before sweeping in with a critique or a "build" while working with a client. The "W" questions (Who, Where, When, Why, What) are the hallmark of good interviewers and coaches (and teachers), but we don't associate this kind of conversation with parents or with traditional, patriarchal parenting.

Old-school parents set rules and enforce them rigidly. They provide resources and nurture growth. They correct. They discipline. They punish. And, yes, they still yell. In conservative cultures, they badger you into careers *they* have chosen for you, often because it is the family business. I never quite understood the logical ground behind a Korean father who runs a dry-cleaning business screaming at his

Harvard-educated son to become a doctor (real person I knew). Sure, it's obvious the doctor makes more money, but what does the Korean immigrant father know about this career? Nothing. Yet, the screaming went on anyway. I'm thinking that that dad is now among those 10 percent who are cut off from their kids.

This old, hierarchical view of parent-child relations makes sense in a society that is not changing that fast. As in Amish America. Or Puritan New England. Or in a survival-oriented society that is experiencing internal chaos due to multiple waves of colonialism (e.g., Korea from 1930 to 1960).

If you've made it this far in the book without skipping your way, you know that this is *not* the America we are living in (stagnant or experiencing violent colonial chaos). Instead, we are living in a society that has seen multiple forms of steady, inexorable change in everyday activities like TV watching, friendship, career pathing, food preferences, and family intimacy.

The problem for my parents and me in 1993 when I was applying for graduate school was twofold: 1) we didn't understand the employment context for academic anthropologists, especially the unwillingness of doctoral programs to throttle admissions given that few could ever find permanent academic employment and 2) my parents and I had no deep understanding of doctoral education and the tightrope walk toward tenure. We all seriously had no clue. I *really* had no clue.

I made the decision to apply without critical context and a huge overdose of upper-middle-class optimism. I told myself I would work hard, do well, and my awesome dissertation would magically carry the day. Even my dad thought this made sense. I would be the grad student as heroic knight jousting with the doubters and faculty haters. My "life coach" parents applauded this highly individualistic, merit-based *plan*. I'll admit all this enthusiasm was largely a WASP projection onto reality. There was *nothing* rational about it. Yet, you could have predicted it like the rising of the sun. For a kid raised like me.

And, more importantly, there was *no* plan B. This is probably one of the better signs of elite class privilege. Optimism with no plan B. What could go wrong?

If we give children the autonomy to select their own careers, even ones we know not the slightest thing about, then we the parents are not very useful at guiding them.

The lack of preparedness that I and millions of older Americans had for multiple career changes in our lifetime did affect us. In some cases, we surfed jobs and never found the career we intended. In other cases, like mine, we drifted into a career of desperation and eventually found a career we enjoy (because I literally confabulated it on the internet using the modern techniques of personal branding and huge gulps of pure desperation as fuel).

Life Coaching Is Time Intensive for a Future-Obsessed World

If parents have become life coaches, fully aware that their children will grow up into a world their early childhood did not fully prepare them for, then, as a society, we are staring at a very bizarre truth.

The modern household with a child or children is *extremely* child-focused, like never before in the cultural history of the world. There are fewer children than ever before in our households, allowing us to focus even more time and energy on each one.

Demographic and fertility changes did not *cause* parents to become life coaches, but they enabled us to think this is a normal and feasible way to behave with our kids. Experts call it "intensive parenting" to give it an air of scientific, child development rationality. And, yes, it skews toward the college educated.

At least two cultural value systems intertwined to send parents in the direction of becoming intensive life coaches in the twenty-first century: romanticizing childhood and anxiety over educational attainment (and, to a lesser extent, social climbing).

We have tended to *romanticize* childhood in the now huge American middle classes (including the upper-middle class) ever since the Victorian elite emerged in the late nineteenth century (those business owners, merchants, and professionals who benefited from the Gilded Age consumer economy). This era was when children were first protected from child labor due to the growing cash income of *some* households. By the 1920s, child labor laws in the United States then expanded this elite view of "innocent" childhood to a much larger audience across most American social classes.

Kids tended to "grow up" real fast in the preindustrial era. They were along for an *adult* ride, so to speak, especially before high school became a global minimum educational standard. Before the 1920s in America and the advent of high school as a mainstream goal, most kids didn't have extended, irresponsible childhoods drifting into long-education-filled Rumspringa periods with late marriages. That was the privilege of a tiny elite.

When I lived in Tamil Nadu in the 1990s, I got my first taste of *unbridled child labor with minimal social outcry*. I even hired one ten-year-old bus boy at a low-end restaurant to clean my home for an inflated fee (my idea of limited philanthropy). I had been living across the street from the restaurant where he worked for months, and he was a curious kid. I discovered later that his father had pushed him to find a way to get in my house for other "reasons." When I noticed 2000 rupees missing one morning, I realized I had been played not by a child, but by the child's father, who'd used his son as a cash generation tool. This is what it means *not* to see childhood as precious, what it means *not* to invest in your child, because you're focused on survival. In an adult-centered and struggling society, children become instruments of family welfare, not individuals who need nurturing and extensive investment. You only invest intensively in children when the future looks bright, and you have the resources to do it. This is why it was affluent Victorian parents who kicked off the intensive parenting trend.

The other cultural force permitting intensive parenting was the increasing desire for higher education (beyond America's famous, free, and ubiquitous primary schools). I suspect that the unemployment horror of the Great Depression accelerated high school graduation rates because it had become clear who had tended to retain employment versus those who stood in breadlines.[1] It was the emerging desk worker, the office worker, the schoolteacher who seemed to be doing fine. At least since this time period, American middle-class parents have sustained a steady anxiety over their children's journey toward educational attainment. This fretting extended after World War II to college degrees.

And later in the twentieth century, this anxiety extended among the upper-middle class to helping their kids obtain some kind of elite professional degree (even if the child *hated* the profession). Something to give them an edge. Anything.

The dark power of educational attainment anxiety comes from its seamless intersection with an emerging American desire to be seen as super-interesting, as *distinct* inside your own curated social network. PhD in anthropology and avid mountain biker? *Sooooo interesting. Let's connect on LinkedIn.* The more we feel the need to stand out as professionals, the more we will project this way of life onto our children unconsciously.

Our cultural fixation on each child's progress and development from infancy onward, combined with the increasing expense of educating kids through college, merged child-rearing (historically an *unconscious* process) right into the broader late twentieth-century consumer rat race many of us reluctantly participate in.

If you've ever studied or lived in societies not oriented to residential nuclearization and intense child development, you'll know that it is *adults*, not kids, who are the historical focus of most human societies. This is intuitive to any student of Chinese history, where the mainland Han Chinese developed ancestor worship and veneration into a nuanced ritual art form thousands of years ago. Worshipping *dead* adults from the past is perhaps the most extreme form of adult-centricity a human society can create. It requires local cultural systems that honor and value large extended family relations and resource distribution within and across these families. Even the child-suspicious Puritans of seventeenth-century New England were vastly more child-centered than most traditional societies. For one thing, each child's spiritual *development* was a matter of great family pride (and status display). The Protestant sects of Christianity kicked off the process of moral self-optimization that easily morphed into education-led objectives with even more years of intensive parental investment.

Intensive Parenting Became More Important as the Family Faded Away

Some have lamented the modern "nuclear family" residency structure, including my wife and I whenever we couldn't find a babysitter. But, as a social scientist stepping back, it appears that the problem of the isolated couple raising kids is less about who is in the residence (i.e., who is in the home) and more about access to alternative adults as on-demand resources nearby (i.e., who is in your neighborhood/vicinity). Infrequent *access* to nearby extended family is the real modern conundrum since World War II. This loss of frequent access to extended family members, or total loss of access, robs kids of high-trust alternative adult role models, even those like Uncle Vinnie and his not-entirely-legal driving academy for middle schoolers.

The frequent presence of other, high-trust adults in the lives of children is key to their social development. Historically, these were *relatives* in most societies, and you could find multiple extended family members (mostly horizontal) nearby, even if they did not live with you. They easily dropped what they were doing to talk with you. Across human societies.

When you grew up with a family-first ethos like my Italian interviewee Anthony had (don't you dare drive through our neighborhood and not stop in to say hi), you don't need to *live with* these other adult influences. They just need to be within that crucial thirty-minute drive distance or closer.

What this external adult access offers is not guaranteed wisdom, but certainly, someone else onto whom to distribute your emotional needs, someone beyond your exhausted parents. More than two people, the romantic couple. And definitely more than one person (for single parents).

While it is easy to say that childcare workers, YMCA staff, or schoolteachers can fill in for absent family members, I think this overstates how vulnerable any child is willing to be with bureaucratically assigned, *paid* adult mentors. Not very. In part, because only a few teachers are even open to this kind of student bonding.

What this yields is what David Brooks points out well in his recent critique of the patriarchal "nuclear family" that peaked in the 1950s and early 1960s (before the enormous lifestyle shifts of the 1970s).

> *That 1950–65 window was not normal. It was a freakish historical moment when all of society conspired, wittingly and not, to obscure the essential fragility of the nuclear family. . . .*
>
> *In short, the period from 1950 to 1965 demonstrated that a stable society can be built around nuclear families—so long as women are relegated to the household, nuclear families are so intertwined that they are basically extended families by another name, and every economic and sociological condition in society is working together to support the institution. . . .*
>
> *Fewer relatives are around in times of stress to help a couple work through them. If you married for love, staying together made less sense when the love died.*[2]

Marrying your best friend and taking off for a life in a far-off city is something we romanticize today in America, but I and other social scientists can assure you that this is a very modern and weird development as a mass orientation. And it apparently peaked as a behavior in the late 1970s and 1980s (as older Baby Boomers were forming families and settling down).[3]

What many Baby Boomers and Gen Xers discovered is that drifting away, or fleeing, from extended family threw away a powerful psychosocial resource, leaving the triumphant romantic couple to handle 90 percent of their problems with primarily "phone support." Your family turned into a patient, but not entirely engaged, customer support call center.

The added socialization burden of modern couples is why so many feel exhausted.

The standard of parenting has risen, and parents are more on their own than ever before. No wonder some are saying "that's too much work" and remain DINK households forever. They are benefiting from the power of individualism to let you learn from society's inadvertent maladaptations.

Chapter Thirty-One

DECLINING GENDER DIVERSITY AT HOME

My maternal grandmother, Frances, married a well-educated widower with a teenage daughter in 1937. They then had two girls of their own together. As part of a blended family, Frances raised three daughters and no sons. She lived in an estrogen-dominant household. When her two biological daughters were teens, my mom remembers her saying to them at one point, "You girls wouldn't be so boy crazy if you had grown up with brothers." My grandmother certainly had experience with brothers. She had five!

It turns out that my grandmother was onto something. Something huge in the cultural background of the twentieth century. Something we just don't discuss: a lack of gender diversity in the modern home *matters*.

My grandmother was a member of the Greatest Generation (b. 1901–1927). These are the long since deceased elders who lived through the Spanish flu, two world wars, and the Depression. That experiential mix made them pretty conservative about many things, especially money. *But this was also one of the last American generations in which you had a high likelihood of growing up in a large residential family.*

When I was interviewing older Americans, more than half of my respondents described very large natal families on either their mother's or father's side. Having five, six, or even eight siblings was much more common in their age cohort (my grandmother's) than it would be after World War II.

Looking at the decade when my grandmother was born (the 1900s), you'll see in figure 16 that households with five-plus kids at home were 35 percent of American households!

Wow. Just think of how many chores you could assign them! Luxurious! You could even assign one child to ferry you cocktails all evening. Hardly.

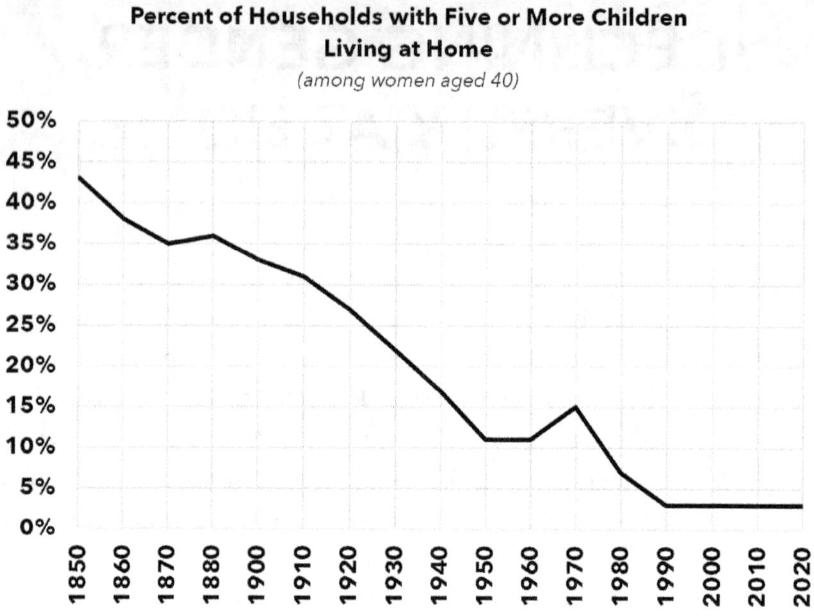

Percent of Households with Five or More Children Living at Home
(among women aged 40)

Figure 16. *Percent of Households with Five or More Kids, 1850–2021. Table data sourced from the United Census via IPUMS; analysis is the author's.*[1]

Then, the percent of large families starts falling off a cliff as war, the Spanish flu, and the Depression sap the fertility rate of American homes. My mother's home must have seemed like a library compared to the one my grandmother grew up in across town.

So, what changes when household size plummets like this?

Many things change, but I want to focus on the *most* overlooked fact in modern social science and popular commentary—the odds of growing up *without siblings of the opposite sex increase a lot.*

Let's use some high school probability math to see what has been going on without our realizing it.

As you reduce the average number of children in a family, the odds grow exponentially that any child will grow up *without* a cross-sex sibling—*without access to platonic, behavioral learnings about the opposite sex from an age peer.*

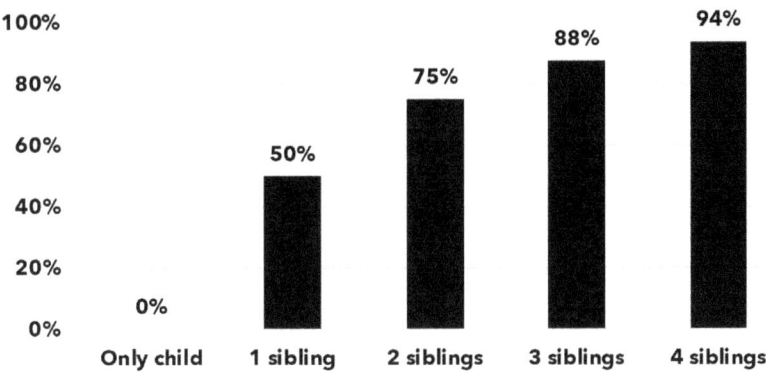

Figure 17. Odds of Having a Sibling of the Opposite Sex.

With the average lifetime number of children born to women today being roughly two,[2] we can see what this yields today's kids in terms of the most fundamental learning labs regarding gender identity and gendered behavior.

Here's what I found in my survey sample of older Americans:

- Thirty-two percent of older women grew up with *no brothers.*
- Thirty-seven percent of older men grew up with *no sisters.*

One out of three older Americans with a sibling did not grow up with a cross-sex sibling.[3]

Fewer births also mean lower odds of having *any* siblings at all (18 percent of older Americans' *kids* are only children), not just lower odds of a cross-sex sibling.[4]

This pushes the burden of mixed-gender socialization training *beyond the home* into our neighborhoods and primarily into our schools. Do you think we've done well with this?

The Tamil Case for Sisters Still Haunts Me

I was regularly interrogated about my family in Tamil Nadu, India, in the late 1990s. My favorite questions from total strangers?

"So . . . How many brothers? How many sisters?"

Notice the emphasis on the *amount*, not the presence, of either sibling type. *Surely, Mr. James has sisters.*

Nope.

Large families were still common in India then (and now), so this is not a silly assumption.

When I told these polite Tamil strangers I had no sisters, most suddenly looked sad. Tamil brother-sister relationships are very intense due to the likelihood of the sister producing children who could marry her brothers' kids. This is called cross-cousin marriage in cultural anthropology, and the practice, though in sharp decline, is not unique to southern India.

Not having a sister was rare when I lived in India, so everyone was confused about me, the guy with one male sibling. So sad. Ever since that time, I have been bothered by their collective look of pity. Was I a freak in America too? Everywhere I looked in my American social world, I saw homes with only children, two brothers, two sisters, or three brothers. It seemed common for American men to have grown up with no sisters (and vice versa). This was before I had sat down to do the probability math above.

The critical power of brother-sister bonding in Tamil culture is the expectation of lifetime flows of cash and resources from the brother to his sister and her children. Most major life-cycle rituals for daughters involve the maternal uncle as both a donor and a ritual participant. These events are very important in Tamil families. Accumulating cash to fund a girl's wedding jewelry is one of the most important rationales for these events. If these rituals (ear piercings, first menses, engagement ceremonies) flounder (or raise little), it signifies great family dysfunction. Which I saw!

Tamil sisters not only allow young boys to learn about gendered behavior patterns early in a low-stakes environment (e.g., fighting for bathroom time), they are critical to binding families together in flows of gifts and other resources.

Why Gender Diversity at Home Matters

My first girlfriend in college was nice enough, but we weren't on the same page about enough things—like dropping acid (not my thing). But that doesn't explain why she accused me of "having a lot to learn about women." Now, you could probably toss that accusation at *most* twenty-year-old men and be correct.

I can't prove it, but I suspect that we are churning out more clueless young men every year (and young women)—clueless about the opposite sex.

As an anthropologist attuned to the complexities of gender and kinship and as a man with no sister or stepsister, I want to share what I believe are just some of the social consequences of this bizarre, very common historical twist in modern family life.

1. A cross-sex sibling living with you as you grow up is a *critical training ground in nonsexual (i.e., platonic) peer interactions* with the opposite sex. They prove that they are possible (even if the person is physically attractive). Without this training, every "hot" female peer quickly becomes a sexual prospect.

2. Those of us in the forty-five-plus age set did not go to schools that promoted group projects in class, let alone mixed-gender group projects common today. Instead, we experienced school as a never-ending individual competition with same-sex peers. Help was outlawed. The boys ignored the girls in class or flirted with them.

3. Gen X and Baby Boomer men could sail through school and *view female peers entirely as potential sex partners* if they wanted to. Or they could ignore them altogether (which is what I mostly did). *There was no ritual*

enforcement of cross-gender collaboration like you would have seen in the nineteenth century on a family farm or in a family business. Brothers and sisters doing chores together is one critical learning lab for later life.

4. Gen X and Baby Boomer boys without sisters socialized with female age peers first in high school and college, when most of those interactions consisted of gender teasing or mating ramp-up activities (or, in my case, awkward fumbles). You didn't have female *buddies* if you were a straight guy. Refer to *When Harry Met Sally* for more details.

5. Gen X and Baby Boomers who chose professional career paths were thrust into 30/70 or 40/60 female/male office settings. But now there was a twist. For straight men, the mere presence of the opposite sex in these age cohorts tends to trigger an immediate erotic sizing up. It takes milliseconds. If the female is attractive, distraction will forever be in the background. Or, much more importantly, there may be a tendency to ignore the female's presence and insist on using male interactional codes (my big problem at work in the 2000s).

One rare researcher, Kimberly Updegraff, studied cross-sex sibling relations in depth years ago and has revealed how much girls absorb opposite-sex gender traits in their public, out-of-home behavior.

Girls growing up with a brother scored higher in both the surveys and the interviews on measures of assertiveness, showing a markedly greater tendency to try to exert control over their friends and playgroups.[5]

She found, however, that boys with sisters acted the same in public settings. There was no feminization of the boys' behavior.

A later study by William Ickes suggests that boys need an *older* sister to really adopt female gender traits like in-depth, empathetic conversation.

> *The males in the study who had older sisters scored significantly higher than those with younger sisters in terms of how much and how openly they talked during the sessions with the females . . . younger brothers with older sisters were an instant hit with the women they were paired with. . . . It seemed that they had learned what a woman thinks and what her expectations are.[6]*

Interesting. Why are cross-sex siblings so crucial for *boys*, especially? Empathy.

Boys gifted with a home that is gender diverse will see the "backstage" behavior of girls and witness their comments and perspective on boys/men in a relaxed environment. They will then be able to notice better what, if anything, women mask in "front stage" public settings later in life. And these lucky men, when arriving at the office as adults, are less likely to be confused by negative responses to male behavior patterns and more likely to be empathetic to the female perspective (including when confronted with their own bad male behavior). Having a sister won't prevent you from becoming a sexist pig, but you will definitely be better informed.

This kind of empathy is amazingly useful in the highly diverse office settings of the twenty-first century. Yet, as I showed above, almost 40 percent of older men did not grow up with a sister to "train" them. And those odds persist due to small household sizes.

I struggle to see how we can continue to permit one third of the male population to simply slip into the office as poorly trained individual men putting their foot in their mouth repeatedly. Surely, this is something workplace training could address in very humorous and engaging ways. The problem is bigger than sexual harassment. It's about basic empathy across gender lines. Leaving individual men (or women) to figure this out independently (like I did) is absurd and the source of needless office stress and miscommunication.

The proportional increase of women in the workplace from the 1970s until the 1990s was a rolling experiment in letting individual men "figure it out" with little community input. And in many cases, these generations of men not only did not, but treated the office like a high school locker room for their own amusement.

I only discovered the broader female perspective once my old company became 70 percent female. That's when I really met my fictive sisters. I also found I was a total misfit as a man raised without sisters in an older generation. When the interactional codes switched to female, I had a big, big problem I hadn't fully acknowledged before.

I eventually left that company for other reasons but spared them in the process.

Part Seven

THE FUTURE OF INDIVIDUALISM IN AMERICA

"Dad, you can really be selfish sometimes."
—a fifteen-year-old American boy

Chapter Thirty-Two

AMERICAN INDIVIDUALISM: A DIAGNOSIS

Across time and cultures, individuals have always had autonomy to varying degrees. It's the scope of autonomy that has varied a lot. And generally, the scope was very narrow regarding major life decisions. The "individual" is not even a Western concept per se, although almost everyone assumes it is because Western democratic governance revolves around a specific view of the individual citizen.

Human beings have always acknowledged idiosyncrasies formed by personal habits. And weirdos and misfits have existed in all societies, defined by local norms. Weird folks like me often became the seer or the shaman or simply took off into the jungle one night.

Most cross-cultural variance occurs in how much to honor, validate, or encourage the formation of eccentric, divergent habits or skills. In highly conformist cultures like the Amish, being eccentric is simply not a value and, therefore, less likely to occur. They use Rumspringa to eject the extremely nonconformist. In modern America, though, we celebrate all manner of eccentric achievements because we are fundamentally an achievement-based society and not one focused on community well-being as the paramount objective. Even our approach to fun, with its desire to showcase eccentric behavior and lively stories or jokes forms another theater for overachieving.

Americans applaud those who stand out most loudly, not those who conform. Even when many of us, deep down, would rather find somewhere secure to conform and ignore the many competitions we find ourselves in (i.e., best career, best marriage, best house, best kids, etc.). It takes an interlocking set of cultural values to make the individual the *primary* focus of a society's culture and public sphere.

In this book, I began by exploring the seven elements of a hyper-individualistic society as if I were an alien trying to make sense of it all for an orbiting mother ship.

Here's a recap of those principles:

- *Unlocking the variables of lifestyle choice* so that we can curate our increasingly idiosyncratic lives, and adapt to a rapidly changing future
- *Silencing the traditionalist power of the elders* so we can pick and choose from their world and curate our own personal futures
- *Making privacy sacred* so that only a few get to critique our behavior—the less critique, the more our eccentricities (and demons) flourish unchecked
- *Making the individual's problems their own to solve* and hanging back until they come asking for help enables risk-taking as if all of life is a never-ending Lakota vision quest in which others should rarely interfere
- *Rewarding productive antisocial behavior*, no matter whom it hurts in the near term, because the autonomy required for personalized achievement is paramount
- *Distracting us all with entertainment* such that social life becomes inconvenient compared to watching TV, even by ourselves
- *Chasing the next new thing to consume* supports both the economy and a constant need for incremental boosts in income

These have been the underlying rules behind the middle-class American experiment since the 1970s. And combined, these forces work relentlessly against solid community bonds, especially at the local level. Our broader economy heavily reinforces them as constructive values despite their mixed emotional consequences at the individual level.

Autonomy, it turns out, is as anxiety-inducing as it is exhilarating. It's volatile, like a Marvel Tesseract.

The additional problem I've mentioned throughout this book at times is that we have not been living in a static system. The forces above that make highly autonomous living possible generate different outcomes as society changes. If you've ever stood in wet sand as ocean waves crash into shore, you know the balancing challenge involved.

In the middle parts of this book (which you graciously made it through), I've explored significant changes in the five major domains of everyday life and how individualism fares as a way of navigating these changes we did not perceive or envision.

And this is what I've perceived as one solitary analyst:

Modern Work Reveals the Tragic Loneliness of an Individualistic Society

We place so much hope for our personal fulfillment and happiness in our work lives. Yet, most of us still work primarily to bring in income from strangers, people we can never control as easily as our passions. We are often apprentices without masters, looking for strong community at work not found in our personal lives.

If we follow the sirens' call to chase ever-rising income, work easily becomes a source of increasing frustration. There are not enough promotions or raises for all of us to beat inflation. Changing jobs to boost income is possible but brings significant emotional risk. You need to be super resilient in case the new job is a bust.

A limited proportion of us who have truly rare expertise *and* learn how to sell it are the most content. These professionals are rare statistically and well-paid. But these are non-scalable models of working.

Some of us may love our work, but most simply put up with it. Work in America tends to ask more and more without raising our compensation. The 2020 pandemic was a wake-up call for employers who finally had to accept the myriad kinds of work-life conflict that they had long ignored, especially those that women face.

The fact that we generally do not live with someone who is in our career, our industry, or even our profession makes the chaos and uncertainty of working for W-2 income incredibly lonely. Those who love us most have the least specific help they can offer.

And our local communities offer only the scantest possible career help—glorified résumé writing, job boards, and "transferable skills" storytelling.

Being autonomous in your career is not only advantageous in our company-first market economy; being superbly autonomous, even sociopathically, is essential. Those looking for community and solace at work usually are maladapted for salary competition. This way of working works against anyone not prepared to be aggressive and self-absorbed. And this is why our approach to work leaves out so many adults who just aren't built for self-promotional careerism. They function better in more protective communitarian approaches to work (i.e., like the family business of yesteryear or union-backed workplaces).

Even a college degree has not saved Americans from career chaos. What older Americans have learned from this career roller coaster is that we have less control over it than ever before. Only elite professionals (again) seem to change careers as a devout practice of calm self-improvement.

This need to constantly adapt and be ready to deal with the next layoff is why *What Color Is Your Parachute* is more of an American *survival* guide than an idealistic career planning guide. Every new postal account opening in America should come with a fresh copy.

Fun is Enjoyable, but It's Also How We Train Ourselves in Noncommittal Socializing, the Opposite of Real Community

America's number one export is "fun." Lighthearted, happy, not serious amusement. Americans all learn its basic rules at our first birthday party. It is about chasing an emotional outcome via parties, recreation, or, in the most common form, simply consuming hours of video.

America may have invented the casual, non-ritualized, informal adult party—a liminal psychic reset from the week's troubles (at school, work, or home). If we did, it owes its ethos to the high school and college party, not the stodgy, status-displaying cocktail party of Jay Gatsby's era.

At virtually any casual American party, we return to a state of childlike autonomy—with no responsibility (unless your kids are at the party!). This hits the spot after a week at work for most of us. Some of us even regress—a lot.

Most of the time, adult parties are innocent. But American party culture is also an unintentional factory of adult alcoholism and self-implosion. Our parties are an ongoing, unacknowledged test of self-control in a world that demands ever more of it for us to thrive. This is partly why partying *sober* is the new elite standard.

Despite all the witnesses, those who freely take party fun too far always get blamed for losing control. *Not we who willingly enable their loss of control* by watching in silence; we who applauded their "fun" behavior at the party are never responsible. In America, we expect the binge drinker to initiate recovery as a conscious act of contrition and self-control—the addict must *seek* recovery. The older American who went down the partying path of self-destruction in the 1980s and 1990s and refused to repent was often abandoned like an injured dog in the wild.

For American youth, fun at a party must also be *un-surveilled*, i.e., not ritualized with elders present and monitoring. Your age peers do the surveilling (with all the conflict of interest this implies). Thus, we learn from an early age that fun is mostly age-fractured. We keep the young in peer-related age bubbles apart from middle-aged and older folks. And the music/entertainment industry wants it this way. They sell more music and concert tickets by *dividing* us into age-based castes of fun.

Recreation is a less controversial but equally noncommittal universe of fun activities that have largely replaced the old social clubs of a gender-segregated pre–World War II era. For young people, recreation is also how they stabilize themselves in periods of romantic or occupational distress during the Rumspringa years. Recreational worlds of all kinds have ironically adopted the achievement ethos of American work, though, making it hard to find real community in them, not like the community at the Elks lodge of your grandfather's era.

Finally, if, as Americans of all ages claim, "fun" is an emotional outcome, it is ultimately context-independent. This allows us to pursue fun in noncommittal, casual, and tenuous social forms. Even alone. This approach to fun has ironically helped weaken the power of friendship, even as recreation increasingly forms a positive way to discover friends (and lovers).

We need to set limits on screen time *for adults*.

Highly Personalized Eating Routines Have Taken Over Everyday Life . . . But at What Cost to Community and Public Health?

We cannot self-actualize ourselves away from harmful food habits any more than we can magically pull ourselves out of a drug or alcohol addiction. In both cases, recovery is a group effort, a community responsibility requiring money, planning, and professional insistence (and expertise).

The American supermarket drowns us in excessive impulse-driven, unhealthy choices in the corporate quest to grow business value. In a way, though, we crave the diversity of food offerings we now have access to because we increasingly curate individualized diets, often unconsciously, as the most feasible thing we can control (other than turning the TV on or off).

The end of evening dinner as a *mandatory*, nightly event involving shared food was the first sign that the individual had conquered the moral and caloric gatekeeping force of the American home.

Daily snacking quickly swept in to take away some of the moral authority of the family dinner. Initially, snacking became an everyday behavior to banish hunger sensations. As it became commonplace in the 1990s, though, snacking absorbed the moral intent of the meal—healthy snacking became a new theater to project individual goals divergent from the rest living in your household.

Twenty-four/seven access to high carb, low nutrition snacks and foods combined with non-ritualized consumption has been a setup for excess calorie intake that we did not foresee because we naively believe in something called willpower . . . the same thing that will magically "protect" the emerging binge drinker at college.

As with obesity treatment, we choose to medicalize food-body interactions, leading to a growth in dietary modifications linked to food sensitivities that set us apart from others at home. I also have a *right* to be gluten-free, even if I do not have celiac disease.

As we have allowed ourselves the freedom to skip dinner, snack all day, and fine-tune our ingredient aversions, we have also allowed our foodways to become a moral and aspirational battleground that divides us from others. Accommodating lactose intolerance is one thing, but militant veganism? The desire to eat for moral advantage has become an under-discussed balm on the perpetual wound of highly ambiguous social status that individualistic societies yield. And college is the perfect time to ignite a hyper-individualistic diet that helps individuals feel in control of something, at least one thing.

Even the fully hosted dinner party could not survive intact because it asks too much of a modern host, whose approach to a party is more like a college student than a stuffy performance of social class. Hosts want to blend *into* the party, not toil in the kitchen for their guests. Or they want to *choose* when they fully host a gathering. And so, the potluck rescues hosts and guests following odd diets no one understands.

Individualism has made eating incredibly complicated and community more difficult to assemble in a very simple act: sharing a meal. However, the potluck shows America at its best, willing to include individual food preferences without debate or snark. Potlucks may be our best adaptation to individualism ever, a modern training ground in tolerance.

Individualism Weakens the Bonds of Friendship in a Post-family Society in which We Actually Need Friends More than Ever

Americans easily neglect friendships as we age. We are masters at this benign neglect. The TV and our pets are such effortless substitutes. Moreover, our best friend romantic partners *seem* to fulfill many of our most intimate friendship needs. As we age and life gets more complicated, many of us realize this just isn't true.

Because we obtain most of our emotional consolation and solace from our sexual partners and, to a lesser extent, from a parent or a sibling, friends have devolved from intense social partners to sources of entertainment.

American notions of reciprocity in friendship are still tied to entertainment. We don't do much for our friends in a practical/logistical sense. We desire independence from a stream of requests for help from them and likewise don't want to impose our needs on them.

Even though we don't rely on them for much that is practical, we still *rank* our friends. We lay them out along a basic trust continuum. This continuum helps us determine who gets access behind our wall of privacy. American individualism leads to a bizarrely guarded approach to friends, not a "more the merrier" social ethos I encountered in India.

As we age, Americans have become more emotionally dependent on their partners, especially men. The historical contraction of close friend networks puts more pressure on spouses and partners than ever. This sets up individuals for real problems if there is a divorce, a premature death, or a prolonged, chronic illness.

It's risky to put all your emotional eggs in one partner's basket . . . it is unprecedented in human societies. And we are not acknowledging the toll on older men.

Individualism Keeps Family Interference and Obligations at Bay While Overwhelming Parents as a Result

Just because your mother moved in with you does not mean "family" is your number one social priority. It's challenging to undermine a century of cultural advantage lent to the romantic couple. The mother-in-law cottage exists precisely to *defend* your autonomy and separation from daily obligations to Mom (or Dad).

The social structural data on American households makes it clear that single adults and couples anchor the structure of contemporary residences. Kids may be there, but there are so few kids in any one family that these homes are not really "groups" in a sociological sense, not like nineteenth-century *families*.

It is easy for the child in today's small, highly permissive families to get loads of attention and service. Spoiling them is easy, especially if the romantic couple is into high achievement, intensive parenting.

The small, weak structure of American residential patterns enables consumer autonomy to a large degree. There are fewer people to object to anything we say or do—the moral force of large residential families before industrialization is mostly lost to history.

Older Americans especially now have a very myopic, vertically biased view of our family trees. The grandparents-to-grandkids axis is the extent of it. They do not visit their extended family much, *even when they are nearby*. This is because family networks are of little use in an achievement and mobility-focused society delinked from cultural traditions. One exception is when we are well-off and about to raise seed money for a start-up (!). Our extended family have little to add to our most important daily activity—work—even when we're on a quest for a new job or career.

Modern parenting styles have also demoted the family. Parenting has evolved from disciplinary apprenticeship into a known adulthood (parenting as training a family clone) into a life coaching model in which we prepare our kids for a life of chaotic and unknown changes ahead.

Good parenting today is about socially upskilling your kids for maximal adaptability. This requires discovering any quirks and disabilities early on, which we increasingly do better at uncovering.

American Mockery of the Incompetent Individual has Evolved from Targeting the Physically Disabled to Marginalizing the Socially Unskilled

I grew up in the last generation that thought it was perfectly OK to use disability put-downs—retard, moron, microcephalic, mentally defective, cripple, etc.—when we wanted to make fun of the *individual incompetence* of our friends, family, or coworkers. For men especially, these physical and mental disability tags helped bolster insecure egos in a hyper-individualistic competition for various kinds of social status. The more you think you compete against everyone else in love, work, and recreation, the more incentive you have to engage in stigmatizing other individuals as permanently incompetent. Some have forgotten that, not long ago, most Americans rejected people with disabilities as broken individuals and most likely to "fail." We used to institutionalize them, lock them away, and refuse to discuss their existence. It's easier to mock people who live in absentia or are otherwise invisible.

In one sense, this old American tendency to mock the biologically weak *individual* is part of a male-dominated frontier and settler mindset, a competitive ethos of dominance over others. But this also epitomizes the "worst" part of individualism as a cultural way of life: the belittling of others to fuel one's own competitive striving—a release of nervous energy inside a brutal form of life historically best suited to the male offspring of the affluent.

You may feel that America has become more accepting of the mentally and physically challenged. Overall, I think you're right. However, *the desire to stigmatize the incompetent individual has not disappeared in America.* Instead, it has shifted to bullying those with social skills deficits. Ironically, Larry David has made a career of being the socially incompetent butt of this new kind of stigmatic talk. We call it "cringe comedy"; again, it is primarily men who enjoy it. I find this ironic because men are most likely to display the cringeworthy behavior.

I suspect that the rise of high-functioning, level 1 autism diagnosis is partly because people with below-average social skills *no longer hide well in adult society*. We no longer get a pass, like I did as a young person. The standards have been ratcheted because we are a fully realized individual labor economy with access to a broad array of talent (i.e., a better array than in a purely male-dominated workforce).

We must be networking and stranger-befriending masters like never before in American history. This is most true for educated elites. But your ability to navigate blue-collar networks is also more important in an era that is post-union. In a society built around an unstable, unpredictable labor economy (whose chaos drives most of our waking hours), adults have to rely increasingly on their own training, upskilling, and clever social skills to stay ahead of inflation. And I know I've spent a lot of time and money upskilling myself from a low baseline.

We have become stranger *dependent* as adult workers, relegating our use of friends and family to sporadic entertainment or amateur psychotherapy. Then fun becomes an emotional balm in an urban world resting on weak ties and few close relationships.

It all works in a clumsy way, but not as well for those who are socially unskilled, the shy, the abused, the traumatized, the depressed, and the wildly disconnected (e.g., a divorced man living alone with few friends).

These "exceptions" add up to a fair amount of people at any given time, though it is not easy to measure. And these alienated adults, hanging by a thin social thread, are too widely dispersed to notice easily.

The beauty of highly individualistic societies like ours is that the socially skilled and dominant can easily escape socially conservative lifestyle prisons and seek relatively un-surveilled opportunities anywhere in the country.

We can become settlers on our own personal frontiers. Some of us.

But, when things go badly, America does not have a ritual way to handle the broken individual. We do have professional interventions, but we refuse to push people into them. And we refuse to make the few proven therapies freely available and easily accessible to all comers. We cannot even staff for the therapeutic demand we are experiencing in America.

The more educated and affluent you are, the more opportunities and lifestyle alternatives you will perceive and encounter. This kind of empowerment has real perceptual consequences for young people. It easily overwhelms them with alternatives—alternative careers, alternative lovers, alternative friends, alternative activities, alternative diets—which leads to the exhausting impulse to curate and re-curate social networks and consumption patterns at the urging of marketing messages that also skew toward the affluent (who spend the most in our economy).

Radical autonomy is terrific if you're trying to *escape* something horrid (abusive husbands, cults, abusive parents, toxic workplaces, etc.). But without constraints, the overwhelming lifestyle choice of the modern urban world is anxiety-inducing for many. It requires enormous cognitive discipline to focus on specific choices and not get spun around constantly by alternatives. Individualism is most confusing and overwhelming *in youth when so many major decisions remain prolonged and unresolved for years.*

America's individualistic Rumspringa years are still a chaotic sh*t show. But, because a decent majority make it through OK, we declare it a fine way to kick off your adult life. Every misfit and failure seems like an anomaly in any social network. The broken are widely dispersed, not gathered together with a public health spotlight on them. We don't notice them.

The fact that 70–80 percent are OK is the standard for evaluating the health of American society. The other 20–30 percent are considered expendable. Individualism gets an easy pass.

"You can't solve everyone's problems," some of us say dismissively.

We all move on with our day.

We can do better than this as an affluent nation and as human beings.

Chapter Thirty-Three

GROWTH AND THE UNDOING OF COMMUNITY

I wrote a best-selling business book in late 2019, right before the SARS-CoV2 pandemic stopped the world in its tracks. It teaches entrepreneurs in physical consumer goods how to design, iterate, and scale a brand exponentially without a war chest of venture capital or inherited wealth.

Like many business books, it taps into the entrepreneur's desire for growth and scale and the social impact that scale can give a business and its founder.

Growth. It's not just an American *cultural* obsession that fuels a massive self-help industry. It's the structure of our entire financial system and everything in the private sector that this system enables.

You may be happy with your income or net worth. I don't know. But the odds are that you still want your savings and income to *grow*, at least as fast as inflation.

The intrinsic nature of modern consumer markets is that they goad you into seeking the next new thing in as many consumption categories as you can afford. This is a systematic intent of the marketplace, not one you consciously feel. Nor is it a conspiracy. Thousands of professionals and entrepreneurs feed this collective desire because they earn a living doing it. And we keep buying their stuff.

Linked directly to our ideology of never-ending growth is the belief in individuals' responsibility to achieve some measure of internal, personal growth for themselves. We no longer admire personal or financial stagnation, fitting in, and keeping things where they are.

An ideologically meritocratic, free-market democracy supported mainly by consumerism focuses on the market's pursuit of growth, not individual happiness. If you can find happiness within the rhythms of an achievement-based, free-market economy in which only social security, Medicare, and unemployment insurance have your financial back, great. But the market doesn't care. At all.

Individuals compete with each other in a startling landscape of indifference for such a wealthy nation.

The illusion of growth in America is very plain when looking at smoothed GDP growth over the long-term—see figure 18. We are trending back toward ultralow, nineteenth-century growth as Thomas Piketty warned years ago. And American consumer spending is a major, hidden reason. It is *not* keeping up with inflation.[1] In part, because wages have not. But also because the US Treasury keeps printing paper money to issue debt, a dangerous illusion of its own.[2] Yet even consumer debt access is not allowing spending to keep up with inflation—so the Emperor of Growth really has no clothes, as was the case with state-sponsored inflation in the late Roman Empire.

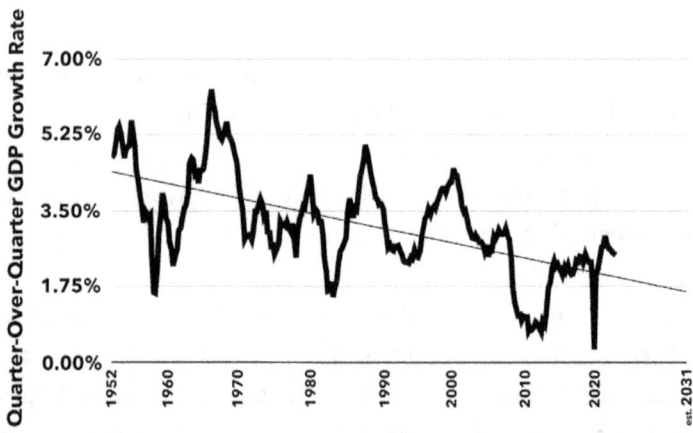

Figure 18. GDP Deceleration 1952–2023 (quarterly data is smoothed on a five-year, rolling basis). Table produced by the author from data provided by Tradingeconomics.com, originating from the US Bureau of Economic Analysis.[3]

Two unhealthy microeconomic variables have artificially propped up subpar growth in consumer spending: 1) tripling inflation-adjusted, revolving debt since 1961 (mortgages, auto loans, and credit cards) and 2) slashing our inflation-adjusted personal savings by 96 percent![4] Eventually, the credit might run out, the savings could disappear, and the debt becomes unsustainable. So, we start spending less permanently and GDP growth transforms into GDP decline.[5]

But there is another layer to the illusion of growth in a consumption-led economy: trading up to unnecessary premium alternatives. This is most widespread among the American upper-middle class (college grads with more than $115K in personal income), who can most easily afford to increase spending ahead of inflation (because their wages have beaten inflation).

By empowering all Americans, as individuals, to develop complex, ever more personalized spending diets across hundreds of categories, we are indeed spending more *per capita* than probably any other society in the history of the world. We wildly overthink our shopping, inserting all manner of aristocratic nuance into this activity that my grandmother (from the Greatest Generation) would simply find ridiculous. And our fragile GDP currently rests on this individualized, overwrought consumer culture and its desire to trade up in multiple categories. Our cultural needs for modern healthcare (to prop up individual longevity), auto transport, and big homes chew through more of our income compared to my great-grandparents' generation because the state does not take housing, public health, or public transportation seriously as a civic right with priority access to the public till.

As growth slows in any society, economists know that wealth creation shifts from labor and personal income to return on capital.[6] In other words, America is headed back in the direction of a nineteenth-century, even an antebellum, low growth, low inflation economy in which the middle class shrinks dramatically more than it already has since the 1970s. (It's diminished 11 percent in 50 years.)[7]

Growth and the New Aristocracy

Because of the enormous wealth concentration in the United States since 1990, the upper-middle class and 1 percent will self-perpetuate at a much larger scale than prior aristocratic elites. I have independently measured the upper-middle class at around 7 percent of the US population and growing.[8] It will do this within zip code–level bubbles of wealth where even getting one's gasoline prevents economic elites from easily encountering ordinary middle-class citizens.

This class-based residential apartheid is not news to many of you. I bring it up because, in an individualistic culture focused on a person's own growth (financial, moral, and otherwise), it is *not* the most important social fact undermining community health in the United States. *However, it is a great way to undermine support for federal wealth redistribution efforts*. Millions of wealthy Americans do not even drive by the forsaken poor any longer.

Our everyday behavioral self-absorption is much more fundamental in undermining the systems of cross-class reciprocity that sustain local communities. Highly educated adults above the age of fifty have been the least concerned with this because we grew up with a solid inherent faith in the state to solve issues of interpersonal inequity.

However, trust in larger government entities is hard to sustain without a strong foundation of local community trust. We project our *local levels of* trust onto the state based on what we feel moving around our local communities. Trust no longer seems to exist even in your average HOA, let alone within municipalities or counties (in the West).

And our way of life does nothing to build that local community trust into our daily and weekly schedules. Our leisure-focused society (leisure is almost as many hours per day as work) either distracts us from social life entirely or focuses us on a small circle of friends and family *who do not live right next to us* (and are not easily accessible in person). My "best friend" could be an online gamer in Manila.

The low-cost social distraction provided by video entertainment keeps us at home more than ever outside of work hours. Entertainment is only 5 percent of average household spending, yet leisure is 30 percent of our waking hours.[9] Imagine if your average hour of television cost you $75, not 75 *pennies*. Would you be more likely to have real watch parties for Netflix instead of sleeping through seven episodes of the latest *Below Deck* release? Or hang out with your kids more?

This would be simplistic because it assumes we have a strong, repressed desire for much more social time if we just didn't possess the cheap distraction of various screens. I have been quietly making the case in this book that most of us consciously *prefer* our individualistic way of life as it is. The issue is one of entrenched *values*, not our deep-seated frustration at being unable to socialize or help our friends more.

We simply have forgotten what we no longer have in terms of the local community and have adapted accordingly. And we don't necessarily see our individual-first adult behavior as a root cause for ballooning problems around us like drug addiction, alcoholism, teen anxiety, adult depression, and suicide.

The discontents of individualism remain largely hidden from public view and our conscious perception.

Community Is Now Bureaucratized, Professionalized, and Even Branded

The challenge with community rebuilding in America is more profound than our lack of desire to participate in communities of mutual obligation. We have adapted to strange forms of community that suit us culturally and are merely pseudo-communities. This is because they do not enforce obligations at all or do not enforce *mutual* obligation. We have lost so much basic understanding of a healthy human community. In some respects, the traits of healthy communities *offend* us. Obligation, especially, cramps our cultural style as modern individualists.

We can best measure the health of communities when individuals are in distress. This is when we see what is really going on. Not after a natural disaster but in every quiet slippage into addiction and in every suicide attempt. After every brutal layoff, corporate firing, or gustatory crossing of the morbid obesity threshold. In America, these events generate collective shrugs from most of us.

Some personal problems are so intense (i.e., addiction) that it takes a group to intervene directly. This has always been the case in human societies, even preliterate ones with minimal technology.

We modern Americans know this intimately if we have ever been to the emergency room. You're not at the ER to interact with *one person*. We expect a team of specialists. But we accept group interventions like this only when a) we *seek* them out and b) when a *professionally managed*, bureaucratic entity offers them.

We may want family or friends to know or pay their respects later, but not to handle or force an informal group intervention common to traditional societies. We have moved beyond inviting the medicine man into what is a family-hosted healing event. That's not modern, because the *family* is the source of the solution.

We trust bureaucracies like hospitals in the modern world—a lot. We depend on hundreds of bureaucracies for our everyday lifestyle in ways we don't appreciate until we watch the first season of *The Walking Dead*.

We criticize bureaucracies all the time. We love to hate them for the slightest problem and for huge letdowns that do occur. But we are entirely dependent on these giant, complex organizations, nonetheless. They loom over us. No Wild West homesteading alternative would deliver a similarly affluent lifestyle or superficial middle-class comfort level. Few of us are skilled enough to go off-grid anyway. We would quit within a month or two tops.

For most of us, our most frequent experience of "community" is interacting with a bureaucratic entity or a retail business. We encounter these *professional* communities as consumers in a capitalist exchange cycle, even at the ER.

For parents, there is also the local school their kids attend—a bureaucratic community where trust is not super high.

At work, we experience "team community," also crafted like a bureaucratic entity (even if the team is small). The trust here is narrowly scoped and variable in strength, depending on the organization.

But, in all these bureaucratic communities, no one we interact with understands us as whole people. They only see slivers of us based on what we enter on forms or choose to reveal at the water cooler. It is the most alienating possible form of community interaction. There is no way to humanize ourselves inside a bureaucracy, not completely.

Beyond these types of everyday bureaucratized "communities," Americans experience their own private thoughts and mostly a series of dyadic interactions at home. Texts. Calls. Video calls. Conversations mostly in homes with two to four people. This is what social life is like in an individualistic society like ours.

Either bureaucratic groups or slivers of dyadic communication between those well-known to each other. *And little in between.*

Rarely do we sit around in informal groups on an *everyday* basis. Think about this for a bit. I'm sure you are trying to contradict me in your mind. But remember that I italicized "everyday" for a reason.

A weekly happy hour with buddies does not count.

A monthly family barbecue is impressive compared to many Americans, but it also does not count.

If we reflect on the individuals who get total access to our lives and to whom we feel most obligated—it's a small list indeed.

A real human community beyond our family members requires regular contact to sustain (weekly or more frequent). And we simply don't commit the time for this. Our everyday time is reserved for *individual* income generation, eating, drinking, and media consumption (fun). The effect of friends and family (not living with us) is hard to measure on a daily basis.

Informal human community (friends and family that comprise local community in eras past) sustains itself in reciprocal sacrifices of time, money, and labor. Not holiday cards. Not birthday calls. Not barhopping. Not bungee jumping once a month. Some of us have one or two friends who might fit into this description, but many of us do not, especially those who see friends primarily as sources of entertainment. Strangers who simply entertain us are not the raw ingredient of community.

The internet chat group, social media group, or social network came into this vacuum for daily group interaction. Except that we've never seen most of these people in real life, only a profile photo. These social media communities are the epitome of "entertainment networks" unless they are focused on an activity you need information about regularly (e.g., electric car groups for newbs).

The *brand* community is the newest form we are invited to join regularly. Often, this occurs in the form of an e-mail newsletter. I run one for my own business as well. I just don't call it a "community." I cannot dishonor the word to that degree.

Marketers have taken the shallow American definition of community and run with it. The reciprocity underpinning these brand communities is that a) the marketing team entertains you, and b) you respond by continuing to buy. Wow.

The brand community cannot be a real community, of course, because the consumer does not interact with the business owners or know them personally for most brands. And they don't need the e-mail per se. It's a somewhat needless reminder to the consumer, even if it does nudge one more purchase that may not have happened.

Americans do not often access informal communities in the ancient human sense. We mostly experience professionalized, bureaucratized communities embedded in capitalist systems of *impersonal* exchange.

Communal Empathy as a Threat to Our Autonomy

If ten of your relatives come over unannounced to convince you *not* to do business with person X or Z or to postpone your home renovation to avoid bankruptcy, we consider this to be rude, even medieval behavior in middle-class America. Some may even associate it with mafioso practices. I can tell you that it does not fly in northern New England.

Who cares, you ask?

When individuals fall off the rails in our DIY society, they suddenly realize how alone they are. When a close relative slides into addiction, for example, we still do not get it. We still don't see the absence of a functioning group intervention as a problem. We look to bureaucracies and professionals.

When a crowd of well-known local people comes to your door unannounced, you immediately know it's a huge deal. You almost assuredly will let them in your home and listen, even if you remain a stubborn mule.

The group versus one solitary person is a powerful human interactional dynamic largely lost to the lives of most Americans. Yet, we view this style of confrontation as a total negative, a horrendous situation that we have evolved away from, moved beyond, etc. We're so much more sophisticated than bullying the wayward soul back into line.

Are we, though?

While we know rehab works and how to de-addict adults from substances, we still rely legally on the addict to raise their hand and ask for help.

"Pardon me, my dear wife, but may I please be driven to rehab?" is not a sentence you will hear uttered by a drug addict in the throes of addiction, and certainly not early in the cycle, when so much downstream pain could be avoided.

So, many American families tend to cut off the addict, demonize them, and eventually abandon them to preserve their mental and economic well-being. I understand why a parent might eventually resort to doing this. Watching your child implode slowly is a form of torture we do not acknowledge as a society focused on the upside.

We all train ourselves to be callous in this way by watching endless news stories about total strangers and blaming these strangers for their problems. We all do it or have done it.

- *Oxy overdose?* Get your sh*t together. Get help! Commit to help!
- *Homeless?* Get a job, take your meds, stop smoking crack.
- *Unemployed?* Apply like crazy, take anything to bring in cash, get on it!

It's easy to play the judgmental puritan cleric watching a TV story about a stranger who means nothing to you. And we watch thousands of these stories in our media lifetimes now. Throw in similar plotlines in films and our lifelong training in callous dehumanization gets amazingly efficient, almost like weekly church attendance once trained us to be *empathetic* about our community. Church, mosque, and temple accomplished this by forcing us to meet and trust people in our community *unrelated to us.*

So, we don't have a local community intervention process composed of people who know the person well (friends and family). We let this kind of community intervention slowly disappear and get replaced by professional intervention. *The problem is that most people never get that professional intervention or get it in time.*[10]

A community led by the bigoted can be a source of social evil when its members attack defenseless individuals or members of a stigmatized group. Yes. But to fear informal community interventions of *any* kind is too easy a cop-out. It allows us to return easily to our leisure time full of individualistic pursuits. Caring is time-consuming after all. Tough conversations can last for hours.

This "cop-out" is why Americans continue to outsource all sorts of disputes and social conflict to the local "cops," who are not trained to intervene like a psychotherapist or social worker. They detest these resident calls, including the domestic abuse ones.

It's interesting that some of us are so threatened by the obligation-heavy, style-cramping reality of informal human communities that we are willing to embrace a view of life and living in which the individual who cannot solve their own problems is *worthy of our passive neglect.* They failed the individualistic ethos so we can discard them. *We can revoke our empathy at will in an individualistic society.*

This is the essence of noncommittal social life in a hyper-individualistic society—revocable empathy. Revocable even from our "friends and family."

Empathy means accepting that others' suffering could easily be your own. This is why it is a critical component of any human community. But in an individualistic society, which is inherently competitive, we cannot imagine ourselves as embedded inseparably within a community of others. We have replaced community with curated social networks of personal advantage or entertainment. The American civic religion of a private, autonomous self corrodes not only community health but also encourages a lack of empathy in the pursuit of one's individual goals.

In traditional societies, harm brought to any individual wounds the community and results in a communal response. Dropping everything to help does not signal the individual was a VIP or more important than anyone else. It signals that the *community* was wounded and needs to heal that wound. In real communities, we see our suffering in the suffering of any one member.

It's possible to find this kind of community in America, but it is rare. And, if you do find it, it is most likely composed of individuals who lie at the margins of our achievement and growth-obsessed consumer economy. They have chosen a life based on community, not chasing wealth or status. I see these native social critics from all walks of life. In many cases, they have survived the trauma cycle and understand what happens in a low-empathy society with weak community (or none).

Chapter Thirty-Four

THE RIGHTS-ENABLED CONSUMER IN SOCIAL RETREAT

In my senior year of high school, I delivered a speech at a student awards ceremony on what I now feel is the central problem of American individualism as a cultural ideology. My talk pointed to our loud American focus on individual rights *and our conspicuous silence on individual obligations to the communities in which we live.*

Since the civil rights era, many Americans have discussed the "individual" in the public sphere as a rights-bearing entity, a bundle of rights. At the time I gave this speech, in 1990, very few beyond the religious right talked about obligations to society or community, even in the simple way of John F. Kennedy at his 1961 inauguration—"Ask not what your country can do for you, but what you can do for your country."

The continuing fight for equality of treatment and opportunity for ethnic minorities, women, people with disabilities, LGBTQ individuals, immigrants, non-English-speaking residents, and others fuels our modern concern with *expanding* the right to be an autonomous, equal, and equally empowered citizen. It's a massive project of inclusion.

For many of the disempowered subpopulations I just listed, discrimination and hate speech make them suspicious of the state, the police, large pools of strangers, and even groups as small as their own neighborhoods and school districts.

In addition, as I've narrated at various points in this book, escaping the suffocating lifestyle constraints of traditional families, towns, and religious groups is something we usually celebrate in the name of individual freedom and autonomy.

For the stigmatized, especially, the local community is always at risk of being the source of their biggest problems in life—hate, violence, and denial of opportunity.

For those who define the individual primarily as an autonomous, rights-seeking being, this all makes sense. But it is also part of a tragic view of communities in America as historically, irrevocably flawed. Community becomes disappointing, hypocritical, brutal, and full of betrayal.

The result is a persistent, understandable belief: *The local community and society tend to infringe on my freedoms and my right to autonomous movement, achievement, and expression.*

So, why try to rebuild it?

Some members of stigmatized groups find it more sensible to retreat socially into their families and carefully curated, narrow communities of "people exactly like me." And among the stigmatized I would also include poorly educated white people shut out of acceptance among the urban elite (even when they are wealthy). This tribal tendency is incredibly normal human behavior—curating circles with minimal lifestyle variation. But it is a *defensive* form of tribalism, a reaction to a broader culture that doesn't take their suffering seriously as a communal responsibility to solve. Insensitivity toward the problems of minority groups is an extension of our insensitivity to the average stranger's problems. Americans largely hate listening to the failure of groups of self-described "victims" in a hyper-individualistic society. It annoys us because it exposes the lie behind our way of life—that individualism as a way of living ever had mass applicability.

Ironically, the more we are left to fend for ourselves, the more most people seek to find the smallest possible tribe to nestle inside of psychologically. Only the white, male, affluent neurodivergents like me seem happy to fight alone for our fortune. It's easy for us to fall for the fallacy of self-reliance.

At the same time as the civil rights movement, the entire American middle class accelerated the overthrow of conservative, ancient human ideas that have limited human autonomy for millennia in both classical civilizations and tribal communities (marriage is mandatory, having kids is mandatory, divorce should be mediated by elders, helping family is compulsory, taking care of babies is women's work, etc.). And Americans did this incredibly fast as a society.

This delinking from tradition and community permitted the appearance of something else—the fully realized, autonomous consumer.

This leads me to the other concept that individual Americans act on in their everyday lives—the individual *as a bundle of consumer preferences*. It is the inner-directed individualist playing with their own desires versus the external individualist fighting for inclusion and respect in the public sphere. This concept of the individual as a bundle of consumer preferences is absent from most philosophical conceptions and most academic political science as well but it is real and inextricably linked to a postindustrial consumer society dependent economically on citizens buying virtually everything they need and even more, everything they simply *want*.

If we combine both latent concepts, we see the American individual as a rights-enabled *consumer* interested in defending her lifestyle autonomy against any confining claims by family or community. These two concepts love each other deeply because, without socioeconomic autonomy, we are extremely limited in what and how we can consume.

The result of training up a nation of rights-enabled consumers is a bewildering number of lifestyle combinations I discussed at the beginning of the book. I suspect no museum is large enough to "display" them all. And they are most likely increasing in number as time goes on.

One major result of lifestyle diversity is the emergence of market niches to serve them—everything from black television, road cycling and gluten-free eaters to LGBTQ travel, nightclubs, and even nudist resorts.

More important than all this lifestyle diversity is what it yields in our everyday encounters with strangers and new acquaintances—at work, on the sidelines of our kid's soccer games, and at the bar.

It is much harder now than two hundred years ago to bump into a stranger near your home and be "on the same page" about *most* lifestyle decisions (marriage timing, sexual orientation, home value, who is the dominant partner in the relationship, car preferences, sexual practices, interest in extended family, recreational passions, TV preferences, etc.). You will quickly bump into a choice the stranger has made that contradicts one you have made. I think most of us know the modern problem of making lifestyle assumptions about new strangers in our lives. Oops. We get it wrong very quickly.

Some of those who recognize this awkward truth caused by lifestyle diversification also remain confused about how many "contravening" lifestyle choices a new acquaintance can have . . .

- *Before we don't feel like continuing the conversation*
- *Before we don't feel like having them over for a beer*
- *Before we don't feel like spending the two hundred hours or so it takes to form a close friendship*

And does it matter that we may increasingly bump into people with lifestyle choices we don't like, agree with, or just don't understand (e.g., reading romance fiction, practicing nudism, transitioning to another gender, becoming a Substack author instead of doing premed, continuing to drink Bud Light, single parenting, seeking random hookups, engaging in polyamory)?

The list you just read deliberately had examples on a continuum of triviality (your continuum probably varies from mine). But all these lifestyle choices are non-majoritarian. Most Americans don't make these choices. Many of these non-majoritarian choices can easily hide behind the veil of privacy and concealment we learn to don early in our lives.

A group of us defiantly believe that our sacred veil of privacy is essential to getting along with all this lifestyle diversity (trivial or not). Don't ask, don't tell has quietly become our de facto code of stranger interaction.

By not communicating much about our lifestyle behaviors, we can skim the surface with colleagues, even with some of our weak friends. We avoid the awkwardness of "too much information."

I'm not here to divulge research on how tolerant we all are of lifestyle diversity in America. That's a huge empirical task I leave to large teams. I doubt there is a hidden tribe of Super Tolerants who Buddhistically accept all, no matter what they divulge about their behavior. There is little in human history to suggest we tend to behave this way when encountering lifestyle diversity that suggests some of our most basic choices (i.e., marital practices) are *optional*.

Yet, I want to raise a troubling question for which you may not be ready.

Is it just too easy in modern America to write off someone for a bit of lifestyle diversity you disagree with, don't like, or don't understand?

I think it's easy to do this. I've even done it myself. It is amazingly easy with a Facebook stranger trolling your post. Still easy with a cousin. And even with a colleague.

I suspect this ease of dismissal over lifestyle divergence is one reason we have fewer close friends than ever. But my larger concern is that urban communities unravel if we cannot even tolerate the lifestyle diversity implicit in what Robin Dunbar calls the outer rings of our 150-max social connections. These "weak ties" are invaluable to us as social actors and connect us to everyone else's social networks.

If we become accustomed to dismissing strangers and weak ties too quickly, without trying to accept and include them, we retreat to our island of three to four close relationships inside a potentially narrowly conceived racial, ethnic, and gender tribe of our own making. And we just stay there. Or we spend more time alone, consuming media. This degree of retreat is also something incredibly new in human societies. Few members of the premodern, preliterate tribes I've studied lived in groups of less than fifty to one hundred nearby relatives, people who were often within earshot all day long.

Our society, on the other hand, allows the disgruntled to live alone, collect social security, and watch TV *for years*.

This kind of extreme social retreat works against feeling obligated to serve a broader community. Because to feel that obligation, we need to accept and tolerate minor to moderate lifestyle differences on a regular basis. To serve the community, we must believe those with other lifestyle behaviors deserve our aid. We simply must be able to be obligated to the annoying. *Isn't this what marriage becomes if we're honest with ourselves? If we can love the annoying spouse, why have we become so stingy with that love?*

The more we make things like drinking Bud Light or single parenting deserving of social rejection, the more we turn down our scope of empathy in an era when, ironically, we need more of it than ever to stay connected enough to make local communities function.

A consumer society of rights-seeking individuals tending toward lazy social retreat and dilettantish consumption does nothing to build empathetic communities. Instead, it encourages the faux tribalism we see all around us but downplays its shallowness as normal. Then, we all return to our Netflix binging.

This leaves an alienated society of seemingly autonomous individuals competitively choosing their way through life (the next promotion, the next relationship, the next potluck, the next Netflix series to binge, the next new consumer object). Yet, the more lifestyle intolerant we are, the more we're vulnerable emotionally to the consequences of a layoff, a failed relationship, or rejection by a child following a wildly divergent lifestyle.

Hate and tyranny love weakened families and communities. Dictators love societies full of people who focus their days on buying things and consuming media more than feeling obligated to interact more and more deeply in their social networks. Such individuals are *defenseless* against a corrupt state.

Cycles of reciprocity sustain local communities, preferably face-to-face ones. Unidirectional philanthropy and charity do nothing to keep them going. This "aid" separates people experiencing poverty from the well-off.

The obligation to get enmeshed in your local community is the most challenging thing to ask of Americans today. And it is not restricted to helping people experiencing poverty (a difficult thing for the inexperienced to do well).

It starts with your friends and colleagues. And your close family members. We must find our way back to being reciprocally obligated to these folks first. That's probably all we need to do to jump-start local communities, thanks to the overlapping nature of all social networks on the planet.

Chapter Thirty-Five

EMERGING COUNTERTRENDS

To surface the hidden influence of individualism inside of our social lives, this book has leant a deliberately lonely feeling to modern America. This is also because my primary research and the academic research focus primarily on older Americans, mostly white, who experienced rapid changes in lifestyle possibilities here in America. And because older Americans are more socially disconnected than other age cohorts.

As immigration has surged in the past twenty-five years and the fertility rate among non-white females has pulled ahead of white females, our country is now on track to be mostly non-white by 2050 or so.[1]

If the approach to analyzing the individual in this book has had an ethnic bias toward the non-Hispanic Caucasian experience (as I followed the experiential wisdom of older Americans), then could it be possible that America's changing ethnic composition will essentially moderate the problem of excessive individualism on its own? Perhaps immigrant cultures will teach us the value of community more effectively?

Does Cultural Diversity Work Against Individualism?

Placing strangers in racial or ethnic boxes is a learned behavior, one learned very young in America. And extremely dark skin has always been a stigma in this country since before its founding. Racial stigma involves more than a simple assessment of skin tone. Behavioral cues tend to let individuals out of this or that racial box in specific contexts (a discussion at work). What reaction dark skin garners you as an individual has varied from place to place and over the decades.

The persistent division caused by racial profiling in everyday life (not just by the police) is sadly ironic. It is *sad* because we are better people than this, most of us, and we should be able to stand up to our racist colleagues, family, and friends when needed (cf. George Floyd). It is *ironic* because my national study of older Americans' beliefs regarding individualism showed no statistically significant differences for non-white Americans in my sample. This held across the multiple measures I used. I looked again and again, yet it is true that we all share a common fixation with focusing on an achievement-oriented, individualist path in life. We believe this is how you succeed in work, in love, and even in fun. Race and ethnicity correlate more to access to opportunity, or to the ability to exercise our culturally desired autonomy.

It is the basis for national unity, even though I have shown how it blunts our empathy, our compassion, even our ability to perceive when huge social forces like the media and the market economy structure our seemingly individual choices.

Individualism has helped us integrate as a divided country before, remarkably quickly. Vietnam War mobilization was a major accelerant in overcoming long-held racial prejudices, because it was the first fully integrated military conflict. It let American men especially understand that the promise and dream of American individualism *were broadly shared*.

One of the less discussed lessons of social integration in the United States was the surprisingly quick spread of interethnic marriage (German-English, Swedish-Italian, Irish-Italian) among Caucasian Americans after World War II. And it drove my maternal grandmother nuts at times if I am to believe the family gossip.

The appeal of ethnic endogamy is still strongest among English Americans and German Americans (most likely because there is so much wealth in these two groups). However, by quickly expanding marriage to *any* European American, white Americans created an enormous marriage market in which individual romantic preferences could dominate.

Creating a "white community" depended heavily on America's ideology of meritocratic individualism as the social glue and may be a precedent for integrating an increasingly multiracial America.

Interracial marriage rates among newlyweds have already grown to 17 percent as of 2015, and the trend is geometrically steady in its slope.[2] The active, bigoted opposition to marrying out of one's race declined dramatically in the 1990s, especially America's opposition to a relative marrying an African American.[3]

If we follow the logic that individualism *promotes* interethnic and interracial marriage by subordinating loyalties to traditional identity groups (by silencing elder opposition to major lifestyle choices), then *a resurgence in tribalistic endogamy would be one way to weaken our dominant cultural ideology.*

Yet, there's nothing of the sort happening, as far as the data suggests. Among postgrad educated elites, there is a recently higher amplitude of ethnic pride since the 2020 George Floyd incident revealed that the great project of multiracial inclusion has not achieved its goals. It's unclear, though, whether this racial or ethnic tribalism has any real broad relevance as a dominant force for most Americans, even for young Americans' view of the world.[4] A broader look at national behavior suggests we are moving away from strict racial filtering for dating and marriage. *I suspect that racial endogamy has more now to do with who you get exposed to in your social network. If it's mostly white, the odds are low you'll marry interracially.*

If we want to find signs of a rebalancing toward community obligation in American life, we have to look elsewhere. Racial and ethnic tribalism does not seem to be it. Even the white nationalists have a *shrinking* audience, which is why their screams are getting louder.[5] Nor do we want to rediscover community through rigid fragmentation like this.

I see reasons for some optimism in the world of today's youth and in the institutions that serve them. Gen Alpha (age two to eleven) and Gen Z (age eleven to twenty-six) are growing up with a different perspective on adulthood from older Americans. I believe they are building a less viciously competitive, callous form of individualism. It remains to be seen if it will translate into a lifelong orientation and if it can overcome the alienated reality of careers and our obsession with personally curated consumption.

What I share below is not meant to be comprehensive; it only highlights three areas where data reveals that our society is trying to adapt in a way that constrains the excesses of individual autonomy that older Americans directly participated in (with very mixed outcomes).

Group Work in School and Colleges Is Now Normative

Today's teens are coming of age with expectations of a flatter, more collaborative work environment than I did, because of how administrators now run America's schools. Older Americans went to schools run much like the command-and-control companies and government offices they would soon join.

When I was in first grade, in 1978, I vividly remember my first-grade teaching pair keeping track of "gold stars" for achievement next to each student's name in a colorful grid. I believe there was a grid for each subject. It was very clear we should compete with each other *as individuals*. And, of course, I only focused on my *male* competitors. The competitive incentives of a fully realized consumer capitalist culture were in plain sight. I don't recall doing a single group project ever in my twenty-four years of schooling. Not once. Only my summer archaeology course in college involved group work, but that involved digging one-meter square pits (and mostly alone). Everything I did academically was a solo effort and judged accordingly with a score or letter grade.

My own children, on the other hand, have been doing group projects, where one grade gets assigned to everyone based on the group's output, since the first grade! And they will keep doing it, off and on, all the way through college. It's not that individual assessments have disappeared. They haven't. But today's youth are growing up without the assumption that they are simply a graded individual competing adversarially with everyone else. Group work is especially important for boys, who must learn to work with girls on group projects (in preparation for group work at the office!). These projects become a perfect laboratory for platonic, cross-sex interaction (transcending any lack of cross-sex siblings at home).

I believe this new group learning approach began in MBA programs in the 1990s. In fact, MBA programs are famous (even notorious) for the group work they mandate. These new ritual processes in business school intend to prepare adults to work collaboratively and cross-functionally in diverse teams at elite companies and consulting firms.

Group work at school is where the less ambitious, less talented, or just plain sloppy students can no longer hide in the back of the class and then receive their poor grades in isolation. Instead, the underperformer gets *shamed* into putting in effort where they might have been left behind to fail in a truly mid-century competitive environment. Or spat out like flunkies. The group has to "carry" them.

Group projects in high school, college, or graduate school allow young adults to learn what it means to fulfill community and team *obligations*, one of which is to display mutual respect for team members. They also provide an opportunity for less gifted or struggling students to get peer support (however reluctant it may be). Teams compete with teams, yes, but individuals can learn from the smarter, more talented kids on their teams. This can't hurt.

Late twentieth-century individualism, on the other hand, focused primarily on assessing and credentialing individual adults to compete with each other for jobs that relied on command-and-control specialized delegation more than collaborative work.

White collar work today is getting more creative, team-oriented, and collaborative. It is less regimented and factorylike than in prior decades. So, employers need highly collaborative workers with stronger social skills than in decades past. Much stronger social skills. Group work in school helps teach those collaborative skills again and again. The overly eccentric and difficult either adapt or get spat out.

Structured Youth Activities Are More Common

There is a nonstop stream of essays about the overscheduling and excessive achievement anxiety of America's youth.[6] To some extent this is mostly a problem of *upper-middle-class parents* or those with extreme class mobility or achievement desires for their children. Parental anxiety about their child's future can lead to intense achievement expectations. And loading kids up on after-school activities from an early age is more common than ever.

The increase in hypercompetitive "club" sports has no doubt been unhealthy for some kids and parents (we even yanked our kid out of one), but the idea of structured group activity supports what has been going on with group work in schools.

When I was growing up in the 1970s and 1980s, there were youth sports (soccer and basketball), but most kids did not participate in them, let alone consistently. The now huge world of private, fee-based club sports was very small and mostly focused on boys. Extracurricular activities largely emerged from your school and were not mandatory or as culturally "essential" as they feel in many college-bound homes today.

Today, the situation is very different. Tossing your child into local club sports from the age of five or six is common. T-ball. Soccer. Flag football. Although many of these sports clubs are pretty chill, others are expensive, pseudo-professional feeders into the professional leagues. I kid you not. This is a middle-to-upper-middle-class phenomenon primarily but represents a massive extracurricular social theater for group work and ritualizing the power of community obligation.

If you add in music, arts, and other possible extracurricular options, today's youth have had access to far more than I did in the 1970s. I'm adamantly opposed to pushing kids into these activities, but they are wonderful social labs for kids to learn the value of group goal setting, obligation to the group, and community formation across households. It's too early to see if these net positives outweigh the pressure-cooker feeling some of these clubs create for young people who don't need this kind of anxiety in their lives. The social benefits of filling your afternoons and weekends with athletic group work versus bingeing TV shows or YouTube videos seems obvious to me.

Mental Health and Addiction Stigma Are Fading

Historically, America's ideology of individualism has failed those suffering from mental health challenges and addiction. Not only do we tend to judge these people harshly for the pain they cause their families and communities, but they also have hidden behind the sacred veil of privacy for as long as possible due to the stigma of confessing their wandering along these twin paths to self-destruction.

One of the more ironic twists of modern politics is that the traditional Republican defense of gun rights has increasingly strengthened advocacy for better detection and treatment for the mentally ill in our society. I completely agree.

And apparently, so does America.

From 2004 to 2022, the number of adult Americans who reported having visited a mental health professional in the past twelve months grew from 13 percent to 23 percent. More importantly, 80 percent who have rated their mental health as fair or poor have sought treatment of some kind. This is a huge, all-ages victory for individual mental well-being and public health. Of course, visiting a therapist is no guarantee of successful outcomes, not when the patient may return to a debilitating social environment which mostly enabled the original problem.

What's interesting and important to note, is that the growth in seeking mental health treatment parallels a separate trend in diagnosis of a major depressive disorder in the past year (from 14 percent to 24 percent), mostly due to diagnoses among eighteen- to twenty-five-year-olds.[7]

Only the severely depressed appear to be seeking treatment, *not the entire population of the mentally unwell*. We are catching people reactionarily, but at least they are not trying to hide as in the past, especially younger people.

We are also getting much smarter about how social alienation and lack of social support and friendship exacerbates the conditions for major depressive episodes and for generalized anxiety. Our uncertainty in work and love provide near-constant fuel for both of these problems. We are becoming smarter about the sociological causes.

America's deadly encounter with OxyContin addiction in the past twenty-five years has been both tragic and oddly helpful. Helpful, because it definitively established that drug addiction can strike anyone from any background or social class.

And it made the case that the distribution and mis-prescription of the drug itself presented the gravest public health threat. Patient misuse of these drugs "to get back to work" quickly (when long periods of rest are necessary for many common sources of severe orthopedic pain) often was the trigger for ramping up dosages to guaranteed addictive levels. Our inability to support the injured worker properly with sufficient leave time provides millions of willing victims for the Oxy demon annually.

Addiction is a lifelong condition, like autism or any other neurological disability. It doesn't get cured or go away. But we are slowly learning that we can coach families to intervene as groups and get even reluctant individuals into therapeutic recovery processes, guiding them to constructing a new social life away from the source and those who provide it.

Addiction survival is about applied repositioning of individuals into new social contexts. The social intensity of recovery reminds me a lot of what used to go on in shamanistic healing rituals in premodern cultures. Rescuing the individual is not supposed to be convenient or easy for the immediate group. It will be exhausting and draining yet hopefully worth the long-term outcome.

I am not in the prediction business. Yet, it appears that slowing growth, economic disruption due to climate change, and younger generations of more collaborative, more socially skilled youth will help America adapt better to the risks of an otherwise highly flexible approach to living.

Individualism can work. But we don't need to accept the outcomes we've seen among older Americans. We can and should do better.

EPILOGUE

This book has often been brutally honest about major social changes in American society and how they've affected older Americans especially. This is not the context in which to offer definitive solutions to the imbalance of power between the individual and the community. I believe this is a group discussion, beginning in local towns and cities, anything that transcends zip code segregation.

But we must first recognize that individualism, as it affected older Americans, has been a public health disaster. And that it continues to be, as long as we can define "public health" broadly as a local system of surveillance and as a system of aid for the whole person.

If we accept this broader definition, then I hope this book has pointed out the implicit need for a different approach to handling specific public health threats posed by individualism:

- Defining individual problems as *psychological* ones
- Obesogenic diseases and the failed cultural practice of dieting
- Domestic assault hidden behind a sacred veil of privacy
- Un-surveilled depression/anxiety (due to career and financial hiccups that are increasingly common)
- Unmanaged mental illness left to roam our streets and parks
- Globally extreme levels of addiction and substance abuse
- Our lack of empathy for individuals who "flop" in an achievement- and growth-oriented culture
- Turning to video media for fun instead of socializing beyond the home

- The extra emotional burden placed on women, mothers, and minorities by a way of life that favors personal independence over making demands of the community

I don't believe that the solution to most of the negative outcomes described in this book is to grab us all by the neck and drag us back into premodern forms of ritual and community in which I, of all people, would never ever participate.

I believe we are largely stuck with a consumer market economy and a culture that affords a large degree of autonomy for adults (even more dangerously so for the wealthy).

So, let's do better to make it work for more people. I can't accept that, if 70–80 percent make it through OK, we're doing great. Even at a population of 334 million that's too many individual exceptions for a country as powerful, as smart, and as wealthy as ours.

Here's an initial list of urgent social needs and possible, even radical, solutions to consider:

1. Mandatory Community Service for All Eighteen-Year-Olds
    - Why is Israel the only country with mandatory national service for everyone?
    - Surely we can learn from the Civilian Conservation Corps of the 1930s and find something for every eighteen-year-old to do for a year *in their local communities.*
    - No one needs to start college at seventeen or eighteen—we can deal with a gap year.
    - Community is built on personal sacrifices of time like this.
    - This is how you teach adults to bridge divisions of race and class.
2. Putting Reciprocity Back into Adult Friendships
    - Ask for help more! Don't do everything as a couple!
    - Do errands with friends.
    - Give your spouse a break from your sh*t and get some hobbies that produce friendships organically.

3. Professionalizing and Subsidizing Career, Mental Health, and Financial Services
    - We need to look at public health departments more broadly in every county—career, mental, and financial health solutions are best delivered at the county and local levels.
    - Every high school graduate in America should experience a therapeutic session series—self-awareness is possible and useful for all.
    - We need federal subsidization of mental health treatment for all—this should not be subject to the whims of private insurers.
    - We need to ensure in-depth financial planning training in high school and college.
    - We need impartial, person-centered career change resources to permit more adaptive use of individual talents in our labor market.
4. Sociological Approaches to Eliminate Binge Drinking
    - Raise liquor prices substantially to decrease binge drinking of the most dangerous forms of alcohol.
    - Limit the number of hard drinks an individual can purchase in *one visit* at bars/taverns.
    - Mandate designated driver bracelets for groups entering bars/taverns.
    - Learn from the stigmatization of cigarette smoking—make binge drinking *uncool* on college campuses.
5. Grant the Addict Constant Companionship
    - When we discover an addict close to us, we must learn to engage in group confrontation and insist that they get help.
    - But we must never let this person be alone again in public—not until their sober social habits have been reestablished—chaperoning is what community is for.

6. Ritualizing *Failure* in Life
   - We need to find ways for a person's social network to gather together and help that person grieve whatever loss has struck them.
   - We have to stop avoiding people in these periods of their lives.
   - We must stop letting people self-isolate when we know they are grieving something.
7. Personal Finance Interventions
   - Universal basic income permits all middle-class people the ability to plan major career changes and escape toxic work environments damaging their mental health.

One guy writing in a shed in the Sonoran Desert certainly does not have all the answers. I primarily wrote this book to make us question our American style of individualism and take off the blinders.

I hope you enjoyed it and am honored that you made it through it all.

If it made you want to change your relationship with your local community, then please let me know what you plan to do differently: james(at)socialawarenessinstitute.org.

And, if you like this writing, please subscribe to my Substack, Homo Imaginari. You'll find material cut from the book draft and more in-depth exploration of many of the similar social issues.

Discounted bulk orders for classroom use are available directly from me. Minimum bulk order size is twenty-five paperbacks or hardcovers.

BOOK CLUB QUESTIONS AND MORE

Delve Deeper on My Substack, Homo Imaginari

Since you graciously made it all the way to the end, I want to offer you a special discount link to gain access to my Substack, Homo Imaginari (https://jamesrichardson.substack.com/OWS).

Through the above link, you'll get a year's subscription at 50 percent off, including access to my Editor's Scraps section with the best research that did not make the cut for this book.

Book Club Conversation Starters

1. Think about a time in your life when you felt overwhelmed by choices. Describe the situation for your club buddies. How did you make a decision in the end?
2. What groups of Americans might not fit the patterns in the book and why do you think this is?
3. Is the problem of friends as entertainment more of an issue for men or women? Explain your thinking.
4. Does your extended family resemble the pattern described in this book? Why or why not?
5. Do you want more close friends than you have? Why or why not?

6. How did you react to the story of Sally and her insensitive workplace? What can we do to improve sensitivity to personal situations in the workplace?
7. Which ideas in the epilogue resonated most with you and why?
8. Which ideas in the epilogue seemed impractical and why?
9. Think of a time when autonomy led you to make a worse choice than you might have made with wiser intervention.
10. Did you come to any conclusions the author *did not*? Please share!
11. Does your club want a *virtual Q and A with the author*?
    - Buy at least ten copies of *Our Worst Strength*.
    - Send your proof of purchase to: james(at)socialawarenessinstitute.org.
    - I'll schedule our virtual Q and A within approximately two weeks.

ACKNOWLEDGMENTS

Most of all, I must thank my parents for encouraging my love of writing (and reading), even though it took decades to get to a position where I could write almost full-time.

In the same vein, I must thank two early mentors, Dudley Cotton and Chuck Sanborn, former teachers at the Derryfield School. They encouraged a love of writing and critical thinking that carried through multiple careers and into the creation of this book.

I also thank Babu, Charles Stephen Gnanamuttu and family, David Ben, Winston, Mrs. Bharati, the late Mr. Erskine, my former cook Aachi, and every one of the people of Tamil Nadu with whom I had the privilege of living and working for a few years in the 1990s. Without realizing it, they all provided a young man with a powerful contrast to the New England culture in which he grew up.

This book would also not have been possible without the incidental, on-the-job training I received in quantitative analytics, demography, and survey design from a former market research colleague, David Moore. For the survey research that went into this book, I also need to thank Tim Scharks, who helped me refine my initial hypotheses, reviewed my survey instrument, and helped significantly with analysis on the back end. I also have to thank CINT, the world leader in global market research sampling, for letting me execute a very slow drip sample to a tough-to-reach population. And at a very low cost.

Additionally, I have to thank Victor Braitberg of the University of Arizona for boosting my literature review on the topic of individualism and for debating lots of content that went into this book.

Finally, there is the team behind this book's production. Self-publishing may be a thing, but no one can create a world-class book without bringing together a lot of specialized talent. This is where I must initially thank Reedsy.com in London for aggregating so much great publishing talent for small presses and self-published authors. This entire book and the related publishing business would not have been possible without this single resource. Specifically, a huge thanks goes out to everyone on my personally curated editorial and production team for their professional wisdom and talent:

- Jasmine Hromjak, for her clever and striking cover design
- Cathy Suter, for her developmental review and line editing, which resulted in the jettisoning of seventy pages of suboptimal thinking!
- Jennie Cohen for her unbelievably sharp, diligent proofreading
- Rosie Wood for her expert help with the index
- Ryan Scheife, Jess LaGreca and the rest of the Mayfly Design for their digital typesetting and layout work

Appendix A

American Consumer Spending in 2023 Dollars	1901	2021	Percent Change from 1901-2021
Average household size	5	2.5	−50%
Total annual	$4,659 per person	$26,771 per person	+474%
Total monthly	$388	$2,230	+474%
Housing	23.3%	33.8%	+45%
Food (at home)	42.5%	7.8%	−444%
Clothing	14.0%	2.6%	−438%
All other	20%	56%!	+180%
Transport		16%	
Insurance/pensions/Social Security		11.7%	
Healthcare	5%	8%	+60%
Personal care		1.1%	
Education	1%	1.8%	+80%
Entertainment	1.5%	4.7%	+213%
Tobacco	1.4%	0.5%	−70%
Reading	<1%	0.2%	

Alcohol	1.5%	0.8%	−50%
Food away from home		4.5%	
Cash contributions (students, alimony, child support, charity)	1.3% (charity)	3.6%	+176%
Miscellaneous (gifts?)	8%	1.5%	−433%

Source: United States Bureau of Labor and Statistics, "100 Years of U.S. Consumer Spending: Data for the Nation, New York City, and Boston," Report 991, 2006.

Appendix B

RESEARCH DESIGN

One of the core inputs for this book was a national study of older Americans that you've seen me reference sporadically. I originally designed the study to explore *class-based* variation in orientations to individualism. I hypothesized that individualism mattered most for the upper-middle class, a small elite with the most economic power and social opportunity to pursue autonomous choices. I also hypothesized that elites had a more pervasively individualistic approach to all the major domains of daily living (work, family, friendship, fun, eating/drinking).

What I found instead was that individualism is really an all-American way of navigating life. It has little to do with social class at its core. The volume of superficial eccentricity and eccentric material displays may go way up among the rich and famous, but the fundamental impulse to make autonomous decisions and to narrate them as personal choices is all—American. One could argue it is now even a feature of the world's top one hundred population centers.

Phase 1–National Survey

The study began with a national survey designed by me and facilitated by CINT, a leading research sample provider for the global market research industry. This twenty-two-minute survey collected 2,983 clean responses used in my analysis. It fielded from May until August 2022 due to the difficult sample design.

Screening Criteria

- Adults aged forty-five to seventy-four (Gen X and Baby Boomers)
- High school degree or higher in educational attainment (ensures the ability to take the survey)

Sample Design

- Half the sample is upper-middle class (college degree plus $115K or more personal income from all sources)
- The other half of the sample represents the rest of the high school graduate population in the United States in this age cohort
- This disproportionate design was used to compare the upper-middle class against a general age cohort across a large set of variables

Survey Design

The survey instrument has seventy-one questions, including standard profiling questions.

I designed the instrument as a mix of polling-type questions and a few more complex modeling question series related to career change, family intimacy, and attitudes toward individualism. The more complex areas aimed to fill holes in family sociology uncovered in my literature review.

The instrument has six major segments exploring attitudes and behaviors related to a) socioeconomic status, b) family, c) friendships, d) fun, e) foodways, and f) gender relations. It ends with question batteries related to measuring the respondent's orientation to political figures, neurological and mental health status, and individualism as an attitudinal orientation.

I had roughly ten major hypotheses going into the survey phase, mostly related to how UMC respondents differ from less privileged members of the same age group. The results were very entertaining and not in line with many of the hypotheses. This has allowed me to write a more compelling, representative book—essentially by getting rid of some big biases. Hypotheses often betray weird biases that scientific sample analysis can help eliminate.

Unless specified in the endnotes, all results cited are weighted to census norms of the broader age cohort only (by reducing the impact of the upper-middle-class half of the sample).

Phase 2–In-Depth Life History Interviews

Design

Surveys are helpful in rigorously measuring the *prevalence* of attitudes and behaviors and whether or not two or more variables are meaningfully correlated. But they are very limited in getting at nuance, the kind that cultural anthropologists like me are trained to *infer* from language and symbols. This includes motivational nuance as well. Surveys require respondents to be largely *conscious* of what is being directly measured in the question. In many cases, though, the felt experience of life requires us to tell stories and share emotions. This is where interviews built around vignette capture can fill gaps in understanding.

The initial point of these interviews was to acquire powerful life event narratives using a standard life history interview technique. The technique involved setting the interviews up as a comparisons of the person's life as a teenager versus their life today. At a minimum, there was a thirty-year gap between the stories they told.

I went through all the major topics in this book twice with each respondent, permitting me to contrast historically the effect of social changes *not* due to life stage. For example, explicit discussions of how parenting styles differed between their parents and the respondent as a parent surfaced evidence for the silencing of the elders finding discussed in chapter two (i.e., grandparents today are asked to refrain from contradicting their children's parenting styles).

I also used life history stories as a source of vignettes to illustrate quantitative findings from the survey or other data sources related to measuring social change.

This follows classic social science reasoning by letting individuals exemplify a separately verified social pattern (versus generating the pattern from one individual, which is prone to error, observer bias, and stereotyping).

When

In March and April 2023, I interviewed twenty folks recruited from within my survey dataset who volunteered to carve out four hours of their time in return for a $200 honorarium. The use of honorariums is a standard market research technique designed to a) get people to show up and b) be more serious and engaged in the conversation.

The primary problem with a sample like this is the self-selection bias for those with a "life story they're desiring to tell about themselves" or who think "my life story is interesting." In the case of this study and book, that bias was very welcome! Boring interviews help no one, including the author. I also have other datasets and contextual information to interpret the "weirdness" of any one respondent and I disclose this in the analysis, where relevant.

Interview sample profile

Here is the demographic and lifestyle breakdown of my life history subsample per the variables most relevant to the experience of individualism:

Age

- 9 Gen Xers
- 11 Boomers

Gender

- 9 women
- 11 men

Class

- 4 of 20 never graduated from a four-year college
- 6 of 20 had ordinary middle-class incomes; the rest were upper-middle class with personal incomes of $115K or more as of 2022
- 8 of 20 went to graduate school

Retirement status

- 9 of 20 retired

Raised kids

- 3 of 20 never raised kids (below survey average)

Only children

- 7 of 20 were only children (above survey average suggesting motive to share stories)

Living alone

- 2 of 20 living alone

Open Access Data—Qualified academics, journalists, and market researchers are welcome to request the survey instrument and de-identified dataset from me at any time: james(at)socialawarenessinstitute.org.

NOTES

Preface

1. My first clue to my own neurodivergence was when I took Simon Baron Cohen's online version of his classic instrument to position individuals along an autism spectrum from neurotypical (most of you) to severe autism. Released online by *Wired* magazine in 2001. You can find it here: https://www.wired.com/2001/12/aqtest/. Accessed May 14, 2023.

Introduction

1. The classic work on ritual was written by Victor Turner—cf. Victor Turner, *The Ritual Process* (New York: Penguin Press, Pelican Imprint, 1969). Available in a new Kindle edition.

2. United States Bureau of Labor and Statistics, "American Time Use Survey," (ATUS), 2021, my analysis.

3. Rosa Hartmut, *Social Acceleration: A New Theory of Modernity*, trans. Jonathan Trejo-Mathuys (New York: Columbia University Press, 2013). Originally published as *Beschleunigung: Die Veränderung in der Moderne* (Frankfurt am Main: Suhrkamp Verlag, 2005).

4. Only 15 percent of Rumspringa participants leave the community, according to recent research. See David L. McConnell, "Leaving Amish" in *The Handbook of Leaving Religion*, edited by David G. Bromley and Lewis F. Carter, vol. 18 of *Brill Handbooks on Contemporary Religion* (Schöningh: Brill, 2019), 154–163. PDF here: https://bit.ly/3bDbAjt. See my Substack essay on the Amish if you desire more info (this content is behind a paywall).

5. See appendix B for the full research design I employed to fuel this book's content.

Chapter One

1. We can even shop our pasts in the form of genetic testing and highly selective tours of our genealogy.
2. Thomas Piketty has done the definitive historical research on the history of global income growth since the classical period and its likely future in the twenty-first century. See Thomas Piketty, *Capital in the Twenty-First Century*, translated by Arthur Goldhammer, (Cambridge: Belknap Press of Harvard University Press, 2017), 127, figure 2.4.
3. "In traditional kinship systems a person's social obligations arise from the fact that they are a mother's brother's child, rather than coming from an individually chosen network of friends who determine their own level of reciprocal obligation." Daniel Miller, Elisabetta Costa, Nell Haynes, Tom McDonald, Razvan Nicolescu, Jolynna Sinanan, Juliano Spyer, Shriram Venkatraman, and Xinyuan Wang, "Individualism," in *How the World Changed Social Media* (California: UCLA Press, 2016), 183.
4. White men could break with the past most easily. Black and Latino men far less. My recent research among older Americans included 14 percent who were non-white. There was no statistical variation by racial background with regard to the diagnostic criteria I set up to measure positive orientation to individualism as a choice ideology. I looked and looked. It's possible that this reflects mimesis of a white majority's dominant ideology in a mid-century era, when this was simply a more pragmatic masking strategy. This orientation to the dominant group's lifestyle ideology may also be changing for younger age cohorts who find themselves increasingly in middle-class settings where white folk are 50 percent or less of the group.
5. Cf. Stephen Mennell, The American Civilizing Process (Cambridge: Polity Press, 2007).
6. For an entertaining immersion, check out the following films: *Rumspringa*, directed by Mira Thiel (Netflix, 2022), 1:41; *Devil's Playground*, directed by Lucy Walker (Cinemax, Stick Figure Productions, and Winstar Cinema, 2002), 1:17. [Note: *Devil's Playground* is a documentary film.]
7. This highly exploratory campus culture increasingly causes a campus crisis of identity for conservative children of immigrants who don't understand this phase of American life.
8. If "individualism" has any usefulness as a concept, it is as a way of behaving, not simply a conceptual framework.

9. It's true that specific individuals may have exercised most of the choice in this table much earlier than 1970, especially in New York City in the 1920s. The roaring twenties was one of the earliest urban experiments with a Rumspringa-like young adulthood. However, it was largely confined to the rich and was not a middle-class or mass societal reality.
10. The huge amount of government subsidization of college education, retirement, and suburban housing after World War II disproportionately went to white (or near-white) Americans. As such, the forces releasing Americans from traditional social constraints on lifestyle choice also skewed white in this period.

Chapter Two

1. 14 million family businesses exist where two or more family members work and control the strategic direction of the company. At a minimum this means that there are 28 million adults working inside their family business. If true, then only 18 percent of the employed, civilian population of 152 million work in their family's business. Sources: Bureau of Labor and Statistics, United States Census, "Employment Status of the Civilian Noninstitutional Population, 1952 to date," 2021, accessed July 24, 2023, https://www.bls.gov/cps/cpsaat01.htm; Daniel Van Der Vliet, "Measuring the Financial Impact of Family Businesses on the US Economy," FamilyBusiness.Org, June 2, 2021, accessed March 29, 2023, https://familybusiness.org/content/measuring-the-financial-impact-of-family-businesses-on-the-US-ec.
2. Native Americans were excluded from this process, though emancipated slaves definitely participated in it (cf. the northern migration).
3. A majority of Americans, 62 percent, are working for a family business, even though most of us don't work in our own family's business. Source: "Measuring the Financial Impact of Family Businesses on the US Economy," FamilyBusiness.Org, June 2, 2021, accessed March 29, 2023, https://familybusiness.org/content/measuring-the-financial-impact-of-family-businesses-on-the-US-ec.
4. It's important to note that two groups still find it much harder to cut off family than the rest of us: 1) the 1 percent with inherited wealth often find themselves constrained in their lifestyles due to family obligations and the maintenance of elite family status in society, which is a lot of

time-consuming work and 2) those from immigrant or poor backgrounds who may also find it very hard to escape obligations to parents and relatives, which can limit their lifestyle options as well unless they are willing to make a sharp, emotional break.

5. My source on historical work hours: Robert Whaples, "Hours of Work in US History," Economic History Association, accessed May 12, 2023, https://eh.net/encyclopedia/hours-of-work-in-u-s-history/.

6. A one-hour, cross-country phone call to someone living 101 miles away or more in 1983, for example, cost roughly $34 in 2022 dollars! It was very easy to measure the worth of extended family before long-distance telephone deregulation in 1993. "Calls of 100 to 3,000 miles to cities in the MCI network cost 33 to 43 cents a minute from 8 A.M. to 5 P.M., 16 to 20 cents from 5 to 11 P.M. and 12 to 16 cents from 11 P.M. to 8 A.M. and on weekends. Calls 100 to 3,000 miles to cities outside the network cost 33 to 48 cents a minute from 8 A.M. to 5 P.M., 16 to 26 cents from 5 to 11 P.M. and 12 to 19 cents from 11 P.M. to 8 A.M. and on weekends." Peter Kerr, "Saving on Costs of Long-Distance Calls," *New York Times*, May 7, 1983, accessed July 23, 2023, https://www.nytimes.com/1983/05/07/style/saving-on-costs-of-long-distance-calls.html.

7. About 37 percent of estranged American adults *are estranged from a parent*, suggesting that parent-child discord is a major issue but also that most elders have learned to adapt. This doesn't mean that America's elders are happy with the behavior of either their kids or their grandkids. Source: Karl Pillemer, PhD, *Fault Lines: Fractured Families and How to Mend Them* (New York: Avery, 2020), 25.

8. Although not all multigenerational households have children under eighteen living in them, many do. Source: Pew Research Center, "Financial Issues Top the List of Reasons U.S. Adults Live in Multigenerational Homes," March 2022, accessed July 24, 2023, https://www.pewresearch.org/social-trends/2022/03/24/the-demographics-of-multigenerational-households/.

9. Social Awareness Institute interview with Sam (pseudonym), living in New York State, conducted via Zoom in March 2023. Some edits made for clarity.

10. This is why hard socialist states control the media directly and totally.

Chapter Three

1. Identity theft with financial consequences is occurring at around 1.4 million incidents per year, affecting one-third of one percent of the US population. It's fairly common, but it probably won't happen more than once or twice in your lifetime at current rates. Source: Jim Akin, "Identity Theft Is on the Rise, Both in Incidents and Losses," Experian.com, October 11, 2022, accessed July 23, 2023, https://www.experian.com/blogs/ask-experian/identity-theft-statistics/.
2. Washington State Department of Children, Youth, and Families, "Child Welfare Overview CY 2022," published August 2023, accessed January 2, 2024, https://www.dcyf.wa.gov/sites/default/files/pdf/OIAA-ChildWelfareOverviewCY2022.pdf.
3. The lower courts initially indicted many suspects based on spectral attack performed during the depositions themselves. Of the initial fifty-six defendants, only three were condemned because a higher court disallowed spectral evidence that most later acknowledged was likely fabricated due to interpersonal grievances. Jess Blumberg, "A Brief History of the Salem Witch Trials," *Smithsonian Magazine*, online edition, October 23, 2007, accessed July 24, 2023, https://www.smithsonianmag.com/history/a-brief-history-of-the-salem-witch-trials-175162489/#:~:text=The%20Salem%20witch%20trials%20occurred,magic%E2%80%94and%2020%20were%20executed.
4. America's greatest disrespect of privacy continues to be shown toward African Americans and Native Americans, who remain the most unintegrated and subordinated social groups in modern America.
5. Katrina Feldkamp and S. Rebecca Neusteter, "The Little Known, Racist History of the 911 Emergency Call System," *In These Times*, January 26, 2021, accessed July 25, 2023, https://inthesetimes.com/article/911-emergency-service-racist-history-civil-rights.
6. Fifty percent of domestic abuse victims never report these crimes for obvious reasons, so I suspect the 4 percent number is a vast undercount. Furthermore, 25 percent of women in the United States will experience domestic violence during their lifetime, suggesting the broad reach of this trauma in American society. A. E. Bonomi, B. Trabert, M. L. Anderson, M. A. Kernic, V. L. Holt, "Intimate Partner Violence and Neighborhood Income: A Longitudinal Analysis," *Violence Against Women* 20, no. 1

(2014): 42–58, doi: 10.1177/1077801213520580, accessed July 25, 2023, https://www.ncbi.nlm.nih.gov/pmc/articles/PMC5486977/.
7. There are clear origins here in the cultural traditions of Anglo-Saxon/Nordic groups who colonized the United States from the seventeenth century onward. However, the ideology here has become the dominant middle-class ethos, observable by me and others even among *middle-class* blacks, latinos, and asians. Our very residential setup as middle-class Americans encourages the adoption of this ethos of extreme privacy.
8. A 2015 research study on how domestic violence victims approach the use of local law enforcement indicates how a lack of trust on both sides has made police involvement a very weak solution. Source: T. K. Logan, PhD, and Rob Valente, "Who Will Help Me? Domestic Violence Survivors Speak Out About Law Enforcement Responses," 2015, National Domestic Violence Hotline, accessed July 25, 2023, https://www.thehotline.org/wp-content/uploads/sites/3/2015/09/NDVH-2015-Law-Enforcement-Survey-Report.pdf.
9. National Survey on Older Americans by the Social Awareness Institute, summer 2022. The study looked at attitudes and behaviors among 2,983 adults aged forty-five to seventy-four with at least a high school degree. Referred to hereafter as SAI National Survey on Older Americans, 2022.

Chapter Four

1. SAI National Survey on Older Americans, 2022, questions 21 and 22: 0–2 on a scale of 0–10 where (0) = prefer to think through life problems alone and (10) = prefer to canvas the opinions of relatives. This finding is not significantly gender biased in my dataset.
2. SAI National Survey on Older Americans, 2022, questions 21 and 22: 8–10 on the same scale as above.
3. The 45–74-year-olds in my recent research study definitely experienced the absolute peak of performance review rituals, even though the practice is in noticeable decline since 2011. A great history can be found here: Peter Cappelli and Anna Tavis, "The Performance Management Revolution: The Focus Is Shifting from Accountability to Learning," *Harvard Business Review Magazine*, October 2016, accessed July 25, 2023, https://hbr.org/2016/10/the-performance-management-revolution.

4. I can't help but speculate that the US Army is exhibiting an unconscious bias against the female spouses of army staff who threaten to bring family drama into the tight discipline of a military bureaucracy. Jon Miele, US Army, "Family Life Matters: Combating Codependency," November 5, 2014, accessed July 25, 2023, https://www.army.mil/article/137572/family_life_matters_combating_codependency#:~:text=Some%20estimates%20suggest%20that%20over,American%20population%20demonstrates%20codependent%20behavior.

5. "Non-Hispanic white adults were most likely to have received any mental health treatment in the past 12 months (24.4%), followed by non-Hispanic black (15.3%), Hispanic (12.6%), and non-Hispanic Asian (7.7%) adults." E. P. Terlizzi and T. Norris, "Mental Health Treatment Among Adults: United States, 2020," NCHS Data Brief, no. 419, Hyattsville, MD: National Center for Health Statistics, 2021, doi: https://dx.doi.org/10.15620/cdc:110593external icon.

6. I looked hard and failed to find trended data on therapy usage rates. The commonly accepted history of CBT's spread in the late twentieth century notes the spread into broader usage in the 1970s. Source: Kelly Miller BA CAPP, "CBT Explained: An Overview & Summary of CBT (Incl. History)," PositivePsychology.com, May 6, 2019, accessed July 25, 2023, https://positivepsychology.com/cbt/#:~:text=The%20practice%20of%20CBT%20grew,understanding%20of%20emotional%20self%2Dcontrol.

Chapter Five

1. *My Best Fiend*, directed by Werner Herzog. Outpost Studios, 1999. 1:35:00; my transcription of dialogue.
2. The full declaration by Kinski's daughter can be reviewed on the Guardian website: Kate Connolly, "Klaus Kinski Repeatedly Raped Me During My Childhood, Claims Daughter," *Guardian*, January 10, 2013. (This article was published more than twenty years after Kinski's death in 1991.)
3. Herzog is not a man who has time for bourgeois moral judgments on behalf of community norms. He is a mid-century European artist obsessed with the extreme margins of society, deviancy, antisocial heroes, and the obliteration of "cruel" norms. He is a connoisseur of madness in all its forms. He is the classic artistic product of post–World War II Germany,

epicenter of the world's greatest mass insanity. His fixation on madness is therefore not his own.

4. *Fear and Loathing in Las Vegas* is a perfect window into the performance of self-destruction that Hunter S. Thompson personally engaged in and loosely glamorized, but then largely stopped as he grew older.

5. Source: Google Ngram database.

6. This is one way of interpreting the madness of wage stagnation that I find more illuminating than charts of median, inflation-adjusted income.

7. Olivia Choy, Adrian Raine, Robert Schug, "Larger Striatal Volume Is Associated with Increased Adult Psychopathy," *Journal of Psychiatric Research,* May 2022, 149: 185-193, doi: 10.1016/j.jpsychires.2022.03.006. Epub March 6, 2022. PMID: 35279510.

8. "Not only did the business execs come out ahead, but psychopathy was positively associated with in-house ratings of charisma and presentation style: creativity, good strategic thinking and excellent communication skills." Robert Hare cited in Kevin Dutton, *The Wisdom of Psychopaths: What Saints, Spies, and Serial Killers Can Teach Us About Success* (New York: Scientific American, 2012), 105.

9. M. E. Thomas, *Confessions of a Sociopath: A Life Hiding in Plain Sight* (New York: Crown, 2014).

10. In the 1990s, the number of North American M&A deals grew from c. 2,500 in 1992 to almost 10,000 by 1999. Most recently, deal counts annually amount to around 8–10K annually prior to the pandemic. Factset.com, "At a Glance: Factset Mergers Datafeed," accessed July 25, 2023, https://insight.factset.com/resources/factset-mergers-datafeed.

11. Deloitte and Touche, "The 12 Critical 'Reorg Routines' for CEOs Embarking on Restructuring," Deloitte and Touche2019.

12. Robert Hare and Paul Babiak, *Snakes in Suits: When Snakes Go to Work*, quoted in Kevin Dutton, *The Wisdom of Psychopaths* (New York: Scientific American, 2012), 106.

13. Thomas, *Confessions of a Sociopath.*

14. Paraphrased from an author interview with Emma R. of Alabama, February 21, 2023.

15. Tessa West, "Jerks at Work: Toxic Coworkers and What to Do About Them," *Harvard Business Review Ascend*, September 1, 2022, accessed July 26, 2023, https://hbr.org/2022/09/5-jerks-at-work-and-how-to-deal-with-them.

Chapter Six

1. Britannica, "The Era of the Mini-Series," accessed July 26, 2023, https://www.britannica.com/art/television-in-the-United-States/The-era-of-the-miniseries. The 2000 figure is calculated based on cable and satellite TV penetration in the year 2000 using data from the United States Census and Federal Communications Commission, "FCC Adopts Seventh Annual Report on Competition in Video Markets," CS Docket no. 00-132, accessed July 26, 2023, https://transition.fcc.gov/Bureaus/Cable/News_Releases/2001/nrcb0101.html and the US Census.
2. The eight streaming giants I'm counting here are: Netflix, Prime Video, HBO Max, Hulu, Paramount+, Disney +, Peacock, and CBS+.
3. The time use data in the next two paragraphs derives from the American Time Use Survey 2021 dataset (ATUS). As defined in the ATUS, "watching TV" refers to any time people said their main activity involved watching TV, videos, or movies. This includes the time they spent watching live programming, viewing DVDs, and streaming shows on their TV sets, computers, and portable devices. Source: United States Bureau of Labor and Statistics, American Time Use Survey, 2021, persons age fifteen and over "watching TV": series ID TUU10101AA01014236; persons age fifteen and over "watching TV," not employed: series ID TUU10101AA01014267.
4. Americans' Use of Time Project survey data, cited in John P. Robinson and Geoffrey Godbey, *Time for Life: The Surprising Ways Americans Use Their Time* (University Park: Pennsylvania State University Press, 1997). This work *precedes* the creation of the federal American Time Use Survey.
5. Although time usage research was not conducted back then to today's standards, it's not hard to believe that most of the usage minutes per day probably went to music, since the entertainment programs were highly time-delimited. It is difficult to determine exact percentages, since this would be highly dependent on the station and the content of the programs. Stephen Smith, "Radio: The Internet of the 1930s," APM Reports, November 10, 2014, accessed July 26, 2023, https://www.apmreports.org/episode/2014/11/10/radio-the-internet-of-the-1930s#:~:text=Surveys%20found%20that%20listeners%20in,day%20listening%20to%20radio%20broadcasts.
6. Smith, "Radio: The Internet of the 1930s."
7. Seventy-five-plus-year-olds read forty-one minutes a day on average versus sixteen minutes a day for the average person fifteen years or older.

Source: United States Bureau of Labor and Statistics, American Time Use Survey, 2021, average hours per day reading for personal interest, seventy-five years and over: series ID TUU10101AA01030212 and average hours per day reading for personal interest, fifteen years and over: series ID TUU10101AA01006315.

8. There is a 71 percent inverse correlation between the two activities, ATUS 2003–2021, United States Bureau of Labor and Statistics, American Time Use Survey, 2021. My analysis of series ID TUU10101AA01014236 and TUU10101AA01013951 for persons aged fifteen and over.
9. US Bureau of Labor and Statistics, ATUS, my analysis.

Chapter Seven

1. Neil McKendrick, John Brewer, J. H. Plumb, *The Birth of a Consumer Society: The Commercialization of Eighteenth-Century England* (Brighton: EER Publishers, 2018) 29.
2. Sugar was a super-elite consumer item until the eighteenth century deployment of slave labor and stolen land in the Americas. In 1500, sugar went for roughly $150 per pound in 2023 currency. This is more than ten times the price of the world's most expensive spice today—saffron. By 1800, slavery had brought the cost down to $10 per pound in 2023 dollars or about the price of premium coffee beans in today's grocery store. By 1900, industrial technology in refining (and low paid labor) brought sugar down to $5 per pound in 2023 dollars, effectively a mass-market good. (Pricing was updated and converted to 2023 USD by the author.) Source: Hillary J. Shaw, "Sugar, Sugar," *New Scientist*, February 1, 2017, accessed July 26, 2023, https://www.newscientist.com/lastword/mg23331111-300-sugar-sugar/.
3. Margaret Walsh, "Automobile in American Life and Society: Gender and the Automobile in the United States," University of Michigan Dearborn and Benson Ford Research Center, 2010, accessed July 26, 2023, http://www.autolife.umd.umich.edu/Gender/Walsh/G_Overview.htm#:~:text=At%20the%20start%20of%20the,buy%20into%20personal%20motor%20mobility.
4. If you have not read it before, *Bobos in Paradise* by David Brooks is a classic of modern journalistic ethnography from an unlikely but perceptive source.

5. United States Bureau of Labor and Statistics, "100 Years of U.S. Consumer Spending Data for the Nation, New York City, and Boston," report 991, 2006. Inflation-adjusted sums used 1913 CPI data, the earliest available data, as the starting point. Thus, these estimates are probably a bit high, but not too much.
6. Sources: 1920 United States Census, Pew Research Center definition of the middle class ($62–$155K household income); Office of the Commissioner of Internal Revenue, *Statistics of Income from Returns of Net Income for 1920*, Washington, DC: 1922. The middle class in 1920 are defined here as those who earned $2–5K in net income in 1920, equivalent to $62–$155K household income in 2023. Only around 11 percent of American adults in 1920 filed an IRS form, making the tax dataset a small chunk of America's most affluent households.
7. Ashfaq Khan, Christian E. Weller, Lily Roberts, and Michela Zonta, "The Rental Housing Crisis Is a Supply Problem That Needs Supply Solutions," Center for American Progress website, accessed July 26, 2023, https://www.americanprogress.org/article/the-rental-housing-crisis-is-a-supply-problem-that-needs-supply-solutions/.
8. Joseph Schumpeter was the scholar who coined "creative destruction" as a key growth element in modern, consumer capitalism. I highly recommend diving into his classic work for more background: *Capitalism, Socialism and Democracy* (New York: Harper & Brothers, 1942).

Chapter Nine

1. The Organization for Economic Co-operation and Development (OECD), "Hours Worked" (indicator), 2022, doi: 10.1787/47be1c78-en, accessed June 8, 2023, https://data.oecd.org/emp/hours-worked.htm.
2. Nineteenth century agricultural workers, mostly family farmers, worked about sixty to sixty-nine hours per week on average, with seasonal fluctuations. Hours declined from 1830 to 1880. Jeremy Atack and Fred Bateman, "How Long Was the Workday in 1880?" *Journal of Economic History*, 52, no. 1 (1992): 129-160. Cited in Robert Whaples, "Hours of Work in US History," Economic History Association website, accessed June 2023, https://eh.net/encyclopedia/hours-of-work-in-u-s-history/.
3. Based on seasonally adjusted averages for May, June, July of 2023, today's average American works *34.5 hours per week*, US Bureau of Labor and

Statistics, "Table B-2. Average weekly hours and overtime of all employees on private nonfarm payrolls by industry sector, seasonally adjusted," *Economic News Release*, July 2023.
4. Migrant farm workers and undocumented meatpacking plant workers may also work more than the average, but data is scattered and unclear for this class of worker and national underreporting of overtime is common.
5. Robert Whaples, "Hours of Work in US History."
6. Derek Thompson, "Workism Is Making Americans Miserable," *Atlantic*, February 24, 2019, accessed June 8, 2023, https://www.theatlantic.com/ideas/archive/2019/02/religion-workism-making-americans-miserable/583441/.
7. Kate Hidalgo Bellows, "What a Shooting at the U. of Arizona Tells Us About Campus Safety," *Chronicle of Higher Education*, November 18, 2022.

Chapter Ten

1. Kenneth A. Simon and W. Vance Grant, Digest of Educational Statistics, Office of Education, bulletin 1964, no. 18 (Washington, DC: US Government Printing Office, 1964), p. 56, accessed January 2, 2024. https://files.eric.ed.gov/fulltext/ED544136.pdf
2. Alexis De Tocqueville, *Democracy in America*, [1835 original] (Chicago: University of Chicago Press, 2000), 50.
3. Simon and Grant, Digest of Educational Statistics.
4. Seventy-three percent of older Americans attempted college: 25 percent dropped out before receiving any degree, 12 percent obtained a two-year degree, and 36 percent received a traditional four-year degree. Data sourced from SAI National Survey on Older Americans, 2022.
5. Vocational course credits taken in American high schools were steadily on the decline from the early 1980s until more recently. See Brian J. Jacob, "What We Know About Career and Technical Education," October 5, 2017, Brookings Institution, accessed April 14, 2023, https://www.brookings.edu/research/what-we-know-about-career-and-technical-education-in-high-school/; Karen Levesque et. al., "Vocational Education in the United States: The Early 1990s," National Center for Education Statistics—November, 1995, NCES 95-024 , accessed April 2023, https://nces.ed.gov/pubs/web/95024-2.asp—.
6. SAI National Survey on Older Americans, 2022.

7. Mikaela Kiner, "It's Time to Break the Cycle of Female Rivalry," *Harvard Business Review: Ascend*, April 14, 2020, accessed June 5, 2023, https://hbr.org/2020/04/its-time-to-break-the-cycle-of-female-rivalry.
8. See J. Lorand Matory, *Stigma and Culture: Last Place Anxiety Among African-Americans* (Chicago: University of Chicago Press, 2015).
9. Social Awareness Institute interview with Nancy W. (pseudonym), living in Alabama, conducted via Zoom in March 2023. Some edits made for clarity.
10. Social Awareness Institute interview with Nancy W.
11. Social Awareness Institute interview with Todd L. (pseudonym), living in Idaho, conducted via Zoom in March 2023. Some edits made for clarity. Modern research on the age of discovery for adopted infants has revealed that telling the adopted child before it can form long-term memories reduces problems later. It's as if a child's adopted status simply melts away unconsciously and the need to keep secrets or tell lies disappears. The child knows *before* it can even speak. Letting a consciously aware young child know their adopted status allows the potential for all sorts of rumination and story-invention without professional therapeutic guidance (which parents do not possess). Todd's parents unfortunately told him at the age of five on the advice of a contemporary professional following best practice at the time. Source: Amanda L. Baden, Doug Shadel, Ron Morgan, Ebony E. White, Elliotte S. Harrington, "Delaying Adoption Disclosure: A Survey of Late Discovery Adoptees," *Journal of Family Issues*, June 1, 2019, vol. 40 (9): 27.
12. These are the ethnic groups who produced virtually all congresspeople and all US presidents (except JFK) until the 1970s.
13. Social Awareness Institute interview with Todd L.
14. Social Awareness Institute interview with Todd L.

Chapter Eleven

1. SAI Older Americans National Study, 2022.
2. Micki McGee, *Self-Help Inc.* (Cambridge: Oxford University Press, 2005), 38.
3. Google Ngram service, "Career Change," accessed April 2023. The decline from 2015 to 2019 is either a blip or a recognition that the "career" concept itself is dying.
4. SAI Older Americans National Study, 2022. Answers to question 8: "How many different times did you completely change your career?" Note:

I'd ignore the folks who checked 8 and above, because they tended to interpret the question as "job change" instead of "career change."
5. Dorie Clark's *Reinventing You* (Cambridge: Harvard Business School Press, 2017) is one of the more successful modern books aimed at women in midlife.
6. My lawyer advised me to caveat that this is a joke, *not a serious offer or contest of any kind.*
7. Richard Nelson Bolles, *What Color Is Your Parachute?*, revised 1978 edition (CITY: Ten Speed Press, YEAR) 13.
8. SAI National Survey of Older Americans, 2022.
9. United States Census, CPS Monthly Survey, July 2022; my analysis.
10. I encourage you to visit a fantastic website, Flowing Data, and see for yourself how unlikely it is that you are married to anyone in your career or even in your career class. The careers where marrying within the profession is most common? Doctors/surgeons, actors, and professors. See https://flowingdata.com/2017/08/28/occupation-matchmaker/, accessed May 8, 2023. Flowing Data used here is sourced from raw 2015 American Community Survey datasets collected by the US Census.
11. Social Awareness Institute interview with Anna W. (pseudonym), living in Virginia, conducted via Zoom in April 2023. Some edits made for clarity.
12. "Job Training & Career Counseling Industry in the US—Market Size, Industry Analysis, Trends and Forecasts (2023–2028)," March 2023, published by IBIS World, accessed June 7, 2023, https://www.ibisworld.com/united-states/market-research-reports/job-training-career-counseling-industry/.
13. Bolles, *Parachute*, preface.

Chapter Twelve

1. Based on a random sample (100) of the top 1000 worldwide grossing Hollywood films with international and domestic revenue. Source: TheNumbers.com, Accessed October 23, 2023, https://www.the-numbers.com/box-office-records/international/all-movies/cumulative/all-time.
2. *Oxford English Dictionary*, s.v. "fun," accessed online May 2023.
3. *Oxford English Dictionary*, s.v. "fun," accessed online May 2023.
4. There is large, U-shaped dip in English print usage of the word "fun" from 1800 to 2019, according to Google's Ngram service, accessed May 22, 2023.

Chapter Thirteen

1. Nonbehavioral causes such as genetics, poverty, and low educational attainment are also at play. See National Institute on Alcohol Abuse and Alcoholism, "Alcohol's Effects on Health," 2020, accessed October 23, 2023, https://www.niaaa.nih.gov/publications/brochures-and-fact-sheets/understanding-alcohol-use-disorder.
2. Center for Disease Control, "Trends in Mortality from Cirrhosis and Alcoholism—United States, 1945–1983," *Morbidity and Mortality Weekly Report*, November 14, 1985, vol. 35, issue 45, 703–05, accessed November 2, 2023, https://www.cdc.gov/mmwr/preview/mmwrhtml/00000821.htm.
3. National Institute on Alcohol Abuse and Alcoholism, "Alcohol Use Disorder (AUD) in the United States: Age Groups and Demographic Characteristics," 2023, accessed November 2, 2023, https://www.niaaa.nih.gov/alcohols-effects-health/alcohol-topics/alcohol-facts-and-statistics/alcohol-use-disorder-aud-united-states-age-groups-and-demographic-characteristics. These last two studies may not be using the exact same definition of AUD, so a precise increase should not be derived.
4. National Institutes of Health, National Institute on Alcohol Abuse and Alcoholism annual survey data: https://bit.ly/43ga5NW; Gallup's yearly poll on Americans who drink: https://bit.ly/3IErBCT. The 1939–1970 results are based on adults aged twenty-one and older. The 1971–2022 results are based on adults aged eighteen and older.
5. Social Awareness Institute interview with Kevin F. (pseudonym), conducted via Zoom in March 2023. Some edits made for clarity.
6. Social Awareness Institute interview with Kevin F.
7. Eleven percent of adults eighteen and over have an Alcohol Use Disorder (AUD). Source: National institute on Alcohol Abuse and Alcoholism (NIAAA), "Alcohol Use Disorder (AUD) in the United States: Age Groups and Demographic Characteristics," accessed May 25, 2023, https://niaaa.nih.gov/alcohols-effects-health/alcohol-topics/alcohol-facts-and-statistics/alcohol-use-disorder-aud-united-states-age-groups-and-demographic-characteristics#:~:text=Prevalence%20of%20Past-.Year%20Alcohol%20Use%20Disorder%20(AUD)&text=According%20to%20the%202021%20National,AUD%20in%20the%20past%20year.&text=This%20includes%3A,12.1%25%20in%20this%20age%20group)

8. Samuel Stebbins, "Here's What a Six-Pack of Beer Cost the Year You Were Born," *USA Today*, November 20, 2016, accessed May 2023, https://www.usatoday.com/story/money/2018/11/20/cost-beer-how-much-six-pack-cost-year-you-were-born/38528543/.
9. Inference made based on an excellent econometric study of data from 1987 to 1999, in which this finding first appeared. Recessions decrease binge drinking and heavy, risky drinking. Source: Christopher J. Ruhm and William E. Black Ruhm, C. and W. E. Black, "Does Drinking Really Decrease in Bad Times?" *Journal of Health Economics*, vol. 21(4): 659–78.

Chapter Fourteen

1. Paul Howe, *Teen Spirit: How Adolescence Transformed the Adult World* (Cornell: Cornell University Press, 2020), 31.
2. Howe, *Teen Spirit*.
3. SAI National Survey on Older Americans, 2022.
4. SAI National Survey on Older Americans, 2022. Thirty-seven percent of older Americans live in couples-only households. And 32 percent live alone!
5. 2022 Google Surveys poll designed by the Social Awareness Institute asking adults to define "fun" in their own words. The survey polled 1,190 adults of all ages, 850 older Americans (over forty-five years old), and 290 younger Americans (age forty-four and younger).
6. IBISWorld, "Retirement Communities in the US—Market Size, Industry Analysis, Trends and Forecasts (2023–2028), accessed June 5, 2023, https://www.ibisworld.com/industry-statistics/market-size/retirement-communities-united-states/ https://www.ibisworld.com/united-states/market-research-reports/retirement-communities-industry/.
7. The preceding analysis of generational orientations to music genres is based on my analysis of data from the Music Business Association, "Audio Monitor U.S.: The Overall Music Landscape," 2018, p. 65. https://musicbiz.org/wp-content/uploads/2018/09/AM_US_2018_V5.pdf.
8. Glenn Peoples, "Millennials and Boomers Love Experiences, But Who Attends More Concerts?" Billboard, August 24, 2015, accessed June 9, 2023, https://www.billboard.com/pro/millennials-and-boomers-love-experiences-but-who-attends-more-concerts/.
9. SAI National Survey on Older Americans, 2022.

10. 2022 Google Surveys poll designed by the Social Awareness Institute asking adults to define "fun" in their own words.

Chapter Fifteen

1. Robert Putnam, *The Upswing* (New York: Simon and Schuster, 2021).
2. Lara B. Aknin and Ashley Whillans, "Helping and Happiness: A Review and Guide for Public Policy," *Social Issues and Policy Review*, vol. 15, no. 1, 2021, 3–34, accessed June 9, 2023, https://www.hbs.edu/ris/Publication%20Files/Helping%20and%20Happiness_41d48a88-0cd1-48ce-8428-4988f6f2ce0c.pdf.
3. 2022 Google Surveys poll designed by the Social Awareness Institute asking adults to define "fun" in their own words. The survey polled 1,190 adults of all ages, 850 older Americans (over forty-five years old), and 290 younger Americans (age forty-four) and younger.
4. And because the music industry specifically gears itself toward youth (under thirty) who tend to prefer partying or recreation as their primary mode of fun.
5. Robert Putnam, *Bowling Alone*, (New York: Simon and Schuster, 2001). He also cites some important work on how TV reduces community involvement.
6. This may not have been visible in the 1990s datasets Robert Putnam used. *Bowling Alone* was published in 2000, right around the time that the new kinds of recreational worlds really began to grow in scale and reach.
7. For the data hungry, please examine this list of popular outdoor recreational activities assembled by online publications: John Spacey, "60 Examples of Outdoor Activities," *Simplicable*, July 25, 2020, accessed June 5, 2023, https://simplicable.com/life/outdoor-activities. Eighteen out of sixty activities listed are post–WWII in origin, relying on modern equipment and chemical engineering to support them. Kayaking, skateboarding, and windsurfing are great examples.
8. Becky Timbers, "A to Z to Mountain Bike Slang & Terminology," twowheeledwanderer.com, accessed June 3, 2023, https://www.twowheeledwanderer.com/posts/mountain-bike-slang/.

Chapter Sixteen

1. ATUS, 2021, average hours per day socializing, relaxing, and leisure, age 15+: series ID TUU10101AA01005370.
2. ATUS, 2021, average hours per day socializing, relaxing, and leisure, age 15+ = 4.77 hours: series ID TUU10101AA01005370; ages 25–54 = 3.85 hours: series ID TUU10101AA01034690; age 65+ = 6.79 hours: series ID TUU10101AA01034702.
3. ATUS, 2003–2021. This is my weekly projection of the average hours per day people age 15+ spent socializing and communicating: series ID TUU10101AA01013951.
4. ATUS, 2003 versus 2021 comparisons of average hours per day of socializing and communicating for my research cohort (aged 27–55 in 2003 and 44–73 in 2021); my analysis.
5. ATUS, 2021, average hours per day people age 15 years and over spent socializing, relaxing, and in leisure activities: leisure = 4.77 hours (series ID TUU10101AA01005370), socializing and communicating (except social events) = 0.52 hours (series ID TUU10101AA01005442). Note: the average I cite in this book won't necessarily resemble you.
6. I calculated this in terms of dollars per hour using the following inputs: typical internet/cable/satellite television packages run $83 per household, assuming streaming subscriptions of $50 per month, 1.96 people per household (2021 CPS), 30 days in a month and 2.9 hours per person per day. Sources: https://www.cabletv.com/blog/how-much-should-i-pay-for-cable-tv#:~:text=TV%20plans%20run%20between%20%2455,costing%20around%20%2483%20a%20month.&text=The%20average%20cable%20TV%20plan%20costs%20around%20%2483; US Census, ATUS 2021 data on TV usage.
7. Americans age fifteen and older spend 0.52 hours per day socializing/communicating face-to-face per the ATUS. If we include group interaction at work as a meeting, then I calculate that American office workers spend about 1.2 hours per day in meetings, using data from LiveCareer's 2023 online poll of 1,033 adult office workers. Source: Live Career, "Workplace Meetings—2022," accessed June 2023, https://www.livecareer.com/resources/careers/planning/workplace-meetings-2022-statistics. I assigned modal hours for each segment in the LiveCareer data and created a weighted average using a five-day work week.
8. SAI National Survey on Older Americans, 2022.

9. "Rooms with a View: Multiple-Set TV Households Provide an Array of Access and Choice for Content-Hungry Viewers," Nielsen.com, February 2022, accessed June 2023, https://www.nielsen.com/insights/2022/rooms-with-a-view-multiple-set-tv-households-provide-an-array-of-access-and-choice-for-content-hungry-viewers/.
10. Mentions of "family" in respondents' open-ended definition of fun = 18 percent for 45+ and 9 percent for those under 45. Mentions of "friends" in their definition of fun are 9 percent for 45+ and 4 percent for under 45. Source: Google Surveys poll by the Social Awareness Institute asking adults to define "fun" in their own words. The survey sample included 1,190 adults of all ages, 850 older Americans (45 and older), and 290 younger Americans (44 and younger).
11. Avery Koop, "Visualized: Who Americans Spend Their Time with," *Visual Capitalist*, October 28, 2022, accessed June 9, 2023, https://www.visualcapitalist.com/who-americans-spend-their-time-with/.
12. Gareth Willmer, "Social Skills Begin to Decline in Late 30s and Early 40s, Study Finds," *Horizon: The EU Research & Innovation Magazine*, European Commission, March 3, 2020, accessed June 2023, https://ec.europa.eu/research-and-innovation/en/horizon-magazine/social-skills-begin-decline-late-30s-and-early-40s-study-finds#:~:text=Old%20age-,Prof.,rather%20than%20in%20old%20age. See also Heather J. Ferguson and Elisabeth E. F. Bradford, eds., *The Cognitive Basis of Social Interaction Across the Lifespan* (Oxford: Oxford University Press, 2021).

Chapter Eighteen

1. In my survey of older Americans, for example, roughly 28 percent (+/− 3 percent) never raised children in their home (most of these never had children intentionally either). SAI National Survey on Older Americans, 2022.
2. Single-parent families as a percentage of families with kids under eighteen at home grew from 1960 (9 percent of families with kids) to 2022 (31 percent of families with kids) with the percent plateauing around 2010. Source: US Census Bureau. CPS surveys. "Table FM-1. Families by Presence of Own Children Under 18: 1950 to Present," accessed July 4, 2023, https://www.census.gov/data/tables/time-series/demo/families/families.html.

3. As of 2022, 35–40 percent of kids age six to seventeen are doing sports activities regularly; when these are games, they tend to interrupt dinner completely (unless the home eats very late by custom). Source: Aspen Project Play, State of Play 2023 Report, accessed December 18, 2023, https://projectplay.org/state-of-play-2023/participation.
4. From eight to twenty-seven minutes of commuting time each way from 1977 to 2019. Sources: United States Census current population reports, "Selected Characteristics of Travel to Work in 20 Metro Areas: 1977," *Social Studies*, no. 105, p. 23; US Census Bureau, "American Community Survey, 2010–2021, 5-Year Estimates Subject Tables, S0801," accessed July 3, 2023, https://www.energy.gov/eere/vehicles/articles/fotw-1284-april-3-2023-average-travel-time-work-was-about-27-minutes-2021#. Note: these two sources use differently collected data and aren't perfectly comparable.
5. Economists who have studied extreme work among Gen X and Baby Boomers from the 1980s through today indicate that the longer hours are largely self-inflicted (only 36 percent of adults claim the organization pressured them to work sixty hours or more per week). "There is very little sense of victimization." The professional workaholic hero archetype is common to men and women still. "Extreme jobs, we've found, are distributed across the economy—in large manufacturing companies as well as on Wall Street, in entertainment and media, in medicine and law, in consulting and accounting." Source: Sylvia Ann Hewlett and Carolyn Buck Luce, "Extreme Jobs: The Dangerous Allure of the 70-Hour Workweek," *Harvard Business Review*, December 2006.
6. The average family size in the United States was around six for most of the nineteenth century. Source: Pew Research Center, "The Number of People in the Average U.S. Household is Going up for the first time in over 160 Years," accessed June 2023, https://www.pewresearch.org/short-reads/2019/10/01/the-number-of-people-in-the-average-u-s-household-is-going-up-for-the-first-time-in-over-160-years/.
7. Abigail Carroll, *Three Squares: The Invention of the American Meal* (New York: Basic Books, 2013).
8. Food Marketing Institute Foundation, "Power of Family Meals," August 2017, chart 1, p. 2. Note: margin of error here on the source survey +/– 6 percent.
9. Fifty-five percent of families with children and 47 percent of couples living without children say this. This is two times greater than the number two

rationale for canceling dinner. It is the master cultural cause. Source: Food Marketing Institute Foundation, "Power of Family Meals," p. 4.
10. I doubt it, since modern snacking is an asocial, often impulse-driven act of eating outside of rituals of food preparation. Stuffing your face by yourself at home is the most basic possible act of self-absorption in the human world. I've read hundreds of ethnographies on tribal humanity, and this is not the vibe they give you. Doing whatever you want is the privilege of elders in most traditional societies, although they usually also have the greatest burden of social obligations to counter their social power.
11. *Oxford English Dictionary*, s.v. "snack," accessed online June 2023.
12. "Frito Company," in Other Sales, Mergers, *New York Times*, August 11, 1965.
13. Based on a US population of 182 million in 1961. Source: US Census Bureau. "Current Population Reports: Population Estimates," series P-25, no. 226, April 17, 1961, accessed July 3, 2023, https://www2.census.gov/library/publications/1961/demographics/P25-226.pdf.
14. Sources: Dirk E. Burhans, *Crunch!: A History of the Great American Potato Chip* (Madison: University of Wisconsin Press, 2008) and US Census Bureau, "Population Profile of the United States: 1989,"
April 1989, report number P23-159, accessed June 2023, https://www.census.gov/library/publications/1989/demo/p23-159.html.
15. Pepsico Corporation, *2022 Annual Report*, accessed July 3, 2023, https://www.pepsico.com/investors/investor-relations and US Census Bureau Population Clock, accessed July 3, 2023, www.census.gov/popclock for December 31, 2022.
16. Inflation-adjusted, per capita consumption of Frito-Lay snacks in 2022 dollars are 1) $7.37 for 1961, 2) $34.31 for 1989, and 3) $69 for 2022. Source: Bureau of Labor and Statistics, accessed June 2023, https://www.bls.gov/data/inflation_calculator.htm.
17. Google, "Ngram Viewer," accessed June 2023, https://books.google.com/ngrams.
18. J. P. Enriquez and E. Gollub, "Snacking Consumption Among Adults in the United States: A Scoping Review," *Nutrients 2023*, 15, 1596, accessed June 2023, https://www.ncbi.nlm.nih.gov/pmc/articles/PMC10097271/#:~:text=Snacks%20are%20a%20staple%20of%20the%20American%20diet%2C%20accounting%20for,occurrences%20per%20day%20%5B3%5D.

19. The Hartman Group Inc., The Hartman Group Compass Eating Occasions Database 2021–2022, adults 18–75. Sample includes data on 13,540 eating occasions.

20. For context, on any given day around 20 percent of adults are on a special diet and 1.8 percent of adults have an eating disorder. Sources: Bryan Stierman, MD, MPH, Nicholas Ansai, MPH, Suruchi Mishra, PhD, and Craig M. Hales, MD, MPH, "Special Diets Among Adults: United States, 2015–2018," NCHS Data Brief, no. 389, November 2020, accessed July 4, 2023, https://www.cdc.gov/nchs/products/databriefs/db389.htm and Deloitte Access Economics, "Social and Economic Cost of Eating Disorders in the United States of America Report for the Strategic Training Initiative for the Prevention of Eating Disorders and the Academy for Eating Disorders," June 2020, p. iii, accessed July 4, 2023, https://www.hsph.harvard.edu/striped/wp-content/uploads/sites/1267/2020/07/Social-Economic-Cost-of-Eating-Disorders-in-US.pdf.

21. When I asked older Americans to agree/disagree with the statement, "Individuals are solely responsible for what they eat and drink," 68 percent said they strongly agreed or agreed. Virtually everyone chose the "agreed" side of the six-point Likert scale. Only when I asked about obesity in the same way, did their opinion change. Source: SAI National Survey on Older Americans, 2022.

22. Obesity rates measured in the NHANES survey dataset show a 30 percent increase in the prevalence of obesity from 1999 until 2018; we now have 43 percent or more of the adult population measuring as obese. Incidence of childhood obesity has also not stopped growing as of 2020 and currently stands at 22 percent for children age two through nineteen. Sources: NHANES online database, my analysis; "Trends in Obesity Prevalence Among Children and Adolescents Aged 2 to 19 Years in the US From 2011 to 2020," *JAMA Pediatrics* 176, no. 10 (October 2022): 1037-1039, accessed July 4, 2023, https://www.ncbi.nlm.nih.gov/pmc/articles/PMC9315946.

23. Examples sourced from University of Rochester Medical Center, *Health Encyclopedia*, "When Your Weight Gain Is Caused by Medicine," accessed July 4, 2023, https://www.urmc.rochester.edu/encyclopedia/content.aspx?contenttypeid=56&contentid=DM300#:~:text=For%20certain%20medicines%2C%20researchers%20aren,%2C%20olanzapine%2C%20quetiapine%2C%20and%20lithium.

24. They tend to be rich, white, alienated men like Bryan Johnson, a wealthy entrepreneur who follows a strict, vegan, calorie-restricted diet and other regimens in order to revert his biometrics to those of an eighteen-year-old man. https://www.bloomberg.com/news/features/2023-01-25/anti-aging-techniques-taken-to-extreme-by-bryan-johnson?utm_source=website&utm_medium=share&utm_campaign=copy (accessed June 2023).
25. Didier Chapelot, "The Role of Snacking in Energy Balance: A Biobehavioral Approach," *Journal of Nutrition* 141, no. 1 (2011): 158–62, accessed July 5, 2023, https://doi.org/10.3945/jn.109.114330.
26. The first mass-produced candy bar was the British-made Fry's Chocolate Cream bar in 1866. American candy came a bit later with Hershey's Chocolate in 1894, Planters in 1906, the Mars Bar and Clark Bar in 1911, and Oh Henry! in 1920. Salty snacks proliferated after the Depression, forming the next wave of snacking.

Chapter Nineteen

1. Professional allergists have located early references to milk intolerances among the ancient Greeks, but nothing like the explosion of anaphylactic allergies that has overtaken young people in the last quarter century. Most references to allergic responses in premodern literature refer to asthma, insect bites, horse dander, etc. Source: *Achoo! Blog*, "A History of Allergies and Asthma, Part One: The Ancients' Perspective," AchooAllergy.com, accessed June 2023, https://www.achooallergy.com/blog/learning/a-history-of-allergies-and-asthma-part-one-the-ancients-perspective/.
2. In large-scale studies of food allergy prevalence by the National Institutes of Health, 19 percent of adults self-report a food allergy. However, only 10.8 percent met the standards of convincing in a survey environment. R. S. Gupta, C. M. Warren, B. M. Smith, J. Jiang , J. A. Blumenstock, M. M. Davis, R. P. Schleimer, K. C. Nadeau, "Prevalence and Severity of Food Allergies Among US Adults." *JAMA Network Open*, January 4, 2019, 2(1):e185630. doi: 10.1001/jamanetworkopen.2018.5630. PMID: 30646188; PMCID: PMC6324316.
3. "Introduction," in *Adverse Reactions to Foods*, NIH Publication no. 84-2442, July 1984, American Academy of Allergy and Immunology Committee on Adverse Reactions to Foods, National Institute of

Allergy and Infectious Diseases, US Department of Health and Human Services, p. 3, accessed July 5, 2023, https://babel.hathitrust.org/cgi/pt?id=mdp.39015063090743&view=1up&seq=1.

4. I use the phrase "food sensitivity" to bridge the allergy/intolerance boundary and reflect people's experience. This is standard practice on health surveys. Source: SAI National Survey on Older Americans, 2022.
5. The reality is that most of the 27 percent of older Americans I mentioned earlier do not have a medical food allergy. Not even close. I can infer this from larger datasets broken out by age. In 2021, *only 5.1–6.7 percent* of adults age forty-five to sixty-four have true a medical food allergy; 6.2 percent for the general population overall. Source: Amanda E. Ng and Peter Boersma, "Diagnosed Allergic Conditions in Adults: United States, 2021." NCHS Data Brief, no. 460, January 2023. CDC, accessed July 5, 2023, https://www.cdc.gov/nchs/products/databriefs/db460.htm. This means that only one out of five older Americans you meet who claim to have a food sensitivity have a medical allergy. The majority are dealing with nuisance symptoms like those caused by lactose intolerance.
6. "My lord you haue very good strawberies at your gardayne in Holberne, I require you let vs haue a messe of them. Gladly my lord, quod he, woulde God I had some better thing as redy to your pleasure as that. And therwith in al the hast he sent hys seruant for a messe of strauberies. The protectour sette the fast in comoning, and thereupon prayeng them to spare hym for a little while departed thence. And sone, after one hower, between .x. and .xi. he returned into the chamber among them, al changed, with a wonderful soure angrye countenaunce, knitting the browes, frowning and froting and knawing on hys lippes, and so sat him downe in hys place." Source: Lumby, J. Rawson, ed., *More's History of King Richard III* (Cambridge: Cambridge University Press, 1883) 46, accessed July 5, 2023, https://www.google.com/books/edition/More_s_History_of_King_Richard_III/xQL154m8wxYC?hl=en&gbpv=1&printsec=frontcover.
7. Google, "Ngram Viewer," accessed June 2023, https://books.google.com/ngrams.
8. Hugh A. Sampson, "Food Allergy: Past, Present and Future," *Allergology International* 65, no. 3 (2016): 363–369.
9. Total dairy per capita output peaked in the 1970s in the United States per the USDA. https://www.ers.usda.gov/amber-waves/2014/june/trends-in

-u-s-per-capita-consumption-of-dairy-products-1970-2012/ (accessed June 21, 2023).
10. There was a twenty-four-fold increase (to 13,000,000) in the immigrant population from countries with known genetic predispositions for low lactase levels (India, Afghanistan, Armenia, Cambodia, China, Greece, Iran, Iraq, Israel, Japan, Kazakhstan, Kuwait, Laos, Lebanon, Malaysia, Myanmar, Nepal, Nigeria, Pakistan, Philippines, Saudi Arabia, Senegal, Sierra Leone, Singapore, Syria, Taiwan, Thailand, Uzbekistan, Vietnam, and Yemen) per the US Census and other public data released by the Migration Policy Institute, accessed June 17, 2023, https://www.migrationpolicy.org/programs/data-hub/charts/immigrants-countries-birth-over-time. Countries with populations prone to lactose intolerance sourced from Medline Plus from the NIH National Library of Medicine, *Genetics Home Reference*, "Your Guide to Understanding Genetic Conditions," Lister Hill National Center for Biomedical Communications, January 24, 2017, last updated March 24, 2023, accessed June 17, 2023, https://medlineplus.gov/download/genetics/condition/lactose-intolerance.pdf.

Chapter Twenty

1. Jasmijn De Boo, The Vegan Society, "Ripened by Human Determination: 70 Years of the Vegan Society," 2014, accessed June 19, 2023, www.vegansociety.com.
2. Although some Brahmin communities in India are vegan by practice, it is considered a caste or communal orientation related to social status reproduction, not a voluntary, ethical statement, as in the West.
3. Today, vegan meat alternatives are roughly 1–2 percent of the total meat market, even after hundreds of millions of venture capital dollars poured into the space in the last fifteen years. In 2022 there were $86 billion in US retail meat sales according to Winsight Grocery Business. And there were $1.4 billion meat substitutes in 2022. (SPINS Natural Grocery Channel, SPINS Conventional Multi Outlet Channel, all outlets, 52 weeks ending 1/1/2023, accessed July 5, 2023, https://gfi.org/marketresearch/.) This means that meat substitutes represent only 1.6 percent in retail sales of the combined meat/faux meat category. Vegan alternatives to cow milk, on the other hand, have done much better in terms of sales and market share. $2.4 billion dollars' worth of milk alternatives sold in 2022 in US

retail. This is a 15 percent market share of the combined $18 billion fluid milk retail market. Brian Berk, "Dairy and Plant-Based Milks Continue to See Strong Dollar Sales," *Dairy Foods Magazine*, accessed July 5, 2022, https://www.dairyfoods.com/articles/96153-dairy-and-plant-based-milks-continue-to-see-strong-dollar-sales.

4. Health beats "animal protection" 2:1 as a motivation for all vegans (current and former). See table 4 of Humane Research Council, "Study of Current and Former Vegetarians and Vegans," 2014, accessed July 5, 2023, https://faunalytics.org/wp-content/uploads/2015/06/Faunalytics_Current-Former-Vegetarians_Full-Report.pdf.
5. An eight-ounce serving is the benchmark here. "Original" or sugar-added almond milk is the top selling UPC for most brands, not unsweetened. Almond Breeze Original from Blue Diamond is the comparison here.
6. www.veganbits.com, accessed November 1, 2023, https://veganbits.com/vegan-demographics/.
7. Medifast survey, April 2022, sample of n=2000 adults cited in Simona Kitanovska, "Majority of Americans Who Have Dieted Report No Lasting Change," June 24, 2022, accessed June 21, 2023, https://www.newsweek.com/majority-americans-who-have-dieted-report-no-lasting-change-1719100.
8. Survey results were derived from online interviews of 1,005 Americans ages eighteen to eighty, conducted March 23 to April 4, 2022, by Greenwald Research, using Dynata's consumer panel, accessed June 2023, https://ific.org/media-information/press-releases/2022-food-health-survey/.
9. Bradley Johnston et al., "Comparison of Dietary Macronutrient Patterns of 14 Popular Named Dietary Programmes for Weight and Cardiovascular Risk Factor Reduction in Adults: Systematic Review and Network Meta-Analysis of Randomized Trials," *BMJ* 369, accessed August 31 2023, https://www.bmj.com/content/369/bmj.m696.
10. Jolie Porter, "I Lost 20lbs While Living Abroad in France," *Illumination*, October 20, 2021, accessed July 5, 2023, https://medium.com/illumination/i-lost-20lbs-while-living-abroad-in-france-445d5101c6d4.
11. Stephanie Heiner, "Helping You Adapt to Life in France," *The American In Paris* (blog), May 10, 2022, accessed July 5, 2023, https://theamericaninparis.com/2022/05/03/how-i-moved-to-france-and-lost-20-pounds/.

12. B. Krupal, "Sober 365 Days and Counting," LinkedIn article published May 4, 2023, accessed July 5, 2023, https://www.linkedin.com/pulse/sober-365-days-counting-krupal-b%3FtrackingId=e1uy3jlaTvKMx03OivZqzQ%253D%253D/?trackingId=giuGW9dSPW6cvqoOBrvD8g%3D%3D.
13. Derek Thompson, "Workism Is Making Americans Miserable," *Atlantic Monthly*, February 24, 2019, accessed July 5, 2023, https://www.theatlantic.com/ideas/archive/2019/02/religion-workism-making-americans-miserable/583441/.

Chapter Twenty-One

1. GfK, "Half of Americans Entertain Guests in Their Homes at Least Once a Month," July 25, 2017, accessed July 5, 2023, https://www.gfk.com/press/half-of-americans-entertain-guests-in-their-homes-at-least-once-a-month#:~:text=Less%20than%20one%2Dthird%20of,(43%25%20versus%2030%25).
2. *Oxford English Dictionary*, s.v. "potluck," accessed online June 2023.
3. Flora Martin, "Potluck Meal Innovation Due to Depression," *Chicago Tribune*, January 27, 1933, p. 14, accessed June 27, 2023, https://www.newspapers.com/image/354875200/?clipping_id=55951150.
4. Google, "Ngram Viewer," accessed June 2023, https://books.google.com/ngrams. We can see the exponential increase in mentions of "potluck" in the printed English language in the 1990s as food preferences fragmented aspirationally and due to perceived allergies/sensitivities.
5. The earliest print article dedicated to modern potluck hosting advice I can find is from 2002 in the *New York Times*: Marian Burros, "Potluck Tips: A Note to the Host," *New York Times*, January 30, 2022, accessed July 5, 2023, https://www.nytimes.com/2002/01/30/dining/potluck-tips-a-note-to-the-host.html?smid=url-share.
6. Google Trends, an online service, "potluck."
7. The Hartman Group, Inc., The Hartman Group Compass Eating Occasions Database 2021–2022, adults 18–75. A sample of 13,540 eating occasions.
8. Stephanie Witt Sedgwick, "Potlucks," *Washington Post*, Lifestyle Section, July 26, 2006, accessed July 5, 2023, https://www.washingtonpost.com/archive/lifestyle/food/2006/07/26/potluck-rules/b4c3179d-168a-48a4-8dca-69875497d3a4/.

9. Some of the earliest national research on declining cooking skills appeared in the early 1990s, often supported by corporations interested in how to encourage less cooking and more buying of prepared, branded foods. Trish Hall, New 'Lost Generation': The Cooking Illiterate *New York Times*, January 15, 1992, p. 43, 48, accessed July 5, 2023, https://timesmachine.nytimes.com/timesmachine/1992/01/15/824292.html?pageNumber=43.

Chapter Twenty-Two

1. Tiruvalluvar, *The Kural*, Translated from the Tamil by P. S. Sundaram (New Delhi: Penguin, 1990).
2. The friendship behaviors depicted here are those of men in public. Since women did not "hang out" in public when I lived in Madurai, these comments may not extend to them.
3. Johann Hari, *Lost Connections: Why You're Depressed and How to Find Hope* (New York: Bloomsbury Publishing, 2019).

Chapter Twenty-Three

1. Around 80 percent in AEI's recent survey indicated that their best friend is someone outside their family (i.e., not their spouse). I believe this may be changing slowly over time. My anecdotal sense is that highly educated couples tend to see each other as best friends as the root of their marriages and lifestyles. Source: Daniel A. Cox, "The State of American Friendship: Change, Challenges, and Loss," American Enterprise Institute, June 8, 2021, accessed August 30, 2023, https://www.americansurveycenter.org/research/the-state-of-american-friendship-change-challenges-and-loss/.
2. Cox, "The State of American Friendship." "Close friends" excluded relatives in the survey design.
3. Cox, "The State of American Friendship." Some of this variance is due to the enormous Baby Boomer generation distorting the averages and trends.
4. SAI National Survey on Older Americans, 2022.
5. Robin Dunbar, *Friends: Understanding the Power of Our Most Important Relationships* (New York: Little, Brown, 2012).
6. Dunbar, *Friends*, 8.
7. This is my inference based on the data presented in Cox, "The State of American Friendship."

8. *Oxford English Dictionary*, s.v. "friends," accessed online May 2023.
9. My analysis of data published in Cox, "The State of American Friendship."
10. Pulling away from our parents was a major mark of Gen X and Boomer cohorts that does not appear to be continuing as strongly in younger generations.
11. Nick Christakis and James Fowler, *Connected: The Surprising Power of Our Social Networks and How They Shape Our Lives* (New York: Little, Brown Spark, 2009), cited in Dunbar, Friends, 12.
12. Women do appear to fold in more solace-seeking than men do with their close friends per Cox, "The State of American Friendship."
13. In my survey of older Americans, 37 percent of respondents said they felt it was harder to maintain friendships than it was for their parents at the same age as they are now. That's a healthy chunk of people who think it is even harder for older Americans to keep their circle of friends intact. Source: SAI National Survey on Older Americans, 2022.
14. Visual Capitalist did a great chart showing how the time spent with various types of social actor (e.g. family, friends, alone) changes as we age. Time with friends drops really fast by the early thirties and never recovers, hovering around forty-five minutes per day (on a crude average). This obviously does not mean we see friends daily. See: https://www.visualcapitalist.com/who-americans-spend-their-time-with/.
15. Social Awareness Institute interview with Tim (pseudonym), living in Connecticut, conducted via Zoom in March 2023. Some edits made for clarity.
16. Cox, "The State of American Friendship."

Chapter Twenty-Four

1. Mark Granovetter, "The Strength of Weak Ties," *American Sociology Review* 78, no. 6 (May 1973): 1360–80.
2. Emily Flitter and James B. Stewart, "Bill Gates Met with Jeffrey Epstein Many Times, Despite His Past," *The New York Times*, October 12, 2019.

Chapter Twenty-Five

1. Anthony Giddens, *The Transformation of Intimacy: Sexuality, Love and Eroticism in Modern Societies* (Stanford: Stanford University Press: 1993).

2. Paul Amato et al., *Alone Together: How Marriage Is Changing in America* (Cambridge: Harvard University Press, 2007).
3. Amato, *Alone Together*, location 196 of Kindle edition.
4. Suzanna Rose, "Same- and Cross-Sex Friendships and the Psychology of Homosociality," *Sex Roles* 12, no. 2 (August 16, 2004): 63–74.
5. Jeffrey A Hall, "Friendship Standards: The Dimensions of Ideal Expectations," *Journal of Social and Personal Relationships* 29 (2012): 884–907.
6. Lawrence B. Finer, "Trends in Premarital Sex in the United States, 1954–2003," *Public Health* 22, no. 1: 73–78, accessed August 30, 2023, https://www.ncbi.nlm.nih.gov/pmc/articles/PMC1802108/.
7. Jill Filipovic, *OK Boomer, Let's Talk* (New York: One Signal Publishers, 2020). Cited in Jill Filipovic, "How Boomers Changed American Family Life (by Getting Divorced)," August 13, 2020, accessed August 30, 2023, https://lithub.com/how-boomers-changed-american-family-life-by-getting-divorced/#:~:text=They%20just%20married%20a%20little,the%20average%20bride%20was%2023.
8. Initially, it was very hard to get a prescription for the pill from most primary care doctors, unless you were married. And even then, it was not possible in every state. Eight states outlawed distribution of the pill including Connecticut and New York after it appeared. Some states even had old laws banning married couples from using contraception!
9. Wendy Wang, "The U.S. Divorce Rate Has Hit a 50-Year Low," November 10, 2020, accessed August 30, 2023, https://ifstudies.org/blog/the-us-divorce-rate-has-hit-a-50-year-low.
10. Forty-four percent of Gen X men currently age fifty-four to fifty-eight had ten or more lifetime sex partners as of 2010 versus 21 percent of similarly-aged Gen X women. L. T. Haderxhanaj, J. S. Leichliter, S. O. Aral, H. W. Chesson, "Sex in a Lifetime: Sexual Behaviors in the United States by Lifetime Number of Sex Partners, 2006–2010," *Sexually Transmitted Disease* 41, no. 6 (June, 2014): 345-52, PMID: 24825330; PMCID: PMC5795598, accessed August 31 2023, https://www.ncbi.nlm.nih.gov/pmc/articles/PMC5795598/.
11. One source of this male benefit was a historically larger population of unmarried, attractive young women who served as sexually available alternatives to one's wife in their offices and country clubs. If women circulate on the premarital sexual "scene" longer, married men have more sexual alternatives beyond prostitution than ever before. This was very

true for the female Baby Boom when viewed from the perspective of older men from much smaller generational cohorts (Silent and Greatest Generations).

12. Social Awareness Institute interview with Alison (pseudonym), conducted via Zoom in April 2023. Some edits made for clarity.

Chapter Twenty-Six

1. IRI/Circana, past 52-week retail sales US Multi-Outlet, week ending August 7, 2020, cited in American Pet Products Association, "Pet Industry Market Size, Trends & Ownership Statistics," accessed August 30, 2023, https://www.americanpetproducts.org/press_industrytrends.asp
2. American Veterinary Medical Association, 2018 and 2022 *Pet Ownership and Demographics Sourcebook*, p.11.
3. According to the American Pet Products Association, "the number of dogs and cats in the United States increased by about 32 percent between 2000 and 2017. At the same time, the human population grew only 15 percent." Source: American Pet Products Association, *Pet Industry Market Size*.
4. American Veterinary Medical Association, 2018 and 2022 *Pet Ownership and Demographics Sourcebook*, p. 14.
5. Kathleen Morrill et al., "Ancestry-Inclusive Dog Genomics Challenges Popular Breed Stereotypes," *Science* 376, no. 6592 (April 29, 2022), accessed August 30, 2023, https://www.science.org/doi/10.1126/science.abk0639?adobe_mc=MCMID%3D84642491739088231094049347991384876828%7CMCORGID%3D242B6472541199F70A4C98A6%2540AdobeOrg%7CTS%3D1651162390&_ga=2.218466969.1066386900.1651162373-689641651.1609118629.
6. Yes, certain pig breeds can be trained to tolerate doglike pet affection, but it's a process. And not all owners of pet pigs bother to get them to tolerate more than a quick pet. Source: American Mini Pig Association, "Socializing Mini Pigs," no date, accessed August 30, 2023, https://americanminipigassociation.com/owners/helpful-owner-articles/socializing-mini-pigs/#:~:text=Pigs%20do%20not%20like%20to%20be%20grabbed%20at%20or%20held,natural%20instinct%20is%20to%20run.
7. Becca Risa Luna, "9 Reasons Dogs Make the Very Best Friends, the End," The Dog People powered by rover.com, no date, accessed August 30, 2023, https://www.rover.com/blog/reasons-dogs

-make-best-friends/#:~:text=Dogs%20provide%20us%20with%20 unconditional,feeding%20them%20a%20second%20dinner.
8. S. M. Jourard, "An Exploratory Study of Body-Accessibility," *British Journal of Social and Clinical Psychology* 5, no. 3 (1966): 221–31, accessed August 30, 2023, doi: 10.1111/j.2044-8260.1966.tb00978.x. PMID: 5975653.
9. Jacob Bogage, "Americans Adopted Millions of Dogs During the Pandemic. Now What Do We Do with Them?" *Washington Post*, January 7, 2022, accessed August 30, 2023, https://www.washingtonpost.com/business/2022/01/07/covid-dogs-return-to-work/.

Chapter Twenty-Seven

1. www.whitepages.com. This and similarly creepy databases are amazingly comprehensive and represent the only public source of the country's names beyond the Social Security database (to which the public has no access).
2. James F. Richardson, *Ramping Your Brand: How to Ride the Killer CPG Growth Curve* (Seattle: PGS Press, 2019).

Chapter Twenty-Eight

1. Post-grad degree holders like me, as of 2020, generally took 1.5–2 years longer to get into their first marriage. School gets in the way. Source: Christopher A. Julian, "Median Age at First Marriage, 2021," Bowling Green State University, National Center for Family and Marriage Research, Family Profile no. 15, 2022, figure 3, accessed August 8, 2023, https://www.bgsu.edu/ncfmr/resources/data/family-profiles/julian-median-age-first-marriage-2021-fp-22-15.html.
2. United States Census, table MS-2: Estimated Median Age at First Marriage by Sex, 1890 to Present.
3. Google, "Ngram Viewer," accessed June 2023, https://books.google.com/ngrams.
4. Romance Writers of America, "About the Romance Genre," www.rwa.org, accessed August 9, 2023.
5. Nikki DeMarco, "Why More Men Should Read Romance," Bookriot.com, March 15, 2023, accessed August 9, 2023, https://bookriot.com

/why-more-men-should-read-romance/#:~:text=According%20to%20a%20survey%20conducted,as%20instruction%20manuals%20for%20relationships.
6. The American Council on Education, "National Norms for Entering College Freshmen," *American Council on Education Research Reports*, 5, no. 6 (fall 1970).
7. Linda J. Sax et al., "The American Freshmen National Norms for Fall 2000," *American Council on Education Research Reports*, (2000).
8. That said, this data is only for two generations. We simply do not know how things will turn out for Millennials and Gen Zers. The declining rates of divorce on a per capita basis suggest loosely that younger folks may be making better marital matches. Source: Yerís Mayol-García, Benjamin Gurrentz, and Rose M. Kreider, "Number, Timing, and Duration of Marriages and Divorces: 2016," *Current Population Reports*, April 2021, table 10, accessed August 9, 2023, https://www.census.gov/content/dam/Census/library/publications/2021/demo/p70-167.pdf.
9. Katherine Wu, "Love, Actually: The science Behind Lust, Attraction and Companionship," Harvard University Graduate School of Arts and Sciences, Science in the News website, February 14, 2017 post, accessed August 9, 2023, https://sitn.hms.harvard.edu/flash/2017/love-actually-science-behind-lust-attraction-companionship/#:~:text=High%20levels%20of%20dopamine%20and,eat%20and%20can't%20sleep.
10. Angie Askham, "Intranasal Oxytocin Ineffective for Autism in Large Trial," Spectrumnews.com, October 13, 2021, accessed Augsut 9, 2023, https://www.spectrumnews.org/news/intranasal-oxytocin-ineffective-for-autism-in-large-trial/.
11. In my 2022 survey of older Americans, we can use employed women age forty-five to sixty-five who live with a partner and have never raised kids to infer the scale of the glorious DINK phenomenon. We just need to assume that women in my survey dataset with a sexual partner have a *working* one. If true, then my sample suggests that 7 percent of older women have lived a DINK lifestyle. (Another 7 percent of women this age live alone and have never raised kids.) SAI National Survey on Older Americans, 2022.
12. I recognize there is a modern move to reclaim "family" to describe any curated network of close, intimate adults and kids (regardless of where they live). This movement originated in the LGBTQ community for the very simple and tragic reason that so many who came out in the Baby

Boomer cohort found themselves disowned and rejected by their own blood kin. Their alienation forced some to reclaim the family concept in their own way. They were on the forefront of transforming networks of friends into a functioning family of their own choosing. See Kate Weston, *Families We Choose: Lesbians, Gays, Kinship*, (New York: Columbia University Press, 1991).

Chapter Twenty-Nine

1. This list is taken from an amazing online linguistic resource maintained by Cree language instructor and historian Chelsea Vowel. Source: *Appihtawikosisan*, "Cree kinship terms," October 24, 2011, https://apihtawikosisan.com/2011/10/cree-kinship-terms/.
2. This analysis only counts people who have living relatives in the specific kin group automatically. It uses the definition of intimacy included in the text. Source: SAI National Survey on Older Americans, 2022.

Chapter Thirty

1. Anonymous, "The Labor Market During the Great Depression and the Current Recession," *Congressional Research Service*, June 19, 2009, accessed August 5, 2023, https://www.everycrsreport.com/reports/R40655.html#:~:text=Those%20who%20toiled%20on%20farms,manufacturing%20reported%20high%20unemployment%20rates.
2. https://www.theatlantic.com/magazine/archive/2020/03/the-nuclear-family-was-a-mistake/605536/.
3. The United States Federal Reserve, "U.S. Internal Migration: Recent Patterns and Outstanding Puzzles by Raven Molloy and Christopher Smith," Federal Reserve Board of Governors, October 2019, figure 3B.

Chapter Thirty-One

1. US Census data 1850–2021 (both decennial and American Community Survey data) courtesy of the IPUMS USA online system. Author's analysis using women aged 40 as the key indicator. Steven Ruggles, Sarah Flood, Matthew Sobek, Danika Brockman, Grace Cooper, Stephanie Richards,

and Megan Schouweiler, IPUMS USA: Version 13.0 [dataset]. Minneapolis: IPUMS, 2023. https://doi.org/10.18128/D010.V13.0.
2. This number corresponds to what is known as the Completed Fertility Rate, or total lifetime births for women age forty to forty-four. It bottomed out in 2006 at 1.86, which can be attributed mostly to Baby Boomer women who were most of this age group in 2006. See Gretchen Livingston, "Is U.S. Fertility at an All-Time Low? Two of Three Measures Point to Yes," *Pew Research Center*, May 22, 2019, accessed November 2, 2023, https://www.pewresearch.org/short-reads/2019/05/22/u-s-fertility-rate-explained/.
3. But wait. What about the high rate of divorce and remarriage in the United States? Stepsisters and stepbrothers might fill the gap, no? Well, only 16 percent of today's US children live in such a household, according to recent research: https://www.stepfamily.org/stepfamily-statistics). The numbers are lower for blacks due to the higher baseline fertility rate among African Americans. African American men age forty-five to seventy-four have an 80 percent chance of having a sister or stepsister. I don't think white men have had those high odds since well before the Great Depression. Only 14 percent of my adult survey sample were only children.
4. SAI Older Americans National Survey, 2022. The US sex ratio is 105. In other words, there is a 5 percent extra likelihood of any newborn being male. This is in line with evolutionary understandings of human sex ratios for a more violent and dangerous world than our own.
5. Cited in Jeffrey Kuger, *The Sibling Effect: What the Bonds Among Brothers and Sisters Reveal About Us*, (New York: Riverhead books, 2011) 201.
6. Kuger, *The Sibling Effect*, 201.

Chapter Thirty-Three

1. From 1961 until 2023, consumer spending grew 26 percent below the rate of inflation, in large part because median wages are not keeping up with inflation. My analysis here is based on data from the United States Bureau of Economic Analysis (BEA) and sourced through www.tradingeconomics.com.
2. Some sources to explore if you want to understand the extreme danger of inflation-dependent growth are Ludwig von Mises, "Ludwig Mises on Money and Inflation: A Synthesis of Several Lectures," Ludwig von Mises Institute, Auburn, Alabama 2010; Joseph Tainter, *The Collapse of Complex*

Societies (Cambridge: Cambridge University Press, 1990); and a Substack publication, Academy of Ideas, recently wrote a nice synthesis of this literature in order to explain how runaway inflation can precipitate social collapse.

3. BEA, smoothed, quarterly GDP growth rate, 1961–2023; my analysis.
4. Based on my comparison of inflation-adjusted, average monthly revolving debt and savings totals for the United States from two thirty-six-month periods (March 1959–February 1961 and June 2021–July 2023). Source: United States Bureau of Economic Analysis data sourced from www.tradingeconomics.com.
5. To be clear, no federal agency is forecasting GDP *decline*. Yet. But, current projections have annual GDP growth at only 1.8 percent on average through 2033. See "The Economic Outlook for 2023 to 2033 in 16 Charts," Congressional Budget Office, December 2022 release, accessed November 28, 2023, https://www.cbo.gov/publication/58957#:~:text=The%20Economic%20Outlook%20for%202028%20to%202033,-CBO's%20economic%20projections&text=Real%20potential%20GDP%20is%20projected,previous%20cycle%20of%20business%20activity.
6. Thomas Piketty, *Capital in the Twenty-First Century*, translated by Arthur Goldhammer, (Cambridge: Belknap Press of Harvard University Press, 2017) 106.
7. Rakesh Kochhar and Stella Sechopoulos, "How the American Middle Class Has Changed in the Past Five Decades," Pew Research Center, April 20 2022, accessed August 28, 2023. https://www.pewresearch.org/short-reads/2022/04/20/how-the-american-middle-class-has-changed-in-the-past-five-decades/.
8. James F. Richardson, "The Rise of Whole Foods Tracks the Ballooning of America's Elite," *Homo Imaginari*, July 13, 2022, Social Awareness Institute, https://jamesrichardson.substack.com/p/the-rise-of-whole-foods-tracks-the.
9. US Bureau of Labor and Statistics, "Consumer Expenditures 2021," accessed August 28, 2023, https://www.bls.gov/news.release/pdf/cesan.pdf.
10. *Less than 10 percent of adults with past-year alcohol use disorder seek any treatment.* Sourcing note: Population prevalence estimates here are weighted by the person-level analysis weight and derived from the Center for Behavioral Health Statistics and Quality (CBHSQ) 2021 National Survey on Drug Use and Health (NSDUH-2021-DS0001) public use data

file, defining "any treatment" as treatment or counseling designed to help reduce or stop alcohol use, including detoxification and any other treatment for medical problems associated with alcohol use, as well as defining AUD as having met two or more of the eleven AUD diagnostic criteria according to the fifth edition of the Diagnostic and Statistical Manual of Mental Disorders. SAMHSA, CBHSQ. 2021 National Survey on Drug Use and Health (NSDUH-2021-DS0001). Public use files, cited February 28, 2023, https://www.datafiles.samhsa.gov/dataset/national-survey-drug-use-and-health-2021-nsduh-2021-ds0001.

Chapter Thirty-Five

1. David Wessel, "The U.S. in 2050 Will Be Very Different Than It Is Today," Peter G. Peterson Foundation, accessed August 30, 2023, https://www.pgpf.org/us-2050/research-summary#:~:text=America%20will%20also%20be%20more,will%20have%20more%20than%20doubled.
2. Gretchen Livingston and Anna Brown, "Intermarriage in the U.S. 50 Years After Loving v. Virginia," Pew Research Center, part 1, May 18, 2017, accessed August 30, 2023, https://www.pewresearch.org/social-trends/2017/05/18/1-trends-and-patterns-in-intermarriage/.
3. Livingston and Brown, *Intermarriage*, part 2.
4. For example, statistical analysis of popular belief in structural racism correlates most to political party orientation, *not to race*. Source: Public Religion Research Institute, "Creating More Inclusive Public Spaces: Structural Racism, Confederate Memorials, and Building for the Future," September 28, 2022, accessed August 30, 2023, https://www.prri.org/research/creating-more-inclusive-public-spaces-structural-racism-confederate-memorials-and-building-for-the-future/.
5. Simon Clark, "How White Supremacy Returned to Mainstream Politics," July 1, 2020, Center for American Progress, accessed November 1, 2023, https://www.americanprogress.org/article/white-supremacy-returned-mainstream-politics/.
6. Alvin Rosenfeld and Nicole Wise, *The Over-Scheduled Child: Avoiding the Hyper-Parenting Trap* (New York: St. Martin's Griffin, 2000); Bruce Feiler, "Overscheduled Children: How Big a Problem?" *New York Times*, October 11, 2013, accessed August 30, 2023, https://www.nytimes.com/2013/10/13/fashion/over-scheduled-children-how-big-a-problem

.html; Jennifer Wallace, *Never Enough: When Achievement Culture Becomes Toxic and What We Can Do About It* (New York: Portfolio Press: 2023).

7. The White House, "Reducing the Economic Burden of Unmet Mental Health Needs," May 31, 2022, accessed August 30, 2023, https://www.whitehouse.gov/cea/written-materials/2022/05/31/reducing-the-economic-burden-of-unmet-mental-health-needs/.

INDEX

Locators in *italics* refer to locators and in **bold** to figures.

academia
  as career plan 69, 71–73
  and gender 72–73
  higher education in the 20th century 89–92
  see also college degree attainment
addiction
  alcoholism 129–135, 201–202, 311, 346
  fading stigmatization 342–343
  mis-prescription 343
  routes out of 327, 343
adolescence 137
  see also youth culture
adult-centricity 294
advertising
  branded food items 167, 168–169
  snacks 175, 179–180
age cohorts *see* generational change
alcoholism 129–135, 201–202, 311, 346
allergies 186–190, *189*, 192–193
American Rumspringa 8–14
  parties and alcoholism 125–135
  sex and relationships 248–251
Amish culture 8, 22, 145
anthropology, academic research in 71–73
antisocial behavior
  jerkism 50–51
  productive 43–51
  sociopathic manipulation 46–49

399

aspirational diets 194–203
autism 317
autonomy 7
   and individualism 101–102, 307–310
   moral difficulties with 261–266
   parents' role in supporting 290–292
   radical 317–318
   romantic partners 274–277
   seeking professional help 42
   sex and relationships 250–251
   see also lifestyle choice

binge drinking 130, 134–135, 346
   see also alcoholism
birth control 242, 246, 248–249
birthday parties 125
bisexual activity 246–247
body image 198–199
book clubs 349–350
brand communities 326
brand identity 167, 168–169
bureaucratic communities 323–326
business
   entrepreneurship 319
   fake business friends and social media 233–240

capitalism
   and academia 71–72, 73
   consumer trends 57–58
   and elders 21–22
   food sensitivities 192–193
career planning industry 116–117
careers
   in academia 69, 71–73
   college degree attainment 89–96
   consistency vs. 'career change' 106–110, *107*, *108*
   distinction from 'jobs' 103–104
   and individualism 104–106

  intentionally changing career 108–109, 110–118, 310
  promotions at work 45–46
child labor laws 292–293
childless-by-choice 105, 170–171, 278, 279–280
children
  child-centeredness 292, 294
  declining gender diversity at home 297–304
  fertility rates and number of children 297–300, 336
  grandparent relationships 15–16, 284–289, *285*
  intensive parenting and life coaching 292–296
  meal rituals and snacking culture 170–184
  media based vs. social leisure time 157
  rise in allergies 187–188
Christianity
  approach to marriage 242–243, 279
  evangelical church example 272–273
  serving community 146
civil rights 330
class diversity, romantic partners 274–280
clickbait 50–51
codependency 39, 40–41
collaborative work 339–340
college-based sexual relationships 246–251
college degree attainment
  careers 103–104
  higher education in the 20th century 89–92
  importance to women 92–96
  men who choose not to 96–102
college parties 125–135
community
  bureaucratized, professionalized, and branded 323–326
  codependent behavior 39, 40–41
  communal empathy as a threat to our autonomy 326–329
  economic growth 319–323
  growth and the new aristocracy 322–323
  improving public health 344–345
  rights-enabled consumers 330–335

community service 345
confluent love 242–243
consumer spending, change from 1901-2021 **353–354**
consumer trends
    creative destruction 60, 63–65
    generational change 57–59
    growth 319–320
    historical context 58–63
    rights-enabled consumers 330–335
consumption-led economies 21–22, 319–320
contraception 242, 246, 248–249
cousins, kinship patterns 281–284
creative destruction 60, 63–65
Cub Foods 164, 165–169
cultural diversity 336–339
cultural shock 163–164

degrees *see* college degree attainment
depression 227–228
dieting
    aspirational diets 194–203
    as self-critique 198–201
    snacking and weight management 178–184
disabilities 315–316
divorce
    dark side of autonomy 261–266
    generational change 278
    no-fault 242–243, 264–265
dog ownership 254–258
domestic abuse
    concealing interpersonal trauma 25–26
    and privacy 32–33
dopamine, starting a relationship 273, 279
Double-Income-No-Kids (DINK) lifestyle 279–280
    see also childless-by-choice
dysfunctional reactions 83–88

eating routines, changes in 170–184, 312–313
economic growth 322–323

educational attainment 294
elders
    absence from youth culture 136–137
    and capitalism 21–22
    critiquing their children 20
    "cutting them off" 17, 18–19
    financial independence 16–17
    geographic distance 17–18, 284–289
    grandparent-grandchild relationships 15–16, 284–289, 315
    "silencing the elders" 16
emergency room (ER) 324
emotional intimacy 226
emotional validation 37–38
emotions
    dysfunctional reactions 83–88
    in friendships 313–314
    kinship patterns 281
    pets as companions 253–255, 257–258
    reliance on romantic partners 243–251, 314
empathy
    communal empathy as a threat to our autonomy 326–329
    cross-sex sibling relationships 303–304
    media based vs. social leisure time 159–160
employment
    competitive labor market 316–317
    intentionally changing 108–109, 110–118, 310
    jobs vs. careers 103–104
    middle-class conformity 95, 96
    promotions at work 45–46
    social skills needed for 340
    working hours 75–77, **76**
    see also careers; work-life interaction
entertainment
    as American export 121–122
    friends as 221, 227–229, 322–323, 325
    media and VHS tapes 52–53
    media based vs. social leisure time 154–160
entrepreneurship 319

estrangement threat, intergenerational 17, 18–19

failure in life, responding to 27, 102, 347
family
    coupling but not starting a family 278–280
    dark side of autonomy 261–266
    declining family intimacy 284–286
    declining gender diversity at home 297–304
    fertility rates and number of children 297–300, 336
    vs. friendship 225, 226–228
    and individualism 314–315
    intensive parenting replacing wider family 292–296
    kinship patterns 281–284
    meaning of 280
    nuclear family involution 287–289
    see also marriage
family dinners 170–184
family relationships
    "cutting them off" 17, 18–19
    financial independence 16–17
    geographic distance 17–18, 284–289
    grandparent-grandchild relationships 15–16
feminist freedoms 4–5
fertility rates 297–300, 336
film making 121–124
food
    allergies 186–190, *189*
    consumer trends 61–62
    creative destruction 63–65
    eating routines 170–184, 312–313
    Indian vs. American approach 164–169
    meal rituals and snacking culture 170–184
    "potluck" meals 205–209, *207*
    sensitivities and intolerances 185–193, 204–209
    see also dieting
foodie culture 63–65, 148–151
foreknowledge 25–26, 37
fractional executives 80–81
Friends-Who-F**k (FWF) 247–248

friendships
    for entertainment and leisure 221, 227–229, 322–323, 325
    fake business friends 233–240
    generational change 221–223
    marrying your best friend 241–251, 267–269
    noncommittal behavior 152–153, 310–312
    number of 229–232
    old boys' networks 92
    reciprocity in 216–220, 345
    romantic partners as priority *226*, 226–228
    social history 223–225
    Tamil vs. American approaches to 213–220

Frito-Lay 174–175, 179

"fun" 122–123, 125
    catering for people 209
    definition **140**, 142, 143, 144–145
    different recreational world 148–151
    media based vs. social leisure time 154–160
    noncommittal socializing 152–153, 310–312
    for older Americans 138–139, 142–143
    for young Americans 136–141

GDP growth *320*, 320–321

gender
    and academia 72–73
    career women 105
    choices for men compared to women 6, 101–102
    college degree attainment 92–102
    cross-sex sibling relationships 300–304
    declining gender diversity at home 297–304
    early feminist freedoms 4–5
    graduate women entering the workforce 92–96
    pursuing a career 105, 111
    romantic marriage 241–243

generational change
    college degree attainment 89–92
    consumer trends 57–59
    family intimacy 284–289, 296–298
    friendships 221–223

    marriage and divorce 278
    meal rituals and snacking culture 170–184
    media based vs. social leisure time 154–160
    sex and relationships 245–251
geographic distance, from family 17–18
    declining family intimacy 284–286, *285*
    nuclear family involution 287–289
governments, trust in 322
graduate degrees *see* college degree attainment
grandparent-grandchild relationships 15–16, 284–289, *285*, 315
grieving practices 82, 83–88, 347
group healing 83–84
group work, in school 339–340
growth, economic 319–323

health, food and snacking 177–184
hero cycle 69–70
higher education *see* college degree attainment
Hollywood films 121–124
house vs. home
    consumer trends 57–58
    lifestyle choice 3–4

India *see* Tamil culture
individualism
    and autonomy 307–310
    basic societal ingredients for 3–14
    consumer trends 61
    countertrends 336–339
    dieting as self-critique 199
    difference between men and women 101–102
    difficulty of coordinating group fun 159–160
    discontents as hidden 323
    family structures 314–315
    food and eating routines 170–184, 185, 312–313
    and friendships 313–314
    interpersonal trauma 25–26
    national research for this book 355–359
    noncommittal socializing 152–153, 310–312

as public health disaster 344
  pursuing a career 104–106, 116
  responsibility for own problems 34–42
intensive parenting 292–296
interpersonal trauma
  loneliness 27–29
  and privacy 25–26
irritable bowel syndrome (IBS) 185

Jenny Craig (diet plan) 200, 201
jerkism 50–51
'jobs' 103–104
  see also careers

kinship patterns 281–284
  see also family
knowledge, interpersonal trauma 25–26
The Kural 213

labor market
  competitiveness 316–317
  intentionally changing career 108–109, 110–118, 310
  promotions and salary increases 45–46
lactose intolerance 185, 186–187, 190–191
law enforcement, and privacy 31–33
leisure time 142–143
  achievement, posturing, and performance 149–151
  from formal to informal 144–146, **147**
  friends as entertainment 221, 227–229
  given for friends 229–232
  in marital relationships 241–243
  media vs. group fun 154–160
  mountain biking versus foodies 148–149
  for older Americans 138–139, 142–143
  parties and alcoholism 125–135
  respite from loneliness 151–152
  for young Americans 136–141
life coaches, parents as 292–296
life history interviews 357–359

lifestyle choice
    American Rumspringa 8–14
    aspirational diets 195–198
    coupling but not marrying 278–280
    generational change 3–6
    house vs. home 3–4
    meal rituals 172
    proliferation of choice in the modern era 10–14, **11**, **12–13**
    radical autonomy 317–318
    rights-enabled consumers 332
    sex and relationships 245–251
    social forces influencing 6–8
lifestyle diversity 332–334
LinkedIn 201–202, 233–240
loneliness
    due to individualism 309–310
    and privacy 27–29
    recreation as respite 151–152
    and work-life interaction 81–82
love *see* romantic partners

Mad Men series 241
mandatory community service 345
marginalizing the socially unskilled 315–318
market research 237–238
marketing
    brand identity 167, 168–169
    snacking culture 174–175, 179–180
marriage
    choices over 8–14
    coupling but not marrying 278–280
    marrying your best friend 241–251, 267–269
    median age 267–268, *268*
    mutual happiness 242–243
    see also divorce
meal rituals 170–184
media 322–323
    America's video entertainment revolution 53–54
    generational change 54–55

    media based vs. social leisure time 154–160
    pets as companions 257–258
    and socialization 55–56
    VHS tapes 52–53
mental health
    and academia 74
    access to help 317, 328, 346
    fading stigmatization 342–343
    work-life interaction 77–80
mergers and acquisitions (M&A) 48
microaggressions 7
middle class
    graduate women 92–96
    intentionally changing career 108–109
    productivity and alcoholism 201–203
    romantic partners 274–277
morality, fake business friends 240
morality of eating
    aspirational diets 195–198
    dieting as self-critique 198–201
    snacking 178
    through food choices 313
mountain biking group example 148–151, 153
music, as part of youth culture 140–141
mutual obligation 323–324
    see also reciprocity in friendships

networking 73–74
    no-fault divorce 242–243, 264–265
    nuclear family, changes in 284–289, 296–298

obesity 180–184
old boys' networks 92
oxytocin 273, 279

parenting
    intensive parenting and life coaching 292–296
    permissive parenting 53, 171, 253
    role in supporting child's autonomy 290–292
    supporting grandparent relationships 15–16, 284–289, *285*

parties
    catering for 205–209
    "fun" 121–124, 125, 126
    noncommittal socializing 310–312
    for young Americans 125–135
permissive parenting 53, 171, 253
personal tragedies, grieving practices 82, 83–88, 347
personalized entertainment
    America's video entertainment revolution 53–54
    generational change 54–55
    media and socialization 55–56
    VHS media 52–53
pets, being treated like family members 252–258
political polarization 231
"potluck" meals 205–209, *207*
privacy
    approaches to friendship 218–220
    concealing interpersonal trauma 25–26
    and law enforcement 31–33
    loneliness 27–29
    noncommittal behavior 152–153
    pets as companions 255–256
    sacredness of 23–25, 27
    stigmatizing busybodies 29–31
    unsolicited advice 35–37
    work-life interaction 79
productive antisocial behavior 43–51
professional communities 40–41, 323–326, 346
promotions at work 45–46
    see also careers
public health, individualism as disaster to 344

race
    busybody neighbour example 29–31
    cultural diversity 336–339
    fertility rates and number of children 336
    marriage practices 275
    profiling by 337
radical autonomy 317–318

reciprocity in friendships 216–220, 345
recreation
    achievement, posturing, and performance 149–151
    emotional component 227–228
    from formal to informal 144–146, **147**
    friends for 148–151, 226–227
    media vs. group fun 154–160
    mountain biking versus foodies 148–149
    noncommittal behavior 152–153, 310–312
    for older Americans 142–143
    parties and alcoholism 125–135
    as respite from loneliness 151–152
    for young Americans 136–141
religion
    approach to marriage 242–243, 279
    evangelical church example 272–273
    serving community 146
research design for this book 355–359
rights-enabled consumers 330–335
romance novels 269–271, 273
romantic partners
    choices over 8–14, 241–251
    class diversity 274–280
    coupling but not marrying 278–280
    dark side of autonomy 261–266
    dopamine at the start of a relationship 279
    marrying your best friend 241–251, 267–269
    median age for marriage 267–268, *268*
    mutual happiness 242–243
    as priority over friends *226*, 226–228
    the unloved 272–274

salary increases 45–46
    see also careers
school work, team-orientation 339–340
self-awareness
    career goals 113–114, 117–118
    and microaggressions 7
    professional solutions 40–42

self-improvement
    aspirational diets 194–195, 198
    career changes 310
    professionalization 41
    serving community 146
self-isolation, when grieving 82, 83–88, 347
self-regulation 7
sex
    birth control 242, 246, 248–249
    changing practices and the sexual revolution 245–251
    negative office behavior 50–51
sibling relationships 297–304
single parent households 171, 280
smartphones 158
snacking culture 173–184, 312–313
social clubs 144–146, **147**
    see also recreation
social networks
    fake business friends 233–240
    lack of true community 325–326
    lifestyle choice 5
social norms
    American Rumspringa 8–14
    choices for men compared to women 6
    social forces influencing 6–8
social pain 159
social retreat 334–335
social skills
    decline with age 159–160
    for employment 340
    marginalizing the socially unskilled 315–318
    middle-class conformity 95, 96
    urbanized societies 224
sociopathic manipulation 46–49
stigma
    intentionally changing career 112
    local community 331
    marginalizing the socially unskilled 315–318

racial 336–337
symbolism
   brand identity 167, 168–169
   "fun" 121–123

Tamil culture
   American entertainment in 121–122
   community support 23–25, 39
   food and cooking 164–165, 166–167
   friendships 213–220
   kinship patterns 281–284
   The Kural 213
   sibling relationships 300–301
therapy
   access to 317, 328, 346
   seeking professional help 40–42, 323–326
touch, cultural norms around 256
tribal societies, kinship patterns 281–284
Trobriand island culture 271
TV viewing 53–54, 322–323
   see also media

veganism 191, 195–198
vegetarianism 195–198
VHS media 52–53
video entertainment 52–54, 322–323
   see also media

weight management
   aspirational diets 194–203
   dieting as self-critique 198–201
   obesity 180–184
   snacking culture 178–184, 312–313
When Harry Met Sally 243–245, 267, 275
work-life interaction
   in American culture 77–80
   dysfunctional reactions 83–88
   fractional executives 80–81
   hours of work vs. leisure 75–77, **76**

    and individualism 309–310
    and loneliness 81–82
    see also labor market
working hours 75–77, **76**
"workism" 202

the Yanomami, Venezuela 32
youth activities 341–342
youth culture
    fun as something enjoyed with friends 136–141
    parties and alcoholism 125–135
    see also generational change

ABOUT THE AUTHOR

James F. Richardson is a Ph.D. cultural anthropologist who has studied American society for twenty years as a market research consultant. He has interviewed Americans in 40 different states and conducted extensive demographic and survey research at the national level. He has also had the privilege of living all over the country, including New England, the Chicago-to-Madison corridor, Seattle, and Tucson, Arizona. For nearly three years in the late 1990s, he also lived in Tamil-speaking South India, studying a very different society than our own. His research focus then was on the experience of middle-class Dalit Christians as post-colonial minorities.

Today, Dr. Richardson lives with his wife, children, and dogs in sunny Tucson, Arizona, where he writes nonfiction under his own imprint and consults virtually with a national client base of fast-growing emerging consumer brands. He also writes a popular anthropology Substack—*Homo Imaginari*—for a growing international readership.